D0816457

WRITER'S CHOICE
A LIBRARY OF REDISCOVERIES

WRITER'S CHOICE

A LIBRARY
OF REDISCOVERIES

with an Introduction by Doris Grumbach

Linda Sternberg Katz
Bill Katz

Reston Publishing Company, Inc.
A Prentice-Hall Company
Reston, Virginia

Library of Congress Cataloging in Publication Data

Katz, Linda Sternberg.
   Writer's choice.

   Includes indexes.
   1. Bibliography—Best books. I. Katz, William A.
      II. Title.
Z1035.K27 1983   011'.7   83-3245
ISBN 0-8359-8799-X

Copyright 1983 by
Reston Publishing Company, Inc.
A Prentice-Hall Company
11480 Sunset Hills Road
Reston, Virginia   22090

Interior design by Annie Guérard

All rights reserved. No part of this book may be reproduced
in any way, or by any means, without permission in writing
from the publisher.

10   9   8   7   6   5   4   3   2   1

Printed in the United States of America

CONTENTS

WITHDRAWN

MAR 8 4

MAR 84

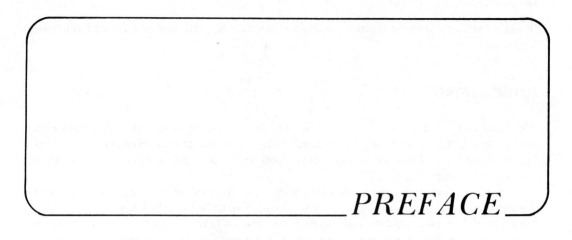

PREFACE

Here is an annotated listing of approximately one thousand books which 400 distinguished writers and a handful of other experts believe to be unjustly neglected, overlooked, or forgotten. In the Introduction, Doris Grumbach discusses the problems of determining what is a neglected book, but few writers have any real difficulty with the definition. Most define it as a book which deserves a wider audience.

Publisher William Jovanovich says, "Maybe books are not really neglected after all. They are just appreciated selectively, as it were. After all, for every book there is at least one believing reader, the publisher." And E. H. Gombrich adds, "Isn't the real point now that books are altogether neglected."

The editor of *The American Scholar* "Neglected Books" series writes, "We were aware, of course, that the phrase 'the most undeservedly neglected' was open to various interpretations. What we had in mind was the selection of a book which, although of striking merit, did not seem to our correspondent to have received either the critical recognition or the general audience that he or she believed it so deserved."

The present compilation should bring some well-deserved attention to numerous books, and serve as a departure point discovering and subsequently savoring truly remarkable works. The list is also a guide for book collecting. Most of the titles are available in used or antiquarian bookstores across America and England. Few, too few, are in print and available from retail bookstores.

Fortunately, many libraries have the majority of the books. If not available at your local library, you may ask the librarian to order the title on interlibrary loan.

No definition or limitation was imposed when asking for nominations. Still, the majority of titles are from the twentieth century, with the preponderance of both fiction and nonfiction from after World War II. The only exclusions were: (1) books in a foreign language (although there are numerous translations included) and (2) standard titles which are so often found in the "best" type of reading lists that they need not have been included although, of course, being mentioned on numerous lists may still not save a book from being neglected.

Arrangement

The book is divided in two main sections. The first is fiction, the second nonfiction. The first is arranged alphabetically by author, while the second part is subdivided into broad subject categories. There is an index of authors and titles, and of those who nominated the books for inclusion.

Each entry includes the name of the author, the title of the book and the place, publisher and date of first publication. No effort is made to indicate if the book has been republished at a later date, although this may be the case. Where the work is a translation, the name of the translator is given as well as the original language and an added note as to when the work was first published in its original language.

A brief annotation describes the primary focus of the book, and indicates why it is of importance. This descriptive annotation is followed by the name of the individual who recommended the book. The writer may have added comments about the work. In most cases, the recommendation and comments are from a letter to the compilers. Where this is not true, we have indicated the source of the recommendation and comment.

Where there is no name after the annotation, the book is recommended by the compilers.

Method of Compilation

Over a period of two years, letters were sent to authors asking for their personal choice of neglected books. Most replied with one or two titles, and some were good enough to add their own annotations and remarks. These are the heart of this compilation, but, in addition, the reader will find some titles discovered in book reviews, essays, and a few listings. In each case this is clearly indicated, and the listings most often used include:

American Scholar, which began a series on neglected books in the autumn of 1956.

Antaeus, which published listings of "Neglected Books of the Twentieth Century" which ran from the summer of 1975 through autumn, 1979.

Antioch Review, which offered essays on "forgotten writers" in autumn, 1981.

Books Abroad, which published a listing by William F. H. Lamont, "Neglected Masterpieces of Foreign Fiction," in 1953.

The Journal of American History, which offered "Historian's Choice" in 1952 and again in 1954.

The Times Literary Supplement, which on January 21, 1977 published a column "Reputations Revisited," and on June 5, 1981 ran one on overlooked detective and mystery fiction.

Daedalus, which devoted an issue to "Twentieth Century Classics Revisited" in winter, 1974.

The New Review, which presented a symposium in the summer of 1978, called "The State of Fiction," which included some overlooked titles.

The Arts Council of England, which along with the publishers Secker & Warburg is now publishing a series of classics which they consider overlooked.

The Washington Post Book World, which, under the guidance of Noel Perrin, began a monthly feature on February 15, 1981 called "Rediscoveries" which features essays on neglected books and authors. Most of the titles suggested in this feature are included here.

Several publishers which have lists of neglected books that they have reissued. Some titles were selectively chosen from those lists. The publishers include: Ecco Press (*i.e., Antaeus*); Second Chance Press; Southern Illinois University Press; Virago; and Secker & Warburg.

To the best of our knowledge, the only book previously devoted to this subject is David Madden's *Rediscoveries* (New York: Crown, 1971), but his emphasis is on presenting about thirty books in "informal essays [by] well-known novelists." Robert Birley's *Sunk Without Trace* (New York: Harcourt, 1962) is an entertaining group of essays primarily on forgotten Elizabethan and eighteenth-century authors.

Acknowledgments

The compilers thank the authors and others who so generously and enthusiastically sent us nominations and comments. Without them, of course, this compilation would not have been possible. Thanks, too, to the scores of librarians who made numerous suggestions. Unfortunately, space does not allow using all of their names, but it is through their encouragement and guidance that this book is possible.

We wish, too, to thank Nikki Hardin our editor who provided so much aid and comfort.

INTRODUCTION

The idea of compiling a list of books which writers think have been overlooked or neglected is intriguing. Immediately, one begins to wonder: why are books of real merit overlooked? Is their neglect a function of the way the publishing industry works, the way the critical fraternity operates, or is it often the result of some characteristic of the books themselves? Is it possible that books of true excellence can disappear from human memory and record without ever being noticed? What role does "fate" or luck or chance play in the rediscovery of such books? Or has the culture made a subtle switch which then becomes hospitable to books hitherto ignored?

It is entirely possible for a fine book to disappear without a trace forever, but since the very conditions of that possibility make it impossible to prove, we must here deal with the reality that such books often disappear in their own time only to find *lebensraum* in another, for some reason. The paths to these rediscoveries vary: a critic—say, Edmund Wilson—finds the book and pushes it into notice, or it is raised up from a long but continuing underground life to wider notice, or an enterprising publishing group (*Daedalus* in its 1974 *Antaeus* issue, *The American Scholar* a few years ago, called our attention to books "most undeservedly neglected," as Ecco Press, Southern Illinois University Press and Virago have done) starts a search for "hidden masterpieces." This volume you are about to study is evidence that there is an inherent immortality for books neglected in their own time that many times provides for their renaissance. Despite bad reviews or no reviews in some prestigious places, and because its language at the time seemed almost private, James Joyce's *Ulysses* took a long time to gain the kind of universal recognition it now has. *Moby Dick* was poorly regarded and obscure much longer than it has been acclaimed an American classic. Franz Kafka, a giant of twentieth-century literature, died in obscurity without knowing the taste of fame. Gerard Manley Hopkins' renown as a poet was the result of a posthumous volume published by his good friend Robert Bridges. But here they all are, with us now, *quand même*.

One age's oddities and curiosities are often another's masterpieces. It may be that it requires a long absorbtive time for a unique style to be understood and then admired, or an original thought to be comprehended and then appreciated. The resistance to such phenomena is great. Most people prefer the easy and familiar; they are encouraged in their complaisance by reviewers and publicists who also feel more comfortable recommending what they think the public will more readily and profitably accept. It is a case of the dog chasing the tail which he holds firmly between his teeth. So it is that posterity, as we see by the list that follows, acclaims ideas vigorous enough to have lasted in obscurity; only the future reveres the original and daring style.

If these sweeping generalizations do not damn my argument too much, let me venture some others: very often the acclaimed work of the present quickly loses its force. I think of my own youth, of the large sales and great reader-interest in this century for the work of "giants" like Romain Rolland, Anatole France, Booth Tarkington, John Galsworthy, Pearl Buck—the list is long. Note how few, if any, of their works are still read or even mentioned when twentieth-century fiction is discussed. We read their contemporaries: Virginia Woolf, D. H. Lawrence, Henry James, Gertrude Stein, recognizing the importance of their stylistic advances for all that was to follow in fiction.

It is of parenthetical interest that the influential critics of the first half of this century in the United States are hardly remembered, yet their views, enthusiasms and dislikes influenced what was read as well as what we never heard about. William Lyon Phelps, Clifton Fadimen, Irita Van Doran, J. Donald Adams, Alexander Woollcott, all had a kind of instant celebrity. They were courted and petted and fed at book parties by "the trade," but their literary mortality is high. Often their names disappear with the names of the books they most highly praised. Sadly, they are remembered, if at all, chiefly for the books they failed to notice.

The lists this book contain were sent to the editors by writers who scoured their bookshelves and their memories to rescue from them, for the guidance of others, books which did not deserve the oblivion heaped upon them. A careful reading of the lists will reveal certain interesting departures from this original stricture. For example:

Three fiction writers—William Gerhardie, Janet Lewis and John Horne Burns—garnered several recommendations each. Burns got all four for his first book, *The Gallery*, a superb and universally neglected World War II novel. Elias Canetti's *Auto da Fé* has three nominators as does G. V. Desani's *All About H. Hatterr* and Leonard Woolf's *The Village in the Jungle*. William Maxwell is represented by three different novels recommended by three writers—clearly a writer's writer. Four different writers were in agreement about John Cowper Powys' three novels, the record for the list.

The list shows how faithful writers are to each other, especially their friends. Friends tend to have the longest and most tender memories for the books of each other. The writing program at George Mason University employs such novelists as Richard Bausch, Stepher Goodwin and Susan Shreve. They are frank about finding their colleagues' books unfairly neglected. Allen Ginsberg calls attention to William Burroughs' *The Job*. Quentin Bell recommends Roger Fry's book; Hentoff is high on Kempton; black writers are faithful to their brothers' and sisters' work: Nikki Giovanni reminds us of James Baldwin, Martin Luther King, and Bessie Head. Ronald Sukenick of the Fiction Collective wants us to remember a novel by Peter Spielberg of the Fiction Collective.

Some recommendations are predictable. Doris Lessing wants to see restored a book by Idries Shah on the Sufis. She also likes a work in psychology by the same author, but recommends no works of fiction. Annie Dillard's recommendation of John Hay's *Nature's Year* might have been foretold, like Frederick Buechner's fondness for G. K. Chesterton's *The Man Who Was Thursday* (not entirely neglected, however: Sheed and Ward reprinted the 1908 masterpiece in 1975). Surprisingly though (to me), it is also on Susan Sontag's list. Julia Child recommends *The Art of Making Sausages, Pâtés and Other Charcuterie* and Berton Roueché, Dr. Pickels' *Epidemiology in Country Practice*. Both are to be expected, but one wonders how special a preference their books are. Southerners predictably prefer the work of their countrymen: Peter Taylor points to Caroline Gordon, Reynolds Price to Romulus Linney.

Writers who admire one work by an author tend to admire others. Thus, Diana Trilling suggests two novels by the obscure and neglected writer Isabel Bolton who wrote her three novels in the Forties after the age of sixty, choices in which I heartily concur. Eve Auchincloss favors two books in the social sciences by Tony Parker. D. J. Enright likes two of Stella Benson's novels, although not the one I like, *Pull Devil, Pull Baker*, and Daniel Halpern likes novels by both the Bowles. Gore Vidal recommends two Thornton Wilder novels and two by Dawn Powell (Edmund Wilson's old sentimental favorite). Anthony Powell cites two novels by Jocelyn Brooke, and Laurie Colwin two by Frederick Buechner, but not my favorite first novel of his, *A Long Day's Dying*.

Some oddities appear on the list: Who would expect James Michener to recommend Mrs. Gaskell's *Cranford*? Or Russell Baker to suggest a return to Trollope's *Autobiography*? Alison Lurie and Alan Lelchuk rather surprised me with their attention to George Gissing, Dwight MacDonald with his to O. Henry, and Betty Comden, that fine writer of musical-comedy lyrics and books, with her recommendation of George Meredith's *The Egoist*.

Instant Action: Susan Sontag and poet John Ashbery suggested Laura Riding's *Progress of Stories*, published in 1935. Recently a new enlarged edition of the book, with commentary by Laura (Riding) Jackson arrived on my desk, published by Dial Press. This new edition contains thirteen stories from other collections and some hitherto unpublished ones.

Understandable oddity: A number of writers state their opinion that their own books have been badly neglected, an opinion most writers hold but are too shy or too proud to admit. Note that Stanley Elkin recommends his own *A Bad Man*, Stanley Kauffmann mourns the neglect of his autobiography, *Albums of Early Life*, Edna O'Brien suggests her book, *Mother Ireland*, and James H. Hall unabashedly names *two* of his own books as his choice for most neglected fiction.

A few of the books deemed neglected were not. Frank Conroy's *Stop-Time*, Rebecca West's *Grey Lamb and Black Falcon*, Jean Genet's *The Thief*, Franz Werfel's *The Forty Days of Musa Dagh*, and some others were not neglected when they appeared and in the case of the first three, are not now. They are much sought after in their first editions: in out-of-print bookstores and libraries they cannot be kept on the shelves.

Others on the list, like Kate Chopin's *The Awakening*, Elizabeth Bowen's *The House in Paris*, Willa Cather's *The Professor's House*, and Joyce Cary's *The*

Horse's Mouth have not been neglected for some time. Cather's novel has been continuously in print since it appeared in 1925, due to the remarkable concern of her publisher, Alfred A. Knopf. Peter Mathiessen's *At Play in the Fields of the Lord*, Jean Stafford's *Boston Adventure* and Delmore Schwartz's *The World is a Wedding* were much admired in their time, and still are. Schwartz's book was reprinted long after it first appeared; *Boston Adventure* is now available in paper.

Some titles reappear here because their publishers continue to nurse an understandable fondness for the works they once published and still believe in. Note the choices (not all, of course, but some) of such notable and loyal publishers as: Aaron Asher, Roger Straus, Gordon Lish, Alfred Knopf, and Virago Press which has recently put its money where its mouth was and reissued its recommended *The Lacquered Lady* by F. Tennyson Jesse.

What is most intriguing about the lists which follow is the number of recommendations I found myself underlining in approval. Among them: the novels of Thomas Savage, although I would have added his most recently published (and equally neglected) *Her Side of It*; Clancy Sigal's underground classic, *Going Away*; Margaret Yourcenar's *Memoirs of Hadrian*; Sybille Bedford's *A Legacy*; and Barbara Deming's *Prison Notes*. The reader can have the same fun, identifying his own favorites, seconding some of the nominations for restoration.

Another pleasure was discovering books I have never encountered by authors with whom I was familiar. I learn from Leon Edel that E. M. Forster wrote a *History and Guide to Alexandria*, that Ford Madox Ford wrote a travel book on *Provence* (from Daniel Halpern). I am grateful to Larry McMurtry for alerting me to Eric Newby's *Slowly Down the Ganges*, a book I did not know existed. I've never read the novelist David Black and his book *Like Father*, but Anne Tyler recommends him so I shall go in search of him.

To the readers of this volume I bequeath the pleasures of following up the nominations, in libraries both public and the private ones of their friends. To publishers and editors with an apostolic attitude toward fine books I suggest a treasure hunt through these pages for books well worth reviving in print. And to those unheralded heroes whose forlorn names appear among the nominations I wish for a revival of their work of such dimensions that it will rival the most grandiose Billy Graham meeting.

Doris Grumbach
Washington, DC
June 1982

WRITER'S CHOICE
A LIBRARY OF REDISCOVERIES

FICTION

Abbott, Edwin. *Flatland: A Romance of Many Dimensions, by A Square* (London: Seeley, 1884) A geometrical romance with a unique twist, this imaginatively explains the fourth dimension. Purportedly written by a genius who has a vision of great dimensional possibilities, the focus is on the men and women of the mythical Kingdom of Flatland. The author exposes their limitations and their intriguing mathematical methods for recognizing such essentials as configurations. Written in a clear, sprightly fashion, the combination of imaginative mathematical theory and social satire has contributed to the book's fame among a small audience for almost a century.

Quentin Bell calls this "the best possible introduction to the understanding of the fourth dimension."

Abele, Rudolph von. *The Party* (Boston, Houghton, 1963) In a single evening late in World War II a party gathers at an Austrian chateau to be entertained by, and pay homage to, a Nazi host. The completely amoral Marshal is as clever as he is brutal and the counterpoint to his dominant will is his ability to charm even his worst enemy. He is pitted against his guests, particularly the benign Steinbaum who proves unable to withstand the alternate cruelty and wit of the Marshal. The careful style and the frank description of a world of uncertain reality work to advance a brilliant analysis of the people who serve and were served by the Nazis.

Roger Sale says that this novel "can quickly be described as being about Hermann Goring and by Henry James. It is a wonderful tour de force, and if it doesn't reread so well as it reads, that is in part due simply to one's amazement the first time that such a book could exist. It takes 400 pages to describe the events of one evening with, obviously, great slowness and concentration" (*American Scholar*, Winter, 1979).

Adams, Henry. *Democracy: An American Novel* (New York: Holt, 1880) Possibly the wittiest and best political novel ever written about and by an American, this was first published anonymously. *Democracy* is a fictional account of Washington, DC, and many of its residents whom Adams was to make famous in *The Education of Henry Adams* (1907). While proud of the work, he refused to let his name be attached to the intimate picture of official political life, and it was not disclosed until after his death that he was the author. Depicting the corruptions, intrigues and political dealings with realism and wry pessimism, Adams is careful to portray his primary characters as human beings, not stereotypes. Many characters are, in fact, real people in Washington *circa* 1870.

Noel Perrin writes, "*Democracy* is a comedy and an extremely funny one . . . but [it] cuts deeper than social comedy. It is also a serious look at American government. . . . That in no way spoils the comedy . . . . It just gives the book a kind of resonance" (*Washington Post Book World*, June 14, 1981).

Aiken, Conrad. *A Heart for the Gods of Mexico* (London: Secker, 1939) A woman, Noni, and two men, Gil and Blom, are on a train bound from New York to Mexico City. Gil, Noni's lover, is unaware that she has only a few months to live. Blom, who knows about her illness, has raised money for the trip. Consequently, the three characters are on slightly different planes of thought and emotion as they journey from one culture to another. There are fine descriptive passages of the country and the people. The literary allusions are some of the best the poet ever achieved.

Hayden Carruth declares that this is "one of the best short novels I know in all American literature, and I wonder why it isn't better and more widely known. It is compact, simple, but beautifully managed in its transition from New England to the subtropics, a transition involving many elements. I think it would make a wonderful movie, though probably not the most popular kind."

Aldington, Richard. *Death of a Hero* (London: Chatto, 1929) Considered one of the most distinguished English novels to come out of World War I, this is the story of the youth and the death of a British captain. Aldington, who was an infantry private, draws from his own experiences. Here there is more indignation than heroism, but the fact remains that the story is powerful enough to carry the reader straight to its predetermined ending. As sensitive as it is ruthless, the novel is timeless in its description of war.

Frank MacShane recommended this in *Antaeus*, Winter, 1975.

Algren, Nelson. *The Last Carousel* (New York: Putnam, 1973) Short fiction, travel sketches, reminiscences, character studies—all are in this collection of material written between 1947 and 1972. Best of the lot are the short stories which show Algren's ability to create tension and credible characters from unlikely situations. For other Algren short stories, see *The Neon Wilderness* (1946).

Clancy Sigal believes that the early Algren stories, such as "The Devil Comes Down Division St." and "A Bottle of Milk for Mother," are "as good as the best Russian/French short stories, grotesque, truthful, funny."

Algren, Nelson. *The Man With the Golden Arm* (New York: Doubleday, 1949) While this was Algren's most famous novel, it is not as well known today as it should be. The realistic story of a Chicago card dealer—the man with the golden arm—is only one among a large cast of hopelessly lost characters. From the first scene, the reader is caught up in a plot with a group of individuals who seem headed irretrievably towards disaster.

Sol Yurick considers this "one of the greatest of American novels." And he calls Algren "one of the few great language stylists of our time, surpassing Hemingway by a long shot."

Algren, Nelson. *Never Come Morning* (New York: Harper, 1942) Bruno is a young fighter and near-gangster who is arrested for murder in the middle of his first professional fight. This powerful, moving story of Bruno, his girl friend Steffi, and their lives of poverty and crime among the indigent of Chicago's West Side is as authentic as it is moving. Few American writers are as able as Algren to create poetry out of the familiar, to avoid the tedium in the realistic, and to render characters with such verity and completeness.

J. F. Powers writes: "When *The Man With the Golden Arm* was published, I liked it a lot, but I remember thinking *Never Come Morning* still Algren's best book. For me, it was one of those rare books with characters whose lives you discuss, whose lines you recite and act out, with others who've read the book."

Algren, Nelson. *A Walk on the Wild Side* (New York: Farrar, Straus, 1956) During the early years of the Depression, an astonishingly varied group of people are depicted as they try to succeed in the slum section of New Orleans. Filled with brilliant little profiles of socially marginal characters, the novel is balanced between outrageous hilarity and moving tragedy. The wild 1931 landscape is portrayed in the best American tradition, and can be compared favorably with more familiar works such as *Sanctuary* and *Tobacco Road*. Still, this novel has a unique, boisterous yet tender quality all its own.

Ken Kesey recommends it.

Allfrey, Phyllis. *The Orchid House* (London: Constable, 1953) The house is on the tropical island of Dominica, and it is filled with three Creole sisters who enjoy a languid, happy childhood. As they develop into young women, some of the mystery and decay of the home becomes apparent, particularly when they all fall in love with the same man. Soon economic reality catches up with the family, and the girls are forced to leave the orchid house for England and America. As a picture of life in a bewitching, extraordinarily beautiful part of the world, the novel can be compared to Jean Rhys's *Wide Sargasso Sea*.

Virago Press is reissuing this novel.

Anderson, Sherwood. *Marching Men* (New York: John Lane, 1917) Two years after this novel was written, Anderson published his famed *Winesburg, Ohio*, and for all intents and purposes *Marching Men* disappeared. Yet, despite its obscurity, it remains one of America's great labor novels, and is equal to anything written on the subject by other authors.

Here Anderson traces the life of Beaut McGregor and the progress of the union movement, while concentrating on its development in the urban centers.

Aragon, Louis. *Aurelien*. *Translated from the French by Eithne Wilkins* (London: Pilot, 1946) The stage is the French political and cultural milieu of the 1920s. Here, the poet and journalist Louis Aragon tells the love story of a veteran of World War I. Since the author has a sure sense of the everyday life of that period, the novel is as lively as it is witty, and few writers have given a better pictorial representation of France.

Piers Paul Read recommends this novel.

Asch, Shalom. *Salvation*. *Translated from the Yiddish by Willa and Edwin Muir*

(London: Gollancz, 1934) Making dramatic use of both Talmudic knowledge and rabbinical teaching, this Yiddish dramatist and novelist evokes an accurate picture of nineteenth-century Jewish life in a small Polish community. The central character, who becomes a famous rabbi, is revered as a righteous man who advocates a beautiful, concrete way to salvation. The narrative is as fluent and vivid as the characters.

Robert Roper, who recommends this work, compares it to the *"shtetl* stories of I. B. Singer" but says that it is "less fevered and richer and more memorable. A good European novel with magic in it."

Ashbery, John and James Schuyler. *A Nest of Ninnies* (New York: Dutton, 1969) The "ninnies" of the title are two American families whom the author-poets humorously envision as falling short of aesthetic judgment in such things as their attachment to shopping centers and six-lane highways. They are followed around the Eastern United States and Europe, their amusing activities and conversations (usually endless discussions about friends) ruthlessly captured and recorded.

W. H. Auden thought the work reminiscent of the best of P. G. Wodehouse, and believed it was "destined to become a minor classic" *(New York Times Book Review, May 4, 1969).*

Azuela, Mariano. *Underdogs*. *Translated from the Spanish by E. Munguia* (New York: Brentano's, 1929) First published 1915. This vivid, fast-paced portrayal of fighters in Mexico's revolutions was assembled from the author's own experience as a revolutionary. His extraordinary and accurate account of these times is written with the cold realism of an idealist who recognized the futility of the countless struggles. The novel simply traces various rebels in their aimless quest for aimless victory. There are no heroes or villains, but there are remarkable accounts of fighting, indescribable confusion, and the chaos of Mexican peasant life.

Robert Roper reports that while the work is "not much known in the United States," it is very well known in Mexico. "The color and ghoulishness of the 1910 (and on) revolution are done impressively. A color-filled sketch for a meatier novel."

Babel, Isaac. *Collected Stories*. *Translated from the Russian by Walter Morison* (New York: Criterion, 1955) During a brief writing career that spanned only twenty years, the Russian short story writer produced many distinguished works which are celebrated in literary circles. Included in this volume are tales and vignettes of life among the Odessa Jews under the rule of the Communists, and stories of the Red Cossack cavalry during the Russian civil war. Babel's ironical, fresh and gifted prose makes him one of the most notable writers of post-revolutionary Russia. Lionel Trilling, in the introduction to this work, analyzes Babel's literary genius and his peculiar racial and psychological characteristics.

Recommended by Daniel Halpern.

Bagnold, Enid. *The Loved and Envied* (London: Heinemann, 1951) At fifty-three, Lady MacLean is "loved and envied" for her beauty as well as for her graceful entrances into, and exits from, love affairs. In contrast to her aristocratic London life, the reader is introduced to her daughter—a woman completely overshadowed by the mother she loves but cannot please. As a story of aging men and women, it is poignant, beautiful and true. Even the satirical touches help to round out the otherwise sympathetic treatment of the aging lady. This is a remarkable novel which deserves to be better known than the author's *National Velvet* .

Howard Moss recommended this in *Antaeus*, Autumn, 1975.

Baldwin, James. *Tell Me How Long the Train's Been Gone* (New York: Dial Press, 1968) Recovering from a heart attack, a black actor looks back on forty years of his life, beginning with his childhood experiences in Harlem. As he grows older and more ambitious, he recalls his dual struggles to find love in his personal life and prominence in his profession. The driving forces behind all his motives are social crisis and violence. This, in a real sense, is a protest novel with an unusual central character.

Nikki Giovanni says she chooses this book as undeservedly neglected because, "I never can seem to find [it] when I want to give a friend a copy. I meet people who . . . think James Baldwin only wrote *The Fire Next Time*." And she feels it is a book which "deserves a reading because [it] not only has something both sweet and crucial to share about the human condition but [it] shares it beautifully."

Baring, Maurice. *Tinker's Leave* (London: Heinemann, 1927) Drawing upon his experience as a correspondent for an English newspaper during the Russo-Japanese War, Baring tells the story of a young Englishman covering this war. The plot, however, is incidental to what is essentially a splendid combination of autobiography and travel book. Few people have understood Russia and Manchuria as well as the author, and this is obvious in the stimulating and refreshing prose.

Isaiah Berlin, who recommends this work, says, "It gave me great pleasure when I read it before the war. . . .I like it because it seemed to me to give a very vivid picture of what it was like to be there then [Manchuria, 1904], for it did what very few novelists do—reproduced the conversation of civilized people accurately and fully. Thus I seem to remember that the journalist disputed whether north or south German literature was the more distinguished—very few characters in novels, whether nine-teenth or twentieth century, ever do what people like us do a good deal of the time—discuss books, opinions about artistic events, and generally behave in an altogether life-like fashion. . . ."

Baring-Gould, Sabine. *John Herring: A West of England Romance* (London: Smith, Elder, 1883) D. M. Thomas recommends this book and describes its author as follows: "Baring-Gould was a Victorian priest and squire, prolific in every way: e.g., seventeen children, one hundred fifty books." Thomas, furthermore, says, "This novel is probably his best: teeming with a quirky vitality. Set in the west of England, where the author lived."

Barnes, Djuna. *Nightwood* (London: Faber, 1936) Moving in a dream-like, surrealistic milieu, five characters seem to be submerged in a nightmare as they serve the whims of a baron desperately seeking to provide an heir for his title. Serving as a kind of Greek chorus, a brilliant doctor explains how the other characters fit into the scheme of life and the novel. The force and distinction of the writing makes character and situation not only plausible but eerily original. The setting is Paris, but the situation and characters are universal. If the plot is bizarre, the invention and skill of the author in constructing a unique psychological situation are marked by genius.

Lawrence Ferlinghetti believes that *Nightwood* includes "some of the greatest prose of our time, especially in the monologues of Dr. Matthew O'Connor. . . ." And he calls it "one of the most important American expatriate novels of the period."

Barnes, Djuna. *Ryder* (New York: Liveright, 1928) While Barnes' *Nightwood* is now a twentieth-century underground classic, this equally excellent, some would even say better, novel is relatively unknown. Wendell Ryder, his various mistresses, his mother, and his wife are the central personalities who discuss their robust world of the 1920s. The construction of the novel, with its amorphous plot and its range of Joycean characters, is unique, and Barnes' wit and humor have never been stronger than in this trenchant satire. *Note:* The 1928 edition was heavily expurgated.

Kenneth Rexroth recommended this in *Antaeus*, Autumn, 1979.

Barrie, James. *Sentimental Tommy* (London: Cassell, 1896) ***Tommy and Grizel*** (London: Cassell, 1900) Endowing Tommy with the temperament of an artist, with a passion for posing and a talent for insincerity, Barrie charts his hero's course from the back streets of London to the fictional village of Thrums. This is a touch of paradise for the boy who becomes involved in the fantasies and romances of the period. Barrie continues the saga with *Tommy and Grizel*, a story that follows Tommy, now a writer, to an unanticipated death. His life of make believe is an admixture of ingratiating himself with his friends and deceiving himself, and it is a marvelous comedy of sentimentality.

Alison Lurie, who mentions these works, says they are "almost unknown, but interesting and often brilliant late-Victorian novels."

Baxter, Walter. *Look Down in Mercy* (New York: Putnam, 1952) The pressure of World War II turns an otherwise mild-mannered English officer into a depraved and brutal monster. The place, Southeast Asia, is as much responsible for his transformation as the war. Actually, battles are almost forgotten when the tropical climate and foreign surroundings undermine the sanity and disposition of the officer.

Henri Peyre calls this "a very remarkable English novel."

Becker, Stephen. *When the War Is Over* (New York: Random House, 1969) Deserted by his family, a teen-aged Kentucky boy becomes a Rebel guerrilla during the last years of the Civil War. The story is narrated by a Yankee officer wounded by the boy. The two become friends and the officer helps the young soldier understand himself in light of his familial deprivation. Based on historical fact, the novel moves to the trial of the boy after the war. In a struggle between his love of the law and the military, Lieutenant Catto tries to save the youth. The story is a brilliant reconstruction of time and place, and while the plot is relatively simple, the dialogue, descriptions and overtones are complex and illustrate a marvelous craftsmanship. The conflicting views of war and justice have never been better drawn.

John Irving recommends this work "highly," and Vance Bourjaily calls it "a lovely novel which is well worth reviving."

Beckford, William. *Vathek* 2 volumes (London: Constable, 1929) First published, 1786. One of the early pseudo-Oriental, Gothic tales with a mad mixture of comedy, magic, and horror, this novel concerns a certain despotic sultan, Vathek. He participates in a series of crimes against his people, and finally is doomed to the Hall of Eblis, an inferno of magnificent dimensions. The hall is depicted with loving detail, and Beckford's ability to portray characters and events has rarely been rivaled in this genre. The torments are graphically delineated in a richly imaginative, extravagant manner.

Quentin Bell recommends this.

Bedford, Sybille. *A Favourite of the Gods* (London: Collins, 1963) Coincidence and free will determine the fate of three related women: Anna Howland, an American heiress who early in the twentieth century marries an Italian nobleman; her daughter, Constanza, who is raised as a European; and, in turn, her daughter,

Flavia, who is raised as an Englishwoman. The contrasts in the various national characteristics, the social mores of the different periods of time, and the distinctive personalities of the three women combine to produce an impressionistic picture of people and events. The plot develops around the changes in European society, the reaction of the three women to those alterations, and, most importantly, the casual decisions of Constanza which have unforeseen consequences. Rich in overtones, beautifully written, this is a substantial work of art.

Liz Smith recommends it.

Bedford, Sybille. *A Legacy* (New York: Simon & Schuster, 1956) Christopher Sykes writes, "I think *The Legacy* . . . is a remarkable book for various reasons. First of all, it deals with a very little known world, that of Kaiser Wilhelm II, though the Kaiser plays a minimal part in the story. It also deals with a Jewish world such as was widespread in the Berlin of that time and the intermarriage of Jews and German aristocrats which was much deplored, especially by anti-Semites. . . .

"Being about a Jewish world, it deals with the comic aspects of Jewish life in a completely unself-conscious way, and in a way that has been lost since the Hitler-ite atrocities of recent years.

"It has certain blemishes, for example: a comic use of one of the character's pet chimpanzees, which is merely tiresome, but this is a relatively small feature of the book and does not seriously damage it.

"The lasting impression of it is of an extraordinarily vivid picture of Berlin aristocratic-Jewish life in the early years of this century in Berlin and in the whole of Germany, notably the Rhineland where the scene of the story is set."

Martha Gellhorn also recommends this work.

Beer, Thomas. *Mrs. Egg and Other Barbarians* (New York: Knopf, 1937) In this collection of short stories, one of America's most effective stylists demonstrates his considerable technique. But beyond his style, Beer has a clear understanding of peculiar characters, especially when they are avid individualists living intensely. The sophisticated, intellectually cool descriptions of these people are matched only by their lusty and recognizable actions.

Glenway Wescott names this work in *Antaeus*, Autumn, 1979.

Bellamy, Edward. *Looking Backward* (Boston: Houghton, 1888) While this is a recognized classic, it is overlooked today by the people who would most enjoy it, i.e., those interested in social issues who also have a predilection for science fiction. The story is as follows: awakening from a one-hundred-thirteen-year, Rip Van Winkle sleep, the narrator discovers himself in the Boston of 2000 A.D. The place is virtually a utopia, and the author is concerned with explaining how it was created as he, incidentally, involves the narrator in a romance. While Bellamy's utopia may no longer be a blueprint for the modern reader's sense of a perfect society, the novel remains outstanding for its profusion of ideas.

Edwin Morgan notes it was "one of the most widely-read and influential works of 19th-century science fiction, dealing with the 'projected future' theme; didactic, but still interesting."

Bely, Andrei. *Petersburgh.* *Translated from the Russian by John Cournos* (New York: Grove, 1959) First published, 1916. *Note:* A better translation is by Robert A. Maguire and John E. Malmstead, published by Indiana University Press, 1978.

A skilled writer reaches heights of genius with this subtle combination of characterization, mesmerizing plot and unerring style. Bely, in this view of Russia before the revolution, is concerned with a high-ranking government official who is loyal to the Czar, and his son, who is a confused revolutionary. The son is ordered to kill his father, but before he is able to resolve his conflicting emotions, the father brings about his own surprise solution to the problem.

Vladimir Nabokov, according to *The New Yorker*, September 11, 1978, "once volunteering on television to list in order the greatest masterpieces of twentieth century prose, placed . . . Bely's novel . . . third, behind Joyce's *Ulysses* and Kafka's *Metamorphosis*." Susan Sontag also recommends it.

Bennett, Arnold. *Buried Alive* (London: Methuen, 1908) Published the same year as *The Old Wives' Tale*, this has been overshadowed by Bennett's most famous novel, although its plot has been the basis of theatrical and cinematic works. The title derives from the central character's changing places with his dead valet. Extravagant complications occur when the "dead" man's paintings suddenly begin to appear in great quantity, and there is a threat to shorten his happy life as a deceased artist. The richly ironical story is one of Bennett's best, particularly in its characterization of the hero.

Russell Hoban considers it "a wonderfully funny story of a shy painter who finds himself living out the matrimonial hopes of his dead butler." He remarks, furthermore, that "it contains some of the best descriptions of painting I've ever read."

Bennett, Arnold. *Riceyman Steps* (London: Cassell, 1923) Henry Earlforward is a middle-aged London bookseller who lives above his small shop and saves every shilling. Despite the distasteful penury of both Henry and his wife, they

emerge as sympathetic characters. Through his novelistic skill, Bennett is able to shade the harsh plot with bleak humor, as well as charm.

John Hollander calls this "a remarkable novel" concerning "a frighteningly powerful and destructive domestic relationship. Bennett's novel is spare, and almost French in its precision."

Benson, Stella. *Living Alone* (London: Macmillan, 1919) Responsible for tending a small general shop in a community of people who wish to live alone, Angela is at the center of a novel charged with whimsical madness and great beauty. She claims to be a witch, but she is always hungry and terribly intolerant of other souls who live in the combined home, monastery and college. Moving as rapidly as Angela claims her broom stick will carry her, the plot includes an air raid which is described from both below and above. Then, as well, there is the wildly humorous chronicle of Peony who has found the perfect man. This work may have little rhyme and less reason, but it is a masterpiece of wonder.

Naomi Mitchison writes, "For some reason none of Stella Benson's novels have been reprinted. I always felt she was one of the best, a really hard-hitting stylist and teller of a story. She wrote a number of novels during the twenties and thirties, but this was the one I liked best."

Benson, Stella. *Tobit Transplanted* (London: Macmillan, 1931) The special flavor of this novel comes from its setting, a White Russian community in Manchuria. Its title is taken from the Apocryphal Book of Tobit, which is added as an appendix. The style of this unusual work is described by the author as follows: "It is my . . . effort to record, as honestly as . . . possible to me, the point of view of people as other people—not as people seen by me or seen through myself, but people seeing themselves—each from the vantage point of his own identity." She succeeds in doing so, and the intricate details and insights of the work give the community a life all its own.

D. J. Enright calls this work "a skillful and engaging version of the events of the Apocryphal Book of Tobit (the angel Raphael helps Tobias to cure the blindness of his father, Tobit) transferred to a group of White Russians. . . ." It was published in America under the title of *The Far Away Bride*.

Berners, Gerald H. *The Camel* (London: Constable, 1936) One day, a camel rings the doorbell of the vicarage of Slumdermere. He happens to be returning a call made years earlier in the Orient by the Reverend Aloysius Hussey and his wife, Antonia. Taking the camel as a pet and a friend, Antonia is helped immensely by the camel's understanding of English. Amusing, at times harrowing, calamities ensue and the reader is engaged by a series of outrageous characters along the way. This narrative of wit, imagination and bizarre humor culminates in a great finale.

Edward Gorey recommended it in *Antaeus*, Autumn, 1975.

Berners, Gerald H. *Far From the Madding War* (London: Constable, 1941) This satirical, delicately malicious novel is about Kimble College, in an English university, and the vital role the faculty plays in World War II. The professors test theories in order to aid the Foreign Office. And little comes of their work except for confusion and, for us, the pleasure of following these characters. War, at least here, is a silent delight, and universal truths about university life are more apparent than battles.

A. J. P. Taylor says, "Oxford in 1940. Very funny."

Berriault, Gina. *The Mistress and Other Stories* (New York: Dutton, 1965) Despite her pessimism, Berriault's stories are as adept as they are convincing, as imaginative as they are insightful. Most of the characters in these fifteen stories live in states of isolation or fear of seeing their lives come to nought. At the same time, the breadth of the author's psychological perceptiveness into individuals of great diversity carries the reader along in fascination.

Raymond Carver recommends this volume.

Berry, Wendell. *The Memory of Old Jack* (New York: Harcourt, 1973) Jack Beechum, a ninety-two-year-old Kentucky farmer, remembers through a series of vivid dreams the experiences of his unsatisfactory life. His loveless childhood, his unfulfilling marriage, his toil on the land are all recalled on this last day of his life. There is a strong sense of compassion for this character as well as for the others who populate the story. The small-town Kentucky milieu is skillfully evoked as is the characters' primary attachment to the land.

Ken Kesey calls this "a Wendell Berry novel that advances his theme of the poetry and the importance of involvement with the land better than his essays."

Bester, Alfred. *Who He?* (New York: Dial Press, 1953) The script writer of a successful television show, "Who He?," is followed through a week of busy activity between Christmas and New Year's in New York City. The television production and its various minions—writers, network associates, advertising executives—provide the focus. While neither a satire nor a renunciation of television, the novel leaves little doubt that the price demanded of its followers by that mass medium might be too high. The accurate presentation of the television writer and the other characterizations give this work a timeless quality.

Samuel Delany commended this work in *Antaeus*, Winter, 1975.

Birmingham, George. *Spanish Gold* (London: Methuen, 1908) While working as a clergyman, Birmingham (pseudonym for James Hannay) wrote a prodigious number of popular novels, although he valued his scholarship on Church history and theology more highly. The title *Spanish Gold* refers to an effort to locate gold on a Spanish galleon sunk during the Armada off the coast of Ireland. The hero is a clever Irish curate who, along with some friends, challenges two similarly enthusiastic competitors. The curate, a man of good humor and compassion, sharply differs from his rollicking, devious and dishonest competitors. Actually, the comedy is more concerned with English notions about Ireland than with gold hunting, and the strength of the novel lies in characterization rather than plot. Among Birmingham's novels, this remains one of his best.

Graham Greene, according to an article in *The New Yorker*, March 26, 1979, counts himself as an admirer of this novel.

Bishop, John Peale. *Act of Darkness* (New York: Scribner, 1935) The mind of an adolescent boy in a small West Virginian community is the sensibility through which Bishop measures the moral worth of the community. The town and its residents often fall short in strength and courage, yet even in failure they help the developing consciousness of the narrator. A startling trial concludes the novel, and as a record of a particular American experience, this is a memorable work. It fully employs the skill of a writer better known as a poet.

Allen Tate noted this work in *Antaeus*, Autumn, 1977.

Bissell, Richard. *High Water* (Boston: Little, 1954) This light-hearted, good-humored tale is told through the eyes of a second mate of a small Mississippi towboat, and focuses on the efforts of the craft to push eight coal barges from St. Louis to St. Paul during a high-water flood. Everything goes wrong. The chaos is conveyed in lively dialogue which reflects a refreshing, river view of life.

Roger Sale, in *The American Scholar*, Winter, 1979, recommended this along with Bissell's *Stretch on the River* (1950) and *7½ Cents* (1953), calling them "wonderfully durable books, funny, sweet, touching."

Black, David. *Like Father* (New York: Dodd, 1978) Moses, an English teacher for over twenty-five years, reads a biography of Tolstoy and decides he must abandon his work in order to find himself. He turns to his son and daughter-in-law who live in rural New Hampshire. When Moses attempts to find a new love in his son's wife, he is driven from the house by his outraged child. Moses then moves to New York and finds his father, a nonconformist who had relegated his son to an orphanage. This sometimes raucous, sometimes sad story is told convincingly and the novel is a superior comment on life in America during the 1970s.

Anne Tyler recommends this work.

Blake, Nicholas. *The Private Wound* (New York: Harper, 1968) H. R. F. Keating writes: "The detective stories that Cecil Day-Lewis wrote under the pen-name of Nicholas Blake have often distinctly dated from their earliest appearance in the 1930s and 40s (though there is much of sociological interest to be grubbed out of them). Even, it must be admitted, some of the ones written later have a smack of the perfunctory about them. But to both of these perhaps not wholly satisfactory groups there can be opposed the last book he wrote in the genre, *The Private Wound.*

"For some reason he chose to pour into this detective story (for such it is, with all the classical trimmings of plot, clues, suspects and surprise) what was plainly a deeply felt private experience. And in doing so he brought off the rare feat of combining a no-holds-barred novel with its bastard cousin.

"The writing is of a high order. Within the first few pages, indeed, you realise you have entered the dense world of the successful fiction. The tiny details of life intermesh like the matted hairs on human skin, each perhaps irrelevant to the body it springs from, all together transforming what would otherwise be a metal-sheathed automaton into something vibrantly alive. Each detail takes its place in a fully realised whole. Not one sticks out as striking, but irrelevant, *trouvaille.*

"The scene is Ireland just before the 1939-45 War, a background real as can be and subtly menaced all the while by the rumours of the conflict to come. Against this scene there takes place a love affair pulsating with truth, and from that affair there grows a murder. The sexual scenes are handled with truth and modesty, nothing burked, nothing exaggerated for titillation's sake. And, equally, scenes of true violence are made real and frightening, again without false effects.

"In sum, here we have a fine detective puzzle and a novel that stays in the memory as a mysterious whole, sad, true and lit with menacing flames from Ireland's violent past and the world's yet more violent future. It should not be a neglected book."

Blasco Ibáñez, Vincente. *Cabin.* Translated from the Spanish by F. Haffkine Snow (New York: Knopf, 1918) First pub-

lished, 1898. The action in this novel takes place in a small irrigated district near the Spanish city of Valencia. Most of the area is deserted until Batiste settles upon the inauspicious land. Batiste, in conflict with landlords, society and the government, is representative of Spanish political tendencies of the time. But apart from the symbolism, this is a superb dramatic narrative and a vivid portrayal of Spanish life.

William F. H. Lamont cited this work in *Books Abroad*, Vol. 27:3.

Bolton, Isabel. *The Christmas Tree* (New York: Scribner, 1949) While involved with Christmas preparations for her grandson, Mrs. Danforth recollects her effortless youth filled with wealth and style. However, her unfulfilling marriage led to the birth of an adored homosexual son around whom the story is built. When he makes an appearance at the Christmas tree, he draws the story to a tragic conclusion.

Diana Trilling recommends this along with *Do I Wake or Sleep* by the same author. Doris Grumbach also recommends these works, calling them "small and marvelous novels."

Bolton, Isabel. *Do I Wake or Sleep* (New York: Scribner, 1946) Set in a twenty-four-hour period in 1939, two women and a man, deeply involved in New York's social and artistic circles, discuss their experiences and their desires. Edmund Wilson compared this novel to the best of Henry James and Virginia Woolf. Wilson commented, "The story has life and moves; it immediately creates suspense without our understanding how or why; it carries to an unexpected climax" (*The New Yorker*, October 26, 1946). The sensitive and satirical eye of the author perfectly captures pre-war America.

Diana Trilling writes: "Although Edmund Wilson in *The New Yorker* and I in *The Nation* reviewed *Do I Wake or Sleep* with the greatest respect and admiration, neither it nor the novel that followed it [*The Christmas Tree*] reached its proper audience. The author, in her early sixties when it appeared, had previously written under the name of Mary Britten Miller."

Bolton Isabel. *Many Mansions* (New York: Scribner, 1952) At the age of eighty-four, Margaret looks back on her life through the pages of her unpublished novel. While the plot is minimal, the author's uncanny appreciation for the thoughts and emotions of an aged woman have poetic vitality. For while Margaret relates the experiences of her early years, the reminiscence is dominated by an old woman's perspective. At the end of the day, the end of the novel, the telephone rings and the story comes to a simple climax.

Babette Deutsch recommended this in *American Scholar*, Spring, 1970.

Borchert, Wolfgang. *The Man Outside.* *Translated from the German by David Porter* (New York: New Directions, 1952) First published, 1949. Kay Boyle writes, "I consider *The Man Outside* (a collection of stories, poems, and the play which gives the book its title) one of the two most stirring literary masterpieces to come out of Germany following World War II. (The other is Theodore Plievier's *Stalingrad*.) Written by a young German in the months preceding his early death in a Swiss sanitarium, the book articulates the fierce anger and despair of the young who have been betrayed by a world gone mad with militarism, a world in which all hope, all man's dedication to his fellow-man, all belief in a future, have been starved, bombed, executed into total extinction."

Bowen, Elizabeth. *The House in Paris* (London: Gollancz, 1935) Henrietta and Leopold are lovers whose romance begins and develops in Paris. The author, who is often compared to Katherine Mansfield and Virginia Woolf, renders every scene, every action with a sense of reality. Not only is this a compelling story, it is an inspired one since it offers profound insight into human nature.

Daniel Halpern recommends it.

Bowles, Jane. *My Sister's Hand in Mine* (New York: Ecco, 1978) First published as *The Collected Works of Jane Bowles*, 1966. With an introduction by Truman Capote, this is an expanded version of the 1966 collection. Included are ten witty, short stories (primarily from *Plain Pleasures*, 1966); the play, *In the Summer House*; a novel, *Two Serious Ladies*; and three fragments.

Daniel Halpern commends this volume.

Bowles, Jane. *Two Serious Ladies* (New York: Knopf, 1943) Reissued in her collected works, i.e. *My Sister's Hand in Mine*. Robert Mazzocco says that *Two Serious Ladies* is "certainly the most *sui generis* novel by an American woman since Gertrude Stein's *Three Lives*. Jane Bowles domesticates the Steinian oddity of syntax and the Steinian arrangement of 'composition,' and uses these difficult properties not so much for narrative ends (though her narrative line is far clearer than anything in Stein) as for dramatic juxtapositions in a cubistic vein, creating, at times, a heartbreakingly comic pattern. Not as formidable as Katherine Anne Porter nor a genius of the stature of Flannery O'Connor, she is, I think, far more 'unique' than either. This book, stupidly received when it first appeared, has for some time now been recognized as an underground 'classic'—and deservedly so."

Bowles, Paul. *The Delicate Prey* (New York: Random House, 1950) The short stories that make up this volume are unforgettable in their violence. The author, who is also a composer, has a refined style which skillfully creates the deadly spiritual environments of his characters. Mr. Bowles' gifts as a writer are never in question, although the horrific nature of his stories can be repellent.

Daniel Halpern recommends this volume.

Boyd, Thomas. *Through the Wheat* (New York: Scribner, 1923) Moving through the wheat of a French field, an American marine enters a battle in World War I. He is fated to become a hero, but the lonely private gains more stature from his moral virtue than from military honors. In its ability to reduce battle to human terms, this book is a match for *The Red Badge of Courage.* Edmund Wilson believes, "This is probably the only candid account on record of what it means to be a hero in the Marines."

Southern Illinois University Press is reissuing it.

Boyle, Kay. *Monday Night* (New York: Harcourt, 1938) One of the best sophisticated horror stories and psychological mysteries, this novel is somewhat reminiscent of Edgar Allan Poe's stories and Alfred Hitchcock's films. The author's style and plot is equal to theirs. Her story concerns two Americans in France who are in pursuit of a certain Dr. Sylvestre. Both her sly descriptions and fast-moving narrative capture the reader's attention through to the surprise ending in the form of a newspaper announcement.

Doris Grumbach and James Laughlin recommend this.

Bramah, Ernest. *Eyes of Max Carrados* (London: G. Richards, 1923) One of the more unusual British detectives, Max Carrados is blind, yet able to solve diverting mysteries in this collection of short stories. Carrados is able to locate a lost book, a lost person, comprehend the true personality of a ghost, and crack a spy case—among other adventures in these ingenious tales.

Patricia Highsmith applauds "the artistry and literary elegance of Bramah's stories [which] entertain as much as the ingenuity of his plots. . . .If their very period flavour has contributed to present day neglect (the rich, blind amateur of criminology, his retinue of able assistants, his man-servant with perfect recall), they nonetheless used to great effect the basic situations of classic detective fiction, such as the 'wrong' body, the trail of red herrings, the opportunity which makes the thief and so on. 'It is as well to look beyond the obvious,' says Max Carrados at one point. The knowing reader of course does this, but the ensuing complexities never unravel in quite the way he expects. This is always satisfying to the true addict" (*Times Literary Supplement,* June 5, 1981).

Brancati, Vitaliano. *Bell'Antonio.* *Translated from the Italian by Stanley Hochman* (New York: Ungar, 1978) First published, 1949. The title refers to Antonio Magnano whose manners and handsomeness insure his idolization by the women in his Sicilian village. The shock comes three years after his marriage when it is revealed that he is impotent. This discovery plunges Antonio, his family and his friends into frenzied despair. The counterpoint to this tragicomic novel of Sicilian manners is the rise of Italian fascism in the 1930s. Without forcing the comparison, the author suggests common traits in Antonio and Mussolini.

John Simon recommends this novel.

Branch, Pamela. *Murder's Little Sisters* (London: Penguin, 1963) In this mystery, the author draws a satirical picture of British magazine publishing. The work is outstanding as much for the imaginative twists and turns of the plot as for the lively and wonderfully amusing dialogue.

Peter Dickinson writes, "Some twenty years ago I must have read getting on for a thousand crime novels during a five-year stint of reviewing—late Allingham, both Inneses, early Keating, Deighton, Le Carré. Just as strongly as those, two or three novels by Pamela Branch stick in my mind. They were black humor (before the vogue) not because of a desire to shock, but because of the author's genuinely bizarre vision. She seemed to see a world in which the aberrations of a psychopath were no quirkier, and no less sympathetic, than those of any other eccentric; and no one but eccentrics inhabited her surreal cityscapes: even the animals had twisted psyches. Though her characters were (to say the least) misfits, who sometimes did appalling things to each other, the effect in my memory is one of warmth, cheerfulness, and of laughing aloud as I read" (*Times Literary Supplement*, June 5, 1981).

Brickner, Richard P. *Tickets* (New York: Simon & Schuster, 1981) Cynthia Ozick says, "This is a masterpiece of its kind, and its kind is wholly original: an 'opera' novel (with an operatic ending), an enthralling love story, a wonderful portrait gallery of New York types. A New York novel the way Graham Greene's *The End of the Affair* is a London novel. His previous novel is *Bringing Down the House* (1971), and he has written a moving and altogether splendid memoir called *My Second Twenty Years* (1976). He has a mind of distinctive beauty and power."

Brooke, Jocelyn. *Conventional Weapons* (London: Faber, 1961) The reader is introduced to a stratum of English middle-class society before and after World War II by following the divergent paths of two English brothers. The younger gains some fame as an artist and novelist. His elder brother, whom he worships and detests, turns from the army to virtual exile from England. With an astonishing appreciation of the deeper character traits which remain unspoken and barely revealed, Brooke turns both brothers into unforgettable personalities. His impeccable prose is never better than in this late novel.

Brooke, Jocelyn. *The Dog at Clambercrown* (London: Bodley Head, 1955) A mixture of travel writing, childhood memoirs, and vivid portraits of English society, this is a rare type of reminiscence. While disarmingly clever, it is equally sincere and sensitive. Appreciating the contrasts between different people and different places, Brooke combines mild malice with obvious affection to carry the reader along in the fashion of a novel.

Anthony Powell, who also recommends *The Orchid Trilogy*, says that here Brooke's "best qualities are to be seen as autobiographer, traveler, critic. The Dog was a pub at a neighbouring village called Clambercrown."

Brooke, Jocelyn. *The Orchid Trilogy* (London: Secker/Penguin, 1981) Composed of *The Military Orchid* (1948), *A Mine of Serpents* (1949), *The Goose Cathedral* (1950). The author, from early childhood, was a solitary youth, a natural outsider in his society which consisted of upper middle-class English people living near the coast in the winter and inland in the summer. These complementary novels, not chronologically successive, salute brilliant moments in the author's early years: long summer afternoons searching for rare orchids, discovering and hoarding and finally exploding gorgeous fireworks; running away from a typically repressive English public school. Neither entirely fictitious nor autobiographical, the trilogy takes the narrator from childhood to adolescence to Oxford in the 1920s and to his service in the army. The books cover a wide range of composite characters who typify phases in the author's life. The combination of Brooke's good humor, his sensitivity to the tension between youth and adults, his sensuality and his unstinting, unsentimental view of society result in a unique literary experience.

Anthony Powell writes, " . . . I had marked Brooke down as one of the notable writers to have surfaced after the war. . . . All writers, one way or another, depend ultimately on their own lives for the material of their books, but the manner in which each employs personal experience, interior or exterior, is very different. Jocelyn Brooke uses both elements with a minimum of dilution, though much imagination. However far afield he goes physically, his creative roots remain in his childhood. He was by nature keenly interested in himself, though without vanity, or the smallest taint of exhibitionism.

"Brooke might, indeed, be compared with a performer at a fair or variety show . . . who arrives on the stage always with the same properties and puppets. The first backdrop is certain to be the landscape of Kent . . . "(Introduction to *The Orchid Trilogy*).

Roald Dahl also recommends this volume saying "this comparatively little-known writer and his books have given me more pleasure this year than anything else I have read."

Brossard, Chandler. *The Bold Saboteurs* (New York: Farrar, Straus, 1953) This evocation of a delinquent childhood is given immediacy by the voice of its young narrator, his brother and his companions. Yogi is a juvenile thief who dodges in and out of areas traditionally forbidden by society. The characterization is wholly believable and the descriptions of this marginal society are striking.

Harlan Ellison recommends this novel.

Brown, Alice. *The Country Road* (Boston: Houghton, 1906) Over a long life (1857-1948), Alice Brown pursued a vigorous writing career. She was the author of numerous novels and short stories. This, a collection of thirteen of her best stories, is set in New England near the turn of the century. Most of the pieces are deceptively mild domestic dramas, often acted out in a kitchen or dooryard. Beneath the calm, we find some of the most winning characters in American fiction—wise, tolerant, sometimes slightly comic. Whether concerned with marriage, an innocent love affair, or a community problem, few writers better capture the spirit of the typical New Englander than Alice Brown. The original characters remain as fascinating today as when they first appeared in popular American magazines.

Judith Fetterley recommends this volume as well as Brown's *Meadow-Grass* (1895) and *Tiverton Tales* (1899).

Brown, George Douglas. *The House with the Green Shutters* (London: Mac-Queen, 1901) Scottish village life at the turn of the century is portrayed as mean and inhospitable to ideas. This author's vision runs counter to typical village novels of the period, and his realistic sketch of the fall of the House of Gourlay is centered on a bully as its major character. In fact few of the many characters, who are drawn with great skill, are sympathetic. And this extraordinary psychological novel with its macabre edge is appreciated only today.

Edwin Morgan, in the *Times Literary Supplement* (October 13, 1978), writes, "The fall in his tragic novel is owed not only to the fatal pride of the bullying central character, but also to the machinations of the sly, gloating, garrulous villagers. The boy . . . does not grow up . . . [H]e kills his father and takes poison; and the author himself, a young man, was dead a year after the book appeared."

Bryher. Roman Wall (New York: Pantheon, 1956) German tribes are massing on the far bank of the Rhine and threaten the existence of a Roman outpost (in what is now Switzerland) and even Rome itself. Three different responses to the impending doom are charted through three characters: a Roman soldier, a migrant Greek trader, and the Roman governor. This is a deft, impressive, historical novel which is particularly strong in plot and characterization.

Noel Perrin believes this to be the "masterpiece by the 88-year-old Englishwoman." Most impressive "is the extraordinary texture of reality. There is not one character whose actions and thought processes do not seem to me at once alien (these people lived 1,700 years ago) and true. . . .More impressive still are the ways in which Bryher shows the powerful but decaying society in which these characters move" (*Washington Post Book World*, March 12, 1982). Bryher is the pseudonym for Annie Winifred Macpherson.

Buckmaster, Henrietta. *And Walk In Love* (New York: Random House, 1956) Based upon the life of Saint Paul, as described in Acts and Paul's letters, the novel follows fairly accurately the historical evidence. The author does allow herself one invention—that Saul knew and loved Stephen the martyr.

Roger Sale notes that Buckmaster "shows Saul persecuting the Nazarenes out of torment and the need to believe in some absolute truth. He is, thus, quite ready for the vision on the road to Damascus when it comes. It does not turn his life around, only clarifies it, sets it on its true path, the one he had long been seeking. No one believes in either visions or conversions who does not want so to believe, that is Buckmaster's assurance, and it gives her her strength, her sense of the kind of love this forbidding man could feel. . . .There's not a cinemascopic moment in the novel . . . there is none of the ordinary historical novelist's fatal need to explain the unexplainable with decoration in details. The world that Paul moves in is there, clear enough at all events, because he himself is clear. The writing is undistinguished, but it is always diligent and serviceable, a rather plain rhetoric that is sufficiently like Paul's own that when he speaks words we all recognize as his we can read without embarrassment . . . "(*American Scholar*, Winter, 1979).

Buechner, Frederick. *Lion Country* (New York: Atheneum Publishers, 1971) Antonio Parr hopes to recover his writing job by exposing the unethical operations of a divinity diploma mill. The Church of Holy Love is lead by Reverend Leo Bebb and Laverne Brown, whom Bebb claims to have restored to life. Parr clashes with Bebb and his grotesque band of followers. The peculiar twist is that an odd yet mature religious belief arises from the conflict in this thoughtful comedy. Not only are the storytelling and characterizations superior, but the description of traditional Christian ideas and actions is outstanding. The same characters and much of the story are further explored in a second novel, *Open Heart*, 1972.

Laurie Colwin says: "I am not much of a critic, just an enjoyer. These books have what all good books have: intelligence, intensity, idiosyncracy, clear, moving and often original prose, and clear, moving and often original insights about the lives of men and women."

Buechner, Frederick. *A Long Day's Dying* (New York: Knopf, 1949) A widow, her son and her mother contend with problems caused by what appeared to be a casual incident. The psychological sophistication in this witty, stylish work resides in characterization which turns uninteresting, though highly cultivated, people into surprisingly complex personalities. The somewhat bizarre impressions are framed with in a baroque plot, which includes three men who are in love with the mother.

Doris Grumbach says, "This is his first novel. Until the recent *Gudric* his most amazing achievement."

Bunin, Ivan. *The Village. Translated from the Russian by Isabel Hapgood* (New York: Knopf, 1923) First published, 1910. The daily routine of two brothers is employed to illustrate life in a typical Russian village before the Russian Revolution. The complexity of living under the Czar and his massive bureaucracy is vividly portrayed. While the brothers are shown to be sympathetic figures, they are depicted with all their flaws, and many readers consider this one of the truest depictions of Russian life to appear. Best known for his short story collection, *The Gentleman from San Francisco* (1923), Bunin was awarded the Nobel Prize for literature in 1933.

William F. H. Lamont cites this in *Books Abroad*, Vol. 27:3.

Burke, Kenneth. *Towards a Better Life* (New York: Harcourt, 1932) A secular ascetic's letters to a rival in a love affair are collected and form a unique novel by this renowned literary critic. The hero finds transitory comfort in the company of another woman, and explains and justifies himself in monologue/letter form. The method is characteristic for one who appeals to his other self (in the recipient of the letters) and to another aspect of his true love (in the other woman). The divisions and oppositions result in ambiguity and paradox which Burke, in his criticism, has so often explored. This combination of comedy, grotesquery and intellectual games is conducted with the aid of hilarious imagery. It is a fine tribute to the imagination of both the writer and the reader.

Howard Nemerov says, "Succeeding . . . years of objective, realistic novels have had the adventitious effect of making this book look better and better." And Malcolm Cowley writes that this is a novel "that tries hard not to be a novel and instead becomes an achieved work of art."

Burns, John Horne. *The Gallery* (New York: Harper, 1947) The setting is Naples in 1944, and the story delves into the lives of diverse Americans and Italians who converged in the Galleria Umberto. Through sympathy with the Neapolitans and antipathy for most of the American soldiers, Burns shows the meaning, in human terms, of changing social and political circumstances. More important, he portrays his characters, confused, lonely and miserable, in their struggle to comprehend their lives and their time.

Edmund Keeley says, *"The Gallery* is, along with *The Naked and the Dead*, the best early fiction written about the Second World War. It was among the very first and the most authentic of those works dealing with the soldier's experience in the European theatre."

Paula Fox, Daniel Halpern, Doris Grumbach, and Derek Mahon also recommend this book.

Busch, Niven. *The Hate Merchant* (New York: Simon & Schuster, 1952) Dissatisfied with himself and his future as a minor henchman of Huey Long, Splane, the rabble rouser, decides to become an evangelist. The development of this soon-to-be-successful preacher is followed from a hitchhiking episode to a fitting conclusion.

Niven Busch writes that this is "a dramatic story based on the career of the notorious demogogue, Gerald L. K. Smith, a man who did more than anyone in history to merchandise racial hate in the U. S., his campaign culminating in the Detroit race riots of 1943. When first published, the novel received highly favorable feature reviews . . . but though I had sold several previous works to movies the filmmakers of that period were afraid of *The Hate Merchant. . . .*"

Butts, Mary. *Ashe of Rings* (Paris: Three Mountains Press, 1925) Ashe is the family; Rings is the English estate. And their history, from the nineteenth century until World War I, is developed in a series of events peopled with a variety of characters. The poetic, staccato style, the emotional intensity of the individuals and the author's sense of place combine to make this a most unusual work. While the surface is typical of the family-historical saga, the creative probing of extremely complex, almost mystical, events gives it a quality all its own.

James Laughlin recommends it.

Butts, Mary. *Several Occasions* (London: Wishart, 1932) The deceptive skill in this series of short stories is witnessed in their flawless development and simplicity of plot. Suddenly there is the sensation that while the surface of the situation is clear its real meaning is perplexing and ambiguous. For example, in "The Dinner Party," only fourteen pages long, one is left wondering what the secret between Angus and Julia and their host is, and what was the explanation for these old enemies meeting. The brilliant descriptions of people in pursuit of unobtainable goals are set in an unusual social context.

John Ashbery recommends this volume.

Cahill, Holger. *The Shadow of My Hand* (New York: Harcourt, 1956) John R. Milton describes this as follows: "A novel of nature and human nature and their related destinies, set in North Dakota following World War II, *Shadow of My Hand* is honest, realistic, dramatic, and highlighted by a few key symbols that bring the sometimes mysterious northern plains into a meaningful relationship with the rest of America. The conflicts, violence, beauty, and drama of human nature are echoed in and reinforced by the same qualities in the immense landscape and forceful climate of the north country. This 'dark sweet land' is everything, everywhere."

Calisher, Hortense. *Journal from Ellipsia* (Boston: Little, 1965) A quasi-science fiction, this is essentially a comedy of manners. A visitor from another planet invades the body of Janice Jamison, an attractive anthropologist. As the creature advances through our unknown world, the author demonstrates a fine understanding of intellectual and sensory awakening. The satire on pulp science fiction is a further delight.

John Hollander says, "*Journal from Ellipsia* was unaccountably unacknowledged when it appeared. It was remarkably prescient of literary feminism's desire to represent a feminine phenomenology; and yet I suspect that subsequent literary feminism neglected it because of its lack of political crudity, or reductive energy. It is far too remarkably poetic, being (like Lindsay's book) a visionary fable framed in an apparent science fiction. It concerns feminine knowledge, power and eros, and imagines as remarkable a group of extra-terrestrials as I have encountered in literature."

Calvino, Italo. *Invisible Cities. Translated from the Italian by William Weaver* (New York: Harcourt, 1974) First published, 1972. A lyrical exploration of cities discovered by Marco Polo during his journey through the lands of Kublai Khan, this is as much a fantasy as a symbolic tale of the quest for understanding. Calvino groups his sketches according to a mathematical formula which is part of an aesthetic game. The eleven categories of cities represent memory, desire, and comparable communities of the mind. The intricate and ingenious stories within stories consider the elegiac landscapes of all people. The uncanny complexity is a challenge well worth taking.

Susan Sontag recommends this.

Calvino, Italo. *The Path to the Nest of Spiders.* *Translated from the Italian by Archibald Colquhoun* (Boston: Beacon, 1956) First published, 1947. The Italian writer's first novel, this is based on his experience as a partisan in World War II. The main character is a boy who joins the partisans not out of a sense of duty but from a desire to escape his loneliness. He soon discovers older men in the same emotional predicament, and the rich characterization and the symbolism of loneliness place this work among the best to emerge from the war. The translation ably conveys the deliberate ferocity of the language.

Daniel Halpern recommends this work.

Camberton, Roland. *Rain on the Pavements* (London: Lehmann, 1951) Growing up in North London in the 1930s is the subject of this semi-autobiographical novel about a young Jewish boy, David Hirsch. The quiet charm of his world emerges from the numerous character sketches and brief episodes, which are as astonishing as they are plausible. The reader is introduced to a schoolmaster who spends his time playing chess with his students, the library patron who can recall meeting Trotsky in 1907, and Uncle Jake with his wild political views. The warmth of family life and community is reinforced by the sparkling light touch of the author's style.

John Lehmann recommends this novel along with the same author's *Scamp* (1950).

Campbell, R. Wright. *The Spy Who Sat and Waited* (New York: Putnam, 1975) An otherwise ordinary man, Wilhelm Oerter is assigned by the German secret service to watch British shipping. Placed in the Orkney Islands many years before World War II, he becomes an accepted member of the community while continually furnishing data to his superiors. The unique quality of the story is somewhat similar to that found in the best of John Le Carré, with the sense that the true spy is only as good as his capacity to blend into the landscape. Along the way, there is unremitting tenseness as the novel builds toward a dramatic climax.

Campbell, William. *Company K* (New York: Smith & Haas, 1933) Robert Mazzocco describes this work as "A series of snapshots about American soldiers in the First World War; a prose equivalent, in a sense, of Edgar Lee Master's *Spoon River Anthology*—that is to say, it employs a variety of characters and a range of disparate actions to embody a portrait of a generation. Though determinedly impersonal, its realistic details are alternately amusing, nightmarish, or theatrical. Far more modest than *A Farewell to Arms* or *Three Soldiers*, a number of its scenes are considerably fresher. It would make a fine film."

Canetti, Elias. *Auto da Fé.* *Translated from the German by C. V. Wedgwood* (New York: Stein & Day, 1964) First published 1935. Victimized by his own compulsiveness, Kien builds a large, personal library where he gradually loses himself. An abstract man, he is defenseless against the chicanery of his housekeeper who cheats him out of his home and his library. As he shrinks into the underworld of Vienna, he has a last successful *auto da fé* when he immolates himself and his library.

This novel, whose author recently won the Nobel Prize, was recommended by several writers including Francis Steegmuller, Susan Sontag and D.J. Enright, who describes it as: "The nightmare world of a mad, misanthropic sinologist: in some degree a study of Fascist/Nazi mentality, full of (sometimes undirected) power, often blackly comic, enormously inventive, a mixture of genius and sledge-hammer ferocity." And Michael Ivens considers it to be "one of the two or three great novels to be published since the war. Powerful, humorous, frightening, and characters worthy of Dickens crossed with Dostoyevsky, and with great psychological depths."

Carpentier, Alejo. *Lost Steps.* *Translated from the Spanish by Harriet DeOnis* (New York: Knopf, 1955) First published, 1953. Traveling up a South American river in quest of primitive musical instruments, the narrator-protagonist considers the symbolic myth of the noble savage and its psychological relevance for modern man. Set against a realistic background, the novel mixes musicology with romance and ideas. Carpentier, a Cuban, is himself a composer, musicologist and writer who has conceived this work of remarkable beauty.

Donald Finkel cites this in *Antaeus*, Autumn, 1979.

Carver, Raymond. *Will You Be Quiet, Please?* (New York: McGraw, 1976) The survival tactics of the American lower-middle to middle classes are the subject of these twenty-two short stories. Carver shows a significant talent for dialogue and the personality quirks which seem to mark otherwise ordinary people when faced with conflict. The author's wicked, ironic imagination draws unsentimental portraits of such instances as: a husband who regains his pride by forcing his wife to diet and the couple that begins to find happiness by assuming the style of another couple's life.

Gordon Lish recommends this volume.

Cary, Alice. *Clovernook, or Recollections of Our Neighborhood in the West* (New York: Redfield, 1852) Short stories and sketches about life in rural Ohio, these are a look backwards by the author who was born in Ohio but decided, at an early age, to settle in New York and live by her writing. She became a regular contributor to American magazines, and her work was extremely popular. In fact, this collection of thinly disguised portraits of real people and the events in their lives on the Ohio frontier became an early best seller in America and England. Today, all but forgotten, Cary's work remains an imaginative, weirdly and sharply observant portrait of a time and people the author knew intimately.

Judith Fetterley recommends this volume as well as the author's *Pictures of Country Life* (1859).

Cary, Joyce. *The Captive and the Free* (New York: Harper, 1959) Not quite completed when Cary died, this last novel remains one of his best. Thanks to careful editing, it is as good as finished and little is left unresolved about its primary character, Preedy, who is a faith healer. A man locked in dissension and combat with an English curate, he strongly influences the lives of several women and an investigative journalist. As a study in character and conflict, it is a triumph.

Mervyn Jones says, "In my view the most unjustly forgotten English writer, since his death, is Joyce Cary." And this novel, he feels is "most remarkable" and "well deserving a revival."

Cary, Joyce. *The Horse's Mouth*
(London: Joseph, 1944) Few novelists have
portrayed an idealistic artist better than
Cary in this day-to-day romp with Gulley
Jimson, the unrefined painter and oppor-
tunist. The character is so perfectly drawn
as to come alive for most readers and works
as a symbol for the full, good, lively life.
The plot is incidental to Gulley's daily existence and his abiding reverence for true
art, such as that of William Blake, yet it is
fascinating throughout. Gulley is just out
of prison, and while he helps a fledgling
artist, he finds himself ensconced in a
magnificent apartment which he is, unbe-
knownst to the owner, turning into a living museum. Wonderfully entertaining,
the novel should be read by many more
people today along with its two related
novels, *Herself Surprised* and *To Be A
Pilgrim.*

Kelly Cherry recommends it.

Cary, Joyce. *The House of Children*
(London: Joseph, 1941) A childhood on
the coast of Ireland *circa* 1890 is the focus of
this part-fictional, part-autobiographical
work. The reminiscences of blissful summers spent sailing, fishing and party-go-
ing constitute one of the most idyllic novels about childhood.

Mary Ann Hoberman recommends this.

Cassill, R. V. *Clem Anderson* (New
York: Simon & Schuster, 1961) Clem Anderson, a writer of genius, is a fictional
amalgam of Dylan Thomas and F. Scott
Fitzgerald going about their respective
ways to self-destruction. After Anderson's
early death, a former college friend recalls
and measures Clem's life through the materials of his novel, stories and poetry.
Clem's mid-western childhood, the period
when his creative powers become evident,
his experience in World War II, are all

punctuated with flashbacks and flashforwards. The largely credible picture of the
artist who fails to fulfill his promise has
rarely been better drawn, and throughout
the novel there is an insightful account of
the post-World War II generation.

Cather, Willa. *The Professor's House*
(New York: Knopf, 1925) This is one of two
attempts by Cather to deal with contemporary affairs. (The other was *One of Ours*,
1922.) The professor teaches European history in a state university and through various circumstances suddenly becomes
wealthy. He and his family move to a new
house, but he degenerates and is compelled
to return time and again to his old home.
The episodic development of the plot is
overshadowed by the treatment of American society and its conflicting attitudes
toward materialism and intellectual excellence. Cather pictures her character reluc-
tantly ejecting a style of American life he
has loved.

Daniel Hoffman recommended this in
Antaeus, Autumn, 1979.

Caudwell, Christopher. *This My Hand*
(London: Hamilton, 1936) This imaginative study is of a murderer's mind and his
reasoned, intellectual justification for
committing a crime. Ian Venning works in
an English industrial town. Upset with his
wife, he takes a lover and concludes that the
solution to his untenable situation is to kill
his wife. The murder appears to be an accident, and the only person who knows the
truth is his mistress. They marry, but when
Ian becomes bored with her, he is trapped
since he fears that if he leaves, she will talk.
His second wife finds a way out of the
dilemma and Ian is free to commit more
crimes. The ironic set of events draws the
novel to a fitting close.

Roy Fuller says, "This is the only 'straight' novel by the famous young Marxist critic killed in the Spanish Civil War—but a crime novel, not at all ideological."

Cela, Jose. *The Hive.* *Translated from the Spanish by J. M. Cohen* (New York: Farrar, Straus, 1953) One of the most admired modern Spanish novels, *The Hive* delineates three days in the lives of over one hundred patrons of a run-down cafe in a working-class section of Madrid. The cafe is the focus, and there are no outstanding characters and little plot. Instead the author creates a devastating vision of poverty and oppression in imitation of the natural flow of life—rambling on without apparent point. Both as a social document and a literary achievement, this novel is most exceptional.

Daniel Halpern recommends it.

Chambers, George. *The Bonnyclabber* (Western Springs, IL: December, 1973) Ronald Sukenick, who calls this "one of those rare innovative novels that is at the same time extremely moving," describes it as follows: "Since this is a novel about getting it together, I suppose it is appropriate that it emerges out of bits and pieces of collage: war stories, fairy tales, news clippings, apparent tape recordings, dreams, pages of typing. . . . It begins with a series of black pages with footnotes—footnotes to nothing, but which sound some of the leitmotifs of the story. . . .There is a great deal of play . . . much of it funny or sexy or affecting. It comes out of an insistence on improvisation over methodical progress toward a particular conclusion . . . " (*New York Times Book Review*, March 4, 1973).

Chappell, Fred. *It Is Time, Lord* (New York: Atheneum Publishers, 1963) A thoughtful, serious farm boy yearns to be a writer, and, when he grows up and becomes despondent over his failures as an adult, he traces his life through a stylistic hall of mirrors. There are flashbacks and flashforwards; characters come and go and reappear; and the deliberate effort to encompass the past in the present results in a startling, innovative novel.

Annie Dillard recommends any novel by Fred Chappell saying he is a "great American writer of intellectual, emotional, gothic power, widely read in France, out of print here."

Chester, Alfred. *The Exquisite Corpse* (New York: Simon & Schuster, 1967) Lacking both a direct story line (despite the tantalizing title) and coherent characters, this novel's camp vision of the world records the humor, anguish and obsessions of people involved in homosexual love affairs. The human condition is explored as though it were a nightmare, and the cast acts out fantastic sequels to dreams within dreams. The surreal atmosphere of the book is puzzling, yet gripping, and the novel is hard to put down. Most of the success is due to Chester's fine style.

Ned Rorem recommends this.

Chesterton, G. K. *The Man Who Was Thursday: A Nightmare* (Bristol: Arrowsmith, 1908) A club of seven anarchists is determined to destroy the world. Only one member, however, is genuinely involved in the mission. The others are police officers and the author traces the frantic efforts of the six to capture one another. The allegory of what is right, what is wrong; who is friend, who is foe, is wonderfully depicted. While better known for his Father Brown detective stories, this is by far Chesterton's most impressive novel.

Susan Sontag and Frederick Buechner recommend this work.

Chirico, Giorgio de. *Hebdomeros.* *Anonymously translated from the French* (New York: Four Seasons, 1966) First published, 1929. Along with Breton's *Nadja* and Aragon's *Anicet,* this is considered to be one of the great surreal novels. For decades after it was written, it was not adequately translated into English, and so was not very well known in America. This version, however, is excellent and a tribute to the novel's combination of prose, poetry and artistic perceptiveness. The aesthetic, sometimes puzzling, impression defies clear description, but as a document from a creative artist, it is unsurpassed.

John Ashbery recommends it.

Chopin, Kate. *The Awakening* (New York: Stone, 1899) One of the earliest American novels to celebrate the struggle of a woman for self-identity and fulfillment in a repressive society, this traces the saga of Edna Pontellier. Married to a dull husband and leading a tiresome life, she decides to make a break with her past. On meeting a young man, she experiences a profound impression which is to change her life. The author was determined to make her heroine no better nor worse than she was, and for this objective point of view she was roundly condemned by contemporary critics. Today her novel is a minor classic.

Kelly Cherry recommends it.

Cicellis, Kay. *No Name in the Streets* (New York: Grove, 1953) The resistance in Greece during the Second World War is the milieu in which a middle-class Athenian youth moves toward maturity and a fresh appreciation of Greek history and myth. The interweaving of actual events with the central character's alienation is beautifully executed and builds toward a powerful conclusion.

Edmund Keeley says, *"No Name in the Streets* is a brilliant novel written by a Greek writer in English—the best woman writer of her generation who suffers from writing in what is, for her audience, a foreign language. She is a stylist with the same kind of gift that Conrad demonstrated."

Claman, Julian. *The Aging Boy* (Garden City: Doubleday, 1963) Aged by unhappiness, alcohol and a pervading sense of failure, Andrew Keogh is a derelict near death. He luckily falls into the company of a migrant laboring family where he discovers love and compassion. As a result, he slowly regains the ideals of his youth. The characters are fully portrayed, the plot moves easily along, and the result is a thoroughly credible examination of one man and his fight for dignity.

Larry McMurtry calls this an "original and too-little-known novel."

Clifford, Lucy Lane. *Aunt Anne* (New York: Harper, 1892) All rogue or all fool? That's the question asked about the central figure in this domestic novel of nineteenth-century America. Aunt Anne is sentimental and foolish as a young girl. Now that she is old, she becomes a headache to her nephew and niece by causing trouble through her thoughtless actions. All the while, however, she is generous and lavish with her gifts. So what emerges is one of the more puzzling, ambiguous personalities in American fiction.

Alison Lurie recommends this "now almost unknown, but . . . interesting and often brilliant late-Victorian novel."

Coates, Robert. *Yesterday's Burdens* (New York: Macaulay, 1933) Young Henderson, who is a kind of "Everyman," wanders through the streets of New York in the 1930s. Using startling stylistic devices, Coates displays the richness of the metropolis, its people and its various milieus. Superimposed over Henderson's wandering are three fictional endings, all believable and imaginative. And the quiet humor and vivid characterizations are outstanding.

Southern Illinois University Press is reissuing this book.

Cocteau, Jean. *Thomas the Impostor.*

Translated from the French by Lewis Galantiere (New York: Appleton, 1925) First published, 1923. Thomas, a French variation on Walter Mitty, lives in a dreamland of his imagination. Unlike Mitty, however, he is able to turn his inventiveness to real situations, and the novel is primarily concerned with his war exploits. Thomas winningly succeeds in a series of dramatic and witty impostures through to the dramatic finale.

Susan Sontag recommends it.

Cohen, Albert. *Solal.* *Translated from the French by Wilfred Benson* (New York: Dutton, 1933) Solal, a young, attractive Jew, rises from poverty to great wealth. His career—its rise and fall—is charted in detail and the novel presents a convincing saga of human nature. The author's style has the mark of greatness, particularly since he is able to portray convincingly his hero in extraordinary, eccentric situations. The plot moves as briskly as its hero, and results in a remarkable literary experience intensified by the author's trenchant comments which are interspersed in the narrative.

Edouard Roditi recommends this novel.

Cohen, Arthur A. *In the Days of Simon Stern* (New York: Random House, 1972) A vastly intelligent novel, this is told by Nathan, a blind Jewish scribe, who relates the life of Simon Stern, beginning with his birth on New York's lower East Side to his success as a rich real estate agent. Enhancing the marvelous character study is the wealth of provocative theological ideas which the author presents.

Cynthia Ozick writes, "Arthur A. Cohen's reputation as an essayist of ideas has, strangely, gotten in the way of his recognition as a novelist. But he has published a number of interesting works of fiction, characterized by inventiveness, curiosity, and extreme intelligence. Some other titles are: *A Hero In His Time* (1976) and *Acts of Theft* (1980). Cohen is a novelist of ideas, a category better understood in Europe and undervalued here, to our detriment. Cohen's strengths are many and fascinating."

Collier, John. *The John Collier Reader* (New York: Knopf, 1972) A master of the fantastic with an individualistic literary style, Collier is the preeminent modern guide to the world of the supernatural. However, he also excels in representing evil. Generally, his writing is spiked with a dash of satire and engaging humor. Here are his best works, the novel *His Monkey Wife* (1931), and forty-seven stories. Collier's peculiar gift is to persuade the reader that the events he details are not only fantastic but perfectly possible, and that the average man or woman might easily fall into them. There are few better raconteurs; certainly the horror story has rarely been conceived more effectively.

Paul Theroux recommends *His Monkey Wife* and Michael Ivens believes that Collier "as a short-story writer (must) be put in the class of H. G. Wells—except that he has much more humor."

Collins, Wilkie. *No Name* 3 volumes (London: Sampson Low, 1862) H. R. F. Keating writes, "Here's a real winter's evening book. A Victorian novel in the full

savour of the term, 600 rich pages of splendidly criminous story with impersonation, a mysterious death, two Wills (nothing less than the capital letter will do) and even a hint of a ghost.

"Quite how it happened that, with Collins's two other similar books, *The Woman in White* and *The Moonstone*, ever-in-print classics, this lively and intriguing work would have been allowed to drop into near-oblivion I do not know. Perhaps its very title somehow stopped people thinking about it; I can find no other reason for the neglect.

"Make 'em laugh, make 'em cry, make 'em wait: this was Collins's formula for success and *No Name* well lives up to it. We are a less lachrymose generation than the 1860s lot, so I admit no tear coursed into my beard as I read; but I did on occasion feel sharply for Collins's heroine (sometimes indeed not far short of anti-heroine) deprived by legal mischance of old home, proper fortune and even a surname. I certainly laughed, too, more than once and out loud. And, by golly, he made me wait all right time and again throughout a corking good story, layered with events like anchovy fillets in a tin.

"Only add that it is told in vivid scene after vivid scene, that the characterisation is always lively yet the people are real (the half-villain Captain Wragge is a creation Collins's friend Dickens would not have been at all ashamed of) and one easily forgives the few touches of melodrama not perhaps to today's taste."

Conrad, Joseph and Ford Madox Ford (Hueffner). *The Inheritors* (London: Heinemann, 1901) An unsuccessful young writer turns to a prominent English family for company and support. At their home, he meets a young, female Fourth Dimensionist (a race of people blessed with superior powers and damned with emotional voids). She claims that her group will inherit the earth, and foretells the future under their influence. As both a political tract (the authors were striking out at the leaders who took Britain into the Boer War) and a satire of leading English figures, the novel is a success. And while the plot is somewhat extravagant, it holds the reader's attention. [In later life, Conrad claimed he had little to do with this novel, and that it was written primarily by Ford.]

William Burroughs recommended it in *Antaeus*, Autumn, 1975.

Constant, Benjamin. *Adolphe.* *Translated from the French by L. W. Tancock* (London: Penguin, 1964) First published, 1816. In one of the first psychological novels dealing with the subject of love, the heroine is trapped by a carefree Adolphe into involvement in a disastrous affair. Adolphe considers it no more than another exciting adventure, a sentimental episode. Ellenore is much more seriously affected, and, in a moment of romantic pique, kills herself. The irony resides in the true poverty of emotion on both their sides. It is a portrayal of self-absorbed egoism which debars real love and affection.

Daniel Halpern recommends this work.

Cooke, Rose Terry. *Somebody's Neighbors* (Boston: Osgood, 1881) This collection of short stories is most representative of the author's remarkable style and talent in capturing the feelings and actions of her nineteenth-century, New England characters. Nothing much happens, at least on the surface. Yet, for local color this is outstanding. In her lifetime, primarily as a contributor to popular magazines, Cooke gained fame for her ability to convey regional milieus. Her use of evocative dialect is matched by her ability to convey the feelings of her characters who live in the rocky terrain of New England. While some of her stories are grim, there is much humor in this collection. Her odd assortment of spinsters and ministers comes alive.

Judith Fetterley recommends this as well as the author's *Huckleberries Gathered from New England Hills* (1891).

Cozzens, James Gould. *Guard of Honor* (New York: Harcourt, 1948) A crisis arises at an Army Air Force base during World War II, and the soldiers are called upon to resolve the difficulty. While the complex, multitudinous characterizations are extraordinary, the novel is also an accurate picture of military life complete with its strengths and weaknesses. So when real trouble is hinted at on the base, the officers form a "guard of honor" to protect each other. The entire episode takes place in a period of three days and builds to a fitting conclusion.

George Steiner recommends this.

Crawford, Stanley. *Gascoyne* (New York: Putnam, 1966) Gascoyne spends entire weeks in his car, eating, sleeping and conducting his business by mobile telephone. This mad fantasia of the Southern Californian freeway culture is as chaotic as it is satirical, yet it remains oddly credible. The deadpan, first-person narration by Gascoyne gives verisimilitude to his preposterous way of living and to the extraordinary plot in which he moves. As a financial success, Gascoyne seems unassailable until one of his associates is murdered. Then, on the verge of ruin, Gascoyne saves himself in a grim and hilarious way.

Frederic Raphael calls this "a real sleeper."

Crawford, Stanley. *Log of the S.S. The Mrs. Unguentine* (New York: Knopf, 1972) Mrs. Unguentine, writing in her log, faithfully keeps track of her experiences during a forty-year voyage around the world on a garbage barge with her hope-lessly eccentric husband. As a reflection of the humorous and fascinating facets of modern civilization, this is difficult to surpass. The author's wit is matched by his sure delight in his marvelous characters.

Gordon Lish says that this is a "work of literature great in the extreme."

Crews, Harry. *Car* (New York: Morrow, 1972) Herman says he will eat a new Ford Maverick at the rate of one ounce a day. His purpose is to draw attention to his family-owned Florida car salvage business. Lovingly supported by the local business community, his venture draws attention not only to them, but to other members of Herman's whacky family. The satiric novel is extremely funny because the author is blessed with a quick and devastating wit and a grotesque imagination. His vision is strong, humorous, and truly uncompromising.

Doris Grumbach calls Crews "the Southern tough who has never had the recognition he so richly deserves, but whose coterie of admirers is furiously loyal." She considers *Car* "his most original" work, she also recommends *Gospel Singer* "his first and most startling (although everything he writes is startling); *The Gypsy's Curse*; *Naked in Garden Hills*; and *A Feast of Snakes*."

Crosby, Harry. *Torchbearer* (Paris: Black Sun Press, 1931) A member of the American lost generation in Paris, Crosby was rich, handsome and talented. In this posthumous collection, some of his more successful poetry is reprinted. The themes are his constant preoccupation with suicide (he killed himself in 1929), his fear of madness, and the overriding joy of sun worship. While most of the poetry is in the form of prose and tends toward the chaotic, it is magical and unique.

Brian Swann recommended this in *Antaeus*, Summer, 1975.

Cusack, Ralph. *Cadenza* (London: Hamilton, 1958) Awakening in a Dublin dentist's chair, Desmond rises, and in a drugged state faces the main events of his picturesque life. The imaginative style may prove confusing, but the narrator has a sure sense of story and a marvelous anecdotal approach to the Irish character. One never knows what will happen next, and this stimulating novel is as vivid as the life of the narrator.

Gilbert Sorrentino terms this "a brilliant comic novel about time and death and love by an Irish writer of extraordinary gifts. This was Cusack's only novel and is, in my opinion, on a level with Beckett's *Murphy*. It is indispensable to the student of Irish fiction, post-Joyce."

Dargan, Olive T. *Call Home the Heart* (London: Longmans, 1932) Ray Olson recommends this novel, and writes, "Olive Tilford Dargan had been a teacher and genteel writer of verse plays until, following her husband's death on the Lusitania, she settled on farm property in the North Carolina Blue Ridge. She watched as her own tenants and other poor farm families were forced into the oppression of the textile mills in such towns as Gastonia. In 1928 there was a horrendous strike organized by the Communist-inspired union. On these events, including the shooting death of the great hillbilly labor songwriter Ella May Wiggins, she based her first novel, written when she was past sixty. It features one of the strongest women protagonists in United States fiction, Ishma Waycaster, and some of the best dialect writing this side of *Huckleberry Finn*.

"Both dramatic and lyrical, the novel reaches its epiphany when Ishma rescues a black worker from a lynch mob including her own former husband, then gives into her residual racism when the man's wife embraces her in thanks. This is powerful stuff, unaccountably forgotten."

Davidson, Lionel. *Smith's Gazelle* (London: Cape, 1971) A bizarre Bedouin tends a herd of rare gazelle which are thriving in southern Israel. The herdsman thinks the animals, believed to be extinct, are sent to him as a miracle. Two young boys, an Arab and a Jew, help the Bedouin tend his beasts. The Arab, the recalcitrant children and the Six Day War combine to offer the reader an involving adventure, as well as a metaphor of Israel's survival.

Patricia Abercrombie calls this "very enthralling and with a peculiar poignant quality which is most original."

Davies, L. P. *Stranger to Town* (London: Jenkins, 1969) By chance, Julian Midwinter happens upon a small British town, and gradually recalls people who should be strangers and places that should be unknown. The ingenious scheme features a dead villager whose wife engineers a business set-up for the retired English publisher. The plot is plausible, the characters real, and the experiences sequentially gripping. One merely has to accept the premise of *déjà vu* and a dash of the fantastic to enjoy thoroughly this cunning thriller.

Ira Levin recommends it.

Davies, L. P. *The White Room* (New York: Doubleday, 1969) Under the impression he has been drugged and his mind altered to that of a murderer, an English industrialist makes a desperate escape from his captors. He meets a young woman, only to discover that somehow he has lost ten years, possibly under the influence of his captors' drugs. But has he really lost a decade? And is he really under the influence of the mysterious people who want him to be a killer? The confused tension between illusion and reality creates great suspense. There is a fitting, yet rational, surprise ending which makes this an exciting mystery spiced with science fiction.

Ira Levin recommends this along with Davies' *What Did I Do Tomorrow?*

Davis, Clyde Brion. *The Great American Novel* (New York: Farrar, Straus, 1938) A newspaperman with the lifelong desire to write "the great American novel" keeps a diary of his day-to-day experiences. He is conforming to the duties of everyday life while indulging in fantasies about the woman he first loved. The diary concludes after thirty-five years when he discovers that the object of his romantic desires led a life very different from the one he imagined. So, ironically, instead of writing the great American novel, he lived it.

James Michener recommends this.

Davis, George. *The Opening of a Door* (New York: Harper, 1931) Eluding any formal classification, this is a unique novel, written by a twenty-four-year-old author. It received almost total acclaim when published, and several critics compared it with the best in American fiction. In a succession of extraordinary yet credible events, the author traces the lives of several members of a Canadian family who have settled in Chicago. The novel has an extreme sense of deeply felt reality about it and leaves the reader with startling insights about life.

Marguerite Young recommends this, as does Doris Grumbach who comments, "[This was] not neglected in its time (four printings), but not read now. His only book, and a fine, autobiographical one. He died sadly in a barroom brawl over some gay boy. Ran the wonderful house on Middaugh St. on Brooklyn Heights, and later married Lotte Lenya."

Davis, Rebecca Harding. *Waiting for the Verdict* (New York: Sheldon, 1868) Race relations in America just after the Civil War were rarely portrayed in contemporary novels with seriousness and ac-

curacy. Here the mold is broken, and the reader discovers what it was like to be a mulatto in the North. While the plot tends toward the melodramatic, the characterization is effective and the situation often grimly realistic. Few novels better demonstrate the toll of racial bias on both the oppressors and the oppressed. It is a remarkably sensitive novel which illustrates the complexity of the race problem in the United States.

Judith Fetterley recommends this.

Decker, William. *To Be a Man: A Novel* (Boston: Little, 1967) The life of a cowboy, from the late 1880s to his death in 1950, is charted. Throughout, he tries in vain to maintain some personal identity in the midst of social change. Since the author has a thorough knowledge of cowboy culture, the novel is as much a documentary as a work of fiction. And it is one of the few authentic records of the fate of the American cowboy after the turn of the century.

Dehan, Richard. *Between Two Thieves* (London: Heinemann, 1912) This highly accurate, literate, historical novel opens with the 1848 struggle in France, and then moves to describe the Crimean War. Here is a remarkable account of the war itself and, thinly disguised, the activities of Florence Nightingale. The correct, yet fictitious, picture of the army at war is particularly impressive since the author was female (Clotilde Graves) and, having no direct military experience, had to base her narrative on painstaking research.

G. B. Harrison recommends this book along with Dehan's *The Dop Doctor* (1910), about a fashionable physician who rehabilitates his lost reputation by demonstrating courage in the South African war.

DeJong, David. *Belly Fulla Straw* (New York: Knopf, 1934) A Dutch family emigrates in the early 1900s and settles in

Michigan. Although the children eventually become Americanized, their father, the main character, cannot renounce his old world traditions, and finally goes back to Europe. The novel is not merely an indictment of American values but a story of a highly sympathetic character.

Peter DeVries writes, *"Belly Fulla Straw* is a sensitive and touching portrayal of a Dutch immigrant family's life in the American Midwest, and the father's eventual return to Holland."

Delafield, E. M. *The Diary of a Provincial Lady* (London: Macmillan, 1930) Quintessentially English, a lady living in a small country house keeps a diary which documents her domestic and social routines and crises, her quiet husband and vivacious children, and the characters in the surrounding village. Her humorous, satirical treatment reveals an exquisite appreciation of human nature. And the minor, homely problems combined with this sharp sense of human flaws make this always amusing and fascinating.

Jilly Cooper says it is a "total enchantment. I read it and was totally hooked . . . all men, all women, all life, really there's something marvellously universal about it, and the gentle heroine is so touching and funny and endearing and modest and yet has lots of bite. I think it's a marvellous book."

DeLillo, Don. *End Zone* (Boston: Houghton, 1972) The mystique and methods of American college football are detailed with wit and skill. The sporting hero, who is also the narrator, is a perpetual outsider who keeps changing colleges but remains true to his obsession: an impending nuclear holocaust. The title comes from the play in which the end zone is free, a timeless yet temporary moment when the game ceases. A visionary novel, beautifully written, it is a major triumph showing tribal patterns against the backdrop of world destruction.

Gordon Lish recommends all of DeLillo's novels with the exception of *Americana* (1971), and those published pseudonymously.

Dell, Floyd. *Moon-Calf* (New York: Knopf, 1920) The well known American socialist tells, in this autobiographical novel, what it meant to be a sensitive young man just prior to, and slightly after, World War I. His skillful portrayal of time and place is matched by his sure and effortless dialogue.

Robert S. Bravard says, "The novel is the hero's coming of age in a small midwestern town, his longing to leave, and the eventual escape to Chicago." He also recommends Dell's *The Briary-Bush* (1921), which he says depicts " . . . the hero's achievement of a measure of success in Chicago. The stories are less grim than Sherwood Anderson or Theodore Dreiser, but are rich with details of a now distant past. There is almost an innocent quality to these."

DeMorgan, William. *Joseph Vance* (London: Heinemann, 1906) In one of England's best novels of character, the author draws upon his first-hand experience with the streets and people of London. DeMorgan's work bridged the transition between the last of Dickens's London tales and modern city stories. Joseph Vance progresses from the slums to middle-class respectability, and in this "ill written autobiography" he explains in the best Dickensian fashion just what was involved in his rise. The reader is introduced to countless memorable characters who surface in reasonable, yet sometimes hilarious, situations. Anyone who relishes Dickens will find this novel a particular delight.

G. B. Harrison recommends this along with DeMorgan's *When Ghost Meets Ghost* (1914), about twin sisters who are reunited in old age.

Denevi, Marco. *Rosa at Ten O'Clock.* *Translated from the Spanish by Donald A. Yates* (New York: Holt, 1964) Someone murders a woman in a cheap Buenos Aires hotel. Four witnesses are called to report on what they observed. Their testimony is supplemented by a half-completed letter. Both the case and the characters are imbued with reality and a dreamlike surrealism. For example, Camilo Canegato, a major character, is the inventor of an imaginary woman with whom he becomes passionately involved. The ingenious plot is heightened by skillful satire.

Barbara Howes recommends this novel.

Dennis, Nigel. *Cards of Identity* (London: Weidenfeld, 1955) This is a rollicking satire on people's natural inclination to change other people. The identity of the characters is determined by the Identity Club, which manages to accomplish such feats as transforming a doctor into a gardener and his former nurse into his aide. The manipulation of these and other personalities is enhanced by the common desire of people to ingratiate themselves and to develop themselves anew. The novel ends with a play, a murder and a police raid. Some believe it is all in horrible taste; others applaud the daring of the author, who attacks religion, politics, the class system, and other sacred institutions.

Richard Wilbur recommends it.

Desani, G. V. *All About H. Hatterr* (New York: Farrar, Straus, 1951) H. Hatterr is a curious Indian whose encounters with his family, gurus and employers are carefully detailed in an elaborate, heartily amusing, and moving series of episodes. While the work cannot be adequately summarized—too much happens in some of the most bizarre settings in fiction—it can be praised as an eloquent and generous view of Indian life.

Anthony Burgess recommends this, as does Herbert Gold, who writes, "This novel is a hilarious satire on East Indian intellectuals, written by an Indian intellectual—more appropriate now, in the time of third-world fermentation, than it was a generation ago when it was published." And Eve Auchincloss says, "*All about H. Hatterr* is a brilliantly funny and sad novel of life in India. [It] seems to have sunk without a trace."

Dostoyevsky, Fyodor. *The Double.* *Translated from the Russian by George Bird* (Bloomington: Indiana University Press, 1958) First published, 1846. In this, his second novel, Dostoyevsky explores for the first time the theme of the divided personality, which became significant in almost all his work. Obsessed by the notion that one of his fellows has taken over his identity, a Russian government clerk produces a self-made split in his personality. The problem of combining the real sensation of the clerk about his doppelganger and the actual fantasy of the situation is beautifully solved. And this translation is particularly good.

Vladimir Nabokov wrote, "The very best thing [Dostoyevsky] ever wrote seems to me to be *The Double*. . . . It hardly exists for the follower of Dostoyevsky . . . because it was written in the 1840s, long before his so-called great novels" (*New York Times Magazine*, August 23, 1981).

Drexler, Rosalyn. *To Smithereens* (New York: New American Library, 1972) A novel about self-actualization, a romantic comedy, an investigation of sexual desires—*To Smithereens* is all of this and considerably more, including a treatment of lady wrestlers. An extremely good book, it centers around the life of a young, naive woman who gets involved with an aging New York art critic. Their affair is described with marvelous skill, and adds up to an absolutely original novel, as authentic as it is hilarious.

Rosalyn Drexler writes, "Did you know that all of my books, except for *Starburn: The Story of Jenni Love* (1979), are out of print! And all were well received by the critics. None of my books is in the book stores."

Dunsany, Edward. The *Blessing of Pan* (New York: Putnam, 1927) Combine a magical style, a theme of magic and a willing suspension of disbelief, and you have a novel with a modern-day Pan as its central focus. The setting is an English village, and the story begins when the young people of the town follow the pipings at sunset. Concerned with this increasing interest in the pipes, which leads the villagers to the Old Stones on the hill, the local vicar writes to his Bishop for help. The Bishop suggests a holiday, but the vicar decides to take action. One night he follows the sound of the pipes himself. After that, peace settles over the town for the vicar becomes the priest of an old, almost forgotten religion. Invention, humor, and a sure sense of characters help the author to create a completely successful fantasy.

Noel Perrin called it "a literally enchanting romance" (*Washington Post Book World*, May 30, 1982).

Eça de Queiroz, José. *The City and the Mountains.* Translated from the Portuguese by Roy Campbell (Athens: Ohio University Press, 1967) First published, 1901. This nineteenth-century Portuguese novel is illustrative of Eça de Queiroz's gentle and sophisticated style, his satirical yet warm sense of character. The focus is on a Portuguese prince returning from exile in Paris for the purpose of appraising his

family's damaged chapel. Through numerous absurd experiences, he begins to fall in love with his own country. Both the descriptions of the countryside and the people give this a place as one of literature's more delightful novels.

Eve Auchincloss recommends it.

Eça de Queiroz, José. *The Relic.* Translated from the Portuguese by F. G. Bell (New York: Knopf, 1925) First published, 1887. *The Relic* tells of the attempt by Dom Raposa to inherit the wealth of his rich, religion-obsessed, spinster aunt. A Latin Tom Jones, the Dom is forced to submit, on the surface at least, to her moral convictions. His religious hypocrisy is temporarily alleviated when his aunt sends him to Jerusalem. On the way, the philandering traveler meets, among others, a pompous German professor and a seller of relics, and the author retells the story of Christ's crucifixion in one of the hero's dreams. The book ends as the Dom returns with a relic which ironically undermines all his efforts. The purity of style, the humor and the play of ideas has made this a classic in Portugal.

Eve Auchincloss recommends it.

Eddison, Eric R. *The Worm Ouroboros* (New York: Boni, 1926) Set in a dreamlike milieu, this is a rigorously conceived modern epic which is reminiscent of the art of Blake and the stately rhythm of Greek drama. The author constructs a whole world, complete with a Witchland and a Demonland, where power is pitted against idealism, and evil seems always about to win. The scheme is grand; and the total effect seems as authentic as the account of this imaginary world is riveting.

Orville Prescott says, "[An] overlooked masterpiece I greatly admire is *The Worm Ouroboros*, a heroic fantasy. . . ."

Eden, Emily. *The Semi-Attached Couple* (London: Bentley, 1860) In the tradition of Jane Austen, this is an entertaining novel of manners among noble Whig families in early nineteenth-century England. The book's huge cast of characters is centered on the persona of an eighteen-year-old Lady and her new husband. As she was not really ready to be married, they are only "semi-attached." The novel develops as the heroine gradually falls in love with her husband.

Noel Perrin writes, "I will . . . confidently predict that almost anyone who picks up the book will be instantly drawn in. And on finishing it will be looking hopefully around for more. Should that happen to you, I have good news. Eden wrote a second novel, almost as good, called *The Semi-Detached House*, (1859)" (*Washington Post Book World*, February 15, 1981).

Edgeworth, Maria. *Castle Rackrent* (London: Joseph Johnson, 1800) The first regional novel to be published in English, this is told from the perspective of an old retainer of the Rackrent family and is delightfully satirical in its debunking of the image of nobility in the nobility. Maria Edgeworth convincingly portrays an unswervingly loyal Irish servant who happens, as well, to be honest. As a result, his disclosures about the upper-class family he serves are unintentionally revealing in their depiction of ineptitude, cruelty, greed, ignorance and folly among the rich. A short novel, it is constantly appealing in its tale of the series of unattractive or misguided inhabitants of *Castle Rackrent*. Additionally, it is a fine introduction to seventeenth-century Irish life and culture.

Eva Figes calls this "a witty, anarchic book, nothing 'feminine' about it and, until *Wuthering Heights*, the most earthy book to come from the pen of a lady."

Edwards, Dorothy. *Winter Sonata* (London: Wishart, 1928) Creating an enchanted mood, the author tells the story of six young people living through a typical English winter in an isolated village. Overtly, nothing out of the ordinary occurs. The charm and satisfaction of the work reside in the abundant details of daily life. Emphasizing descriptions of places, the author presents an almost abstract arrangement of life's patterns.

Gerald Brenan said, "[Dorothy Edwards wrote] novels with a special flavour that is unlike anything else" (*Thoughts in a Dry Season* [Cambridge: Cambridge University Press, 1979]).

Ehle, John. *The Land Breakers* (New York: Harper, 1964) The land breakers are the settlers of the mountainous region stretching from the Carolinas to Tennessee during 1779-1784. Here is a truly literary, historical portrait of these early pioneers. Essentially, the plot involves numerous conflicts between the various characters and is not as important to the book as the sense of what it meant to push into a new frontier. The author captures the suspense, the boredom and the daily work of the people in a totally credible fashion.

Olivia Cole recommends this.

Elkin, Stanley. *A Bad Man* (New York: Random House, 1967) Leo Feldman uses his department store as a base to provide illegal services ranging from prostitution to drugs. He is caught and sent to prison where he is soon judged to be "a bad man" by the warden. Trapped in this Beckett-like purgatory, Leo treats his life as a tragicomedy, attempting to work out a solution to his catastrophe. His story is lightened by numerous comic turns which dramatize his pathetic illusions of freedom.

Stanley Elkin recommended his own novel in *Antaeus*, Autumn, 1975.

Elkin, Stanley. *Criers and Kibitzers, Kibitzers and Criers* (New York: Random House, 1966) In his first collection of short stories, Elkin is concerned, as he is in his novels, with outrageous yet recognizably human characters always on the brink of disaster. Black humor prevails, and even the doomed characters can be bitterly funny. Often realistically, sometimes symbolically, the stories move along at a brisk pace towards unexpected conclusions.

Gordon Lish recommends this collection.

Ellis, Humphry F. *The Papers of A. J. Wentworth B.A.* (London: Evans, 1949) A. J. Wentworth is the generally dour mathematics master in an English preparatory school. His diary entries focus on the scores of mischievous, tirelessly inventive students who live in order to harass him. The ingenious pranks of the students are in the best tradition of English humor. Most of this hilarious book first appeared in the pages of *Punch*.

Helen Muir cited this in *The New Review*, Summer, 1978.

Enquist, Per Olov. *The Legionnaires.* *Translated from the Swedish by Alan Blair* (New York: Delacorte Press, 1974) First published, 1968. Combining fact and fiction, Enquist describes the experiences of a group of Baltic legionnaires who were interned by Sweden during the Second World War. When the war was over, despite public outcry, they were delivered back to the Soviet Union where they expected to be killed. The human dimensions of the story are effectively interwoven with the documented materials, and the result is a striking novel.

Esfandiary, Fereidoun M. *Identity Card: A Novel* (New York: Grove, 1966) Returning to Teheran after spending most of his life in exile, Daryoush Aryana becomes locked into a Kafkaesque situation. He loses his identity card, and is therefore unable to quit the country. In his search for a way out and another card, he must wander through an endless bureaucratic maze. His frustration, coupled with his growing comprehension of a vast system of bribery and mendacity, creates a modern nightmare.

Anne Tyler says, "I mentioned *Identity Card* because it is both powerful and subtle—a book that makes a devasting point; but unlike most such books, it does so with humor and matter-of-factness, in a way that pulls the reader in."

Evans, Caradoc. *My People* (London: Hutchinson, 1915) Evans, a native of Wales, is known for short stories which are astringently wry and realistic in their portrayal of the peasantry in his homeland. Here, in his first collection of stories, the focus is on the difficulty of surviving both a rugged economy and a troublous society. The grim, often stark, stories perfectly capture his subjects, down to their peculiar dialects.

Quentin Bell recommends this as a "masterpiece of love-hate."

Farrell, J. G. *The Siege of Krishnapur* (London: Weidenfeld, 1973) Here is an old-fashioned and unsensational treatment of an historical event. Set in India at the time of the Sepoy Rebellion of 1857, the main character is an English civil servant who must organize the defenses of Krishnapur. Farrell's attention to detail is matched only by his remarkable style. While deeply sympathetic to their individualism, the author has scorn for the ignorance and prejudice of his countrymen. He combines wit, a dramatic, fast moving plot, with a serious evaluation of English colonization.

Mary McCarthy recommends this work.

Farrell, J. G. *The Singapore Grip* (London: Weidenfeld, 1978) This beautifully planned and executed plot carries the reader from the Singapore of the 1930s to the city's fall to the Japanese in 1942. Few novels have displayed such a sure grip on the imagery of place and history. Each of the characters, primarily British employees of a great merchant corporation, is developed in light of the ironic perspective of the author.

Mary McCarthy recommends this novel.

Faulkner, William. *Pylon* (New York: H. Smith, 1935) While it is difficult to imagine any of Faulkner's works being neglected or overlooked, *Pylon* is a novel which is not as popular as his other fiction. It charts four days in the lives of fliers who are performing at a Mardi Gras celebration. Using flight and daring stunts to escape from mundane lives, the small group preserves the integrity of individual aspirations. But they are finally defeated as much by the world of business as by their own naive suggestibility. The ability of Faulkner to illustrate this legend of contemporary life with a brilliant plot and convincing characters makes this one of his fine achievements.

Harvey Breit wrote, "It is a poem, told in one deep, intense, anxious breath. The gray nightmare gradually dissolves into flesh and blood, head and heart, ecstasy and humiliation. And it has some of the deepest insight and vision into the business of the flying machine and the men who ride them" (*American Scholar*, Autumn, 1956).

Fielding, Gabriel. *In the Time of Greenbloom* (London: Hutchinson, 1954) Two youngsters, John Blaydon and Victoria Blount, are bound by love, and then by tragedy, in this novel of pre-World War II England. Greenbloom, a friend of John's older brother, is an Oxford undergraduate of great wealth, sophistication and sensitivity who is determined to break the spell of grief which envelopes the young boy. Through humor, wit, and erudition, the eccentric Greenbloom opens the door back to human society for the youth. The characterizations are dazzling and the sympathetic, subtly argued propositions about life are absorbing.

Laurie Colwin recommends this work.

Finney, Charles. *The Circus of Dr. Lao* (New York: Viking, 1935) While this is a minor classic, it is still neglected by the reading majority. It appears to be about the effect of a traveling circus on a small Arizona town, but it actually is a fantastic, ribald satire. An ageless Oriental operates a circus with an odd assortment of animals and men. Among the chief features are a unicorn, a hermaphroditic sphinx, a male chimera and a hound of the hedges. This remarkable excursion into the bizarre is extraordinary entertainment, as well as being downright lethal in its satire on literal-mindedness.

Edward Hoagland says it is "*the* masterpiece of circus literature. Combines Depression-era realism with surreal mythology into an elixir of what circuses are."

Fisher, Vardis. *Dark Bridwell* (Boston: Houghton, 1931) John R. Milton describes this novel as follows: "The Idaho wilderness spawns a reckless and carefree natural man who marries a lonely and frightened woman and sires a son who is nearly the personification of evil. The story is told dramatically, poetically, and concisely through these three characters' separate points of view, providing three intimate reactions to the wilderness. The climax, as the three people reach their most important decisions, is close to classical tragedy. Uniquely American in setting, *Dark Bridwell* is also a story of Western Civilization in its essence."

Flanner, Janet. *Cubical City* (New York: Putnam, 1926) Delia Poole arrives in New York, the "cubical city," to further her career in stage designing. The cast of

Broadway characters range from a brilliant portrait of a producer to lesser sketches of actors and writers, all of whom support the heroine's romantic inclinations. The novel is as cynical as it is realistic, as witty as it is stylized. After the novel appeared, the author, writing under the pseudonym Genet, began her famous "Letter from Paris" column for *The New Yorker*.

Southern Illinois University Press is reissuing this book.

Footman, David. *Pig and Pepper*
(London: Heinemann, 1936) Lionel Davidson recommends this, writing, " . . . the story is marvellously beguiling. Told by one Mills, a young man in 'H.M. Levant Consular Service,' it concerns the advent and activities in 'Tsernigrad' (where the narrator is stationed) of a raffish adventurer called Vickery. There are dubious Balkan goings-on and an escape down the Danube. Despite lack of commercial success the book has had knowledgeable admirers (including General Philby, KGB). . . . Today it would probably be classed as a kind of up-market thriller, although nobody gets hurt much except perhaps the reader" (*Times Literary Supplement,* June 5, 1981).

Davidson adds that one memorable character, Mausi, a Sally Bowles type, "actually pre-dates Isherwood's [creation]."

Forbes, Bryan. *Familiar Strangers*
(London: Hodder, 1980) Published in the United States as *Strangers* (1980). While tracing the lives of two English cousins from the 1920s to the 1970s, the author takes a fictional tour of the events surrounding the notorious British spies, Burgess, Maclean and Philby. Meticulously, he draws the reader into the workings of the espionage ring. At the same time, the author limns the development of England during this period, its upper-middle classes and its social attitudes. All the characters are extremely convincing as are the situations, and there is an objective, even sympathetic, insight into the vulnerability of certain personalities which pervades the entire work.

Anthony Price recommends this, saying, "It fell into that no-man's-land between the spy thriller and the novel lacking 'action,' on-stage espionage and explicit menace in the conventional manner. But I think it had all three unconventionally in full measure, and that it was in some sense a grown-up 'Dimitrios' [*The Mask of Dimitrios*] of our times" (*Times Literary Supplement,* June 5, 1981).

Forbes, Esther. *The Running of the Tide* (Boston: Houghton, 1948) From 1795 to the end of the War of 1812, Salem, Massachusetts, reached its height in prosperity and influence. This novel describes the community and the families which engineered the development of this seaport. The color and life in the town when the fleet is getting ready to sail are as authentic as the characters. In this way, a lost epoch is revivified and convincingly portrayed with style and skill.

Janet Lewis recommends this, writing, "I wanted to teach these [*Running of the Tide* and Forbes' *A Mirror for Witches* (1928)] at the University of California at Berkeley a few years ago, and almost had to drop them from the course, . . . because they were unobtainable except for a few copies."

Ford, Ford Madox. *The Fifth Queen*
(New York: Vanguard, 1963) Republication of an early Ford trilogy, including: *The Fifth Queen* (1906), *Privy Seal* (1907), *The Fifth Queen Crowned* (1908). A trilogy depicting the life of Katherine Howard in the court of Henry VIII from 1540 until her execution, this is an impressive and historically accurate account. While Ford is clearly sympathetic to Henry's fifth queen,

the treachery of Tudor intrigue is wonderfully documented. This is a virtuoso performance in historical fiction and one of its author's most significant achievements.

William Gass recommends this as does George Core who writes, "Ford has often been praised, and at the moment there is a modest Ford revival underway, but no one seems to read anything but *The Good Soldier* and *Parade's End*. These novels . . . are fascinating reading for anyone who relishes good fiction and who is interested in the tone and language of the Tudor period."

Ford, Ford Madox. *Parade's End* (New York: Knopf, 1950) A collection of four novels: *Some Do Not* (1924), *No More Parades* (1925), *A Man Could Stand Up* (1926), *The Last Post* (1928). This is a magnificent recreation of the years of the First World War. The four novels which constitute this work are considered by many to be the major literary accomplishment of that period. A work of great brilliance, it follows the life of Tiejens, his friends and foes, and the social history of Tory England. Some scenes are as dazzling as anything found in literature, and Ford brings into focus a major turning point in history.

Martha Gellhorn writes that this is "one of the finest works of our time." And Naomi Mitchison says, "They were among the very best books about World War I and the even more forgotten British society of the same period. [Ford] was a very important writer."

Fox, George. *Without Music* (New York: Holt, 1971) X. J. Kennedy writes, "*Without Music* . . . is a sardonic comic novel no less worth reading than *The Day of the Locust*. It concerns a bunch of expatriates and social outcasts, one of whom has been amputated down to little but a head, cigarette smuggling, and religious frenzy. The most remarkable scene in the book recounts the hero's attempt to make love while suffering from burns all over his body. Description fails: Fox is a laconic, highly original humorist who at his best writes like a dream. One of that group of writers who at one time all worked for *Male* magazine (including Bruce Jay Friedman, Mario Puzo, and Martin Cruz-Smith), he is to my mind the most amazing of them, and the least widely recognized. (He has also written a commercial thriller novel, *Amok*, some paperback mysteries, fiction in *Paris Review*, and the script for the film *Earthquake*.) *Without Music* was clearly written not for money, but for joy."

Frank, Waldo. *The Death and Birth of David Markand* (New York: Scribner, 1934) One of the earliest American novels about a disenchanted character who seeks to find himself and some meaning in life by setting out on the open road, this begins in 1913 when David Markand gives up a good job and his family to strike out on a four year journey. For the next five hundred pages, the reader is introduced to a rich assortment of characters and situations which skillfully summarize the social, economic and political patterns of America in the period stretching from 1910 to 1920. The work has a uniquely vigorous tone, and its marvelous concept is executed unerringly. Few novels are as realistic and as imaginatively conceived.

This will be included in the Soviet Union's "Library of the Literature of the United States," which comprises the works of sixty prose writers and eighty poets.

Frayn, Michael. *The Tin Men* (London: Collins, 1965) Drawing upon sophisticated humor and slapstick clowning, the author describes how a group of computer experts prepares for a visit to their institute by the Queen. Concerned that the visit may not go well, the scholars are persuaded to enter into a number of preparatory rehearsals. These take so much time that the top security official and the leading scientist are both torn from their work. Their duties consist of such things as automating football results and working out a programmed newspaper. There is also an ethical decision-making machine. One begins to appreciate what might happen to civilization if computers, security people, and government gain control of daily living. The completely deadpan case is made with wit and hilarity rarely found in such social commentary.

Virginia Clark writes that this is "a wonderfully wry look at the personnel and computerisation complications of a research institute in Britain that is automating everything from research in ethics to daily newspaper production and sports competition. I think this the sharpest and best of Frayn's fiction."

Frederics, Harold. The Damnation of Theron Ware (New York: Hurst, 1896) The nineteenth-century American author's masterpiece, this is a finely rendered, realistic, psychological study of a minister's spiritual degeneration. As one of the earliest analyses of character and motive, it remains an entirely credible, subjective study of a personality. Theron Ware, moving from a narrow position of orthodoxy to one of broad doubt, is bombarded by arguments against his religion. The logical and devastating attacks emanate from a variety of citizens in his small town. Few novels have so carefully studied the basis of religious belief.

Robert S. Fogarty recommends this.

Fremlin, Celia. The Hours Before Dawn (London: Gollancz, 1958) Ruth Rendell, who recommends this, writes, "Celia Fremlin's 'mysteries' or thrillers—they are not really crime novels at all—concern ordinary people, usually in conventional domestic relationships, living in suburbs or provincial towns, who are brought under pressure from some kind of appalling stress. Mostly, but not invariably, her protagonist is a woman, and the stress always derives, though not always apparently at first, from the intrusion into her life of another human being. This person is seldom overtly antagonistic to her, may indeed appear in the guise of a friend or near and dear relation, but will always trigger off the stress, acting the while as a catalyst. Violence of some kind, accident, attempted murder, murder, will result.

"Identification with her characters is very easily made, partly because Fremlin is very skilled at creating character and partly because the awful situations her people get themselves trapped in, the tedium of running a home, the stress of never having quite enough money to live comfortably, the nagging demands of small children, the pressures of a boring or unsuitable job, are familiar to most of us at some time or another through personal experience. Thus, we soon come to live in them and their tensions become more real to us than I think is usual in what must be called light fiction.

"The build-up of suspense is created through this and by means of Fremlin's breathy climactic way of writing, a style that approaches hysteria. Indeed, if I am asked to detract as well as praise I should say that sometimes the hysteria is reached, not merely approached, and were there fewer adjectives and adverbs in her descriptions, fewer gasps and exclamations, she might have produced fine novels instead of just good entertainments."

Frisch, Max. I'm Not Stiller. Translated from the German by Michael Bullock (New York: Abelard-Schuman, 1958) First published, 1954. Stiller abandons his career in an effort to change his identity. His failure to alter his existence is a lesson in self-acceptance, as well as a sign of the ultimate power of the state and one's own family to hold radical change in check. The drama is also one of personal conflict between Stiller and his wife. Their tortured relationship is matched in intensity only by the final fifty-page postscript in which the public prosecutor summarizes Stiller's case.

Lore Segal writes, "If you mention the Swiss writer Max Frisch to members of the American reading public there is a look of recognition: some have seen some of his plays, usually Off Broadway or in college productions: *The Firebugs; Andorra; The Chinese Wall.* They recall that they have always meant to read his first great novel *I'm Not Stiller.* They should also read *Homo Faber, A Wilderness of Mirrors, The Sketchbooks,* and his brief but monumental *Man in the Holocene.* What can one say of such large productions in brief? Frisch writes about the modern world and its politics, the subtlest motions of his own nature, and about his doom, and ours, as if he were holding his eyelids forcibly open to stare at what cannot be looked at."

Fuchs, Daniel. The Williamsburg Trilogy (New York: Vanguard, 1934-1937) The three novels are: *Summer in Williamsburg* (1934), *Homage to Blenholt* (1936), *Low Company* (1937). The setting is Williamsburg, Brooklyn, where the author grew up and discovered the rich material for his brilliant trilogy. From the speech of the characters to the perceptions of events and places, Fuchs proves himself a rare observer. While the plot is ostensibly about the desperate lives of the Jews who dwelled in that section of New York, it equally concerns the life of America's cities in the first quarter of the twentieth century. Fuchs weaves a series of individual stories, all of which are united and completed in the trilogy.

Mordecai Richler calls it "a trilogy, ahead of its time, that anticipated Bellow,

Roth, and many others. A work I greatly admire."

Fülöp-Miller, Rene. Night of Time. *Translated from the German by Richard and Clara Winston* (New York: Bobbs, 1955) There is Hill 317. The army must take the hill, although they are on a hopeless mission and scores of men are likely to be slaughtered. Their captain, in the line of Ahab, leads the men to destruction while the author graphically records the realistic and surrealistic conversations and struggles of the soldiers. The novel is a clear protest against war, any war, and the German author appreciates the pathological drive of men and armies to take pleasure from capturing bits of land. A complex, beautiful book which is in the tradition of Kafka, and is slightly reminiscent of *The Trial.*

Hiram Haydn called this "a striking and vivid novel about war that transcends the all too familiar limitations of this genre" (*American Scholar,* Autumn, 1956).

Gaddis, William. The Recognitions (New York: Harcourt, 1955) One of the most ambitious and revealing novels of modern life, here is a large canvas (close to one thousand pages), illustrating chaos, dissimulation, and egotism. Moving from New York and New England to a monastery outside Madrid, the narrative introduces dozens of well-delineated characters. Each is involved with his or her own pursuits, yet each shares the common goal of trying to beat the system, usually by wild plans and mass hypocrisy. The vast panorama of interlocking plots and personas is carefully organized and easy to follow. The erudition is as impressive as the enormously convincing dramas and deceptions.

David Madden recommends this.

Gallant, Mavis. The Pegnitz Junction (New York: Random House, 1973) Reminiscent of people in her first book of short stories (*The Other Paris*, 1956), these are a group of the lonely and displaced. Most of them are acted upon and seem helpless when it comes to putting their lives back together after the confusion of World War II. And yet, somehow, they do live on. The author's sophisticated style, her sure grasp of character development and analysis, and her moderately hopeful attitude about people makes this a particularly satisfying experience.

Laurie Colwin recommends this volume.

Gallegos, Rõmulo. *Dona Barbara.* *Translated from the Spanish by Robert Malloy* (New York: Cape, 1931) First published, 1929. Having completed his studies in Caracas, Santos Luzardo returns to his run-down homestead in a rugged section of Venezuela. He finds that the notorious Dona Barbara has stolen his cattle, corrupted his workers and destroyed his lands. The fight to gain justice is the subject of this novel, but beyond that the reader is given insights into the history of Venezuela. Widely acclaimed in the Spanish-speaking world, this work deserves more attention in the United States.

William F. H. Lamont cited this in "Neglected Masterpieces of Foreign Fiction," *Books Abroad*, Vol. 27:3.

Gallico, Paul. *Love of Seven Dolls* (New York: Doubleday, 1954) Mary Allen Johnson, in describing this book, says, "A young Breton girl, Mouche, falls in love with seven puppets each of which represents a facet of the puppeteer's character, which as a whole is crude and brutal. I have a particular distaste for this word which is overused, but 'poignant' sums it up. Mouche's love for the dolls changes the personality of the puppeteer. It's hard to think of words to describe how the book affects me without sounding like an advertisement for a Gothic novel: 'moving', 'touching'. . . ."

Garrett, George. *Do, Lord, Remember Me* (New York: Doubleday, 1965) Red Smalley is a fundamentalist preacher and when the novel opens he is about to begin his revival meeting. These scenes are as authentic a representation of this phenomenon as any found in American literature. The author not only thoroughly understands the interactions in the revivals, but portrays the encounters in all their glory and devious showmanship. The group of characters, from wandering faith healers and bums to true believers, offers a memorable reading experience.

Annie Dillard mentions that this is a "newly-topical novel, a study of [a] Southern fundamentalist preacher who wrestles with God. Good characters."

Garrigue, Jean. *The Animal Hotel* (New York: Eakins Press, 1966) Barbara Howes writes, "This curious little work, by the mid-Western poet who lived for many years in New York, is necessarily about animals, but inferentially of course about people too. The hotel has been set up by the wise and intelligent bear, whose cooking, for so many varied customers, evidently excelled. 'So the hotel prospered though the bear worked hard, and the animals met at meals or convened in the evenings with the utmost geniality. The birds would sit on the prongs of the deer, the chipmunk would nestle beside the cat while the blind mole would softly sit by himself in a dream of tunnels. . . .'

"So the tone is set for revealing the bear's story, and how through often bitter experience she had developed to her present level. Soon a horse was seen by the animals galloping about their environs, and this put them into a fit, as they could imagine him bringing about the downfall of their happy circle. The bear had noticed him too. 'But he's a horse!' said the cat emotionally. But the bear retorted quite rapidly for one who usually spoke with such thorough weightiness: He's not a horse, he's a colt!' Thus is set in motion the telling of the tale of her early life, her great love, its denouement and its echo later on.

"Miss Garrigue has kept a remarkable balance between the two worlds she has imaginatively entered—that of the animal and that of man. The creatures are portrayed as one might understand them to be, except for the bear, whose sage comprehension of life could be honored by us as entirely human. To come right down to it, is this not a skillfully drawn metaphor of the human condition? It is a moving tale, a pleasure to read, and the writer has avoided those excesses of sentimentality any lesser talent would have indulged in."

Gascar, Pierre. *Beasts and Men.* *Translated from the French by Jean Stewart* (Boston: Little, 1956) First published, 1953. As the title implies, the six short stories are concerned with men and their unexpected, even shocking, communication with animals. In addition, there is a longer story set in a Russian P.O.W. camp. Most of the surrealistic tales reveal sinister relationships which exist beneath the surface of life. Described as both "eloquent" and "horrifying," the stories have an undeniable power which holds the reader's attention. A remarkable and original effort, this volume will explain to non-French readers why Gascar is the winner of France's highest literary awards.

Philip Levine recommends this book.

Gaskell, [Mrs.] Elizabeth. *Cranford* (London: Chapman, 1853) By far the best of her numerous novels, *Cranford* is a classic, but one that is not that well known. For wit, dry humor, and an uncanny understanding of small-town people, the novel compares favorably with the best nineteenth-century novels. A finely graduated group of characters live out their lives in a peaceful country town. Their primary concern is with etiquette, gossip and the inevitable afternoon tea. Several episodes are among the most amusing in literature, while at the same time there are sketches of almost tragic proportions. It is a completely satisfying novel and one which many readers return to time and again.

James Michener recommends it.

Gellhorn, Martha. *The Trouble I've Seen* (New York: Morrow, 1936) Skilled as both a journalist and a novelist, Gellhorn drew on her experiences as a worker in the Federal Emergency Relief Administration for this marvelous collection of short stories. The focus is on the Depression. The warm, moving and credible characters manage to survive almost intolerable situations and the author's sympathy for, and sensitivity to, them makes this book compelling. Never has her power of observation been better demonstrated.

Gellhorn's *Face of War*, while better known, (New York: Simon & Schuster, 1959) also deserves wider attention. It is a collection of articles on wars in Spain, Finland, China and Europe during World War II—reports which are as emotionally stirring as they are intellectual reminders of the horror of battle.

Genet, Jean. *The Thief's Journal.* *Translated from the French by Bernard Frechtman* (New York: Grove, 1965) First published, 1949. Wandering about Europe in the 1930s, a young homosexual beggar (actually, a fictional disguise for Genet's own persona) recalls in vivid detail his successful pursuit of obsessive pleasures. A work of almost unparalleled consistency in poetic style, it is concerned with the least traditional poetic subject matter, *i.e.*, the beggars, prostitutes and thieves whom the narrator meets in and out of jail. The aesthetic justification of crime makes this one of the great anti-heroic novels of our time; but the reversed values do not in any way conceal the celebration of the human spirit that pervades the work.

Francois Truffaut recommended this in *Antaeus*, Autumn, 1979.

Gerhardie, William. *Futility* (London: Cobden-Sanderson, 1922) This English author was born in St. Petersburg and spent much of his life in Russia. He was posted with the British Military Mission to Siberia in 1918-1920, and his firsthand experience of Russian life and the revolution prepared him for this first novel: the story of a madcap St. Petersburg family. The adults are entangled in amusing love affairs in which the author spoofs the romantic tradition, but the brilliance of plot and character is such that the good-natured criticism is not grating. A rare novel, this turns the traditional, tragic Russian scene into comedy.

Francis Steegmuller recommends this work, as does Michael Ivens who writes, "William Gerhardie—the only novelist who combines English wit with a Chekhovian sense of futility and a Proustian sense of time. A novelist's novelist. Evelyn Waugh and Anthony Powell have bowed the knee and acknowledged his influence. His finest novels are *Futility, Pending Heaven* and *Resurrection*."

Gerhardie, William. *Pending Heaven* (London: Duckworth, 1930) A quintessentially bohemian writer, Max Fisher, is off from London to the south of France to complete his latest novel. Max's delightful ineffectuality is carefully documented as he becomes involved with friends, lovers and strangers during his travels and adventures. As a satire of the literary style of living and loving, the story is filled with good humor and comedy.

Michael Ivens recommends this.

Gerhardie, William. *The Polyglots* (London: Duckworth, 1925) Intervening in Russian affairs immediately after the Rus-

sian Revolution, the English army proved somewhat less than effective. Just how ineffective they were is shown with wit and good humor in the person of a British captain. He meets a vast number of Russian characters in his daily work. The minute descriptions of the British military administration, the wildcap insanity of the army followers, and the surprising relatives of the captain are drawn with great skill. Few novels better capture the chaotic years immediately following World War I than this devastating account.

Michael Holroyd says, "First published in 1925, William Gerhardie's second novel *The Polyglots* is probably the best-known work of this 'best known unknown writer of today,' as he once referred to himself. Drawing largely on personal experience in the First World War, during which he served on the staff of the British Military Attaché in Petrograd and joined the British Military Mission at Vladivostock, it combines in a fashion very rare in English a lyrical and a humorous vein."

Gerhardie, William. *Resurrection* (London: Cassell, 1934) During a nap, the narrator dreams that resurrection is not only possible, but certain. Anxious to share his discovery with friends, he goes to a fancy dinner and ball. Interwoven with his metaphysical discussions are memories of a year's travel and visions of his past. The intelligence of the dialogue and the frothy, satirical scenes are reminiscent of the spiritedness of Aldous Huxley. The novel remains true and thoughtful in regard to its spiritual ideas, and yet proves to be an amusing picture of London life and society.

Michael Ivens recommends this.

Ghali, Waguih. *Beer in the Snooker Club* (New York: Knopf, 1964) Barbara Howes writes, "This unusual novel, by the Egyptian Waguih Ghali, was written in English, though one might say it is the achievement of many voices.

"Set in Cairo after the Nasser triumph, the book depicts the moneyed miseries of those leftover upper classes through the eyes—bright though at times veiled by his favorite drinks, of Ram, the protagonist. This educated young man drifts back and forth from dunning his rich relatives to evenings with his University friends who read Kafka and Sartre; he plays, one might say, his game of snooker—a variety of pool—with them all.

"It's a remarkably sensitive and original novel. Scenes familiar to us are yet dusted over with Oriental psychology, which causes these same scenes to shimmer, as it were, in a bizarre light. Ram, perched wavering between his intelligence and his irrationality, is a perfect reporter of the many voices he hears, as Ghali himself, in a larger way, is reporter and satirist."

Ghose, Zulfikar. *The Murder of Aziz Khan* (London: Macmillan, 1967) According to the publisher, this is the first novel on Pakistan by a Pakistani to be published in America. It is noteworthy in that the plot and characterization are excellent. Aziz Khan is a Pakistani cotton farmer in conflict with a new breed of industrial entrepreneurs. His situation is symbolic of the division between the natural virtues of peasant landownership and the less humane dictates of modern civilization. Carefully conceived and effectively executed, this novel offers insights rarely found in fiction, and its language is eloquent.

Thomas Berger calls this, "A superb novel the scene of which is modern Pakistan; its author is a well-known British poet."

Gibbons, Floyd. *The Red Napoleon* (New York: Cape, 1929) The author, a popular American radio commentator and journalist, draws a general plan of World War II a decade before it actually was declared. The enemy of the West is a Russian dictator who marches across Europe in order to dominate it. He then moves his troops to the North American continent, but there he is finally defeated. While the plot is in the tradition of the rugged, popular novel, the carefully described battles, the characterization of the military and the understanding of politics give the work an added dimension.

Southern Illinois University Press is reissuing this work.

Gill, Brendan. *The Trouble of One House* (New York: Doubleday, 1950) Elizabeth Cullinan writes, "This is the most beautifully constructed book I've ever read, and if that sounds like dry praise, the structure is so close to life and breath that the book itself is anything but dry. The heroine, who is dying of cancer, is so full of light and love that I still live under her influence, twenty years after I first read about her."

Ginzburg, Natalia. *Voices in the Evening. Translated from the Italian by D. M. Low* (London: Hogarth, 1963) First published, 1961. Set in the Italy of Mussolini, this is a story of a factory owner's family and friends, and an accurate and sensitive portrayal of small town life. The primary focus is on the sad romance of Elsa and the trials of her gossipy, hypochondriac mother. While there is little plot, the characterization is as effortless as it is sensitive. The reflective conversations are masterpieces of delicate feeling contrasted with implicit irony. The author has a unique, personal tone and approach which sets her apart from most novelists today.

William Trevor recommends the works of Natalia Ginzburg.

Giono, Jean. *The Song of the World. Translated from the French by Henri Fluchere and Geoffrey Myers* (New York: Viking, 1937) First published, 1934.

One of the earliest novels by this French author to appear in America, the story is set in the Basses-Alpes country. The author, drawing heavily upon peasant life and customs, explains the search for love and meaning among the peasantry. There is a grandeur and zest for life here which is rare.

Henri Peyre recommends this, and William Kennedy recommends Giono's *Horseman on the Roof*.

Giraudoux, Jean. *My Friend from Limousin.* *Translated from the French by Louise Willcox* (New York: Harper, 1923) First published, 1922.

Are there differences between German and French personalities? In a whimsical, sometimes satirical response, Giraudoux comes out with a resounding "Yes," and, of course, favors the French. His vehicle is the story of a brilliant young French writer who is believed killed in the war, but reappears writing for a German newspaper. While suffering from total amnesia, the poet had been identified as a German and thus believes himself so to be until his friend "rescues" him from his fate. The cultural analysis is as correct as the intellectual game is brilliant.

Philip Lyman cited this book in *Antaeus*, Winter, 1975.

Giraudoux, Jean. *Suzanne and the Pacific.* *Translated from the French by Ben Redman* (New York: Putnam, 1923) First published, 1921.

Having won a newspaper prize for the best apothegm on boredom, the intelligent Suzanne sets out from France on a trip around the world. Her boat is wrecked, and she becomes a modern, female, Robinson Crusoe on a South Sea Island. The narrative concerns her imaginative letters, her loves, and the descriptions of the local flora and fauna. The minimal plot is developed in a suspenseful manner—the reader wonders how Suzanne will solve still another problem. And the zest and color of the narrative are superb.

Georges Borchardt recommended this in *Antaeus*, Summer, 1975.

Gissing, George. *New Grub Street* 3 volumes (London: Smith, 1891) As a serious observer of nineteenth-century English social conditions, Gissing naturally had an interest in writers and publishing. In what many consider to be a classic portrayal of the pitfalls of the literary life, particularly revealing since much of it is autobiographical, Gissing tells the familiar story of a writer of genius who fails to gain an audience, while an author of meager talent and little interest in anything besides money becomes a great success. Gissing is often compared to Balzac, and he is at the height of his powers in this penetrating study.

Alan Lelchuk calls this, "A powerful novel written in the 1890s with a modern perspective and tone, concerning a serious writer's fate in the slick new world of literature."

Gissing, George. *The Odd Women* (London: Sidgwick, 1893) The meaning of being a spinster in the nineteenth century is explored, in sometimes painful detail, as the "odd women" progress in this much overlooked novel. The ineffectual struggle of individual single women, having been raised for a middle-class existence as wife and mother, is contrasted with the fate of a young woman who, desperate for a home, marries a totally unsuitable man. The realistic prose, the obvious care and sympathetic attention to the fate of his characters are evident throughout the novel. One of the most serious and conscientious students of contemporary conditions, Gissing is never better than in this work.

Alison Lurie refers to this as a ". . . now almost unknown, but interesting and often brilliant late-Victorian novel."

Glasgow, Ellen. *The Sheltered Life* (New York: Doubleday, 1932) A person who lives in Queensborough, Virginia, can truly be said to be leading a "sheltered life," particularly in the period from 1905 to the outbreak of World War I. But that life is about to be shattered from within, and this change is signified by the breakdown of gentility on a street which the author affectionately describes. Here lives seventy-five-year-old General Archbald with his widowed daughter-in-law, her child, and two unmarried daughters. The General had, years before, returned from the Civil War to make a loveless marriage out of chivalry, and he afterwards acquired a small fortune through hard work. Looking at the past and the probable future, the General's thoughts represent the glories of early America, while the continuing saga of the people around him focus on the uncertain future. There are passages in the novel which are outstanding for their sheer beauty of expression, and the plot is relentlessly engaging.

Virago Press has reissued this, along with Glasgow's *Virginia*.

Glynn, Tom. *Temporary Sanity* (New York: Fiction Collective, distributed by Braziller, 1976) An upstate New York, modern Gothic thriller, this opens when two brothers set out in a pick-up truck, loaded with high explosives, to free a third brother currently in jail. Along the way, they meet an Indian who claims he has the gift of flight. The group, whose collective intelligence is considerably lower than their soaring escapades, spring the jailed brother, and the narrative then follows them in their rush for freedom. Other characters and events are worked into the pattern, and the result is a satisfying, unusual approach to the traditional thriller.

Ronald Sukenick terms this "a brilliant study of stupidity."

Goes, Albrecht. *Arrow to the Heart.* *Translated from the German by Constantine Fitzgibbon* (London: M. Joseph, 1951) Published in the United States as *Unquiet Night,* 1951. In October, 1942, a Protestant German army pastor tells how he has come to be at the terrible battle on the Russian front. Although he abhors Hitler's war and knows it is lost, he risks his life in a promise to deliver a letter to the sweetheart of an executed deserter to whom he has administered last rites. Remarkable for its simplicity and restraint, the novel is as swiftly moving as it is vivid.

Christopher Fry calls this an "immensely moving" novel and says, "It does seem to me to be a work not to be lost to view."

Golding, William. *The Inheritors* (London: Faber, 1955) While best known for his *Lord of the Flies* (1954), Golding produced a masterpiece just a year after his literary debut. *The Inheritors* is a daring effort to present early pre-historic man who as yet has no language. The novel opens by considering eight Neanderthalers who are mild mannered, live near a waterfall, and are peaceful until they are invaded by another group, the homo sapiens, i.e., the inheritors. Unable to adjust to the new ways of behaving, the group of eight is lost. Not only is this story fascinating, but it is blessed with a vibrant style. The author's use of image and symbol perfectly duplicates a sense of primitive mentality.

Arthur Koestler recommends this "imaginative reconstruction of the mentality of Neanderthal man in fictional form."

Goldman, William. *Father's Day* (New York: Harcourt, 1971) Amos McCracken is on the brink of total despair. His marriage is finished and his career in the theater seems doomed. He decides to have his small daughter spend Father's Day with him, but a disaster occurs which is heightened by Amos's frantic fantasies. The striving for a way of life richer than that offered by the traditional model of success is also the theme of Goldman's first novel, *The Thing of It Is . . .* (1967), which likewise featured Amos.

Harlan Ellison recommends *Father's Day*.

Gombrowicz, Witold. *Pornografia.* *Translated from the Polish by Alastair Hamilton* (London: Calder, 1966) First published, 1960. This resumes the theme of Gombrowicz's first novel, *Ferdydurke* (1937), which considered the conflict between the old and the young. *Pornografia* concerns two old men who sojourn in the Polish countryside during the Second World War. They are seized with a voyeur's compulsion to mate two adolescents who seem to have no interest in one another. Despite its prurient theme and title, the novel is developed almost in the style of a fairy tale. Gombrowicz (1904-1969) is considered, along with Czeslaw Milosz, one of Poland's two modern literary masters, and this novel makes his reputation understandable.

Piers Paul Read recommends this work.

Goodrich, Marcus. *Delilah* (New York: Farrar, 1941) Niven Busch writes, "I loved this magnificent book, the Odyssey of a World War I destroyer in various parts of the world and the inter-relationships of its crew members. In tone it is a work like a heady blend of Conrad and Gide, philosophic yet full of action, written in a style surging and luminous like the wash of the seas through which, in southern climes, the destroyer Delilah pushes its prow. Marcus Goodrich was a journalist, a filmmaker and a dealer in many literary wares, but this book occupied him for nearly twenty years and in my opinion, and that of certain contemporary critics, it ranks with the best United States and European fiction produced in the thirties and forties."

Goodwin, Stephen. *The Blood of Paradise* (New York: Dutton, 1979) A writer and his artist wife leave the city to find themselves and the real America in the mountains of Virginia. The civilization versus wilderness theme and its effect on the characters is carefully constructed. The rich physical environment, the humanity of the puzzled, sometimes angry, but always loving couple turns this novel into a small masterpiece of understatement.

Richard Bausch calls this "a beautifully written novel about love, the forces which break it down, and the forces which keep it intact. Goodwin writes like an angel, and *The Blood of Paradise* is a marvelous testimony to his gift."

Gordon, Caroline. *Aleck Maury, Sportsman* (New York: Scribner, 1934) Passionate about hunting and fishing, both as a youth and then as a college professor, Aleck Maury narrates what essentially is his autobiography. The novel is a rare combination of serene, unpretentious events coupled with exciting scenes of hunting and fishing. As both a story of character and out-of-doors action, it is exceptional for its form and lyricism. Even those readers who are less than enthralled by blood sport will come to appreciate the simple, good-natured, candid Aleck Maury.

Peter Taylor cited this in *American Scholar*, Spring, 1970.

Gordon, Caroline. *The Malefactors* (New York: Harcourt, 1956) As intricately structured as the later novels of Henry James, this is based on Dorothy Day and the Catholic Worker group. The protagonist is a middle-aged poet who has to adjust to an emotional challenge presented by his wealthy wife and her charitable work. This is a novel of ideas and manners, a form in which the author excels, and *The Malefactors* is considered by many to be her best work.

Brainard Cheney writes, "... the elusive miracle is the dramatic presentation of the freedom of God's grace. . . .[M]an's idiosyncratic distinction among the animals is based on his reflective realization of death, natural death—by deduction, his own death. All of his peculiar monuments, institutions, dreams are characterized by this realization. And its mystery. . . .He realizes that God's grace is essentially a free gift. And the measure, the very definition of maturity, are the supernatural virtues of faith, hope, and charity that dispose him to the gift. If one reads *The Malefactors,* along with [Hart Crane's] "The Bridge" . . . he will surely perceive this intuition in the action of Caroline Gordon's story" (*Rediscoveries,* ed. David Madden [New York: Crown, 1971]).

Graham, Carroll and Garrett Graham. Queer People (New York: Vanguard, 1930) This is a truly picaresque American novel, which sets T. A. White, an ex-journalist, down in the middle of Hollywood. It is the 1920s and White's adventures are depicted not in order to prove any point but only to entertain. Aside from the delightful experiences of this cheerful rascal, the reader is also given a view of early days in the film capital.

Southern Illinois University Press is reissuing this book.

Grahame, Kenneth. The Golden Age (London: J. Lane, 1895) A series of short stories which reflect Grahame's delicate writing style and his joy for life, these may be enjoyed as much by adults as by children. (In the original introduction to the stories, Grahame makes the point that they were not intended only for children.) It is an art to be able to write adequately and

acceptably about youths, and here the author is a consummate artist. The stories are filled with the imagination of the young, not only of the late nineteenth century, but of any period.

Maxine Kumin terms this "... a seminal work for me, [a] book I read in childhood and early adolescence. . . .Grahame confirmed me as an Anglophile, both in temperament and orthography."

Graves, Robert. Seven Days In New Crete (London: Cassell, 1949) Published in America as *Watch the North Wind Rise.* Turning from the Greeks and Romans, Graves looks to the future. His late novel is set about a thousand years from now. The place is a kingdom in the area of southern France. A poet, who has been summoned magically into this magical future, tells the story. To his surprise, the poet discovers that a female-oriented goddess has replaced the male-dominated religions, and high technology, including printing and clocks, has vanished. In fact, everything seems to have improved markedly.

Noel Perrin writes, "It is not inevitable that imagined futures be dreary. . . . [Graves] has replaced time, money, and machinery [with] ritual, handicraft, and love. . . . [This is] a book so rich in style and plot, so profoundly mythic and at the same time so lightly comic, not to mention so full of twists, turns, and reversals, that there is simply no way to communicate its full flavor" (*Washington Post Book World,* August 16, 1981).

Green, Hannah. The Dead of the House (New York: Doubleday, 1972) Reaching back two centuries, a southwestern Ohio woman, growing up in the 1940s, tries to discover her family history in an effort to understand the peculiar qualities in herself. With singular refinement, the tale discloses the quasi-mythic grandfather and the father who lolls around drinking and talking in the family living room about his past and future. A unique, almost dreamlike novel, this is particularly American in its search for roots, and the author satisfies both her heroine's emotional and historical needs for self-discovery.

Willard Trask cited this novel in *Antaeus*, Autumn, 1979.

Green, Henry. Back (London: Hogarth, 1946) After years in a German prison camp, Charley Summers returns to his position in London and his memory of Rose who died during the war. He visits her family, only to discover that his grief is more probably for the ideal than for the real woman. Finally, he meets someone similar to Rose, and the novel ends with promises of happiness. Lacking the satire of Green's better known *Loving*, this still retains his refreshingly distinct style. Few writers have so nicely communicated what V.S. Pritchett calls "the concealed originality of ordinary human beings."

Lore Segal writes, "Henry Green is sometimes dismissed as a coterie writer with a great ear—a writer's writer. As a member of the coterie, I've delighted in the ear, the felicity of his wit and a verbal skill not unlike the admirable skill of the juggler, which Green has so skillfully admired. He will take on the description of a dancing couple reflected in the facets of a chandelier; he will write a whole novel, wonderfully, restricting himself to dialogue. You can live your reading life sans Henry Green, but you may wish, for delight's sake, to join the coterie."

Lore Segal also recommends Henry Green's *Doting* (1952) and *Loving* (1945).

Green, Julian. Moira. *Translated from the French by Denise Folliot* (New York: Macmillan, 1951) First published 1950. Deeply influenced by his puritanical heritage and rural upbringing, Joseph Day enters an American university in the 1920s.

The contrast between the sophisticated life at the university (a thinly disguised portrait of the University of Virginia, where Green studied) and Day's austerely religious background results in a wryly imagined story. From Day's warped perspective, he believes he is tempted by Moira and must rid himself of her influence. His method of doing so carries the reader along to the ghoulish ending. The heritage of Puritanism in America and its sometimes tragic consequences are extremely well documented.

Henri Peyre recommends this.

Green, Julian. The Pilgrim on the Earth (London: Blackamore, 1929) A psychological thriller, ghost story, and portrait of eccentric personalities, this novel opens in Virginia in the 1890s. An orphan boy lives with his uncle and aunt and the latter's terrifying old father. While no education is provided for Daniel, he spends his days deep in books. His favorite works are *Frankenstein* and other horror stories. In his late teens, he goes to a university and arrives at school two weeks early in order to meet a mysterious young man. The youth is visible only to Daniel, and in a short time, he ruins Daniel's future. The novel draws to a dramatic close, and the true story is revealed through fragments written by Daniel.

William Burroughs recommended this in *Antaeus*, Autumn, 1975.

Greenberg, Alvin. Going Nowhere (New York: Simon & Schuster, 1971) After losing a leg, a former physics student spends ten years hitchhiking around the East Coast until he is accosted by a flying saucer. Controlled by his former teacher, the vehicle is the professor's way of advertising his discovery that nothing in life has purpose. The imaginative fable moves on to explore the weaknesses and humor in the human situation. The author has the ability to make the wildly improbable seem not only probable, but moving and amusing. This is an artful, thoughtful story.

Griffin, John H. *The Devil Rides Outside* (Fort Worth: Smith's, 1952) As a guest in a French monastery, a young American begins his study of Gregorian music. Initially detached, he slowly becomes involved with the faith of the monks. As he does so, he becomes devastated by their moral perspective which contrasts sharply with his sexual promiscuity. Sometimes compared with the early novels of Henry Miller, this work has the same vivid self-revelations about sex, although here they are tied to mysticism. The energy and religious fervor in this novel are astonishing.

R. G. Vliet recommended this in *Antaeus*, Autumn, 1979.

Grossmith, George and Weedon Grossmith. *The Diary of a Nobody* (Bristol: Arrowsmith, 1892) Written by brothers, one of whom became a star in Gilbert and Sullivan operettas and the other a theater manager, this is a minor classic. Weedon Grossmith furnished the drawings for the text which started as a series of illustrated sketches on suburban life in *Punch*.

Bernard Bergonzi writes of the hero, "Mr. Pooter not only makes terrible puns, but he tells the reader how good they are and goes on savouring them for a long time. . . . The [work] is . . . not so much a test of a sense of humour as of a sense of the ridiculous. . . . [Mr. Pooter] is extravagantly pompous and complacent, but he is also remarkably honest, concealing nothing of all the bad things that happen to him. . . . Mr. Pooter is more than just a late Victorian figure of fun. He is a memorable literary type, like Emma Bovary or J. Alfred Prufrock or Leopold Bloom. Such figures focus much of our own experience and ways of feeling."

Paul Theroux also recommends this work.

Grubb, Davis. *Shadow of My Brother* (New York: Holt, 1966) A master of the novel of crime minus detection, here Grubb explores the motives and backgrounds of various people in a small Southern town. The plot turns on the lynching of a black youth. The hanging is seen by two white youngsters. The girl recognizes her father as one of the killers. From there, the author takes the reader into the history of that father and the community. The thought-provoking events and contingencies which made him and the town into murderers of an innocent boy are delineated in sometimes painful detail.

Roger Sale recommends this as well as other Grubb novels: *The Night of the Hunter* (1953), *The Voices of Glory* (1962). He writes, "Grubb can be both pretentious and wearyingly sentimental, but he can also be haunting and exciting. . . . The major reason is Grubb's wonderful sense of the dreariness of the West Virginia landscape; . . . Grubb invents a place, and a way of living to fit it, that is all his own, and unique" (*American Scholar*, Winter, 1979).

Guetti, James. *Action* (New York: Dial, 1972) A young English professor who is a compulsive gambler becomes bored with teaching. More inclined to gaming than erudition, he turns relentlessly toward the life of chance. A number of fascinating underworld characters, as well as more ordinary gamblers, are introduced as the professor gradually destroys his marriage. While the plot is minimal, the strength of the novel lies in the excellence of its characterization and in the author's authentic portrayal of the world of the fast dollar.

Roger Sale calls this "the best novel I know about gambling, and indeed is so much better than most that the others cease to count. Furthermore, it has a grand opening sequence that is, by itself, a first-rate short story, and, to boot, a wonderful indicator for any wary reader of what is in store." (*American Scholar,* Winter, 1979)

Bill Ott says *Action* is "perhaps the best contemporary novel about gambling; this book did everything the overrated film, *The Gambler,* was purported to have done."

Gulik, Robert van. *The Chinese Nail Murders* (New York: Harper, 1963) Using the unexpected time and place of seventh-century China, the author constructs an historically accurate scene in which he places the philosopher Judge Dee. Here, the brilliant detective is involved in a trio of cases which finally cause the end of his career. This is one of the best of the extraordinary Dee adventures.

Jon Anderson recommended it in *Antaeus,* Winter, 1975.

Gysin, Brion. *The Process* (Garden City: Doubleday, 1969) A black American professor sets out on a trip to the Sahara to learn more about the slave trade. While smoking keef, he embarks upon a series of unlikely adventures which serve as a convincing depiction of North African life. Lesser writers have taken volumes to describe what this author manages to convey in a relatively few, vivid pages.

William Burroughs recommended this in *Antaeus,* Autumn, 1975.

Hall, James B. *Mayo Sergeant* (New York: New American Library, 1967) James B. Hall describes his novel as follows: "The materials involve a man from the midwest (Mayo Sergeant) who becomes a successful builder/realtor in Southern California. It has comic aspects—a few—but mostly it is a study of Southern California, a place called Cutlass Bay (Newport Beach). Good sailing and yachting background and details of construction. Circumstances of publication: this was the final hardcover novel printed by NAL. The book was published, but apparently only a few

copies were bound. Only two or three review copies ever got distributed (by the author!). I believe the editor(s) were gone well before publication. In any event, it's a rare item in hardcover and a recent catalogue quotes $200. Obviously, the novel is a collector's item."

Hall, James B. *Us He Devours* (New York: New Directions, 1965) In these fourteen vigorously written short stories, there are satires of university life, tales of the grotesque, symbolic fiction, and emotional vignettes. Many of the characters are down at the heel and are viewed both subjectively and objectively, with a dual perspective which makes them particularly affecting. The extremity of action is worked out beautifully, and the reader leaves these stories with a clear sense of satisfaction.

James B. Hall writes, "This is the first collection of my own stories. They have been widely reprinted and I have been called, 'America's most anthologized short-story writer'—in an encyclopedia article on my short fiction. The title story 'Us He Devours' is said to be a modern classic. . . ."

Hamilton, Patrick. *Slaves of Solitude* (London: Constable, 1947) Although remembered today for his play *Angel Street* (later made into the film *Gaslight*), Hamilton was a tortured author who specialized in novels of loneliness. He intently explored the tribulations of the English middle and lower middle classes. In this novel he perfectly captures what it means to live in a boarding house. The primary character is a forty-year-old spinster who is constantly attacked verbally by one of the bully borders. While apparently helpless, she finally is successful in a rebellion that completely vanquishes her opponent. The author's combined skills of maintaining suspense and granting insight into characters gives this novel a particular place in modern fiction.

Clancy Sigal says, "Set in a London suburb at the start of World War II. Superb, tense evocation of civilian's war, and emergence of timid woman to autonomy."

Hamilton, Patrick. *Twenty Thousand Streets Under the Sky: A London Trilogy* (London: Constable, 1935) First published as *The Midnight Bell, Bob* (1929), *The Siege of Pleasure, Jenny* (1932), *The Plains of Cement, Ella* (1935).

Concentrating on the working class and the poor of London, Hamilton draws an almost perfect picture of the absolute hopelessness of this unsentimental group. The protagonists are Ella, the homely but charming barmaid, Bob, the handsome barman whom Ella secretly loves, and Jenny, who completes the local triangle.

Keith Waterhouse writes, "A trilogy of London novels by, to quote J. B. Priestley, 'one of [a] small company of originals . . . a real novelist, that is, a writer to whom prose fiction seems the natural mode of expression, not one who produces novels simply because novels are what the public wants.' Once highly regarded as a naturalism-school author, somewhat in the tradition of Gissing, but now neglected."

Hampson, John. *A Bag of Stones* (London: Verschoyla, 1952) A young boy has the habit of collecting stones of a peculiar size and type. His father is cruel to him, and his mother cannot intervene. The boy is sensitive and intelligent, but driven almost to insanity by his father. With a simple, realistic style, Hampson carries the reader to the point where the son writes an essay on the boy David, and suddenly the place of the stones in the future of the beleaguered child is understood. A gripping and thoroughly credible development of plot and character give this story an extraordinary feel of reality.

John Lehmann recommends this work.

Hampson, John. *Saturday Night at the Greyhound* (London: Hogarth, 1931) A small pub in an English village is the scene of a Saturday night confrontation between the owner, his wife, and her brother. Added to the group is the barmaid who is having an affair with the pub's owner, a local gossip and several other villagers. The swiftly moving dialogue soon makes the relationships, thoroughly unpleasant ones, clear. And it is very nearly impossible to forget the characters, each of whom is etched so finely, and the dramatic setting of the struggle which lasts only a period of twelve hours.

John Lehmann recommends this work as well.

Hamsun, Knut. *Pan.* *Translated from the Norwegian by W. W. Worster* (New York: Knopf, 1921) First published, 1894. A subtle game of love between a young lieutenant and a merchant's daughter takes place in an idyllic summer setting where the officer is occasionally more devoted to hunting than to his woman. The affair is stormy from the start, particularly as she fails to understand his character, and he is quite lost when she becomes moody and temperamental. The contrast between the lyrical beauty of the country and the pathos of the love affair heightens the interest and drama of the novel.

Robert Roper recommends this as does Shirley Ann Grau, who says it is "the best love story ever written—but *only* in the translation published by Knopf in New York. Hamsun (in senile old age) was a Nazi sympathizer and he has been damned for it ever since. Our loss."

Hamsun, Knut. *Victoria.* *Translated from the Norwegian by A. G. Chater* (New York: Knopf, 1923) First published, 1898. The miller's son and the daughter of a landlord fall in love, have a short spell of happiness and then are separated by the daughter's ultimate loyalty to her father. While only a novelette, an otherwise common story becomes a minor classic due to the author's sureness of feeling and vivid style. There is something both idyllic and passionate in the two characters, and the slim plot, which borders on the sentimental, captures the true romantic sense of life. It is a fresh and delicate love story.

Robert Roper recommends this Hamsun work as well.

Hanagan, Eva. *The Upas Tree* (New York: St. Martins, 1979) Devoted to her aged mother, a Scottish, middle-aged woman is left, after her mother's death, to an eccentric fate. She has had no experience with men, but decides avidly to pursue an infatuation with her young gardener. Their affair ends in disaster, and she orders the destruction of a tree which represents her family and her past. This is a convincing, extremely sensitive story.

Barbara H. Lord recommends it.

Hanley, James. *The Closed Harbor* (London: Macdonald, 1952) In the oppressive heat of Marseilles, a French captain who has lost his ship during the war attempts to find a solution to a personal tragedy. Obsessed with getting back to the sea and regaining his lost pride, the merchant captain tries to live down the suspicion that he murdered his nephew. The simple, naturalistic struggle of the captain ends in abysmal failure. But the sense of the sea, which pervades most of Hanley's work, is a vivid presence for the reader.

John Lehmann recommends the novels of James Hanley, who wrote over two dozen from the 1930s to the mid-1970s.

Hardwick, Elizabeth. *The Ghostly Lover* (New York: Harcourt, 1945) In this, her first novel, the author explores the complex relationships of a bourgeois Kentucky family. Through the eyes of a young girl, presumably some aspect of the author, the extraordinarily sensitive drama is conveyed. The portrayal of the characters' ephemeral emotions is as effective as the style is subtle.

Daniel Halpern recommends this.

Hartley, L. P. *The Go-Between* (New York: Knopf, 1954) It is England at the beginning of the twentieth century, and a thirteen-year-old boy is the go-between in the clandestine affair between a friend's older sister and a local tenant farmer. The story develops as the boy begins to recognize he is playing a part in an action which has ramifications far beyond his understanding. As an accurate recreation of English country life, the absorbing story introduces the reader to other members of the family and community. But the impact of the story has to do with the emotions of the young boy which are permanently shattered as he learns of the troublous situation in which he is enmeshed. The first sentence sets the tone and the scope of this unforgettably evocative work, "The past is a foreign country: they do things differently there."

Hauser, Marianne. *Dark Dominion* (New York: Random House, 1947) A surrealistic, psychological tragedy, this novel moves from present day life in New York back to the heroine's childhood in Switzerland. Told by her brother, it is a study of both the conscious and subconscious acts and emotions of the woman and two men: her husband (a psychiatrist) and her lover (who becomes her husband's patient). Somehow, the incredible set of characters seems plausible, and the exercise in Freudian interpretation is believable and intriguing.

Anais Nin wrote, "When people tire of noise, crassness and vulgarity, they will hear the truly contemporary complexities of Marianne Hauser's superimpositions" (*American Scholar*, Spring, 1970).

Head, Bessie. ***When Rain Clouds Gather*** (New York: Simon & Schuster, 1969) Writing from her life-long experience in Botswana, the author takes the reader into the world of a young, black, South African refugee, Makhaya. This gentle novel is a love story, yet it is accented by drought, tribal rigidity, and clashes between various cultures. The colorful descriptions are matched by the dialogue. The values of African society become both real and immediate.

Nikki Giovanni writes, "i meet people who have never heard of bessie head . . . i choose [*When Rain Clouds Gather*] because . . . [it] would inform both the heart and the conversation . . . [it] deserve[s] a reading because [it] not only has something both sweet and crucial to share about the human condition but [it] shares it beautifully. with words well chosen, emotions properly harnessed, thoughts well formed."

Heinemann, Larry. ***Close Quarters*** (New York: Farrar, Straus, 1977) Operating heavily armored yet terribly vulnerable personnel carriers, an American combat troop is bogged down in Vietnam. The horrifying swamp is not only the actual war, but the ever-present doubts and drugs, as well as the elusive yet deadly enemy. In total command of the GI speech and range of emotions, the author, who was a combat veteran himself, recreates the texture of a war which was unlike any other that America fought. Few novels so well create the glory and the gore of combat, the cynicism and, at times, childish optimism of the soldiers.

Lucian Truscott III writes: "The single best book (novel) ever published about Vietnam. Makes Michael Herr's *Dispatch-es* look like just what it is: a bunch of dispatches from a guy who longed to carry a gun, but never had the courage to carry one—not the moral or physical nerve—not the willingness to risk life—but the *courage* to carry a rifle, which in and of itself demands shooting back at anything or anybody shooting at you. *Close Quarters*, however flawed (it lacks a complete narrative structure as a novel), is at least true and to the point. And extremely well written."

Hemley, Cecil. ***The Experience*** (New York: Horizon, 1960) The title derives from the experience of a New York lawyer. He has a mystical insight which results in his abandonment of job, marriage, and friends in order to become a modern-day pilgrim in search of spiritual salvation This uncommon plot is handled quietly and earnestly, so that the reader has both sympathy and understanding for the central figure.

Ann Stanford recommends this novel.

Hemon, Louis. ***Monsieur Ripols and Nemesis.*** *Translated from French by W. A. Bradley* (London: Macmillan, 1925) M. Ripois, a sensualist and a scamp, is in pursuit of amorous adventures in London, when he unexpectedly meets, and just as promptly loses the affection of, an idealized young woman. The rise and emotional defeat of M. Ripois is shrewd and entertaining. It is an almost perfect portrait of one type of Don Juan—first in, then out, of action. An added aspect is the wealth of detail and intimate knowledge of the London scene.

Francois Truffaut recommended this in *Antaeus*, Autumn, 1979.

Henry, O. ***The Gentle Grafter*** (New York: McLure, 1908) The master of the surprise ending, with a genius for establishing character and setting in a few phrases, O. Henry is one of America's greatest short story writers. In this collection, the focus is on Jeff Peters, who is a type of urban Robin Hood. He victimizes only the rich, and is known among friends as a "reducer of surplusage."

Dwight MacDonald cited this in *Antaeus*, Winter, 1975.

Heppenstall, Rayner. *The Greater Infortune* (New York: New Directions, 1960) First published, 1934, in a somewhat different version and under the title of *Saturnine* (London: Secker).

After a brief, less than encouraging, business career, Leckie decides to throw over everything, including his family, and retreat into the world of Bohemian London. This is in 1938, just before World War II. The situation is reminiscent of an English version of Isherwood's *Berlin Stories*, including the picaresque characters and events. The extraordinary, sometimes exasperating, Leckie is in constant vascillation between the various versions of himself. A fine evocation both of period and people existing on the brink of change, the novel is sometimes funny, sometimes chilling, but always a pleasure to read.

Edward Gorey recommended this in *Antaeus*, Autumn, 1975.

Herbert, Xavier. *Capricornia* (Sydney: Publicist, 1937) An epic of northern Australia, this is often referred to as the finest Australian novel of the 1930s. The plot concerns an English settler who labors to make a home during the first three decades of the twentieth century. The satirical jabs and the indictment of racism are elaborated on in the interrelated stories of settlers who fight year in and year out against the unpredictable weather, economic collapse, and the malignancy of their neighbors. This is a miraculously energetic and invigorating novel.

Robert Roper calls this "a superb realist novel of pioneering in Australia—astringent comedy—the author is at war with the

'sublime' in literature and achieves victory most artfully. This is a great book and should cause Patrick White to surrender his [Nobel] Prize."

Herbst, Josephine. *Money for Love* (New York: Coward-McCann, 1929) Harriet Everist is a young, sensitive actress desperately in need of understanding and affection. She moves in a world of emotionally limited and repressed people, incapable of giving her the love she needs. Her search for fulfillment is tolerably suspenseful, and the story is very effectively told. Beyond that, the author achieves perfect understatement in the realistic dialogue. There is much here to remind the reader of the early novels of Jean Rhys.

Elizabeth Hardwick recommended this, as well as Herbst's *Nothing is Sacred* (1928), in *Antaeus*, Fall, 1977.

Hergesheimer, Joseph. *The Party Dress* (New York: Knopf, 1930) To fall in love again at forty, although married and the mother of two, is the fate of a middle-class woman whose husband is a prosperous businessman. The realization of love comes slowly, and is revealed as the novel builds towards the section in which Nina puts on her first real Paris dress. The rest follows, and in the process the author gives a glowing description of houses, parties, and the inevitable dinner where everyone is totally unaware of the major turn in Nina's life.

William Haggard writes, "I don't know that I would say that Joseph Hergesheimer was 'neglected'; he must have done very well in his time. But I do think he was very underestimated as a novelist. With the exception of H. L. Mencken (*Selected Prejudices*, q.v.), I have seldom seen him praised by anybody of weight, and this is even truer in England.

"When I was a young man my egghead contemporaries were reading Aldous Huxley, Richard Aldington, Rosamund Lehmann—that lot. I couldn't take them so turned to America. Hergesheimer wasn't the only one. . . . What first hooked me was that Hergesheimer wrote about people, particularly men, with whom I, though English, could instantly identify; whereas the protagonist of the English novel of the time was as alien to my own upper-middle-class ethos as a professional jockey. And then the local colour is superb."

Hergesheimer, Joseph. *Quiet Cities* (New York: Knopf, 1928) Combining a keen sense of the dangers in human relations with a sense of our historical past, the short stories in this collection are concerned with the transition in American culture between the eighteenth and twentieth centuries. Moving from Pittsburgh to Natchez, from a steamboat card shark to an amateur in black magic, the tales are as varied in setting as they are in intention. The author is at his best in dealing with the macabre, and few writers have been able to reconstruct the American past in such true detail.

William Haggard writes, "No doubt Hergesheimer wrote his quota of magazine pulp, and jolly good luck to him. To balance that there are some fine short stories. [Some in] *Quiet Cities* would go on my private list of the world's dozen." Haggard also recommends Hergesheimer's novel *Balisand*, saying, "It is impossible that Hergesheimer could ever have lived on a slave-owning plantation in the deep South, but Richard Bale is entirely credible. You can smell the rum punches."

Herrick, William. *Hermanos!* (New York: Simon & Schuster, 1969) A veteran of the Spanish International Brigade, the author takes as his protagonist Jake Starr, who leaves his job in New York as a union organizer and goes to fight in Spain. Unlike many war novels, this has the distinction of

actually clarifying the tortuous conflicts among the various Loyalist groups—conflicts which helped Franco conquer and win. At one level this is a fast moving war novel; the battle scenes are among the best ever written. At another, it is an accurate history of the betrayal of political idealism.

Thomas Berger calls it an "authentic and overpowering novel about the Spanish Civil War, worthy of being placed alongside Orwell's *Homage to Catalonia*."

Higgins, Aidan. *Langrishe, Go Down* (London: Calder, 1966) Here are the Langrishes, genteel people with a country home in Kildare and a sense of the importance of family life. It is just prior to World War II, and, to complicate matters, a young German student becomes part of the narrative. This novel is a masterful evocation of time, place, and human sensibility.

Joseph McElroy recommended it in *Antaeus*, Winter, 1975.

Hill, Susan. *The Bird of Night* (London: H. Hamilton, 1972) The strange relationship in this novel centers on an introverted scholar and a poet whose life of intense creativity frequently costs him his sanity. Despite the bizarre and frightening events that tie its central characters together, the story is utterly convincing. Primarily, this is due to the author's fine style and her matter-of-fact treatment of events. Few novels provide such an unforgettable experience of insanity in everyday life.

Doris Grumbach recommends it.

Hill, Susan. *Strange Meeting* (London: H. Hamilton, 1971) During World War I, two young British officers meet on the Western Front. Despite their differences in outlook and personality, they become friends. The action centers on the war and the effect each friend has on the other. The author describes the terrors and privations of trench warfare including such details as a battle to take an unimportant hill and night-time reconnaissances. All in all, this is an unforgettable, understated novel.

Doris Grumbach recommends it.

Hoagland, Edward. *The Circle Home* (New York: Crowell, 1960) On the road, Denny Kelly is at the end of a fighter's career and the end of his marriage. Willing to drift where fate takes him, he recalls his great days as a fighter and his ultimate downfall. The particular strength of the novel lies in its finite descriptions and understanding of prize fighting, fighters, and their strong dialogue. While the ending is not wholly convincing, the combination of a chronological plot with flashbacks is marvelous and holds the attention from beginning to end.

Bill Ott says, "Despite Hoagland's reputation as a prose stylist, his novels don't seem to have the readership they deserve. *The Circle Home*—in print only in paper— is our best boxing novel. It uses the sport metaphorically, but never loses sight of the gritty reality. As in his essays, Hoagland's fiction displays a reverence for precise detail."

Hofmannsthal, Hugo von. *Andreas.* *Translated from the German by Marie Hottinger* (London: Dent, 1936) First published, 1932. The Austrian poet's first novel, this was left incomplete, probably because of the collapse of the Austrian Empire. It is as much a poem as a story. Drawing from the character of Wilhelm Meister, the work concerns the development of a young, eighteenth-century Viennese. His youthful dreams and aspirations are considered in the first, highly symbolic, sections of the book. The suffering hero is midway through his life when the novel ends. The plot, however, is incidental to the moving prose style.

Lore Segal writes, "The interest of *Andreas* is twofold. The, perhaps, one third of the novel which exists in finished form is very weird and very beautiful. For the rest we have only the writer's stray observations, themes, preoccupations, meditations, sketches. It is our chance to catch the artist in the act: he is not thinking *about* writing, he is making. The reader will find *Andreas* in Hugo von Hofmannsthal, Selected Prose, in the Bollingen Series XXXIII (Pantheon, 1952) and will want to keep turning the pages for more of Hofmannsthal (for instance a little essay on coming across Van Gogh's paintings, before he had heard of him)."

Holmes, John Clellon. *Get Home Free* (New York: Dutton, 1964) "You can't go home again" is the haunting fear of a Bohemian couple, who, breaking up, try to return to their respective homes in New England and the South. In Louisiana, May finds herself confronted with her old self, and admits that the solution to her problems lies not in others but in her own personality. In Connecticut, Dan encounters the town drunk, who is one of the author's triumphant creations. The character seems right out of Dickens. Finally, after a series of subtle insights about themselves, May and Dan return to New York with a certain degree of resignation.

Raymond Carver recommends this.

Holtby, Winifred. *Anderby Wold* (London: J. Lane, 1923) Anderby Wold is a farm in East Riding, and the story opens when the Rusbons gather around a festive board to celebrate the last payment on their mortgage. Mary, 28 years old and married to a man she does not love, is the owner of the farm. Into her life comes a Manchester reporter who covers local activities. Mary falls in love with him, but after a strike by laborers, their affair comes to a tragic conclusion. As an accurate picture of a way of life now gone, and as an accurate, sympathetic portrait of people torn by change, this novel is excellent.

Virago Press has reissued this along with Holtby's *The Crowded Street, Mandoa, Mandoa,* and *The Land of Green Ginger.*

Housman, Clemence. *The Life of Sir Aglovale de Galis* (London: Methuen, 1905) Edith Pargeter writes, "Clemence Housman, sister of A. E. and Laurence, wrote very little; she was known more as an artist. *Sir Aglovale* is her chief novel, and I think by far the finest work on an Arthurian theme since Mallory, in whose writings she is obviously steeped, though her book takes a very individual line philosophically. I know of nothing in literature more intense, nor of an intensity so held in control. Hard to come by, and I wouldn't part with my copy for a fortune. I read it almost every year and still find something newly enlightening."

Howard, Maureen. *Bridgeport Bus* (New York: Harcourt, 1965) Trapped into supporting her widowed mother, Mary Keely finally tires of it all and runs off to New York where she has an affair with an artist. She has a baby, which she gives up for adoption. Mary's departure from the routine to the extraordinary, from the staid to the Bohemian, is as much a working out of dreams as it is reality.

Roger Sale calls this "a very sad and funny novel about a smart, dowdy single woman who discovers admirable ways to accept life as she busily tells us how it ought to be better than it is" (*American Scholar,* Winter, 1979). Doris Grumbach commends this as "a first novel, a real, unforgettable achievement."

Howells, William Dean. *Indian Summer* 2 volumes (Boston: Houghton, 1886) A sparkling comedy, this was written by the indefatigable author and editor of the *Atlantic Monthly* and later *Harper's Monthly.* Howells was often called the father of the American novel. He wrote close to fifty volumes himself. While best known for *The Rise of Silas Lapham* (1885), a year later he introduced his readers to an emotional girl who throws herself at an elderly American living in Florence. She fails to realize that he is in love with her chaperone. In the best tradition of Henry James, the reader is treated to a subtle and delicately moving comedy of manners.

Noel Perrin says this "flashes with wit, gleams with intelligence, glows with sense. . . . It's a true minor classic" (*Washington Post Book Week,* April 19, 1981).

Howells, William Dean. *A Traveler From Altruria* (New York: Harper, 1894) Combining humor and acute observation, Howells has a traveler from a foreign land (Altruria) examine the American economic and social system. His moral appraisal is in the form of a romance, which is an abandonment of Howells' better known realistic genre. Here the hero, Aristides Homos, contrasts the ideal social system of Altruria with the somewhat defective American approach. The characters are representative of various perspectives and are systematically questioned by Mr. Homos. In this way a novelist, a professor, a society woman and others reveal the weaknesses and some of the strengths of their country. While the dialectic is not always successful, it usually is impressively intelligent and the humor and social criticism more than make up for the insignificant plot and hasty characterization. As a picture, albeit a slightly biased one, of American life near the turn of the twentieth century, this has few rivals.

It will be included in the Soviet Union's "Library of the Literature of the United States," comprised of the works of sixty prose writers and eighty poets.

Hower, Edward. *The New Life Hotel* (New York: Avon, 1980) In the process of evolving into an independent nation, an African country tries to rid itself of old superstitions and old governing patterns. Within this political drama are placed a white American teacher, a black owner of The New Life Hotel, and a half-caste barmaid. The stormy relationship between the teacher and Salome is counterbalanced by the more realistic attitude of the barmaid who understands them both. With realistic and probing descriptions of Africa and the moving love story, the author strikes a fine balance between a fast moving plot, intrigue, and character development.

William Kennedy recommends this.

Hubbard, Elbert. *Selected Writings* 14 volumes (East Aurora, NY: Roycrofters, 1922) Hubbard was born in 1856 and had the distinction of developing a kind of poor man's William Morris crafts and printing center in East Aurora, New York. He published numerous books, including many of his own, the most famous being the best seller *Message To Garcia* in 1899. A theatrical personality, Hubbard was a national success before he died on the Lusitania in 1915. Today, he remains as controversial as he was during his life, but the writings are an excellent reflection of American ideas and ideals at the end of the nineteenth and early twentieth centuries.

Marguerite Young recommends these works.

Hudson, W. H. *A Little Boy Lost* (London: Duckworth, 1905) While ostensibly a children's story, this novel is actually an autobiographical sketch of Hudson's childhood. Thus, it may be enjoyed on many levels. Some critics, in fact, claim that only adults will be able to understand its significance. So, as with any classic children's work, it is first a well-plotted story, in this case about Martin who lives alone with his parents on the great pampas. His companions are the animals; his joy, the natural environment. As he grows older, he ventures further and further from home until one day he cannot return. The vivid beauty of the story, the keen love of nature, the rich metaphors and philosophical overtones are as impressive as those in any of Hudson's better known books.

Paul Bowles recommends this.

Hughes, Richard. *In Hazard* (New York: Harper, 1938) Five days in hazard, a modern cargo steamer fights out a Caribbean hurricane. Drawing upon almost every terror known to sailors, Hughes recreates the storm as it comes smashing in with destructive force. As a modern maritime drama, it compares favorably with Conrad's classic *Typhoon*, particularly in its accuracy and the lucidity of its portraits of men battling the sea. While clearly an adventure story, it is also a devastating allegory of the decline of the British Empire.

Paul Bowles says this "was rather like a longer *Typhoon;* I might not find it as compelling now as I did at the time it was published."

Humes. H. L. *The Underground City* (New York: Random House, 1958) A first novel of some seven hundred pages, this is concerned with World War II and its effect on France as well as on a group of participating figures caught up in a political trial. As a meticulous observer, the author draws the reader into the post-war prosecution of a collaborationist, and then focuses on the French resistance in 1944. The final section resolves the trial, although not the problem of guilt associated with many of the participants. The effectively drawn characters, including an American ambassador and a French "Major Owl," are as powerful as the plot is suspenseful. If the moral judgments remain elusive, at another level there is the direct, unencumbered adventure to enjoy.

Ted Morgan recommended this in *Antaeus*, Autumn, 1977.

Huntington, Gladys P. *Madame Solario* (New York: Viking, 1956) Published anonymously. Mary Renault, calling this "a distinguished work," writes, "The only reason, I am sure, for its present neglect is that the author never supported it with further work, and published it . . . anonymously. It is however definitely the work of Gladys P. Huntington; this was well known in the British publishing world, but surpressed in her lifetime in accordance with her wishes.

"The book was published in 1956, received critical acclaim in England, . . . was a Book Society Choice, and had a second printing. The action, which takes place in an upper-class Italian lake resort, is set in the first decade of the century; and its brilliant sense of period is due to the fact that the author, writing in old age, described it from personal recollection. It is Henry James territory, but quite underivative, and very differently, though stylishly, handled. The close is tragic, but done with impressive restraint. One would have supposed it the work of a writer in her prime. I am told however that this was not her first book; that when much younger she had written several novels which attracted no attention and have now disappeared; that from discouragement she gave up writing, and after a long silence produced this remarkable book shortly before her death. It was perhaps the theme (brother-sister incest) which made her publish anonymously, unless she was still sensitive about the poor reception of the earlier books."

Hurston, Zora Neal. *Their Eyes Were Watching God* (New York: Lippincott, 1937) Janie is a beautiful black woman who enjoys an independent life in Florida. Her three marriages (to Logan Killicks, Joe Starks and Tea Cake Woods) are part of her sometimes touching struggle to find a sense of herself in line with her racial identity and despite her poor economic situation. Shining with humor and understanding, the story is an accurate portrayal of black society before World War II. There is an irresistible quality about both the characters and the setting, and the dialect is true and vital.

The Feminist Press (1981) has published a collection of Zora Neal Hurston's works, edited by Alice Walker, entitled *I Love Myself When I Am Laughing*. . . .

Christopher Cox wrote, "Hurston is one of our most important and most underrated writers. . . .Janie became, I believe, the first black heroine who was neither a doomed mulatto nor a mammy" (*Soho News*, September 22, 1981).

Isherwood, Christopher. *Prater Violet* (New York: Random House, 1945) Looking back to London before the Second World War, the narrator details the trials and joys of a refugee filmmaker. Here Isherwood is the narrator who speaks intimately about the role of the creative individual in a world fairly unresponsive to ideas, as well as about mysticism, love, and the commanding figure of the film director.

Brian Glanville writes, "I still think, of its kind, the novel is a delight. *Ars est celare artem;* an apothegm so often forgotten in this age when (in America, alas, especially; but in Britain too) seriousness is so often confused with solemnity, and heavy, strained bad writing flourishes. Isherwood's book, though so light in touch, is beautifully evocative, ultimately moving, and superbly evokes the character of Bergmann. Nor does it have all that come out of the closet tiresome homosexual pick up detail which blemishes his latest books; and those of others who now dare to be 'gay.' Gay!''

Jackson, Shirley. *Hangsaman* (New York: Farrar, Straus, 1951) With a father inculcating upon her the importance of becoming a writer, Natalie retires into a dream world and remains there even after being sent to a progressive college. In the tenuous borderland between reality and disturbed emotions, Natalie manages to live on both sides of the border, until a sudden turn of events pulls her securely into the realm of the real. Each character stands out clearly, and the author's graceful and accurate prose surely delineates the eerie quality of the struggle.

Roy Fuller terms this a "crime novel in the psychiatric genre, somewhat forgotten.''

Jacobs, W. W. *Sea Whispers* (London: Hodder, 1926) One of Jacobs' better collections of short stories, this includes ten irresistibly drole tales of sailors. Jacobs, who is often compared with O. Henry, is best known for his humor. The irony is that he is associated in many readers' minds with only one story, "The Monkey's Paw."

Graham Greene, in an interview, was said to be an admirer of W. W. Jacobs (*New Yorker*, March 26, 1979).

Jacobs, W. W. *Snug Harbour* (New York: Scribner, 1931) An omnibus volume, this contains fifty eight of the author's best known short stories about sailors. The characters' strong passions and vigor are matched only by their highly entertaining activities. The undiminished good nature of the stories, coupled with the sometime tricky endings, reveals this consummate storyteller at his best.

Jan Morris says these are "stories mostly of sea life by a most endearing English

humorist, very popular in his day, now almost forgotten except by his small cult of admirers.''

Jacobsen, Jens Peter. *Niels Lyhne*. *Translated from the Danish by Hanna Larsen* (New York: American-Scandinavian Foundation, 1920) First published, 1880. A spiritual autobiography in the form of a novel, this concerns primary characters who seem to move in daydreams, shunning reality. But the strength of this charming tale lies in the vivid descriptions of Niels' Danish childhood and his gradual discovery of love. After a happy marriage, the hero marches off to war, and, naturally, the end of dreams.

This work was cited by William F. H. Lamont in *Books Abroad*, Vol. 27:3.

Jefferies, John Richard. *Amaryllis at the Fair* (London: S. Low, 1887) One of England's best observers of outdoor life, Jefferies wrote many novels of English fields and woods. This is one of his best and it is concerned with the Iden family and their almost pantheistic relationship with the out-of-doors. The belief in the purity of nature and the picture of the joyful family leaves the reader with a firsthand impression of a significant facet of English thought at the close of the nineteenth century.

Quentin Bell writes, "nearly all Jefferies is too little known, but this is the best of the novels.''

Jerome, Jerome K. *Three Men in a Boat* (London: Collins, 1889) While a minor classic in England, this novel is still not that well known to modern Americans. It tells the story of three men who, one summer day, begin a journey up the Thames River. Their picnic is a mad medley of humor and musings on the human condition. The situations are as funny as the dialogue, and the overall impression is one of great delight and good will.

Paul A. Peterson recommends it.

Jesse, F. Tennyson. *Moonraker* (New York: Knopf, 1927) Subtitled *The Female Pirate and Her Friends*, this story takes place during the Napoleonic period both at sea and on the island of Santo Domingo. Narrated by a young English West Country boy who has gone to sea, the novel begins when the boy's vessel is captured by the pirate ship *Moonraker*. The pirates are relatively conventional, but as the story progresses the boy discovers that the captain is a woman in disguise. A great strength of the tale is the glittering portrait of this captain in all her glory and infamy. The author, by the way, is a woman.

Virago Press has reissued this work.

Jesse, F. Tennyson. *A Pin to See the Peepshow* (London: Heinemann, 1934) Married to a dull man and bored with her life, Julia Almond longs for a lover and the death of her husband. Both wishes are granted. But the twist is that Julia is accused of murder. She is put on trial and her dreams become nightmares. The author's intense sympathy with Julia is matched by the vividness with which she describes London life. The novel is based on a real English murder case, the Penge murder.

John Betjeman, praising some novels by Ernest Raymond, says, "On the same theme F. Tennyson Jesse's *A Pin to See the Peepshow* comes equally high."

Johnson, Pamela Hansford. *Cork Street, Next to the Hatter's: A Novel in Bad Taste* (London: Macmillan, 1965) Produce a most outrageous play, label it absurd or avant garde, give it inordinate publicity, and you will have a success. In order to test this theory, Tom Hariot writes a play so awful that it is sure to bomb. Instead, it is hailed by critics and the pub-

lic. This novel's calculated attack on taste is augmented with a subtle charm and witty dialogue and characterizations.

Nancy Loughridge recommends this.

Jōkai, Maurus. *Timar's Two Worlds.* *Translated from the Hungarian by H. Kennard* (London, Blackwood, 1888) First published, 1872. Here is a type of Hungarian *Count of Monte Cristo*, complete with impossible events, heroic characters, and melodramatic adventures. But because the author is faithful to the essential elements of his country and its people, the story emerges as a glowing tribute to the fantasies and Oriental traits of nineteenth-century Hungarians. Beyond that, it is a fine story which demands attention.

William F. H. Lamont recommended this in *Books Abroad*, Vol. 27:3.

Jones, David. *In Parenthesis* (London: Faber, 1937) Some, including T. S. Eliot, claim that this is one of the finest works to come out of World War I. Based on Jones' experiences as a Welch Fusilier, from late 1915 to early 1918, the narrative concerns the meaning of trench warfare, and is strongly influenced by Jones' Catholic faith. This mixture of prose and poetry has many literary and religious allusions which challenge the reader. Jones has a close following, particularly in England, where some regard him as the best English poet since Blake.

George Steiner referred to him as one of the "two great outsiders in modern British literature" along with John Cowper Powys. And said, "In imaginative stature, in audacity of . . . form, they tower over the *petits maitres* . . ." (*The Sunday Times*, June 18, 1978).

Jünger, Ernst. *On the Marbel Cliffs.* *Translated from the German by Stuart Hood* (New York: New Directions, 1947) First published, 1939.

One of the few public critics of the Nazis and Hitler to survive World War II, Jünger wrote this parable to condemn the Hitler regime. Against the peaceful setting of Germany before the war, not terribly well disguised as a never-never land, the author describes the rise of a chief ranger who sets out to conquer the modern paradise. Again, the ranger is clearly modeled on Hitler. What makes the novel so readable is not the allegory, but the marvelous, imaginative style and the counterpoint of peace and impending doom. Apparently, the German censors never got the point of the novel since it was freely circulated under the Nazi regime while Jünger headed an infantry company in the invasion of France.

Donald L. Poroda recommends this.

Kaplan, Johanna. *Other People's Lives* (New York: Knopf, 1975) Painfully boring, sometimes downright pretentious, and psychotic people are the concern of these brilliant short stories. The author somehow turns even the dullest individuals into fascinating characters. The title story, for example, concerns a psychiatric patient who is lodging in the Manhattan apartment of a once well-known ballet dancer. The patient carefully watches the dancer's wife and family, as well as other people in the apartments around them. She senses that their routines and conversations are almost meaningless. The sweet, tedious Jewish girls who people many of the other stories are likewise adrift. This is a highly successful collection with marvelous characterizations.

Cynthia Ozick recommends this volume.

Kapstein, Israel. *Something of a Hero* (New York, Knopf, 1941) This novel depicts, with warm humanity, life in a Midwestern town from 1907 to 1929, where John Cantrell, whose ancestors were some of the town's founders, is the main character. The story concentrates on men's desires to achieve some form of success. Within the scope of the town's population, many characters are portrayed. Most of them fail in their attempts to attain the American dream, but a few discover a small degree of success. John Cantrell, who is "something of a hero, something of a saint" stands out among them.

J. H. Plumb recommends this book.

Katz, Steve. *The Exaggerations (slc) of Peter Prince* (New York: Holt, 1968) In his quixotic adventures, Peter Prince moves through a loosely constructed plot with memorable typographical elements which range from excised passages to overprinting. The format catches the spirit of Peter who sometimes wanders off in three or four directions, almost defying the reader to follow him. A fine example of contemporary fiction in its charting of atypical forms.

Ronald Sukenick says, "The Katz book . . . is one of those rare innovative novels that is at the same time extremely moving."

Keating, H. R. F. *Inspector Ghote Breaks an Egg* (Garden City: Doubleday, 1971) Inspector Ghote (pronounced *Gotay*) is an intrepid detective for the Bombay CID. Honest, humane, capable, clever, and winning, Ghote also has a number of all too human failings, such as vanity, impatience and pride. The series of novels in which he appears are extremely literate, gently humorous, and fascinating for their portrayal of another culture and its methods of dealing with crime. In this novel, Ghote is sent, disguised as an egg salesman, to a small community far off the beaten track to get information on a murder that was perpetrated fifteen years ago. The motive for the sudden interest in this case is entirely political—an eminent figure wants to see a local leader brought down. The intricacies of a network of influence in a small town are vividly dramatized, the characterizations are vibrant, the action swift, and the effect of the novel wholly entrancing. Keating is one of the best novelists writing mysteries today.

Kennaway, James. *The Bells of Shoreditch* (London: Longmans, 1963) In the world of London business, Andrew and Stella Vass are successful. They are emancipated and deeply imbued with left-wing views. Stella is attracted to her husband's Shavian employer, J. T. Sarson, and around these three characters whirl the bankers and business people who naturally give rise to moral questions which are as toughly intelligent as they are difficult to answer. As a sardonic comment both on business and on success, the novel is a resounding triumph.

Elizabeth Cullinan writes, "Kennaway's characters are so vivid and exciting, so thrilling to be with, so in the throes of love and loyalty and moral confusion. I also recommend *Household Ghosts* and *Tunes of Glory*—which was made into a film that, I think, eclipsed the book. *Tunes of Glory* (the novel, I'm speaking of, though it's also true of the film) is one of the rare books, in recent years, to deal imaginatively and beautifully with a question of morality."

Kennedy, Margaret. *The Ladies of Lyndon* (London: Heinemann, 1923) In a satiric, sympathetic, humorous analysis of English society, the author traces the development of eighteen-year-old Agatha who, at the novel's opening, has married an eligible baronet. The baronet's complex, zany family requires most of Agatha's attention until she comprehends the petty materialism of her situation. She flees with a lover, and upon her return finds her husband deceased. She then begins a new way of life. The combination of insight and humor in this work, its attention to detail

and its balance of different social strata, make this a delicate picture of time past.

Virago Press has reprinted it as well as the author's *Together and Apart*.

Kennedy, William. *The Ink Truck* (New York: Dial, 1969) Considerable originality, allied with ironic humor and vivid dialogue, characterizes this dramatic and artistically rewarding novel. In the devastation of a newspaper strike, the author brings forth Bailey, an exuberant syndicated columnist of heroic hopes and less luck. Determined to foil the newspaper's owners, he launches a wild attack on an ink truck. The operation to drain the truck fails, but not before Bailey has set fire to the store which houses gypsies hired to break the strike. This triggers off a series of real and surreal episodes, chases, conversations, situations, and madcap events which include a burial service for a cat and Bailey's hunger strike on the picket line. As sympathetic and varied as it is humorous and readable, this novel is not only an affectionate portrait of a medium-sized American town's newspaper, but of America itself.

King, Grace. *Balcony Stories* (New York: Century, 1893) Looking back on Louisiana during the Civil War and postwar period, the author writes stories which wander in and out of Creole society, including the fringes of slavery and marriages between whites and blacks. Ultimately realistic, and not, as some claim, an apologia for Creole society, the stories compare favorably with the better known *Old Creole Days* of George Washington Cable. In fact, Edmund Wilson in *Patriotic Gore* (1962) devotes several pages to Grace King and notes that one of her stories "deals with the same theme as Cable's *Madame Dolphine,* the white skinned mulatto daughter of a white father and a

Negro mother; but it is even more tragic than the other story. . . . In another of [her] stories . . . the author . . . presents a 'negro trader' . . . as sinister as anything in *Uncle Tom*." The fine style and the deep concern with truthful portraits make her stories fascinating and enjoyable.

Judith Fetterley recommends this volume.

Kirkland, Caroline. *A New Home— Who'll Follow?* (New York: C. S. Francis, 1839) Many consider this the first realistic American fiction about frontier life at the turn of the nineteenth century. In many ways, it is autobiographical. The author and her husband moved to a small community about sixty miles northwest of Detroit in the late 1830s. Her work remains the most accurate account we have of daily life on the frontier, not as it was romanticized in later novels, but as it was really lived. In fact, it is so realistic that the author was the target of much local animosity. With an unrelenting ear for dialect and eye for manners, she portrays a wide spectrum of characters. And it is all mixed with the overriding humor of easterners trying to adapt to frontier life. A significant landmark in American literature, this is a major novel which deserves much wider attention.

Judith Fetterley recommends this as "early regional realism."

Kitchin, C. H. B. *The Auction Sale* (London: Secker, 1949) Miss Elton, a middle-aged spinster, is attending the auction sale of the property of her former employer. The three-day sale will dispose of everything in his large Kent home. During the proceedings, the reader is introduced not only to the aging Miss Elton, but to other middle-aged people in a country district in the late 1930s. The tone is slightly regretful with a tinge of malice. The mes-

sage concerns the pleasures of love, retirement, and English country life. Kitchin is sometimes linked with the better known L. P. Hartley as a master of the novel in which apparently repressed characters are revealed as internally vital.

John Lehmann recommends this along with the author's *Mr. Balcony* (1927), a masterly character study and tale of murder.

Kitchin, C. H. B. *Death of My Aunt* (London: Hogarth, 1929) "Who, if anyone, killed the aunt?" With that, this clever English detective novel begins. Its primary interest is in the penetrating psychological portraits of various suspected villains, most particularly, the family relations of the aunt. The mystery is truly baffling, and the ingenious solution is exceptional. Best of all, the story is a marvel of good writing and compact plotting.

John Lehmann recommends this, calling Kitchin in general "a really first class and original author."

Kleist, Heinrich von. *Michael Kohlhass* (New York: Macmillan, 1964) First published, 1810. The longest and one of the most famous of Kleist's short stories, this is concerned with the universal struggle of man against injustice. In the process, the author raises more questions than he actually answers about the relation of man to the state. Set in the sixteenth century, it involves horse dealer, Michael Kohlhass, who sets off on his rounds only to be delayed by a Junker. The nobleman takes illegal possession of two of Michael's horses, and when the law fails to right the crime, Michael sets off a local rebellion.

Russell Hoban says this is "a strangely memorable story in which the terrible steadfastness of a just man unjustly treated works great evil on many people and ultimately destroys him."

Konecky, Edith. *Allegra* (New York: Harper, 1976) Allegra Maude Goldman is a superchild whose life, from childhood to adolescence, is a confirmation of her particular genius. As jaded as she is witty, Allegra must battle a loving but materialistic family, including a less than sympathetic older brother. Due to the careful weaving of events and characters, and the novel's sure style, this is a unique literary experience.

Jane Lazarre writes, "This was sold as a teenage book—but it's really a sophisticated story about a smart little girl trying to make sense out of life—a sort of Jewish/female *Catcher in the Rye*."

Konrad, Gyorgy. *The Case Worker.* *Translated from the Hungarian by Paul Aston* (New York: Harcourt, 1974) A Hungarian welfare worker describes a typical day of sessions with children who are burdened with an unrelenting series of woes ranging from incurable illnesses, sexual and emotional perversions, child abuse, and social outrages. The narrator also conveys his memories of equally horrifying cases during his ten years on the job, and his fantasy of escaping from this devastatingly depressing and seemingly ineffectual career. The writing is brilliant and this novel, though terrifying to read, is excellent.

Susan Sontag recommends it.

Kramer, N. Martin. *The Hearth and the Strangeness* (New York: Macmillan, 1956) An inventor, with no sense of monetary limitations, Sumner Grange is easily excited by any technological possibility, and he helps to shape the destiny of his children whose lives, from the turn of the century, the author is concerned with. In defiance of chronology, moving back and forth from 1908 to 1953, the form turns out to be just right. The first chapter deals with January, 1908, when Sumner marries his slightly dotty and unnerving wife. There is a leap in time in the second chapter to 1927. Each episode offers a special insight into these passionate characters and their period.

Joseph Chaikin recommends this, saying it is "an American novel—written a couple of decades ago by a woman who wrote under a pseudonym, thinking appropriately that she probably would not be taken seriously as a novelist otherwise. It is excellent and haunting."

Kuprin, Alexander. *The Duel* (New York: Macmillan, 1916) First published, 1905. Romashov is a young Russian officer serving at a German frontier post. He falls in love with a superior officer's wife, a woman somewhat less interested in love than in ambition. An affair begins, and as the novel unfolds the reader not only watches the two people in the game of love, but also sees the intricacies of the Russian military bureaucracy. This novel is as intriguing as anything written by Gogol, particularly in the acid characterizations of the military.

Jerzy Kosinski mentions that "*The Duel* . . . was considered by Leo Tolstoy [to be] one of the best Russian novels."

Kusenberg, Kurt. *The Sunflowers.* *Translated from the German by George Bird* (London: Chatto, 1972) Although most of these German short stories run to no more than three or four pages, they are remarkably effective in portraying the ridiculous aspects of everyday life. For example, one story concerns a city where looking disdainfully at a policeman is illegal. The book successfully communicates feelings of uneasiness. For instance, the police might eventually consider disgruntled thoughts to be criminal. This uneasy edge, the humor, and the often peculiar endings hold the reader's attention throughout.

Shirley Ann Grau calls Kusenberg "a German Roald Dahl but very much better."

Lambert, Gavin. *The Slide Area* (New York: Viking, 1959) The Pacific Pallisades, which are an integral part of Hollywood, have a habit of breaking off and sliding into the sea. The seven interrelated stories, by this former British film critic, employ this metaphor of the slide area in their penetrating look at fantastic people headed for collapse. The narrative method of panning groups of people, then having close-ups of intimate conversations, fits the film technique. The eccentric characters are treated with humorous objectivity, and the vivid world of Hollywood is shown with skill and sensitivity.

Ned Rorem recommends this volume.

Lardner, Ring. *Best Short Stories* (New York: Scribner, 1957) The twenty-five best, and best known, of Lardner's short stories are included in this collection. Considered to be one of America's most original writers, Lardner gained fame among the literary critics as a short story writer only after his death. As a successful columnist, sports writer, and humorist, he rarely was appreciated by the literary establishment, although he had a large following of common readers. Today, his colorful stories of American life are as fascinating, satirical, insightful and funny as the day they were written. While he may not be neglected or overlooked by some, he still deserves a much wider audience.

John Kenneth Galbraith writes, "My recommendation runs to Ring Lardner's short stories, now published in various collections. The humor is the best after Mark Twain and it has the same American resonance—a nearly perfect ear for the idiom."

Lartéguy, Jean. *The Centurians*. *Translated from the French by Xan Fielding* (New York: Dutton, 1962) First published, 1960. A French paratroop officer is cap- tured during the French involvement in Vietnam, and is shipped off to a prison camp. Upon release, he goes to Algeria to battle with the Algerians. The action is well supported by sound knowledge of the military background and the politics of the wars. This is an accurate description of war, stress, and divided allegiances.

Eugene McCarthy recommended this in *Antaeus,* Winter, 1975.

Lavin, Mary. *Collected Stories* (Boston: Houghton, 1971) Often compared with O'Flaherty and O'Faolain as a master of the Irish short story, Lavin has an unmatched ability to tell a gripping tale, invent marvelous characters, and evoke convincing settings. Her vivid speech and sudden moments of perception hold the reader from the beginning of her stories to the end. In this collection, she moves easily from a farm family, to the life of a servant girl, and to that of an Irish bachelor. All her works have great compassion and beauty.

Elizabeth Cullinan writes, "Mary Lavin excavates truths that the rest of us seldom recognize, but what most surprises me about her work is always its usefulness to any given moment of my life. Her characters live in a world that seems, at first glance, small but turns out to be the universe."

Lawrence, D. H. *The Lost Girl* (London: Secker, 1920) Drawing from the same mining community that was the setting for his better known *Sons and Lovers,* Lawrence examines the efforts of Alvina Houghton to escape her surroundings. She finds her way out by marrying an Italian, a member of a travelling theatre group. The marriage and its subtle effects on Alvina are considered in detail. This is a thoughtful, artistic and absorbing novel.

Joyce Carol Oates recommended it in *Antaeus,* Autumn, 1979.

Laxness, Halldor. *The Atom Station.* *Translated from the Icelandic by Magnus Magnusson* (London: Methuen, 1961) First published, 1948. In the looming nuclear showdown between East and West, the United States proposes to purchase land for an atomic war base in Iceland. This is the central action in an otherwise Brechtian story about a country girl who comes to Reykjavik as a housemaid and goes home shortly afterwards, pregnant, as a Communist. She has fallen in with Brilliantie, who passes the time strumming a salted fish as one would play a ukulele. Soon the girl returns to the city where the debate has shifted to fathoming the contents of two crates imported from Denmark. Some believe they contain the remains of a poet; others believe they carry clay sardines. The sardonic, wildly imaginative prose, in style and in content, is suited to any reader who has enjoyed the works of Gabriel Garcia Marquez or Jorge Luis Borges. Laxness was awarded the Nobel Prize for Literature in 1955, but is little known here.

The Second Chance Press has reissued this work.

Leahy, Jack Thomas. *Shadow on the Waters* (New York: Knopf, 1960) In an Indian village on the Washington coast, sixteen-year-old Jerrod Tobin and the Northwest Indians manage to establish a relationship of tenderness and understanding. While the disastrous effect of the white man's civilization on the Indian is in the background, the primary concern is with depicting the authentic individuals involved.

Roger Sale says that "in its best moments [it] achieves a wonderful harmony of a Huck Finn story of a lad coming to learn of the corruption and ineffectuality of his elders. . . . Since Leahy, writing in the late fifties, had no Third World or environmental fashions to buttress him, had to invent for himself a method that would bring the boy and the Indians into a single

focus, he sometimes stumbled. By the same token, since the fashions weren't there, he could bring real freshness to his details and sense of place. *Shadow on the Water* is a fine little book, one that needs no regionalist, no fashionable perspective. . ." (*American Scholar*, Winter, 1979).

LeFanu, Joseph Sheridan. *Green Tea and Other Ghost Stories* (London: G. Newnes, 1900) One of the world's greatest ghost story writers, (some would claim *the* greatest), the Irish novelist who lived from 1814 to 1873 is not that often read today. In these stories, he demonstrates his supreme mastery of the supernatural. The characterization is as good as the ingenious plots, and among connoisseurs of tales producing gooseflesh, these are considered to be among the very best. "Green Tea" is a masterpiece of terror, and "Carmilla" is a moving story of vampirism.

William Trevor recommends this volume.

Leffland, Ella. *Mrs. Munck* (Boston: Houghton, 1970) A tale of suspense and vengeance, this story depends on the patience of Mrs. Munck, a woman wronged twenty-five years before the novel begins. There is savage momentum in her deadly scheme which, in Pinteresque fashion, is blocked and baffled by commonplace events. For instance, a development company suddenly negotiates to buy her house, and neighbors who have been oblivious to her suddenly take an interest in her life. The unique and startling plot is enhanced by a fine sense of life in a small San Francisco Bay community. Terrifying and utterly credible, this is a rare novel of revenge.

Raymond Carver recommends it.

Lehmann, Rosamond. *Dusty Answer* (London: Chatto, 1927) Young, intelligent, sensitive Judith Earle lives next door to a fascinating family of cousins who are essentially on their own and seem mysteriously beautiful and glamorous. She hungers after them. As she grows up, Judith also comes to admire some romantic figures at Cambridge. And only at the end of the novel does she realize that she will have to find her happiness in herself. The novel is lyrically written, with many beautiful, evocative passages which make this adolescent experience pleasurable.

John Simon recommends it.

Leroux, Etienne. *Seven Days at the Silbersteins.* *Translated from the French by Charles Eglington* (Boston: Houghton, 1967) First published, 1962. Set in contemporary South Africa, the novel concerns an arranged marriage followed by the groom's seven-day visit to the parents of the bride. The days are filled with parties and conversation about the hierarchial power structure in the country. The efforts of the ruling class to shut out the racial problems from their consciousness is evident every moment. This true, sometimes lamentable, sometimes tender view of a troubled society captures the texture of life among the Cape Dutch people.

Paul Theroux recommends this novel.

Leskov, Nickolai. *Selected Tales.* *Translated from the Russian by David Margashack* (New York: Farrar, Straus, 1961) Best known for his short story *Lady Macbeth of Mtsensk* (1865), Leskov was a master of all aspects of Russian character and situation. As one critic notes, "His longing for righteousness and righteous men contending against evil never left him. . . .There is much wonderful fun in his stories as well." In this collection, one discovers a representative selection of his stories which made him one of the greatest and most popular of Russian authors. Unfortunately, that popularity has not been established in other countries.

Leslie, Eliza. *Pencil Sketches* 3 volumes (Philadelphia: Carey, Lea & Blanchard, 1833-1837) One of the best early writers for women's magazines—ranging from *Godey's Lady Book* to *Graham's*—the author, an early American realist, won popularity for her accurate portrayal of urban social life. Here, in a collection of her stories, she concentrates primarily on figures in Philadelphia and its environs. She manages wickedly satirical attacks on those who have pretensions foreign to the clear-headed democratic fundamentals of their country in such stories as "Mrs. Washington Potts." Dwelling on defects of people in high society, she draws from her imagination and her experience to give the reader a just, often comic, description of class distinctions and relations in an early period of the nineteenth century.

Judith Fetterley recommends this.

Lewis, Janet. *The Ghost of Monsieur Scarron* (New York: Doubleday, 1959) The musty, historical episode surrounding the publication of a scurrilous pamphlet against Louis XIV and Madame de Maintenon (formerly Mme. Scarron) serves as background to this novel which brilliantly explores the excesses of the French court. Seventeenth century life is examined in terms of both the aristocracy and the working people. In fact, one of the most effective elements in the novel is the description of the daily life of a bookbinder and his family. The essential humanity of the characters dominates the sometimes grim plot which blends truth and imagination. And, as always, Janet Lewis writes with wonderful lucidity.

Evan S. Connell, Jr. recommends this work.

Lewis, Janet. *The Invasion* (New York: Harcourt, 1932) The invaders of the North American continent who stole land from the Indians included Frenchmen, Englishmen, and Americans. But here the focus is on a single Irishman and his descendents. The link between him and the Indians is solidified when he marries an Ojibway chief's daughter shortly after the Revolutionary War. The gradual transformation of the Indians' way of life is charted from then to the early twentieth century. This novel is important, first because it is an excellent history, and second because it is an accurate picture of the interrelationships of pioneers and Indians. Once again, the style is flawless.

Donald Davie says, "Janet Lewis, still alive and writing (her *Poems Old & New, 1918-1978* is a new book from Ohio University Press), is known to a never large but loyal and fastidious public for her historical fictions. These have been reprinted, but never her first book, *The Invasion*, which is no fiction but a long chapter of neglected American history told out of the papers of the Johnston family of Sault Ste. Marie in Northern Michigan, territory known to the author from her childhood. Her narrative is exquisitely sober, yet vividly imagined and in many places indignant."

Lewis, Janet. *The Wife of Martin Guerre* (San Francisco: Colt Press, 1941) In this unique tale based on historical court records, the author tells of a sensitive, sixteenth-century farm girl whose family arranges for her to marry a man she has never met and who turns out to be somewhat brutal. Since she is deeply religious, she adjusts herself to her husband, and remains committed to him even after he deserts her. Several years later, a man comes to town claiming to be her husband. She has strong doubts. How she responds to her suspicions and the consequences of the actions she takes are at the center of this unforgettable, cruel, beautifully written novel.

Evan S. Connell, Jr. writes, "The intensity pervading [her novels] makes it clear that Miss Lewis is obsessed both by the possibility and by the actuality of injustice. She investigates this theme repeatedly, with the knowledge and the cold skill of a laboratory technician. . . .Recently I reread *Martin Guerre* for the first time, although I have been mentioning it and handing out copies for quite a while. I had no interest in reading it again because some books, like certain scenes, print themselves permanently on the mind. However, it is not tedious to read a second time, and it remains for me one of the most significant short novels in English" *Rediscoveries*, ed. David Madden (New York: Crown, 1971).

He adds, "I cannot think of another writer whose stature so far exceeds her public recognition." And he cites as well Janet Lewis's *The Trial of Soren Qvist* (1947). Phillip Levine also recommends *The Wife of Martin Guerre*.

Lewis, Wyndham. *The Revenge for Love* (London: Cassell, 1937) Considered by some to be the best of Lewis's numerous novels, this is a devastating, sometimes bitter, portrait of a group of Englishmen who become involved with Communists in Spain and at home. Out of the disorderly group emerge several sympathetic, respectful individuals who show that the typical Communist of the thirties was more accurately perceived as a person, first, and a party member, second. There are, too, vivid word pictures of the era. A tumultuous, rich story, this builds to an emphatic and dramatic conclusion.

The Arts Council of Great Britain recommended this as an "overlooked twentieth-century classic" in 1982. It has been republished in England by Martin Secker and Warburg.

Lewisohn, Ludwig. *The Case of Mr. Crump* (New York: Farrar, Straus, 1947) First published, 1926. Banned in America when it was first published (in France) in the 1920s, this *roman à clef* is a great and powerful novel about a failed dream. It features one of the most unforgettably abhorrent women in literature. The bitter theme of an older woman forcing a young man into marriage is as challenging today as when it was first created, and just as powerful.

Robert Boyers recommends this.

Lie, Jonas. *The Family at Gilje.* *Translated from the Norwegian by S. C. Eastman* (New York: Doubleday, 1923) First published, 1883. Gilje is a Norwegian mountain district where Captain Jager, his wife, and four children reside. The story concerns the everyday life of this family, and the author spins a moving tale with wonderful naturalness and very lively characterizations.

William F. H. Lamont cites this work in *Books Abroad*, Vol. 27:3.

Lindsay, David. *A Voyage to Arcturus* (London: Methuen, 1920) John Hollander writes, "David Lindsay's *A Voyage to Arcturus* is a very great prose romance (*not* a novel), with the uncannily profound mythopoetic power of Blake's long poems. It may have been neglected because of the trivial shell of apparent science-fiction which it uses as a kind of framing device for its radically poetic vision. Harold Bloom has not only written extensively on this book. but based a gnostic fantasy of his

own upon it. The peculiar condition of major prose romance in the era of the novel (how many books are there of the poetic stature of *Frankenstein* and the two *Alice* books of Carroll?) is to have been forced into hiding among the minor conventions (Gothic, Mystery, the Literature of Childhood, etc.) and only in the guise of the American novel (*Moby Dick, The Scarlet Letter, Miss Lonelyhearts, Gravity's Rainbow*) does romance claim major critical attention. Lindsay's book is still read by consumers of 'fantasy fiction' and the like, but awaits its major readers—the situation is rather like one in which the only readers of *Wuthering Heights* were the buyers of trash 'romances' and 'gothics' of the contemporary paperback world."

Colin Wilson also strongly recommends this work.

Linney, Romulus. *Slowly, by Thy Hand Unfurled* (New York: Harcourt, 1965) Slowly, through the diary of a country storekeeper's wife, the self-deception and horror in the lives of several characters are "by her hand unfurled." The documentation of the occasional pious righteousness of the middle-aged, semiliterate narrator is a remarkable literary feat. She develops the story of her sons and daughters. And in the beginning, the reader sees her as she sees herself—virtuous, self-sacrificing. Gradually, it becomes clear she is not exactly the woman she wishes to appear to be. Finally, the reader is led to the dramatic climax which only a skilled writer could have realized.

Reynolds Price recommended this in *Antaeus*, Autumn, 1975.

Lodge, David. *Changing Places* (London: Secker, 1975) The title describes the positions of two professors, an American who goes to an English midland city to teach and, in exchange, an Englishman who comes to the State University of Euphoria. The time is the late 1960s, and both teachers, who are liberal, fit nicely into the milieu of student rebellions on both campuses. The absurdly pleasing symmetry of the two experiences works beautifully, and the novel is filled with humor, insights into education, the cultures, the period, and the people who populate universities.

A. N. Wilson, in *The New Review*, calls Lodge "a very accomplished comedian" (Summer, 1978).

Loeb, Harold. *Professors Like Vodka* (New York: Boni, 1927) Two young American professors meet two Russian entertainers in a Parisian cafe, and immediately one of the latter tells how she helped kill Jews in her homeland. She is paired off with the professor who happens to be Jewish, but who only reveals the fact after they have been to bed. Meanwhile, the other teacher has had better luck; he falls in love and decides to take his woman back to America. While this is a trifle melodramatic, the author's confidence in manipulating his material and his complete understanding of his characters turns the story into a realistic, sometimes amusing, study of personality in the traditional game of love and hate.

Southern Illinois University Press has reissued this book.

London, Jack. *The Star Rover* (New York: Macmillan, 1915) Darrell Standing, serving a life sentence in San Quentin, is placed in solitary confinement. He learns from a fellow prisoner how to free his soul from his body and travel through time and space. The reader accompanies him through episodes in which he relives his past through astral projections.

Leslie Fiedler writes, "I must have read *Star Rover*, picking it up quite by accident, when I was 13 or 14 and it has resonated in my head ever since. I keep thinking it should be reissued, since it combines an interest in the occult, a dedication to radical politics and a concern for the injustices of the jail system very much in tune with thinking at the end of the twentieth century."

Lortz, Richard. *Lovers Living, Lovers Dead* (New York: Putnam, 1977) In Christine's room is a padlocked chest which puzzles her husband. He suspects it may hide many things, including the remains of her famous father who was an explorer. It turns out not to be that, but as the mystery grows deeper, the reader discovers Christine's fascination with devil worship. Due to a total command of the obsessive character of Christine, which makes her immensely vivid, the author is able to weave suspense and mystery into a convincing tale of horror.

The Second Chance Press is reissuing this novel.

Lowery, Bruce. *Scarred* (New York: Vanguard, 1961) Published in England as *The Scar*. The scar is a harelip, and Jeff, who is entering his teens so afflicted, is driven to desperation by his tormenting peers. He strikes back, but not, unfortunately, at his enemies. Instead, he turns on those closest to him who have tried to provide some solace. As a fine rendition of guilt and suffering, the novel does not always explicate the boy's motives, but they are always clear.

Paula Deitz writes, "First written in French and then in English by the same author. This is a touching story of the relationship between two brothers, one of whom has a harelip. The author is able to create a child's mind and describes the pain of rejection and the realization of love in a way that makes this an outstanding work."

Lowry, Malcolm. *Hear Us O Lord From Heaven Thy Dwelling Place* (New York: Lippincott, 1961) In this posthumous collection of five stories and two novellas, Lowry demonstrates the technique which now serves as a model for many writers, and shows why his style is so arresting and his imagery so exceptional. Originally, the stories were planned as part of a series of six or seven books, of which *Under the Volcano* (1947) would have been the center.

William Gass says, *"Under the Volcano* seems to be the only Lowry anyone is willing to remember, but many of the stories in *Hear Us O Lord* are extraordinary, not simply the best known, 'Forest Path to the Spring,' but the almost unknown, 'Through the Panama,' which is one of modern experimental writing's unacknowledged masterpieces."

Lumpkin, Grace. *The Wedding* (New York: Furman, 1939) A bitter quarrel twenty-four hours before the wedding of Jennie Middleton to a young, potentially prosperous, doctor upsets their plans. The author details the effect of that dispute on the lives of the primary participants and those around them. She also offers a convincing picture of a small Georgian town in 1909, and a sense of the ritualistic importance of these nuptial events.

Southern Illinois University Press is reissuing this.

Lytle, Andrew. *The Long Night* (Indianapolis: Bobbs, 1936) Vengeance is the driving force behind the actions of Cameron McIvor. He is only a young man, but he is determined to find the rural Alabama gangsters who killed his father. The fast moving, episodic narration pits the youth against the murderers whom he brings to justice one after the other. All of this satisfying action takes place against a regional and historical background (the father was murdered in 1859), which is as vivid as the author's immaculate treatment of the various characters. This is a thrilling novel which demonstrates considerable virtuosity.

Robert Penn Warren recommended it in *Rediscoveries*, David Madden ed. (New York: Crown, 1971).

Lytle, Andrew. *The Velvet Horn* (New York: McDowell, Obolensky, 1957) The Civil War shatters the lives of four brothers and a sister who have sought isolation in the Cumberland hill country. The war effectively highlights the story within stories of the individuals who are torn apart by their passions. This episodic tale is enhanced by the author's faithful characterizations and marvelous poetry.

John Hawkes recommended this in *Antaeus*, Autumn, 1975.

McCarthy, Cormac. *The Orchard Keeper* (New York: Random House, 1965) Set in the Smoky Mountains of Tennessee in the early 1930s, the story opens with the justifiable murder of a local bully. From this incident, the author weaves a pattern of intrigue which alternates between passionate tension and stunning beauty. While the plot is complicated, it is often incidental to the emotions that the principal characters have for the land, the seasons, and their way of life. The narrative power, the sympathetic treatment of the milieu and the people make this an outstanding novel.

Daniel Halpern recommends it.

McCarthy, Cormac. *The Outer Dark* (New York: Random House, 1968) Skillfully combining the action of Greek drama with the horrors of the Gothic novel and the background of Appalachia, the author dramatizes the wanderings of a brother, a sister and three vague yet unrelenting and terrifying men. The plot is minimal, and of no great importance. What carries this exceptionally rewarding novel is its original style and admirable characterization. The dialogue is sparse and accurate, and matched by the superb descriptions of the land and its people. The parable of the wanderers is never strained, and the simple, direct narrative holds the reader's attention from the first to last words.

William Kennedy recommends this novel.

McConkey, James. *Crossroads: An Autobiographical Novel* (New York: Dutton, 1968) An ordinary man, by his own account, tells how ordinary people live and what they actually feel and do. The absence of excitement in his stories of family, friends, and occurrences gives this novel a rare sense of authenticity and, ultimately, a satisfying tone melding together the separate episodes which form this novel. As it conveys the gulf between outer serenity and inner conflicts and anxieties, this becomes a genuinely affecting work about the unexceptional life.

Allison Lurie recommended this in *Antaeus*, Autumn, 1977.

McCourt, James. *Mawrdew Czgowchwz* (New York: Farrar, Straus, 1975) The heroine pronounces her name "Mardu Gorgeous" and opens her story with a solo airplane flight from Prague to Paris in 1940. She has other talents as well. As a singer, she is an instant success, and she moves on to New York and the Metropolitan Opera House. The accounts of the heroine's appearances in opera, at social events, and in concerts are usually hilarious and accurate. This robustly comic novel with its wild love of opera and language is extremely entertaining.

Aaron Asher recommends it.

McElroy, Joseph. *A Smuggler's Bible* (New York: Harcourt, 1966) Erudition and vibrant humor shine through this first novel which is divided into eight episodes, and concerns David Brooke's effort to project himself into the lives and minds of many other characters. The creation of the world of Brooke and his friends involves one aspect of the smuggler metaphor, i.e., the central character smuggles himself into their lives. There is dazzling range exhibited here and much subtlety as well.

McFee, William. *Casuals of the Sea* (Garden City: Doubleday, 1916) A North London family, "those poor casuals of the way-worn earth," is featured with all its aimless struggles and hopeless activities until two of the members rebel. Minnie turns to profitable sexual liaisons, and eventually makes a materially successful marriage. Hannibal goes to sea, and experiences pleasure in its drama. The central part of the novel is not so much the devastatingly real scenes of impoverished family life as the portrayal of relative success in its midst. This convincing, always interesting work is now considered to be McFee's best.

James Michener recommends this.

Machado de Assis, Joaquim. *Dom Casmurro. Translated from the Portuguese by Helen Caldwell* (New York: Noonday Press, 1953) First published, 1900. Bento Santiago, later to be known as Dom Casmurro, narrates this tale. He speaks of his childhood love for Capitū, whom he comes close to rejecting because he has promised his mother he would become a priest. But ultimately he does wed his sweetheart, only to separate from her. Using a literary style of digressions, interior monologues and deceptively irrelevant discourses, the author shows the ambiguity of all parties concerned. No one seems to move in a straight direction; no one seems to know precisely what he desires. The motivations and conduct of the characters is a reflection of the modern dilemma of uncertainty. This novel shows why this Brazilian author of *Epitaph for a Small Winner* deserves an international reputation.

Michael Ivens calls Machado de Assis "the greatest of all Latin American writers. His *Epitaph for a Small Winner* is moderately known, but the rest of his splendid works remain unknown."

Piers Paul Read and Eve Auchincloss also recommend this novel.

Mackay, Shena. *Toddler on the Run* (London: Deutsch, 1964) The toddler is twenty-three-year-old Morris Todd, a midget with a talent for robbery and a desire for normal sized women. The toddler rushes through numerous adventures and affairs. The mockery and the satire are matched by the sympathy the author has for the basic goodness of the characters. But, primarily, this is a genuinely amusing and fascinating series of episodes which cast the English in a new light.

Brigid Brophy, who also recommends Mackay's *Dust Falls on Eugene Schlumburger* (1964), writes, "These two short novels were published (in the British edition back to back) in 1964, when their author was twenty. They are savage, surreally funny and tragic, and they are written, with extreme simplicity, by an angel. Shena Mackay has gone on to more mature and elaborated fictions (*Music Upstairs, Old Crow, An Advent Calendar*) and is on the point, I don't doubt, of developing into a great baroque artist, but twentieth-century fiction would be wronged if people forgot these two early instances of pure Mozartian talent."

Maclaren-Ross, Julian. *Of Love and Hunger* (London: Wingate, 1947) Having lost his job in India, Richard Fanshawe settles down in an English south-coast seaside town to sell vacuum cleaners. The process of his transition from an average person into a salesman is developed in detail. Depressed, but never in despair, he starts his door-to-door rounds, and the reader is thereby introduced to the middle-class, slightly impoverished, residents including the woman with whom he will have an affair. In the final chapter, Richard leaves vacuums for the army and goes off to fight in World War I.

Richard Cobb called this, "a fine piece of social observation, humorous, compassionate and never angry" (*The Times Literary Supplement*, January 21, 1977).

MacLennan, Hugh. *The Watch That Ends the Night* (New York: Scribner, 1959) John R. Milton writes, "With 1951 as the 'present,' MacLennan's novel is an exciting and readable blend of Canadian setting, the hopelessness of young people in the depression of the 1930s, the flirtation with Communism as a solution, and the love of two men for the same woman. The narrative and the background are so well done that the reader becomes emotionally involved even in the intellectual probing into the spirit of life and the great mystery behind it. With beauty and brutality as apparently contradictory evidence, we are asked to believe that life is a gift for which all of us should be grateful. I know of no other novel that so convincingly recommends an ethic of gratitude, something understood in Japan but sadly ignored in America. MacLennan's novel is a brilliant evocation of place, time, and spirit. It has touched my heart as very few works of art have been able to do."

McMurtry, Larry. *Moving On* (New York: Simon & Schuster, 1970) Patty Carpenter is a woman of the modern West, and this novel not only charts her progress but also documents the quality of life on the new frontier. She is consumed by the tasks of daily living, including the caring for a husband, a baby and social obligations. Her sister, a victim of a society she is unable to contend with, is another of Patty's concerns. This is an extremely well written and carefully plotted novel which measures up to the author's better known *The Last Picture Show* (1966).

Cynthia Buchanan recommended this in *Antaeus*, Winter, 1975.

Madden, David. *The Suicide's Wife* (Indianapolis: Bobbs, 1978) The title signifies the content. A young woman is suddenly faced with the colossal task of coping with the suicide of her husband, an English professor and a poet. Ann, unlike her spouse, is of working-class stock, sadly lacking in friends and without a clue to her husband's despair. Left with three children, she is forced to fight for survival. Her personal strength and the development of her character is memorable. What begins pathetically ends in hope.

Eugene Rachlis recommends this novel.

Mahfouz, Naguib. *Midaq Alley. Translated from the Arabic by Trevor LeGassick* (London: Heinemann, 1975) First published, 1947. Egypt's leading novelist concentrates on a single alley in Cairo for the setting of this precisely detailed, cleverly plotted story. Hamdia is a poor girl who dreams of modern Cairo. Although it is the 1940s, her prospects for sloughing off poverty are no better than they were for her ancestors. The constant tension in the characters' lives and the authentic descriptions of everything from food to housing give the novel a vital and spontaneous quality. The dialogue is rivetting.

Daniel Halpern recommends this.

Mailer Norman. *Why Are We in Vietnam? A Novel* (New York: Putnam, 1967) The discussion about why America got involved in Vietnam may go on for centuries, but here Mailer gives his answer. It is the American character that got us embroiled in it, the flaw of the macho man. Agree or disagree, you are soon swept into the argument by a series of actions which show the coarse, violent character of the narrator and his family. An eighteen-year-old Dallas boy describes how he, his father, and his friend go bear hunting in Alaska. With great integrity and some of the finest dialogue he ever wrote, Mailer gives the reader a direct, unvarnished insight into the power and brutality of the American ethos. The hunters' murderous impulses are made worse by sexual and, to a lesser extent, occupational frustrations. The plot, the writing, the characters, and the outcome may strike some as perverse, while others will see it as true. No matter the judgment, Mailer exposes at least one major reason why we went to Vietnam.

Marilyn French writes, "It's hardly been overlooked, but it should be in print. It's Mailer's best book in my opinion, and a great one, a classic."

Mallet, Francoise. *The Illusionist. Translated from the French by Herma Briffault* (New York: Farrar, Straus, 1952) First published, 1951. A short, well-crafted story about a fifteen-year-old girl who falls in love with her father's mistress, this is a direct, sympathetic portrayal of an unusual love affair. The relationship is an agonizing and enlightening experience for the girl, and the author does full justice to the unusual theme.

Henri Peyre calls this "an amazingly skillful story by a then eighteen-year-old Belgian girl."

Manning, Olivia. *The Balkan Trilogy: The Great Fortune* (1960), *The Spoilt City* (1962), *Friends and Heroes* (1965) (London: Heinemann) A British professor and his wife come to Rumania where he is scheduled to lecture at the University of Bucharest. In a historical tragicomic series of events, the Second World War breaks out, and the reader is introduced to a wide variety of Rumanian social figures. The conversations and oddities of the events and the characters build towards the second novel. Here, the couple witnesses the switch from lighthearted gaiety to the grim reality of Nazi occupation. In the final novel, the couple flees to Greece only to meet Italian invaders in Athens. This amazingly full and colorful trilogy is similar to a large painting which requires careful attention in order to observe all the details. It is as authentic as it is successful in its recreation of a society now gone; this is one of the finest works to emerge from World War II.

Eve Auchincloss, who also recommends Manning's *The Levant Trilogy*, writes, "[Manning] is not unappreciated in England, though always had less notice than she deserved, and seems to be unknown in this country in spite of the fact that the last three volumes of her two World War II trilogies were published by Atheneum, without fanfare. She is unique in at least one way: one could not guess her sex, she is so perfectly attuned to every character she writes about, and can uncannily write about such things as battle where women have not been present. Her sense of history too is very far indeed from that of the usual woman writer. There is a big ominous sense of obscure lives being shuffled by events beyond their grasp, tragic and sometimes hilarious, all this handled by an astringent, ironic sensibility. In short, she is one of the most original and intelligent writers of her generation, I think."

Markfield, Wallace. *Teitlebaum's Window* (New York: Knopf, 1970) Simon Sloan's life in Brooklyn from the age of eight to eighteen is captured through quotations from his journal. Covering the decade between 1932 and 1942, the novel is a mosaic of occurrences in the Jewish community during those years. More important, it is a literary triumph, marvelously capturing the people, the times, and the place.

Gilbert Sorrentino writes, "This is Markfield's second novel, a *bildungsroman* of a young Brooklyn Jew growing up in Brighton Beach from the early days of the Depression to the outbreak of World War II. It is wildly comic, bitter, and heartbreaking, one of the best, if not the best example of what was once called 'the Jewish novel' by a greatly neglected American writer."

Marshall, Paule. *Brown Girl, Brownstones* (New York: Random House, 1959) The brown girl, Selina, is the daughter of immigrants from Barbados. The brownstone in which she lives with her family is located in a once fashionable section of Brooklyn. This deeply affecting and true picture of life among the blacks in this section of New York conveys their struggle for economic and social recognition during the Depression and World War II. The conflict between the two races and cultures, while a primary issue, is kept in the background as the author relates the story of Selina who is trying to come to terms with a new country and the dreams of her parents.

Virago Press is reissuing this book.

Martin, Peter. *The Landsmen* (Boston: Little, 1952) The pleasures and traumas of poor Russian Jews in a small Russian village is the focus of this novel set in the late nineteenth century. The various experiences of such diverse characters as Yeersel, the tailor, and Laib, the musician, are developed in this humane, vivacious pastorale, which combines a dark wit with a sense of romance and a knowledge of folk life.

Southern Illinois University Press is reissuing this book.

Martin, Valerie. *Set In Motion* (New York: Farrar, Straus, 1978) A social worker in her mid-thirties with a few psychological and social problems of her own, Helene Thatcher is involved with men even more troubled than she. The setting is New Orleans, and the novel charts Helene's reactions to evocative emotional entanglements with both men and passive female friends. The style is true of the situation, and effectively summons up the elusive characters.

Aaron Asher recommends this novel.

Martin Du Gard, Roger. *Jean Barois.* *Translated from the French by Stuart Gilbert* (New York: Viking, 1949) First published, 1913. One of the earliest novels by the Nobel Prize winner, this deals with the Dreyfus affair and the French anti-clerical movement. In that context, Jean Barois' fate is worked out mainly through direct dialogue. The daily life of Barois, a free thinker, is contrasted with the turmoil in the French socio-political scene, and his decision to return to the church climaxes his struggle. The story is a novel of ideas—as absorbing as any well-conceived argument or narrative—and the translation is fine.

Henri Peyre says *Jean Barois* "has solid value."

Masefield, John. *Dead Ned* (New York: Macmillan, 1938) In this story of eighteenth-century England, young Ned Monsell has completed medical training and is about to embark on his career when he is accused of murdering an old friend. He goes to trial, is convicted, and hanged at Tyburn. However, two friends of his father, one of whom is a surgeon, get hold of

his body and restore him to life. Ned then escapes on a slave ship to Africa to evade the authorities. A second volume follows, entitled *Live and Kicking Ned* (1939).

T. J. Binyon wrote of John Masefield that the novels are "the most undervalued of his works. . . .The best, all equally enjoyable—it would be difficult to name a favourite among them—are: *The Bird of Dawning* (1933) and *Victorious Troy* (1935), two rousing sea stories; *Sard Harker, Odtaa* and *The Taking of the Gry* (1934), three novels of adventure set in Santa Barbara and the Sugar States—a South American Tatshire; and *Dead Ned* (1938) with its continuation *Live and Kicking Ned* (1939). . . .Unlike the narrative poems, the best of the novels seem, within their own limits, almost perfect: the nautical detail is obviously impeccable, and it is combined with fluent narrative, vivid dialogue, a fine alertness to period and place, and a poet's sense of occasion . . . " (*The Times Literary Supplement*, November 17, 1978).

Masefield, John. *Odtaa* (London: Heinemann, 1926) Hi Ridden, the hero of the piece, arrived in Santa Barbara from England at an inopportune period—during the rebellion of the Whites against the tyranny of Don Lopez and his Red followers. The heroine, Carlotta, surfaces long enough to enchant Hi, but then is captured by the Reds. Hi's travels through the mountains to notify Don Manuel, Carlotta's fiance, of her capture, and his gruelling experiences in the course of this journey are menacingly described.

T. J. Binyon also cited this novel in his *Times Literary Supplement* article (See preceding entry).

Mason, A. E. W. *The House of the Arrow* (London: Hodder, 1924) Did the niece murder the wealthy aunt? The famous French detective Monsieur Hanaud sets out to find the answer to that question posed by the niece's legal adviser. The plot is one of the best conceived by Mason, and it remains puzzling down to the last sentence. The style is beautifully polished.

Nicolas Freeling writes, "The suggestion . . . that I would think worthy of notice would be the 'Hanaud' books that were Mason's contribution to the 'detective' genre. Assuming unfamiliarity, there are four. All are striking, original and well written. The first, *At the Villa Rose*, is an interesting and exciting tale; the last, *The House in Lordship Lane*, is tired and rather perfunctory. The other two are more remarkable. *The House of the Arrow* is a classic suspense story of a quality much above the usual level in the genre. . . ." (See next entry for Freeling's comments on Mason's *The Prisoner in the Opal*.)

Mason, A. E. W. *The Prisoner in the Opal* (London: Hodder, 1928) A beautiful English woman is killed in a French château. Her body is discovered in a basket along with an opal bracelet of another guest at the chateau. The bracelet's owner has disappeared, and the mystery lies in the circumstances surrounding the missing guest as well as in discovering the killer. The detective, Monsieur Hanaud, is more than up to the challenge, and he moves quickly so as to avoid another murder.

Nicolas Freeling recommends the mysteries of A. E. W. Mason, saying *"The Prisoner in the Opal* is to my mind the best and the one most worth recalling, for it is a deliberate effort to enlarge the 'detective story' of the English 1930 convention into a human and psychological dimension. The plot is melodramatic but the interest is in the nature of criminal behavior, not just 'who done it' and in this approach the writer was a long way ahead of his time. The 'thriller' has become a work of art, and this remains a rarity today—fifty years later. . . ."

Matthews, Jack. *Hanger Stout, Awake!* (New York: Harcourt, 1967) A high-school dropout who loves cars and works as a gas station attendant in a small town, Clyde Stout has a peculiar talent—he can hang by his hands for several minutes at a time. The skill soon brings him notoriety, and a gambler begins to take bets on how long he can last. Clyde makes enough cash from his exhibitions to keep his girlfriend happy and to keep his car on the road. In the end, he simply quits. The language is extraordinary, a combination of poetry and narration, and the setting is superabundantly American. The economy of the tale (it is under one hundred sixty pages) is in keeping with its originality and honesty.

William Stafford writes, *"Hanger Stout, Awake* has an appealing, unassuming, consistent main character, whose voice is just right for telling the story of apparently ordinary days that yet have their surprises and satisfying confirmations. There is just a good feel about this book; it is easy to love its pace and flavor."

Matthiessen, Peter. *At Play in the Fields of the Lord* (New York: Random House, 1965) The "fields" are a South American jungle, and the "Lord" is supposedly represented by four fundamentalist American missionaries. Delightfully and vividly written, the novel underscores the thesis that native Indians may be better off than the advanced Americans. Fittingly, the story strikes a blow at old-fashioned missions, both political and religious, which fail to appreciate the needs of the individual peoples they purport to help. The author's detailed portrayal of Indian customs and his penetrating characterizations are fascinating. And, what is more, this is an excellent adventure story.

Martha Gellhorn says this is "far and away the best book [Matthiessen] ever wrote," and she calls it "a wonder."

Maxwell, William. *The Folded Leaf* (New York: Harper, 1945) The friendship of two young men from high school through college is carefully documented in this work. Set in midwestern America in the 1920s, the author gradually develops not only the characters but a fine picture of ordinary middle-class American styles of living. The narrative is beautifully written, and the drama of the adolescents finally reaching maturity is unusually sensitive.

John Unterecker writes, "William Maxwell's *The Folded Leaf* is simply one of the finest novels of adolescence ever written. Perhaps because prudish reviewers treated it as sensationalistic or because prudish librarians felt more comfortable with it off their shelves, the book has never had the very wide readership—particularly among young people—that it clearly deserves."

Maxwell, William. *They Came Like Swallows* (New York: Harper, 1937) The weeks during the killing influenza epidemic which struck in the autumn of 1918 is the time of this heart-warming story about an American family. The novel delineates the lives of the Morisons, and in a simple, direct way, without sentimentality or melodrama, the author recreates a significant moment in American history. The genuine sadness and humor add to the nobility of the story which is always convincing and absorbing.

Robert Fitzgerald recommended this in *Antaeus*, Autumn, 1979.

Maxwell, William. *Time Will Darken It* (New York: Harper, 1948) It is 1912 in a small Illinois town when some visitors from Mississippi arrive. They are foster relatives of Austin King, a local lawyer, who has invited them as his guests. Out of this ordinary turn of events, the author creates a sense of period and characters who are wonderfully alive. The people move within a limited midwestern environment to recreate several distinct approaches to love, marriage, and envy.

Howard Moss recommended this novel in *Antaeus*, Autumn, 1975.

Menen, Aubrey. *The Prevalence of Witches* (London: Chatto, 1947) Many believe this to be the author's masterpiece. It is his first novel, and Auberon Waugh observes that it "seems to have grown funnier and more topical with every year which has passed since then" (*Spectator*, December 26, 1970).

The story takes place in a backwater area of India just prior to the British departure. Hopelessly indolent, the natives' lives are steeped in superstition. The novel brilliantly considers the foolishness of inflicting European standards of conduct on these people. The center of the quiet turmoil involves a native who is tried for murdering his wife's lover. The accused, quite reasonably, asserts that the lover was a witch and that he was acting in self defense. As a "prevalence of witches" is a keystone to his culture's way of life, he convinces the English agents of his innocence, but fails to sway an Indian judge. The effort to save him is a marvel of imaginative humor on the part of all involved. Waugh rightly concludes, "So well does [Menen] write, that he makes the reader feel that he, too, belongs to the select company of the truly first rate. . . ."

Doris Grumbach writes, "[Menen] has gone on to write many other books, none as funny or fine as this one."

Meredith, George. *The Egoist* 3 volumes. (London: Kegan Paul, 1879) Developing each dramatic moment with extreme care, Meredith offers a psychological comedy about an outwardly conventional person with a burning, secret egoism. Sir Willoughby Patterne becomes engaged to

Clara Middleton but there soon is a rupture in the wedding plans, and the furor around all this is at the heart of what many believe to be Meredith's best novel. While it is not really overlooked, it is not read enough today. This is a pity because it is an outstanding example of intensely real characters slowly revealing themselves to the reader.

Betty Comden recommends this.

Metcalf, Paul. *Genoa: A Telling of Wonders* (Highlands, North Carolina: Jargon, 1965) *Genoa* has an ingenious structure and is a brilliant combination of fiction and fact. The author has witnessed moral monstrosity and sees it clearly. Here, the primary figure is Michael, a club-footed sadist, whose life is punctuated by murder and destruction. Providing a mythic parallel to Michael's own life, there are factual sections on Herman Melville (the author's great grandfather) and Christopher Columbus. The large factual fragments work to give perspective to the fictional parts.

John O'Brien says, "Written in a tradition of William Carlos Williams and Charles Olson, this novel is a collage of its narrator's attempt to establish connections between his tragic life and those of Melville and Columbus."

Meyerstein, Edward. *Terence Duke* (London: Constable, 1935) Terence begins the novel as an irredeemable young reprobate. Some five hundred pages later he is a sensitive English gentleman. In between, the evolution of his character is depicted as the reader follows him on a leisurely domestic tour of pre-World War I England and is introduced to groups of characters who would have been comfortable in a Dickens novel. There is Terence's eccentric aunt, with whom he spends some time in Hertfordshire; there are a number of flames

whom he seduces; there are several tutors in crime who teach him to be a thief and a forger; and there is his runaway, criminal father. The episodic development of this boy to his manhood is as skillfully achieved as the dialogue is real and the humor all pervading. The author combined in this one volume two earlier novels: *Pleasure Lover* (1925) and *Terence in Love* (1928) and then added a third, new section.

Edward Gorey recommended this in *Antaeus*, Autumn, 1975.

Midwood, Barton. *Phantoms: A Collection of Stories* (New York: Dutton, 1970) Hallucinations are the primary concern of this first-person narrator who conducts a search for meaning in modern civilization through such emblematic productions as television news broadcasts and commercial hair restorers, and leaves it to the reader to make sense of his report. There is a talking horse, a neurotic Edsel and other unlikely figures lurking in these thirteen stories. The combination of farce, horror and hallucination gives these tales a unique quality. They are vivid and compelling reading.

Gordon Lish recommends this volume.

Miller, Carolyn. *Lamb in His Bosom* (New York: Harper, 1933) In pre-Civil War days, Lonzo Smith brings his bride back to a rural Georgian cabin. The story follows the life of the bride from youth to old age, and, without melodrama, the author effectively portrays American pioneer life. The adventures and excitement of the frontier are contrasted with the everyday activities and the round of births, deaths, and marriages. The lyrical descriptive prose enhances the subject matter.

Conrad Richter wrote of this, "Much of my younger life was spent among the remnants of American pioneer stock but the original mind of these simple people, their life wisdom, rich human lore and poetic turn of thought was almost never found by me in fiction about them. . . .Not until a schoolteacher's wife in Georgia set down her . . . people in the hills did I come upon their manner of thinking faithfully expressed in a novel" (*American Scholar*, Fall, 1961).

Miller, Walter M. *A Canticle for Leibowitz* (New York: Lippincott, 1960) After the world is almost completely destroyed, Leibowitz, a technician turned monk, founds a monastery in the American southwest. Closely following the historical pattern of the fall of Rome, the Middle Ages, and the Renaissance, the author traces the modern development of man. In the final section of space travel and hydrogen bombs, he raises the provocative question of whether man will once again destroy the world. It is an extraordinary *tour de force*, with a wide, growing number of readers. And while many consider it a classic of its type, it still remains relatively obscure. This is superb, allegorical, science fiction, in the same category as Orwell's *1984* or Huxley's *Brave New World*.

Walker Percy says, "*Canticle* is remarkable for its grasp of current issues, its unobtrusive insight into the heart of the Christian view of man's nature—and the projection of both into a highly imaginative and entertaining narrative."

Harry Levin also recommends this book.

Miller, Warren. *The Cool World* (Boston: Little, 1959) It is the summer of Duke Custis's fourteenth year in Harlem, and his most urgent need is to acquire a short barrel 45 revolver. This will insure his leadership of the Royal Crocodiles. In his quest for money, he sets out on an adventure which takes him into the perilous country of dope, prostitution, and crime. The strong characterization of the youth is matched by the infallible accuracy of the setting. Told in the argot of the ghetto streets, the story is both convincing and alarming. Few novels have more effectively portrayed the horrifying reality of street life.

Doris Grumbach calls this "the best novel about Harlem by a white ever written."

Mirabelli, Eugene. *No Resting Place* (New York: Viking, 1972) A middle-class, cultured, liberal, and fairly well educated group is profoundly discontent with what life has dealt them. They have vague longings for a better way of living, and to fulfill these dreams they embark on various love affairs and other activities. Set in a small New England community, the novel is particularly rich in details of everyday life. The craftsmanship of the author is matched by the truthfulness of his chronicle.

George Starbuck recommended this in *Antaeus*, Autumn, 1979.

Mitchell, Gladys. *The Saltmarsh Murders* (New York: Macrae, 1932) Eccentric characters, a keen sense of humor, and a gift for concocting a puzzling mystery—these are only some of the attributes of this perfectly delightful detective story. It is one of a series which deserves wider attention.

Patricia Craig wrote that Mitchell's detective fiction has "wit, learning, assurance, vigour and stylishness. . . .Julian Symons, in *Bloody Murder*, placed her among those writers of the Golden Age whose work is now seldom discussed. Perhaps it's time for a reappraisal" (*The Times Literary Supplement*, August 8, 1980).

Mitchell, Silas Weir. *Hugh Wynne, Free Quaker* (New York: Century, 1897) A best selling novel by this famous American physician, this remains a brilliant historical work. Now all but forgotten, it is a detailed, accurate picture of the events surrounding the War of Independence. The contrast between the Quaker philosophy and the necessity of battle tortures the central character. But his portrayal is secondary to the characterizations of Washington, Lafayette, Howe and other historical figures. The author's lively style and carefully constructed plot carries the reader through battles and duels to debates.

Frederick Buechner recommends this.

Mitford, Nancy. *The Pursuit of Love* (London: Hamilton, 1945) In the pursuit of love, a young woman of the English upper class first marries a banker, then a communist, and finally finds what she desires in a wealthy Frenchman. Tracing Linda Radlett's adventures, the author presents an entertaining and perceptive portrait of an age, as most of the action takes place between the two World Wars. The combination of irony and social satire raises the narrow, somewhat absurd plot to a touching, moving profile of a war-haunted generation.

Lucy T.Vecera recommends this as well as other books by Nancy Mitford, including *Love in a Cold Climate* (1949) and *The Blessing* (1951).

Mittelholzer, Edgar. *Shadows Move Among Them* (London: Nevel, 1951) Set in a remote British Guianan settlement, the novel is concerned with a British pastor, his family, and a young man who fled civilization in an effort to forget his dead wife. The sharp insights and humor are set against a bewitching community whose characters are as enchanting as the mad plot. Within this context here emerge a tender love story and many serious ideas about philosophies of life.

Doris Grumbach calls this "the most original, peculiar and subtle novel written in 1951. About life in British Guiana, later

made into a play by Moss Hart (*The Climate of Eden*, 1953)."

Montherlant, Henry de. *Desert Love.* *Translated from the French by Alec Brown* (London: Elek, 1957) First published, 1954. Isolated in a Morrocan outpost, the spoiled son of a French middle-class family finds escape from military routine by the calculated domination of a fourteen-year-old Arabic girl. The exploitation of the child is a parable of the exploitation of Africa, but beyond that, there is a remarkably exacting story of lust and carnal love. All this is accomplished with great dignity, and the two main characters emerge as authentic as the novel's principal message.

Daniel Halpern recommends this novel.

Montherlant, Henry de. *The Girls: A Tetralogy of Novels In Two Volumes.* *Translated from the French by Terence Kilmartin* (London: Weidenfeld, 1968) In a masterly, kaleidoscopic structure which binds the four novels into a complete work, a story is developed around the nature of women and the role men play in their lives. The point of view is that of Pierre Costals, himself a writer and a bachelor, who seems to be the consciousness of the author. (In the introduction to the second half of the series, Montherlant is interviewed and talks about the third novel in relation to Costals.) While not homosexual, the hero is Byronic in his approach to women whom he tends to dislike and, in at least two cases, whom he helps to destroy. Another theme concerns the French character and its relation to sexual matters. The writing is fine, witty and sensuous. A difficult hero and an even more complex theme are established with considerable skill.

John Simon recommends this novel.

Moore, Brian. *Fergus* (New York: Holt, 1970) On the brink of divorcing his wife, confused about this current romance, a failed novelist who has become a Hollywood screenwriter takes a long look at this life. Suddenly, old friends materialize, and within the structure of this experimental novel there are many surprises and twists of plot and character. The whole experience is so convincingly achieved that the reader wishes to read still more about Fergus. This is an impeccably written and constructed story which shows off Moore's considerable talents.

Alison Lurie recommended this in *Antaeus*, Autumn, 1977.

Moore, George. The Lake (New York: Appleton, 1905) Kay Boyle writes, *"The Lake*, which I first found in Paris in 1923 among the tattered second-hand books on one of the stalls along the Seine, gave me the courage then, and through the years, at least to attempt to live and to take action without moral or physical fear. The young Irish priest, whose story this book tells, spoke to all my uncertainties, and I came to see his love story not only as metaphor for his country's long political and religious conflict, but metaphor as well for the condition of all mankind."

Morante, Elsa. History: A Novel. *Translated from the Italian by William Weaver* (New York: Borzoi, 1977) First published, 1974.

Prefacing each episode of her novel with a three or four page summary of world political events, the author demonstrates how little and how great an effect they have on average, poor people during the era she is concerned with: the turbulent 1940s. Here, the poor are typified by the Ramundo family, particularly a young boy whose life is marked by one violent episode after another. Much of the story is seen through the eyes of Ida, the mother of the boy Useppe. Half-Jewish, she is terrified by the war and what may become of her family. Another part of the narrative is related by Useppe. Not only does the author characterize the little people of Italy extremely well, but her settings are magically real. This chronicle of one insignificant family reaffirms Morante's belief in the value of people.

Doris Grumbach calls this "a magnificent book about imprisonment in Italy during Hitler's era which never got noticed and should have. Beautiful translation by William Weaver. Parenthetically, [Morante was] Alberto Moravia's long-time mistress."

Morgenstern, Soma. The Third Pillar. *Translated from the German by Ludwig Lewisohn.* (New York: Farrar, Straus, 1955) A symbolic novel with Old Testament overtones, this is set in Poland toward the end of World War II as the Russians converge on a town and the Germans flee. The rusticity of town life is dramatized while the major question of what is in the mysterious wooden box that defies opening is explored. This is the fourth and last novel in an epic of Central European Jewish life, and it is considered to be one of the most successful in its treatment of the holocaust.

Gary Giddins wrote, "This lean, sinewy novel . . . weds realism and fantasy with a skilled poise we've come to associate with Garcia Marquez" (*Voice Literary Supplement*, October 8, 1981).

Morley, Christopher. Parnassus on Wheels (New York: Doubleday, 1917) This is a very amusing, stylish story of a bookseller who wants to sell off his business and his varied ideas about literature and life.

Mary Allen Johnson writes, "*Parnassus* is a travelling bookshop owned by Roger Mifflin whose philosophy can be summed up in the quotation: 'When you sell a man a book you don't sell him just twelve ounces of paper and ink and glue—you sell him a whole new life.' Although the book was written almost sixty years ago, as a bookseller I can still identify with Mifflin, regretfully though at his point that 'books aren't a substantial world after all, and every now and then we get hungry for some closer, more human relationships.' "

Morris, Wright. *The Home Place* (New York: Scribner, 1948) Combining his own photographs with his fiction, the author tells the simple story of a New York family's visit to a Nebraskan farm. Vivid and realistic photographs are judiciously placed to emphasize the points in the text. The result is a new fictional form which has rarely been repeated.

Martin Marty writes, "As Wright Morris is finally being recognized for his contribution to American letters, newcomers to his lore have begun to reach for earlier works. Among them, *The Home Place*, an exactly right blend of spare prose and simple pictures, has its distinctive appeal. I am convinced that Morris's approach to photography and prose will help readers of the book look not only at *his* world but at *their* worlds with freshness."

Morris, Wright. *Man and Boy* (New York: Knopf, 1951) A Freudian mother, famous as a lecturer on bird lore, rules the lives of those around her, especially her husband. The satirical story climaxes on the day when "mother," as she is called by her spouse, is scheduled to christen a ship named after her son who was killed in World War II. Morris, a master of portraying American life with a comic touch, focuses on a theme familiar to most readers.

Richard Wilbur recommends this book.

Mosher, H. F. *Disappearances* (New York: Viking, 1977) It is the early 1930s, and young William Bonhomme is on a bootlegging trip with his father and uncle near the Canadian border. The setting is a way of resurrecting the history of the Bonhomme family, as the boy journeys from past to present. Surrealistic flashbacks of family members in the Indian War and even a time when Bonhomme discovered a young saber-tooth tiger are depicted. Throughout, the smuggling venture itself progresses. The melding of reality, history and illusion is nicely realized, and the narrator's meditations on the repetitive nature of human experience is fascinating.

Ken Kesey recommends this.

Mosley, Nicholas. *Impossible Object* (London: Hodder, 1968) Two characters are in love. How do they appear to others? In eight cleverly arranged encounters, the couple is seen by different narrators in different locales. As the novel moves from England to Italy to North Africa, the variations on the theme result in more than character studies. They become explorations into differing interpretations and methods of love. The intricate construction gives unity to these carefully wrought stories. The brilliant prose makes these forays into the difficult terrain of love continually absorbing.

John O'Brien writes, "[These are] a collection of interweaving stories that form a novel. With an absolutely original sense of style and structure, this novel should have ended rumors that British fiction died in 1930."

Mottram, R. H. *The Spanish Farm* (London: Chatto, 1924) A substantial farmstead in French Flanders, within sound of the guns of World War I, provides the backdrop to this novel. Madeline, the competent daughter of the farmer, helps to ease the pain of numerous British troops who are billeted on their property. This determined young woman is wonderfully drawn and is as true to life as are the soldiers and the battles. Full of detail about peasant existence, this work is antiromantic in its picture of the French countryside at a crucial period in French history.

John Lehmann recommends other novels of R. H. Mottram as well, including *Sixty Four, Ninety Four* (1925) and *The Crime at Vanderlynden's* (1926) which continue the story of the farm and Madeline. The three novels are collected, with connecting links and epilogue, in *The Spanish Farm Trilogy* (1927).

Mount, Ferdinand. *The Man Who Rode Ampersand* (London: Chatto, 1975) Harry Cotton takes an opportunity to sneak a ride on Ampersand, the greatest chaser of his generation. Although he is ordered to dismount by its owner, for the remainder of his life he is known as the man who rode Ampersand. The novel traces his path from jockey to soldier, to barman, to recruiter in Ireland for English factories during World War II. This irrepressible character is matched by other unforgettable figures who wander in and out of his life, including an eccentric millionaire. The novel has the rare quality of being highly amusing and totally credible. Each episodic section leads naturally to the next, even more outrageous, one.

A. N. Wilson called it "a wonderful book. I have read it three times and anticipate reading it often again" (*The New Review*, Summer, 1978).

Muntz, Hope. *The Golden Warrior* (London: Chatto, 1948) The setting is England just before the Norman conquest, and the novel vibrantly relates the story found in the familiar Bayeux Tapestry and in other, more accurate, historical accounts about Harold of England and William of Normandy. [The eminent historian G.M. Trevelyan writes an appreciative foreword.] Dealing with real occurrences and personalities, the author avoids the faults of much historical fiction. Her subtle technique and luminous style build to the battles of Stamford Bridge and Hastings, both of which are minor masterpieces of description and action.

Orville Prescott calls this a "great novel," adding that "*The Golden Warrior* is a majestic, glittering heroic book of epic stature and stark magnificence. Too austere and strange to catch the popular fancy quickly, it is destined, I believe, to be read with amazed admiration for many years to come. It is . . . at once a triumphant *tour de force* and a major work of fictional art" (*In My Opinion*, Bobbs, 1952).

Murasaki, Shikibu. *The Tale of Genji*. *Translated from the Japanese by Arthur Waley* [4 volumes] (London: Allen, 1925-1928) First published, 1650. Probably written in the early part of the eleventh century, this is a classic Japanese story of the gallantries and amorous adventures of Prince Genji, the emperor's son. Lady Murasaki, as a member of the court, offers a vivid account of court life, political intrigues and love affairs.

Ursula Vaughn Williams writes, "*The Tale of Genji* is . . . gloriously long—both Genji and Murasaki are real, three-dimensional people. Again, a vivid world of other customs and other idioms, but authentic for certain, as it was written by an eleventh-century court lady. Great sophistication, and great compassion, and people-one-has-met in this century. Also, I get the feeling from reading translations of modern Japanese novels that they have all learned from Murasaki, and her influence is still a lively one. I know the Arthur Waley translation which I find beautifully written—I haven't tried the recent one yet. The Waley is timeless in idiom and I believe that for my generation his creation of both China (translations of poems) and Japan (Murasaki) has given us a world as remote and as convincing as the pictures that show us the India of princesses and scholars, gods and milkmaids, without which we'd be less aware of the foundations of those great oriental cultures and the world from which they have sprung."

Myers, Henry. *The Utmost Island* (New York: Crown, 1951) Recalling and recasting the Icelandic sagas, the author weaves his version of the story of Leif Ericson. Set near the close of the tenth century, the novel superimposes fast-moving accounts and adventures against a rich tapestry of folklore and classical mythology. A thoroughly intriguing tale, with the added merit of being extremely well-written, this makes for delightful reading.

Millen Brand recommended it in *Rediscoveries*, David Madden ed.(New York: Crown, 1971).

Myers, Leopold. *The Near and the Far* (London: Cape, 1929) What was life like during the reign of Akbar, the mogul emperor of India from 1556 to 1608? Through a variety of character studies, from a hill chieftain to a Buddhist and his Christian wife, the author scrupulously details styles of living and patterns of thought. The plot is gripping and helps to focus on the major religious, political and social events of the era. Due to the multiple points of view and the glowing characterizations, the period comes to life.

Ursula Vaughn Williams writes, "I read *The Near and the Far* when it was first published—it has, and had, for me many attractions. It's a long story; the people are interesting in a timeless way; it's full of beautiful places, like the Indian pictures, brilliant figures in a romantic and dangerous landscape, and their relationships, philosophies and adventures are timelessly real, though removed into the perspective of a seemingly historical past. I don't know Rajput history, so I accept it as all quite likely—intrigues and power struggles are all too usual [in the] fabric of everyone's history. It has, too, a long perspective, the young grow middle aged and old, the beautiful children become contenders for their own, usurping, places."

Myers, Leopold. *The Root and the Flower* (New York: Harcourt, 1934) This is a trilogy composed of *The Near and the Far* (1929) [see above], *Prince Jali* (1931), and *Rajah Amar*, the final novel in the series.

Ursula LeGuin calls this "a philosophical novel set in sixteenth century India—a very powerful and original book and a good read. . . ." And Michael Ivens writes, "*The Root and the Flower* is probably the only novel in the world that produces a dramatic sense of choice between the aesthetic, carnal, Christian and Hindu choices for life. It does this quite amazingly by evading the trap of making its characters 'ideas on legs,' but rather highly individual human beings. It is probably the most philosophical novel in any language and, although Myers himself was a rather tormented figure, has a strange sense of peace. If one could imagine Prince Genji written in the twentieth century but with religious and philosophical overtones, one would be reaching towards the quality of *The Root and the Flower*." Orville Prescott also recommends this work.

Naipaul, V. S. *A House for Mr. Biswas* (New York: McGraw, 1961) Mr. Biswas, a West Indian Hindu, is meek and kindly and coerced into a marriage in which he must live under the thumb of his new family. Despite his mildness, Mr. Biswas proves stubborn. He desires a house of his own in Trinidad. Finally, realizing his dream, he comes to possess a tumbledown shack in disrepair where he dies at the age of forty six. While the plot is minimal, the delight of the novel resides in the teeming picture of West Indian life. The author's sardonic wit and ironic sense of humor are matched by his sympathetic appreciation of subtle changes in enduring relationships. Beneath the surface Mr. Biswas is noble, and the author succeeds in making this felt.

Paul Theroux recommends this novel.

Nesbit, Edith. *The Bastable Children* (New York: Coward-McCann, 1928) This trilogy is composed of *The Treasure Seekers* (1899), *The Wouldbegoods* (1901) and *The New Treasure Seekers* (1904). It deals with a family of six children in London who are involved in all sorts of adventures and whimsical exploits. Many of the stories autobiographical. The author, who was the youngest of six children, lived in London from 1858 to 1924. Her exploits are told through the voice of the twelve-year-old Oswald Bastable, and they are imbued with the pleasures of a close-knit and loving family. While ambivalent towards adults, the Bastable children take immediately to strangers and know exactly what their fantasies mean.

Maxine Kumin writes, "[These were] seminal works for me, books I read in childhood. . . .Nesbit . . . confirmed me as an Anglophile, both in temperament and orthography."

Nicolson, Harold. *Some People* (London: Constable, 1927) A collection of nine biographical sketches, some of these are purely fictitious and others are composed of half-truths. Among the characters are: Jeanne de Henaut, a tutor of Englishmen; J.D. Marstock, an adored but spoiled little boy; Marquis du Chaumont, a socialite; Miss Plimsoll, a governess; and Miriam Codd of Tennessee, an avid discourser on sexual repression.

Virginia Woolf wrote, "He has devised a method of writing about people and about himself as though they were at once real and imaginary. He has succeeded in making the best of both worlds" (*New York Herald Tribune*, October 30, 1927). Henry Cabot Lodge says that *Some People* "takes a few widely different people and in a hilarious way describes them and their foibles. His style can only be described as unique. Has any book ever caused so much laughter?" And Jilly Cooper writes, "It's just a portrait of his governess, of a boy he was at school with, of various people in the diplomatic service, Firbank the writer and various other people. It's so witty and funny and beautifully written. . . ."

Nissenson, Hugh. *In the Reign of Peace* (New York: Farrar, Straus, 1972) Six of the eight stories are set in Israel during the Six Day War of 1967. All involve contemporary people who have lost religious faith without finding a reasonably sufficient substitution. Written with restraint, but with fervent imagination, the stories are as wise as the unabashed moral quests they depict.

Cynthia Ozick writes, "[Nissenson] possesses what can be called the theological imagination. . . .The strength of his prose is not in what he puts in—the clean dialogue avoids idea-mongering, and there is no luxuriant visual or verbal surface in this fiction—but in how he omits. . . .His stories might almost be recent translations from the Hebrew" (*New York Times Book Review*, March 19, 1972).

Nye, Bill. *Complete Works of Bill Nye* (Various Publishers, 1881-1896) One of America's best nineteenth-century humorists, Nye began his writing career as a columnist for a Laramie, Wyoming, newspaper in 1876. A decade later, he was writing for a New York newspaper and was a national celebrity. Sometimes writing as much as thirty thousand words a week, he continually published until his death in 1896. John Dewey, one of his many fans, called him a great satirist, exposing pretense and superstition at almost every level of American life.

Marguerite Young recommends his works.

O'Brien, Edna. *August Is a Wicked Month* (New York: Simon & Schuster, 1965) Ellen vacations on the Riviera while her estranged husband and young son are in Wales. In the middle of her "fling of freedom," she receives word that her son has been killed. The vivid, episodic development of this novel and the sensitive characterizations make this absolutely haunting.

Adele Satz says that "Edna O'Brien comes recommended as a female version of Hemingway."

O'Brien, Edna. *A Rose in the Heart* (Garden City: Doubleday, 1979) This collection of twelve short stories details the turmoil of women driven into unwelcome solitude by emotional misfortunes. While most stories are set in Ireland, some take place in America. But the setting is not as important as the tragicomic situations which always leave women just this side of happiness. Each story is memorable as much for the precise, masterly style as for the wise treatment of her subject matter. Edna O'Brien is an unforgettable storyteller.

This volume is recommended by its author.

O'Brien, Flann. *At Swim-Two-Birds* (London: Longmans, 1939) As in his brilliant, surrealistic novel *The Third Policeman* (1967), O'Brien works his material so that it resonates at many levels. Here he is concerned with a young man living in his uncle's home in Dublin. He is attending college in a desultory fashion while indulging in what he terms "spare-time literary activities." These are incorporated into the narrative, and it is frequently difficult to separate the character's series of stories from O'Brien's writing. All are wonderfully funny.

V. S. Pritchett called this " . . . the finest piece of learned comic fantasy to come out of Dublin since the Treaty. Despite the praise of James Joyce, Graham Greene, Anthony Burgess, John Updike, and Dylan Thomas—the last said it was 'just the book to give your sister if she's a loud dirty boozy girl'—the book did only moderately well" (*The New Yorker*, May 15, 1978).

O'Brien, Tim. *Northern Lights* (New York: Delacorte, 1975) Two brothers (one tested by the Vietnam war and now home, the other older and settled) go off to a ski lodge. The time is the mid-1970s and the tension is created through clashes between the brothers themselves and their relationship to their father. The marvelous characterizations are matched by the sheer adventure which begins to develop midway through the book. The brothers decide to ski all the way home from the lodge. In their wild trip through the woods, complete with a blizzard and a hopeless loss of direction, they become involved in a breathtaking exploit.

Bill Ott says, "Although *Going After Cacciato* brought O'Brien notoriety, *Northern Lights*, his little-read first novel, is the more memorable. An existential drama pitting men against nature."

O'Faolain, Julia. *Women in the Wall* (London: Faber, 1975) A historical novel, this is based on the life of Queen Radegund, but it is also a means of addressing the essential questions about women's place in society. Queen Radegund, born in 518, was forcibly captured and married to the Frankish King Clotair. Later, she established a monastery where she lived as a nun. There are depictions of other lives which touched Radegund's, and several different meanings to immurement that the novel explores.

Doris Grumbach calls this "a wonderful recreation of sixth-century Gaul."

O'Hagan, Howard. *Tay John* (New York: Potter, 1960) In this collection, legends of the Canadian Rockies are combined with the author's own stories about the outdoors. The title is the English variant for the French term for "yellowhead," the name given to the half-breed character whom one meets in the various stories. In an imaginatively sensitive style, O'Hagan manages to capture the first intrusions of man on an unspoiled wilderness.

Joyce Carol Oates recommended this in *Antaeus*, Autumn, 1979.

Olivia (London: Hogarth, 1949) Sybille Bedford writes, "*Olivia* by Olivia. (*Note:* this is how the book was originally published—pseudonymously.) It is, of course, by Dorothy Strachey Bussy.

"A novella of classical economy; beautifully written and paced. Subject treated with delicacy and candour: first love (Lesbian) innocent and disasterous, of a young girl. Locale—a girls' school in France. Disaster because of the corruption of some elder women. I found it perfect, and original, and delightful to read. (Must add that I've not looked at it again for some twenty years. . . .)

"Must also point out that *Olivia* is not strictly an 'overlooked' book. When it did come out at last, in the 1940s, it found immediate and entire recognition and acclaim. Certainly in England—I don't know about the United States. But: it had been written some thirty or forty years earlier, the manuscript was shown to Andre Gide, the author's friend, who said '*No good. Stick to translating*, etc., old girl.' She believed him and did, and that was that. (Just as Gide turned down Proust's first volume of *A La Recherche.* . . .) So what I feel must have been a born writer did not attempt to write again. When *Olivia* was published at last, D.S.B was over seventy or more. . . . Too late. A prevented writer."

Olsen, Tillie. *Tell Me A Riddle* (New York: Lippincott, 1961) In this fine collection of four short stories, the author leaves her imprint on the reader's imagination. Her situations and her characters tend to be subdued, but their thoughts and feelings are vitally alive and moving. A fine psychologist of human motives and reactions, the author creates characters that are absolutely believable and their pains poignantly affecting. Her rendering of interior monologues, such as that of the tired, depressed mother in "I Stand Here Ironing," is marked by a flawless sense of speech patterns as well as a gripping sense of drama.

Gordon Lish recommended this volume.

Ozick, Cynthia. *Bloodshed* (New York: Knopf, 1976) The intellectual strength of these four short stories is found in the astonishingly true character studies and the strange beauty of the language. Each story is concerned with a different aspect of the American character, particularly the modern Jew who is in conflict with Western culture. For example, "Bloodshed" depicts a confrontation between a Hasidic rabbi and a man who is both drawn to and disgusted by Hasidim. "Usurpation" features a group of stories within stories in which the ghost of a poet materializes. A superb storyteller, the author is as witty as she is profound.

Gordon Lish recommends this.

Ozick, Cynthia. *Trust* (New York: New American Library, 1966) Allegra Vand, a wealthy and eccentric mother, and her husband Enoch are part of the high financial, policy-making, intellectual, decision-making circles in Europe and New York from the thirties to the sixties. Their story and the stories of people around them are told from the point of view of a young woman as she grows up. The novel, a Jamesian one, is beautifully written and crammed full of characters, events and ideas. The work received critical praise as a brilliant, always fascinating, first novel.

Cynthia Ozick writes, "A big difficult novel, perhaps too densely devoted to language to read. I have promised to have a gold medal struck for anyone who claims to have gotten through it. But I still (secretly) like it best of everything I've written: I feel strongly that I've gone downhill ever since."

Paley, Grace. *The Little Disturbances of Man* (New York: Doubleday, 1959) A collection of eleven short stories, these are alternately humorous and vigorously realistic. The dialogue, in particular, is filled with energy. Most of the stories are Jewish in character, and one of the highlights of the group concerns a number of Jewish children who perform in a school Christmas play. The deft style and the compassionate understanding of characters makes this an exceptional collection.

Gordon Lish recommends it.

Pardo-Bazán, Emilia. *The Son of the Bondwoman.* *Translated from the Spanish by Ethel Hearn* (London: Lane, 1907) First published, 1886. The novel by the Condesa opens in a quiet Galician village where a marquess is being robbed by his steward. Not only is the marquess too lazy to alter these affairs, but he also succumbs to his desire to take the steward's daughter as a mistress. Determined to marry, he considers possible brides. The conflicting forces between the characters, and the problem of the marquess' personality, end in tragedy. The novel is noteworthy for its realism and its accurate, colorful picture of the Spanish landscape.

William F. H. Lamont cited this in *Books Abroad*, Vol. 27:3.

Parker, Robert. *The Godwulf Manuscript* (Boston: Houghton, 1974) Spenser is the detective, a private eye in the tradition of Philip Marlowe, Lew Archer and Archie Goodwin. In this, one of his earliest forays into public, he sets out to investigate the theft of a fourteenth-century illuminated manuscript from a college library. He comes into contact with a wide variety of people, from mobsters to student activists, and due to his quite literary, wisecracking, essentially heroic attitude he is well able to cope with all. The very exemplar of the best detectives in fiction, Spenser is a fine achievement.

George V. Higgins says, "Robert Parker of the Spenser detective stories is a writer most unjustly neglected in America. The principal character is a rogue and a scoundrel and a good cook. I am unable to account for the failure of the cinematic world to seize upon his books" (*Times Literary Supplement*, June 5, 1981).

Parrish, Anne. *All Kneeling* (New York: Harper, 1928) A best seller of its time, this novel retains its biting wit and satire, and has much to suggest to modern readers. The title derives from the fact that the heroine has everyone kneeling at her feet, except for the reader who is privy to her intellectual and emotional posing. It is charming for its picture of the period in which the antiheroine lived disguised as a typically sweet, lightweight, American girl.

Maxine Kumin says that this was a "seminal" work for her, "Parrish delighted my most savage and vengeful side, [and] . . . taught me to honor characterization above all else."

Parry, Dennis. *Sea of Glass* (London: Hamish, Hamilton, 1955) The mysterious Vavara appears in the English townhouse of her rich grandmother after spending her childhood in Turkestan. The Amazonian heroine proceeds to rebel against the conventional, tame London society and its stuffy members. The struggle is completely one sided, and throughout the dramatic intrigue and high comedy she lavishly succeeds. The characterization of the London social scene is as winning and true as is the unconventional heroine.

Edward Gorey recommended this in *Antaeus*, Autumn, 1975.

Peake, Mervyn. *Titus Groan* (London: Eyre, 1946) Two years of life in Gormenghast Castle is lovingly narrated. The story begins with the birth of Titus, and ends with his being crowned on his second birthday, since he is heir to the earldom of Gormenghast and the son of the seventy-sixth lord. The plot consists of absorbing palace rituals and the introduction of many human grotesques. The action, while particularly strong, is not gothic, despite the setting. Its cast of characters is marvelous.

Mervyn Jones writes, "... I do think that *Titus Groan* was one of the few books of genuine originality to appear during a rather drab period of English literature. Also, it maintained the tradition of fantasy—a long tradition, stemming from Sterne—which I regard as complementary to the tradition of realism, and which has never received enough recognition from critics."

Peck, Robert N. *A Day No Pigs Would Die* (New York: Knopf, 1973) A remarkably intense, detailed novel of American farm life in the 1920s, this work falls somewhere between fiction and autobiography. It is filled with authentic episodes from animal mating scenes to a boy helping to slaughter his beloved pig. It is highly accomplished and moving.

Frederick Forsyth calls it " . . . an absolute gem. . . .It was the tale of a small Shaker family, told through the eyes of the son, whose father slaughtered hogs for a living and hated it. The day the father died gave rise to the title. I never heard of the book before or since, but for sheer evocative writing it ought to be on a lot of curricula."

Pen, John. *Temptation. Translated from the Hungarian by Ralph Manheim and Barbara Tolnai* (New York: Creative Age, 1946) This Hungarian author (whose real name is John Szekely) is talented enough to make you feel the misery of being a child and a young man in the oppressive poverty of Hungary after the First World War. He vividly portrays the corruption which poverty supports and concentrates on the political consequences. Most effective when dramatizing the routine events of urban and peasant life, the novel offers an accurate and emotional view of Hungary at a crucial time in its history.

Clancy Sigal says, "Novel, juicy and vivid, of a bellboy's life in [a] posh hotel [in] Hungary between World Wars I and II."

Pérez-Galdós, Benito. *The Disinherited. Translated from the Spanish by Lester Clark* (London: Folio Society, 1976) First published, 1881. Driven by a delusion, believing herself to be the illegitimate daughter of an aristocrat, Isidora Rufete can ignore her poverty in Madrid. But soon reality forces itself upon her, and she is reduced to prostitution. A book full of skillful writing, lively characters and evocative descriptions, it is one of its author's best.

Pamela Hansford Johnson says Pérez-Galdós is "worthy to stand in the first half dozen of European writers of all times." She also recommends the author's *Fortunato and Jacintha.*

Phelps, Elizabeth Stuart (Ward). *The Story of Avis* (Boston: J. R. Osgood, 1877) A highly intelligent and capable woman has to sacrifice a brilliant career as a painter in order to maintain her marriage. Her husband, while good intentioned and apparently kind, is incapable of understanding his wife's desire for a career of her own. As a worker for women's rights, the author advocated equal employment for women, and here she draws not only upon her convictions but on the experience of her mother who failed to combine a career with marriage. A polished style and a deep understanding of her characters keeps the story from seeming burdened by overt moralizing. The reader is left to draw her own conclusions from the situation—one that develops slowly but finally engulfs the characters in an ultimate challenge.

Judith Fetterley recommends this along with the author's *The Silent Partner* (1871) and *Old Maids and Burglars in Paradise* (1887).

Phillips, David. *Susan Lenox, Her Fall and Rise* (New York: Appleton, 1917) Growing up in a midwestern town, Susan Lenox soon discovers her illegitimacy. By the age of seventeen, she is forced to support herself, and she turns to prostitution. Breaking away from this for a time, she soon returns, primarily because the income is better than that from legitimate work. The novel is based on harsh realism and is marked by its individual tone.

Glenway Wescott recommended it in *Antaeus*, Autumn, 1979.

Pieyre de Mandiargues, André. *The Margin*. *Translated from the French by Richard Howard* (New York: Grove, 1969) First published, 1967. A classic story with an ominous beginning, this novel is set in Barcelona and chronicles one man's struggle with a sardonic fate. His wife commits suicide, and, unable to accept her death, he wanders through the streets of a red light district trying to pretend that his life has not collapsed. The novel was the winner of the 1967 Goncourt Prize for Literature.

Nadine Gordimer recommended it in *Antaeus*, Autumn, 1979.

Pilnyak, Boris. *Naked Year*. *Translated from the Russian by Alec Brown* (New York: Brewer, 1929) First published, 1922. During the Russian famine of 1921, the Red and White armies continued to struggle while foreign navies blockaded ports. With crops decaying and industrial production halted, a state of abject horror exists for those people who are depicted in

this panoramic view of one year in Russian history. The narrative reaches an eccentric pitch as the author's style reflects the total disorder of his subject. The reader is trapped in a maze of ornate prose and sympathy for people who strive for life and for values amid social anarchy. This is a significant and remarkable novel.

Pilnyak, Boris. *The Volga Falls to the Caspian Sea*. *Translated from the Russian by Charles Malamuth* (New York: Cosmopolitan, 1931) A great construction project is underway and three engineers are completing a dam below the Oka and Moscow Rivers in order to create a new river designed to improve Russian industrial power. Both the 1930s project and the lives of the engineers are the focus of this sweeping, elaborately plotted novel. The characters move effortlessly through various emotional tides as a method of highlighting the progress and problems of the Russian revolution. The immediate action occurs in a twenty-four hour period, but the various threads of the story are traced to their origins. While some of the novel glorifies the Russian government, the skills of the author are such that propagandist aspects fade and finally disappear as the compelling story unfolds.

Harvey Swados recommended this in *Rediscoveries*, ed. David Madden, (Crown, 1971).

Plante, David. *The Family* (New York: Farrar, Straus, 1978) A French-Canadian working-class family living in Providence, Rhode Island, is the primary focus of this realistic, touching novel about the development of a young man and his familial attitudes. Daniel, at age twelve, has turbulently mixed feelings about his parents and six brothers. His adolescent sensitivity widens into an understanding of the complex relationship of his parents. In a pattern reminiscent of Eugene O'Neill's in *Long*

Day's Journey Into Night, the novel works both as a realistic story and as a metaphor. For its meticulous description of family life and the development of a personality, it is exceptional.

Anne Tyler recommends it.

Plomer, William. *Turbott Wolfe* (London: Hogarth, 1926) The former South African's first novel, this work reflects one white person's humane attitudes towards himself and the native black inhabitants. The plot is minimal, concerning the life of Wolfe, a "man of genius," sympathetic to the blacks whom he joins, along with others, in order to secure the country for the natives. He has, as a man of sensitivity, been torn by his growing disillusion with his people and his country. The reader is escorted through the early years of South African history as Wolfe recalls his past.

Nadine Gordimer recommended this work in *Antaeus,* Autumn, 1979.

Popkin, Zelda. *Time Off for Murder* (New York: Lippincott, 1940) Take an inexplicable disappearance, add a murder, garnish it with a word association test, and you have the ingredients for an intricate mystery. The setting is New York and the characters are dessicated aristocrats, rich playboys, and hard-nosed cops. The detective is Mary Carner, and the story is first rate.

Fay Blake notes that this mystery and several others by the same author are "especially interesting because the detective is a thoroughly liberated young woman." She also recommends the author's *Murder in the Mist* (1941), *No Crime for a Lady* (1944), and *Death Wears a White Gardenia* (1939).

Portis, Charles. *The Dog of the South* (New York: Knopf, 1979) In a wildly funny trip of recovery, Ray Midge sets out from Little Rock, Arkansas, one afternoon to find his wife who has run off with her first husband and most of Ray's possessions, including his credit cards. The trip leads him to Texas, through Mexico, and finally to a remote section of Honduras. Along the way, there is what one reviewer terms "a classic piece of American gab" about people and places. Certain of the correctness of his view of life, Midge is a first cousin to many Ring Lardner characters, and just as convincing. This absurd junket is pure Americana, in the form of an exceptionally fine novel.

Sam Shepard recommends this.

Powell, Anthony. *From a View to a Death* (London: Duckworth, 1933) Arthur Schlesinger, Jr. writes, "*From a View to a Death* is the masterpiece of Anthony Powell's early (i.e., pre *A Dance to the Music of Time*) period. This brilliant work had, I believe, a profound effect on the tone as well as the technique of British social comedy. In it Powell devised or refined a variety of effects that moved the comic novel beyond both traditional farce and the more modern homosexual whimsy of the Douglas-Firbank sort into a new dimension, at once more comic and more serious. Some of these effects had been or were soon to be employed by Evelyn Waugh; most were adopted after the war by the younger generation of Amis, Newby, Bradbury and so on—the precise, deadpan description of cumulatively dotty scenes, the complex and sardonic use of slapstick and the readiness to grapple in a comic novel with poverty, madness and death."

Powell, Dawn. *The Locusts Have No King* (New York: Scribner, 1948) Rarely has satire so precisely dissected New York's literary circles and social life. We witness the foibles of Frederick Olliver, a little-known writer who savors his solitude and has the misfortune to hook up with a famous magazine. His frailties are typical of everyone's. The author combines satire with a strong feeling for humanity and produces a work which is sharply and intelligently amusing.

Gore Vidal says, "Dawn Powell is perfectly unknown. This is sad but fairly typical of what happens when academic bureaucrats are allowed to order things. She is a comic writer as good as Evelyn Waugh and better than Clemens. *The Locusts Have No King* is a good introduction to her" (*The Antioch Review*, Autumn, 1981).

Powell, Dawn. *The Wicked Pavillion* (Boston: Houghton, 1954) Two artists manage to convince critics and buyers that the work they are selling is their own. It is not. In fact, it is the work of a dead genius. In order to prevail in their deception, they become involved with a proper Bostonian, a sex-charged patron, and several New Yorkers of questionable reputation. But the plot is not especially important since the author is far more devoted to anatomizing the loves, schemes, and quarrels of café society in the early 1950s. The stiletto-like portraits have been equalled only by such writers as Evelyn Waugh.

Gore Vidal says, "Dawn Powell is our finest comic novelist. As Americans are, perhaps, after the Albanians, the least humorous of people, she will never have with us the success that she deserves."

Power, Crawford. *The Encounter* (New York: Sloane, 1950) A priest, Father Cauder, comes face to face with his own human failings as a result of an "encounter" with two people from a markedly different milieu—the world of a circus carnival. The characterizations are deeply perceptive and the book moves relentlessly to its conclusion.

James Dickey wrote, "It seems to me to be the best and most mysterious and compelling statement of the strange ways in which the Lord works—or doesn't work—

that I know. It is a moving and original book" (*American Scholar*, Spring, 1970).

Power, Richard. *The Hungry Grass* (London: Bodley Head, 1969) Father Conroy is a crusty, old, compassionate, Irish parish priest who is nearing the end of his life. The author slowly lays bare the texture of life in his small Irish community. The people are often so banal as to irritate Father Conroy who has little to occupy him between morning and evening Mass. Still, his life is not without purpose, and the novel ends on a note of acceptance rather than bitterness. The style and the plot are deceptively simple, so it is not until the end of the novel that the full power of the work is felt.

Elizabeth Cullinan calls this "a loving, glowing evocation of life, full of praise and sorrow, with one of the most passionate and generous heroes I know of. He happens to be a priest—a greathearted, exacting, impulsive, shrewd man whose pure heart is in the faithful service of his unsparing eye. Or maybe it's the other way around."

Powys, John Cowper. *A Glastonbury Romance* (New York: Simon & Schuster, 1932) The entire life of the town of Glastonbury is revealed in a conflict between two opposing groups of townspeople. One faction wishes to restore the town's image as one of the world's major shrines by sponsoring a Passion Play. The opposing group hopes to turn the community into a prosperous industrial center. The plot centers on the activities of several characters, and the large-scale satire (the book is over one thousand pages) never lacks for romance, love affairs, and even murder. The grandeur of the novel insures its place alongside Hardy's better known writings.

Annie Dillard calls this a "long, very strange novel, a fine neglected genius." And she also recommends the author's *Wolf Solent* and *Maiden Castle*.

Powys, John Cowper. *Porius: A Romance of the Dark Ages* (London: Macdonald, 1951) Covering eight autumn days in the year 499, the story concerns the invasion of North Wales and the repulsion of those invaders by King Arthur's men. Filled with supernatural acts, peculiar rites of worship, bloodshed and romance, this is first and foremost a novel of action and place.

Angus Wilson recommends this, and George Steiner calls it a masterpiece, noting that it was written by an outsider in modern British literature. Steiner remarks about Powys (along with David Jones) that, "In imaginative stature, in audacity of . . . form, they tower over the *petits maitres* . . . " (*The Sunday Times*, June 18, 1978).

Powys, John Cowper. *Weymouth Sands* (New York: Simon & Schuster, 1934) Against the backdrop of Weymouth, England, the mystery of life is acted out in intricate patterns of human behavior. The impressive writing weaves an eccentric list of characters (including a clown, his brother, a Latin teacher and the clown's insane wife) into some of the strangest situations in literature. Within this self-enclosed world, Powys impersonally surveys the movement of men and women in a world which still feels very familiar.

Anthony Bailey wrote, "It brings to mind . . . the romantic ferment of the film *Les Enfants du Paradis* or one of the works . . . of J. M. W. Turner" (*Observer Magazine*, July 15, 1979).

Pritchett, V. S. *Dead Man Leading* (London: Chatto, 1937) Harry Johnson is on an expedition exploring a South American jungle where his father was lost seventeen years before. In what is both a thriller and a careful study of characters under stress, the author follows Johnson as he moves through the treacherous wilds of Brazil. The protagonist is secretly in love with the expedition leader's stepdaughter, whose former lover is also a member of the party. Harry's fear of disclosure, his hallucinations about the fate of his father, and the leader's demise culminate in a dramatic climax. A fascinating and rich novel, this is one of Pritchett's best works.

Paul Theroux recommends it.

Prokosch, Frederic. *The Seven Who Fled* (New York: Harper, 1937) Seven Europeans who are stranded in Central Asia, two thousand miles from both the Caucasus and Peiping, are forced to separate. This philosophical novel follows each of them as they try to survive desert heat, poverty and the plague. This is a distinguished work which is beautifully written.

Harlan Ellison recommends it.

Purdy, James. *Children Is All* (New York: New Directions, 1963) In reviewing this collection of short stories and two plays, the late Edith Sitwell remarked, "I think James Purdy will come to be recognized as one of the greatest living writers of fiction in our language. . . ." Much of what she predicted has come to pass, yet the short stories in this collection are some of the best. His uncanny skill with characterization, his ability to dig beneath the familiar surfaces of life, usually with only a few carefully selected words or phrases, and his comprehension of loneliness never is better illustrated than in these pieces.

Gordon Lish recommends this, calling it "a work of literature great in the extreme," and recommends as well Purdy's *Color of Darkness* (1957).

Puzo, Mario. *The Dark Arena* (New York: Random House, 1955) In his first novel, some fifteen years before *The Godfather*, Puzo tests the grounds which produce an outlaw. Here, his primary character is a former soldier who returns to Germany as a civilian employee after

World War II. Mosca's frustrations and his inability to concur with the new attitude of America toward post-war, industrial Germany are incorporated into a love affair which ends tragically. The betrayals of the American occupation prove too much for Mosca, and he turns to crime.

James B. Hall comments, "This shadow world of compromise and confusion—partly of our own making—was a world the midfifties forgot or ignored or denied. Nevertheless, it is a world captured by *The Dark Arena* and still kept alive for our consideration. The novel is a hard look at an almost totally unregenerate world, an unpretentious book in a well-recognized, strong American vein" (*Rediscoveries*, ed. David Madden, Crown, 1971).

Pym, Barbara. *Jane and Prudence* (London: Cape, 1953) Jane, a former Oxford tutor in English poetry, has chosen to settle down in a small community as a vicar's wife. Her younger friend, and former pupil Prudence, at the age of twenty nine, is settled in London where she pursues her amorous adventures and works for a tiresome scholar. The plot revolves around the unexciting lives of these women, but with typical élan Pym builds a wonderous story about the development of their friendship and their growing understanding of life.

Jilly Cooper describes Barbara Pym as "a novelist who's just died who wrote very gentle, homely kinds of books but . . . with lots of bite. They're basically about country women or single women living in flats and working in London offices. But particularly they always get involved with the local church and you have this marvellous bitching between the Parish ladies who all have crushes on the vicar. They're tremendously English but . . . tremendously universal." She also recommends Pym's *Excellent Women* and *A Glass of Blessings*.

Queneau, Raymond. *The Bark Tree*. *Translated from the French by Barbara Wright* (New York: New Directions, 1971) First published, 1933. Etienne, in middle age, asks what life is all about. He plunges into puzzling fantasies, adventures, and even a few tentative solutions for the problem of life. Along the way, he meets people who attempt to shape their own existences or those of others. The work is a forest of meaning and no meaning, a land familiar to those who read Joyce or Beckett. The author's ingenious style is matched only by his baffling design and genuine dialogue. The characters discuss unreal events in the vernacular. The genius of Queneau makes this extremely rewarding reading.

Raphael, Frederic. *Lindmann* (London: Cassell, 1963) One of Raphael's finest achievements, this novel concentrates on the necessity of love and patience. Sharing a room with a black American painter, Lindmann, an Austrian Jew, is one of countless refugees in London. Gradually, through a film script written by another refugee, the reader discovers that Lindmann is the sole survivor of an illegal immigrant ship which tried to reach Israel in 1942. Due to lethal indifference by the British and Turkish governments, the ship sank off the Turkish coast. Lindmann refuses to comment on the script, and gradually we learn that he is, in fact, an impostor. A British civil servant whose real name, significantly, is Shepherd, and whose mother's name is Mary, he was involved in the sinking of the ship. The transformation of the civil servant into Lindmann is a masterly accomplishment.

Other titles by Raphael which are recommended are *The Limits of Love* (1960) and *Like Men Betrayed* (1970). The author is, of course, well known to Americans as the writer of Public Television's *The Glittering Prizes*.

Raucat, Thomas. *The Honorable Picnic*. *Translated from the French by Leonard Cline* (New York: Viking, 1927) First published, 1924. Combining humor and satire with a curiously wistful eroticism, the plot is spun around the efforts of a foreigner to seduce a young Japanese woman on a picnic. He is blocked, almost effortlessly, by a deceptively obsequious Japanese merchant. As a delicate comedy of Oriental and Occidental manners, this has few equals. It is stunningly light, and the theme is enhanced by the exquisite literary form.

Paul Bowles notes, "Thomas Raucat is a *nom de plume* for the unidentified Swiss diplomat who wrote [this]." And, he adds, "I reread it occasionally for the amusement it always provides."

Rawicz, Piotr. *Blood from the Sky: A Novel* (New York: Harcourt, 1964) There is an incongruous strain of humor and lyrical joy in this story of a Jewish philosopher and poet caught in the Nazi invasion of a Ukrainian village. As the narrator pieces together the life of Boris, usually from tantalizing scraps of poetry and prose, the pathetic fate of the town and its chief characters is revealed. Boris, with an apparent revulsion toward life, is the perfect foil for the overwhelming terror and suspense of this ultimately satisfying story of courage.

Stanley Kauffmann recommends it.

Raymond, Ernest. *A Family That Was* (London: Cassell, 1929) Skillfully directed, this is a rambling view of a clergyman's family from the end of the nineteenth century to the outbreak of World War I. Sharing much of Trollope's affection for the average cleric, Raymond draws a sympathetic, yet lively, portrait of the family. Also, he relates in detail the lives of a variety of loosely connected characters while maintaining a direct, essentially gripping story line.

John Betjeman recommends this, as well as the author's *We the Accused* (see next entry), and he calls Raymond's *A Family Tree* "another powerful novel."

Raymond, Ernest. *We the Accused* (London: Cassell, 1935) Some fail at everything, and with a mixture of humanity and devilish love of plot, the author takes a gentle, common person and turns him to murder. The teasing possibility that the antihero represents many readers adds to the thrill of the chase through London. Actually, the narrator makes it clear that the killer is a failure, even in his dramatic evasion of the law. Although sometimes compared with Dreiser's *An American Tragedy*, this is distinctly English and can be enjoyed as much for the effectiveness of the London background as for the skillful characterizations.

John Betjeman says, "Atmosphere of suspense, great sense of place, clear prose. Ernest Raymond is the Dickens of middle-class pretension and sadness with great narrative power."

Read, Herbert. *The Green Child* (London: Heinemann, 1935) Recounting the half world of dreams and imagination, the author engages the reader in an uninhibited fantasy. In quest for the "green child" of his youth, an English schoolmaster who has become a South American dictator launches into a romantic search. Finally, after a mock assassination, he slips back to England. Here his goal is achieved, the child is discovered, and the two go away to the country of the imagination. Babette Deutsch called it "one of those books, rare in any time and especially in our own, that a writer envies the author the joy of having composed it."

Thomas McGuane recommended this work in *Antaeus*, Winter, 1975.

Reich, Tova. *Mara* (New York: Farrar, Straus, 1978) An amusing novel, this takes as its subject young Orthodox Jews in America. Rabbi Lieb owns a chain of somewhat shady nursing homes, and he is faced with the dilemma of "making it" while at the same time not offending his religious peers. His daughter Mara (meaning "bitter" in Hebrew) is married to a hippie. The newlyweds go their own way, and the author follows the tension between the father and his offspring as the story hops from one mad and irreverant scene to another. The black, hard-edged comedy is populated with a colorful cast of characters who may be vulnerable and poignant, yet always are eager for the next exciting moment.

Aaron Asher recommends this book.

Reid, Forrest. *Tom Barber* (New York: Pantheon, 1955) Against the setting of the author's homeland, Northern Ireland, this is a trilogy about boyhood from the age of eleven to fifteen. It is comprised of three novels written in reverse chronological order: *Uncle Stephen* (1931), *The Retreat* (1934), and *Young Tom* (1944). Tom is a contemplative and imaginative boy whose daily activities are followed with extreme interest by the author. The peculiar dimension of the novels is their gothic quality. For example, in his carefully recounted dreams, Tom battles magicians. The blending of fantasy and reality is the stuff of childhood, and the author's winning account of the life of an average boy is outstanding.

John Lehmann, who recommends Reid's works, mentions that E. M. Forster admired them very much.

Renoir, Jean. *The Notebooks of Captain Georges.* *Translated from the French by Norman Denny* (Boston: Little, 1966) The famed film director's novel concerns the period just prior to World War I, when an aristocrat could fall in love with an angelic prostitute, and the reader would be more than willing to accept the course of events, the dialogue, and the neat diary entries of the captain. Filled with gossip, firsthand descriptions of society and its milieu, the novel retains a boundless urbanity which provides a suitable accompaniment

to this frankly sentimental story. The marvelous technical control of the author makes the scenes move and the characters come alive.

François Truffaut recommended this in *Antaeus*, Autumn, 1979.

Rhys, Jean. *Sleep It Off Lady* (London: Deutsch, 1976) Drawn from the experiences of the author's own colorful life, these sixteen short stories move from the West Indies (her birthplace) to Paris (scene of her numerous novels) to London. While the heroines inevitably seem helpless, they manage to survive as much through their wit as through a wistful sense of perspective about themselves and the people whom they know. Several of the stories are observed through the eyes of a clever child, and these show the drama in the commonplace when viewed by innocents. Rhys' observant, astringent intelligence is particularly strong in these late stories.

A. Alvarez states, "As always, her writing is precise, poignant, deeply personal yet detached, an equal combination of feeling and craftsmanship."

Rhys, Jean. *Wide Sargasso Sea* (London: Deutsch, 1966) At the center stands Antoinette, the Creole heiress whom Mr. Rochester married on his father's orders, and who was later to appear in Jane Eyre as the madwoman hidden in the attic. The author goes back in time to examine the likely childhood of Antoinette in the lush tropics of Jamaica, and the circumstances of her meeting with her future husband, as well as their fatal honeymoon. The imaginative reconstruction of Antoinette's early life is related in an unsentimental, sparse style. It is deeply affecting.

Shirley Ann Grau writes that his work is "just reviving in England but quite unknown here. The Caribbean scenes are of a breathtaking beauty. I read it thirty years ago and can still quote page after page."

Richardson, Ann. *Digging Out* (New York: McGraw, 1967) In this first novel, the narrator sits by her dying mother's bed and recalls the history of her family that emigrated from Russia in the late nineteenth-century. In an irresistible way, the narrator portrays the events surrounding the large, rich, Jewish family to which she belongs and from which she plans to secede upon the death of her mother. Due to the right blend of wit, irony and compassion, the reader's interest in the family continues to grow until the beautiful design of the novel is complete.

Alison Lurie recommended this in *Antaeus*, Autumn, 1977.

Richardson, Henry Handel. *Maurice Guest* (London: Heinemann, 1908) Strongly influenced by Flaubert and by music, this female author (Ethel Lindesay) examines the personality and the love affair of a young musician. Nothing comes of his affair, but this compact, well-constructed novel offers a dramatic picture of a wasted life near the turn of the century. The dialogue and background are particularly vivid, and the characterization of the tortured, hypersensitive musician, Maurice Guest, is first rate. While the author is better known for her *Getting of Wisdom,* many consider this early novel to be one of her best.

George P. Elliott recommends it.

Richter, Conrad. *The Trees* (1940), **The Fields** (1946), **The Town** (1950); (New York: Knopf) A trilogy of American pioneer life, this is outstanding for its attention to detail, its historical accuracy, and a total lack of conventional pioneer-hero sentimentality. At the same time, the story of settling Ohio from the eighteenth through the twentieth centuries is so beautifully written, so alive with everyday people performing everyday tasks that the novels provide one of the truest pictures of frontier life to be found in fiction.

Isaac Bashevis Singer recommends *The Trees,* and Carlos Baker says, "Conrad Richter's authentic and moving trilogy of the westward movement of the settlers and the spread of civilization through the wilderness strikes me as a flawless and memorable series of books which richly repay reading—and rereading."

Riding, Laura. *Progress of Stories* (London: Constable, 1935) The "progress" in the title refers to the divisions, or steps, which the author takes the reader through in this distinctive series of explorations into manners and meanings. More fables than typical short stories, the series begins with events and people, moves to stories of ideas and then on to attempts at capturing truths. The fourth part is "A Crown for Hans Anderson," a tribute to the writer whom the author believes to be superb. The progression runs from a preoccupation with the immediate and ordinary details about daily existence to a comprehension of the universal through the ordinary. The form is unique—modern years before the current wave of modernity.

John Ashbery and Susan Sontag recommend this volume.

Rilke, Rainer Maria. *The Notebook of Malte Laurids Brigge.* *Translated from the German by M. D. Herter* (New York: Norton, 1950) First published as *The Journal of My Other Self,* 1930.

An autobiographical novel with existential overtones by the great German poet, this traces the development and growth of a child surrounded by countless relatives in an ancestral home. As a young man, Malte Brigge escapes to Paris, and there he assumes the narration of his own life. There are numerous shifts in place and time, in mood and plot, and much of this carefully constructed work reads like a poem. Its particular strength is the author's subtlety in comprehending a great scale of human emotions. The novel closes with an exceptionally moving short story.

Nancy Ryan recommended this in *Antaeus,* Winter, 1975.

Rivera, José Eustachio. *The Vortex.* *Translated from the Spanish by Earle K. James* (New York: Putnam, 1935) First published, 1932.

Set in the plains and jungles of South America, here is the reverse of W. H. Hudson's romantic masterpiece, *Green Mansions.* Although Rivera employs lyrical romantic images, he is primarily concerned with the reality of a couple who plunge into the jungle in order to avoid entanglements in civilization. Here they are driven from one crisis to another, leading to a point where the man, Cova, becomes involved with a small rubber organization. After that, the couple and the company simply disappear into the vortex. The narrative style, while complex and erratic, serves to make the picaresque highly credible, often as amusing as it is exciting. This novel is a fine blend of observation and introspection.

William F. H. Lamont cited this in *Books Abroad,* Vol. 27:3.

Roberts, Elizabeth Madox. *The Time of Man* (New York: Viking, 1926) A moving story of Kentucky hill-dwellers, this first novel relates the struggle of a poor white family to find some stability by owning their own farm. Ellen Chesser and her husband finally achieve their goal only to have it threatened by a mountain family feud. The author appears to be so intimately aware of the nature of these people and their lives that she is able to draw them freely and originally. Her tone is powerful and warm as she blends the poetic and the real, the individual personas and their universal meanings in wonderful, lyrical prose.

Janet Lewis recommends this as well as Roberts' *The Great Meadow* (1930). She writes, "*The Great Meadow* was lately in print. But *The Time of Man* may soon be reissued. *My Heart and My Flesh* (1927) should be remembered too, as well as her poems, *Under the Tree* (1922)."

Robertson, E. Arnot. *Four Frightened People* (London: Cape, 1931) The plague has struck the Malay state, and four frightened people are on a coastal steamer making their way to a port where they can board a ship for home. On discovering that plague has broken out on the steamer, the four English colonials decide to leave it and make their way overland through the jungle. The story takes a new twist when one of the four, a young nurse, is given the opportunity to choose a lover among the three men. A combination of humor, love, philosophy, terror and adventure makes this a highly readable story.

Robison, Mary. *Days* (New York: Knopf, 1979) Fascinated by the mid-American way of life, the author presents ambiguous, at times explicitly satirical, sketches about what it means to participate in such events as an Independence Day celebration, a wedding, or a May Queen festival. The short stories are as authentic in tone as they are precise in capturing the emotional impact of small, yet sometimes devastating, disasters in the lives of the characters. Her style is concise, literate and intelligent.

Gordon Lish recommends this volume.

Rølvaag, Ole Edvart. *The Boat of Longing.* *Translated from the Norwegian by Nora O. Solum* (New York: Harper, 1933) First published, 1921.

A poetical and mystical novel, this in many ways rivals the more popular *Giants in the Earth* (1927). The title is the name of a legendary vessel which symbolizes the heartache caused by emigration, in this case the departure of an eighteen-year-old boy from Norway to America. The boy eventually settles in Minneapolis, but fails to write to his parents. His father sets out to find him, is turned back at Ellis Island, and upon returning home weaves a beautiful story of his visit. This combination of folktale and realism as a means of delving into the minds of people torn between cultures and countries makes this an extraordinarily moving work.

Rosa, João Guimarães. *The Devil to Pay in the Backlands.* *Translated from the Portuguese by J. L. Taylor and H. De Onis* (New York: Knopf, 1963) First published, 1956.

This highly original fusion of trends in the modern novel was written by Brazil's greatest contemporary novelist. Riobaldo, a former bandit, narrates the story much in the manner of Conrad's monologists. Set near the end of the nineteenth century, the focus is on revenge. Riobaldo relates his attempt to right a wrong, and he discusses his relationship with his friend Diadorim. As the narrator progresses, it becomes evident that he believes he is in league with Satan. Diadorim, on the other hand, is almost angelic. The powerful language and the mythical qualities of the story have led some to compare this work to *Moby Dick.*

Alastair Reid calls this Rosa's masterpiece and "perhaps the most brilliantly inventive and encompassing Latin American novel of our time" (*The New Yorker*, January 26, 1981).

Rosen, Norma. *Touching Evil* (New York: Harcourt, 1969) While this is a sharp, ruthlessly observed novel, it is also frequently comic in its relentless examination of modern life. Jean, a New York book designer who is thirty six years old has been so touched by the evil of the Nazi concentration camps that she was determined never to have children. Now, the Eich-

mann trial she is watching on television causes her to desire a child and her absent lover. Instead, she takes in a Puerto Rican waif. This proves disasterous, and as she drifts toward suicide she is saved by a fortuitous decision. The author's vivid style and her sensitive appreciation of humanity turns this away from a potentially self-pitying wallow into a special pleasure.

Cynthia Ozick writes, "Norma Rosen, whose just published *At the Center,* (1982) ends a silence of thirteen years, is surely one of the best novelists in America. It is a scandal that she has not received suitable recognition. Her first novel, *Joy to Levine!* (1962), published by Knopf, is a kind of American *Pride and Prejudice.* Her second novel, *Touching Evil,* is an astonishing book: a kind of moral conflagration, and thronged with splendid characters. Between these two novels there was a collection of stories, *Green,* (1967), which are among the finest in American fiction. It is a mystery of American letters and an exasperation of literary justice that Norma Rosen's name is not better known. She is an important artist of immense talent."

Rosenfeld, Isaac. *Passage from Home* (New York: Dial Press, 1946) In his passage from home, a fourteen-year-old Jewish boy decides to leave his parents and go to live with his modern Aunt Minna. He discovers that while the home he left may have been excessively well organized, his aunt errs on the side of chaos. Her untidy life is another side of the structure of families with which the author is deeply concerned. The moral intensity of the novel is outstanding, and while the style is traditional, the author has the daring to attempt new methods for understanding and explaining his characters.

James Atlas says, "Rosenfeld's novel, about a sensitive Chicago boy coming of age in a family that doesn't understand him, is a masterly evocation of the Jewish middle class and of the traumas of growing up.''

Ross, James. *They Don't Dance Much*
(Boston: Houghton, 1940) A brutal crime and the twist of criminal turning on criminal reveal a stratum of life in midcentury America which is entirely devoid of sympathy or romanticism. Narrated by Jack McDonald, the novel takes place in a small roadhouse outside a Southern mining town. The characterizations, the accurate picture of the roadhouse and its patrons, and the social resonances are vivid and imaginative. The ugly story is told so well and the plot moves so quickly that the reader is enthralled.

Southern Illinois University Press is reissuing this.

Roth, Henry. *Call It Sleep* (New York: Ballou, 1935) An American classic which seems to be discovered and rediscovered from generation to generation, this is on many standard reading lists and is frequently recommended by experts on the American novel. Still, it is not that well known. Roth tells the story of Jewish immigrant life in Brownsville and the lower East Side of Manhattan. Many rightfully consider it the most truthful and profound study of an American slum childhood ever written. The author's virtuosity, his sensitive realism, and his sheer magical style create an exceptional book filled with intelligent observations and sympathetic characters.

Erich Segal and Robert S. Fogarty both recommend this book.

Roth, Joseph. *The Radetzky March.*
Translated from the German by Eva Tucker (London: Lane, 1974) First published, 1932. In what may be one of the most amazing novels of the twentieth century, Roth works out the meaning of people and their real place in history. He tells of a common family, raised to transient fame when one member saves the life of the Austrian emperor. This ordinary man's son becomes a minor official who, in turn, trains his son, Carl Joseph, for the army. Carl realizes at an early age that something is wrong with his life, but he lacks the imagination to fathom the solution. He moves from episode to episode, from friend to friend with almost blind faith both in fate and the love of his father. His father, in turn, has complete faith in the emperor. With extraordinary skill, Roth offers a sympathetic yet cooly detatched view of the events which lead Carl into battle in World War I. The admirably drawn characters are matched by the subtle style. Although this is a European classic, it is too little known in America.

Mavis Gallant, also recommending Roth's *Hotel Savoy* as "a flawless novel," says, "I'd like to see every novel of Joseph Roth, the Austrian writer who died in 1939, translated into English and published." By 1982, there were at least twelve novels by Roth which remained untranslated.

Roussel, Raymond. *Locus Solus.* *Translated from the French by Rupert Copeland-Cuningham* (Berkeley: University of California Press, 1970) First published, 1914. The narrative opens when a rich scientist and famous magician, Martial Canterel, shows a group of visitors around his estate on the outskirts of Paris. The expedition takes up most of the book, and consists of a series of magical occurrences visited upon the group and upon individuals. The author is never quite clear about what is real and what is fantasy, but the freakish and perplexing tableaux are brilliant in their conception. The genesis of each event is later explained by Canterel to his guests. Roussel seems intent on displaying the boundless freedom which is possible by using the imagination.

John Ashbery recommends this.

Rubiao, Murilo. *The Ex-Magician and Other Stories.* *Translated from the Portuguese by Thomas Colchie* (New York: Harper, 1979) First published, 1973. Recently rediscovered in Brazil, Rubiao is a master of the fantastic short story. This collection includes twenty works from as early as 1947, and follows the pattern of working out magical events within closely described, realistic landscapes. Finally, reality takes over, even to the point of a town's formal acceptance of the presence of dragons, and a magician's renounciation of magic in favor of a civil service job. This is material in line with Garcia Marquez's *One Hundred Years of Solitude*, and it is similarly outrageous, surrealistic and completely beguiling.

Alastair Reid wrote that although this work caught few people's attention when it was published, "it ought to have been pounced on, for it has much of *lo real maravilloso* in it" (*The New Yorker*, January 26, 1981).

Rulfo, Juan. *Pedro Páramo.* *Translated from the Spanish by Lysander Kemp* (New York: Grove, 1959) First published, 1956. Juan promises his mother to find his long lost father, Pedro Páramo. What he discovers is that his father has murdered his way to a position of absolute power in a remote Mexican village. Due to stylistic liberties, though most of the characters in the novel are dead, they constantly appear and reappear throughout this gripping story. The novel is considered one of Rulfo's finest, and while it is short, it has the impact of an epic.

Carlos Fuentes recommended this in *Antaeus*, Autumn, 1977.

Sackville-West, Victoria. *All Passion Spent* (New York: Doubleday, 1931) Lady Shane is old and widowed, and now has time to contemplate the contours of her life. She dwells not on the pleasures of the previous epoch nor on the romance which led to her long, prestigious marriage and her large family, but rather upon an image of herself as a young woman on the threshold of making a choice which was to shape her entire life. She remembers walking along the side of a lake, casually swinging her hat in her hand, and pushing the end of her parasol into the earth while deep in thought. What she was considering was whether to focus on her own career, one that she had never even spoken about to anyone, or on the career of her future husband. Her choice, as it turned out, was the traditional one, but in her old age she sees with pleasure that her great-grandaughter is facing a similar dilemma, and probably will decide in favor of her own aspirations. This is a fine novel of mood and nostalgia, and an affecting work.

Laurie Colwin recommends it.

Said, Kurban. *Ali & Nino.* *Translated from the German by Jenia Graman* (London: Hutchinson, 1970) First published, 1937. Barbara Howes writes, "As John Wain remarks in his able introduction: '*Ali & Nino* would be well worth reading even if it were not the brilliantly achieved novel that it is.... It allows us, for a few hours, to see life through the eyes of a Mohammedan. This, by itself, would be reason for reading the book, since Mohammedan beliefs and attitudes are usually opaque to the Westerner, and this story helps us to see how natural and right they seem in their own setting. . . .'

"Wain's comment is a valuable one; we of the European west and of the United States and the 'new world' in general do not have the faintest comprehension of the culture and psychology of Asia, of Islam. This book can indeed open our minds to basic differences of which we need to be aware.

"The story has its start in the early years of this century. Early on we meet Ali Khan

Shirvanshir, scion of a patrician Mohammedan family, and Nino Kipiani from that
of a wealthy Russian Georgian one, all of
whom reside in the Transcaucasian city of
Baku. Ali formulates the reality of his life
thus: 'God let me be born here, as a Muslim
of the Shiite Faith, in the religion of Imam
Dshafar. May he be merciful and let me die
here, in the same house where I was born.
Me and Nino, a Christian, who eats with
knife and fork, has laughing eyes and
wears filmy silk stockings.' Never, of
course, the veil.

"This theme runs, a dividing line, all
through the novel: the basic differences between European and Asiatic in general, between Nino and Ali in particular; yet
through painfully achieved understanding, each comes to accept the other and
their creative and very moving relationship. It is a deep and wonderful book."

**St. Martin, Thaddeus. *Madame Tous-
saint's Wedding Day*** (Boston: Little,
1936) This portrait of a Creole French,
deep backwater community is witty and
humorous. From the moment one meets
Madame Toussaint, rocking and fanning
herself, as she waits for her second marriage to be conducted, one is enchanted.
She had intended to take it easy that day,
but so many things interfered—there was a
stabbing in town, a murder, an operation
and, most disturbing of all, a particularly
good run of shrimp. And Madame Toussaint is nothing if she is not good at
shrimping. This is a perfectly delightful,
absorbing novel.

Shirley Ann Grau says, "Published by a
small New Orleans press, this novel had no
distribution. Yet it is quite wonderful. It's
like a primitive painting. In its utterly unsophisticated way, it makes a splendid
statement on man and his hopes."

Salas, Floyd. *Tattoo the Wicked Cross*
(New York: Grove, 1967) Fifteen-year-old

Aaron D'Aragon is sent to a prison farm
only to find that his friend, who had been
sentenced before him, has become a homosexual queen. In an effort to avoid his
friend's fate, he listens both to his family
and girl friend who urge him to serve his
time unaggressively. However, his attempts
to make some positive adjustments to prison and to his family result in his adopting
the code of the underworld which ends in
personal disaster. The extraordinarily evocative setting and characterizations result
in an extremely impressive, powerful novel.

Roger Sale says, "Salas is so completely
inside his experience that what in many
other novels is treated as sensational lore is
here only the setting for the boy's experience. . . . He has trusted the truth of his
experience to give him the truth of his novel, and it has not failed him. Salas has, so
far as I know, written nothing after *Tattoo
the Wicked Cross;* perhaps he has nothing
else to write, but this book should not have
been allowed to disappear" (*American
Scholar*, Winter, 1979).

Salter, James. *A Sport and a Pastime*
(Garden City: Doubleday, 1967) A Yale
dropout, living abroad, and an eighteen-
year-old French girl are involved in an affair which is patiently described by an un-
named, voyeuristic narrator. Since the
reader is never absolutely sure which part
of the story is imagined and which part is
real, the events involving the young couple
are dubious. The impressionistic story is as
subtle as it is mysterious, as romantic as it
is fragmented dream. This dramatic exploration into sex charts startling areas of
eroticism and love.

Raymond Carver recommends this work.

**Sarrazin, Albertine. *Astragal.* *Trans-
lated from the French by Patsy Southgate***
(New York: Grove, 1968) First published,
1965. An undisguised autobiographical
novel in the tradition of Jean Genet, this

begins when the narrator jumps to freedom from a prison wall. She is picked up by a sympathetic driver, and a love affair develops as she waits for her broken ankle bone (astragal) to heal. The two have only a brief time together when the girl is rearrested. A motif of the story is the pain of her broken ankle which constantly reminds her of imprisonment. The author, who spent nine years in French prisons, died at the age of thirty. This, one of her three novels, is developed almost like a Greek tragedy with its bleak details of prison life and its chilling love story.

John Fowles recommended this in *Antaeus*, Autumn, 1977.

Saunders, John Monk. *Single Lady* (New York: Brewer 1931) On the surface, this is simply another convincing glance at the lost generation of World War I drinking and carousing through Paris and Portugal. There is much of Hemingway in the style, yet the characters are individuals whose dialogue and diverting lives are exciting. What originally appears superficial becomes essential, and the reader is caught up with these individuals who are much more than simply representative of a lost generation.

Southern Illinois University Press is reissuing this novel.

Savage, Thomas. *The Liar* (Boston: Little, 1969) Over a forty year span, moving from coast to coast, Hal Sawyer discovers the power of the commonplace and the joy in getting older and wiser. When the novel opens, Hal is beaten by his dying father for refusing to admit to a theft. Although innocent, Hal finds that he is mistaken for not confessing—a well-told lie would have prevented the thrashing and thus spared his father. From then on, Hal believes in the redemptive power of lying. Savage establishes this theme as the governing one

in this excellent exploration of human wisdom.

Laurie Colwin recommends this novel.

Savage, Thomas. *The Power of the Dog* (Boston: Little, 1968) Roger Sale recommends this novel describing it as "a Western about two ranching brothers that does not falter once in a tremendous evocation of details and their power to articulate whole lives.... We have five major characters, and for each there are telling characteristic objects and habits of life, so that when they clash in some grand climaxes, the objects all become supercharged with a marvelous sense of inevitability." And Sale says that this novel "is very good indeed" (*American Scholar*, Winter, 1979).

Schmidt, Arno. *Zettel's Traum* (Karlsruhe: Stahlberg Verlag, 1970) Although at this writing the work has not been translated from the German, it is remarkable as much for its physical appearance as for its content. It is a book seventeen inches by thirty inches, weighing seventeen pounds, and consisting of thirteen hundred large format pages of facsimile of the author's typescript. It is concerned with the life of four people in a twenty-four hour period, and is notable not so much for their actions as for their conversations, which are riddled with puns and references to James Joyce, Edgar Allan Poe and other cultural heroes.

S. S. Prawer says, "In *Zettel's Traum* and a number of later novels, Arno Schmidt manages to convey an arresting (if often jaundiced) view of recent German history and culture through the medium of a quirky individuality embodied in protagonists who know a great deal of English and American literature. The arresting experimental techniques in which he does so derive mainly from Joyce and German Expressionism, but have been developed in an original way."

Schmitt, Gladys. *Rembrandt* (New York: Random House, 1961) Both the period and the Dutch painters of the seventeenth century are captured in this stunning biographical novel. The tormented temperament and brilliance of Rembrandt, from youth to old age, is displayed on every page. A succession of excellent dramatic scenes follows each major event in the artist's career. And the abundant human qualities of Rembrandt are worked into the novel and complement the magnificent series of Rembrandt's own self-portraits.

Roger Sale says, "The book is best on Rembrandt at work, Rembrandt taking the people around him and making them St. Peter and Aristotle and Danaë, Rembrandt's rapacity in being able throughout a long career to do just that, to see everything as the subjects of his works. He emerges as a great bear, insolent, warm, sensual, often naïve, convinced of his greatness, never capable of or interested in removing that greatness from the world he moved in. It is a book to read with a book of reproductions open at all times right alongside" (*American Scholar*, Winter, 1979).

Schor, Lynda. *Appetites* (New York: Warner, 1975) Appetites for food, sex, power and fantasy are the central themes of these sometimes outrageously offensive short stories. If the primary focus is on the exploitation of women and their strategies to ward off abuse, Schor usually ventures beneath this surface to a more potent truth, namely that men and women are doomed always to be in conflict because their politics and appetites clash. Due to the author's intelligence, wit and lively style, the stories are captivating reading.

Jane Lazarre says, "These are very funny, short stories which blur all lines between fantasy and reality, 'inner' and 'outer' and which revolve around daily dilemmas in an ordinary woman's life—struggling to work, mother and also have a sexual and artistic life."

Schorer, Mark. *The Wars of Love* (New York: McGraw, 1954) Three boys and a girl spend a summer together in an upstate New York resort. The author traces the development of what will become a lasting friendship and love affair. In the second part of the novel, the youths have become adults who are briefly reunited as they tragically work out the end of their affair. This beautifully perceptive study of children and the significance of their relations is played out against rural havens and urban realities. It is a nightmarish tale of love.

The Second Chance Press is reissuing this.

Schulz, Bruno. *Sanitorium Under the Sign of the Hourglass*. *Translated from the Polish by Celina Wieniewska* (New York: Walker, 1978) First published, 1937. This is the second collection of short stories by the modern Polish writer who is often compared to Kafka. Both the unique form and originality of the material make this author exceptional. John Updike claims that he "was one of the great transmogrifiers of the world into words." In this case, it is the world of Joseph, the narrator, his mother and father and Adela, a servant girl. The tales of the four of them swing between reality and fantasy, childhood memory, and the mythic vision of the artist. Schulz, aged fifty, was killed by the Nazis in 1942.

Schuyler, James. *Alfred and Guinevere* (New York: Harcourt, 1958) The title refers to two children. The author has an excellent ear for the dialogue of young people, and particularly excels in presenting in a deadpan style their wildly amusing conversations and situations. For example, in an effort to get out of some difficulty, Guinevere lets it be known throughout the town that her parents are divorcing. She conceives of that ploy after seeing a film "Twin Beds." Still, the events and the plot are minimal. What makes this work such a success is its witty, poetic and always truthful depiction of children.

Kenneth Koch considers this "a remarkable American novel . . ." and William Weaver recommended it in *Antaeus*, Autumn, 1979.

Schwartz, Delmore. The World is a Wedding (New York: New Directions, 1948) The poet's famous collection of short stories, while hardly neglected, deserves much wider attention. Here are some of the most authentic tales of middle-class American Jewish family life ever to be written. With great skill, Schwartz charts generations of family tensions and frustrations. The title piece is the best example of his talent, as he presents a moving description of the torments and dreams of young people, caught in the Depression.

Mary Gordon recommends this volume.

Schwarz-Bart, André. The Last of the Just. *Translated from the French by Stephen Becker* (New York: Atheneum, 1960) First published, 1959. In what is virtually a tragic history and lyrical analysis of European Jewry, the Jewish-French author opens this work with the pogrom at York, England in 1185 and ends it at Auschwitz, some seven hundred sixty years later. The focus is on the Levy family and the "thirty six just men" or martyrs, one of whom is produced by the family in each generation. Actually, much of the work is devoted to a relatively modern generation of Levys and, as such, it conveys a curiously beautiful and tender story of nineteenth- and twentieth-century Europe. Admirably translated, this magnificent first novel won the 1959 Goncourt Prize.

Martha Gellhorn writes, "It is a great book; I do not exaggerate."

Scott, Evelyn. Narcissus (New York: Harcourt, 1922) Embarked on a second marriage, Lawrence Farley discovers that his new wife is more involved with clubs and movements than in the cause of making him feel important. A thoroughly modern woman, Julia is torn between real love for her husband and the fear that she lacks self-fulfillment. In addition, we see Julia's fifteen-year-old stepdaughter and her boy friend who have similar problems. The novel's characters proceed through their daily lives, always hoping that something better is about to be offered them. The author's exuberant style is a match for the obvious intellect which shapes the complex characterizations.

David Madden recommends works by Evelyn Scott which include *The Narrow House* (1921), *Background in Tennessee* (1937), and *Shadow of the Hawk* (1941).

Scott, Paul. The Raj Quartet (London: Heinemann, 1976) This is a collection of novels: *The Jewel in the Crown* (1966); *The Day of the Scorpion* (1968); *Towers of Silence* (1971); *A Division of the Spoils* (1975).

No one has written with more understanding and verisimilitude about the last years of British rule in India than Paul Scott. He lavishly combines lovers and enemies, servants and military men, Indians and English in a series of interrelated stories. The novels make most sense when read in sequence, since Scott often has characters referring to events of previous periods. The interplay between characters is sometimes compared favorably with nineteenth-century masters, and the delight of this carefully crafted scheme is that each character and situation feels real, and the reader becomes immersed in the monumental sadness of the raj.

A. R. Frewen wrote, "Am I alone in thinking *The Raj Quartet* are better than anything we have had since the end of the war and can stand without apology in the ranks of the Great Victorians?'' (*The Times*, London, August 4, 1978).

Segal, Lore. *Lucinella* (New York: Farrar, Straus, 1976) In residence at Yaddo, a northern New York writers' and artists' colony, Lucinella begins the story of her experience as a poet and a woman. The scenes are entirely peopled by writers, either in New York or at Yaddo or on the college circuit. There is much humor and wit in the portrayal of this community as they yearn toward ever greater fame. And there is also fantasy in the writing. But underneath, there are cold, hard perceptions of the nature of writers and their craft or art.

Cynthia Ozick writes that although Lore Segal's *Other People's Houses* (1964) had a "certain celebrity . . .[h]er extraordinary novel, *Lucinella*, . . . appears to have gone almost entirely neglected. It is a burnished and witty exploration of the psychology of sophistication, and simultaneously of the psychology of dread. And beyond that, it should be said that Lore Segal's prose is itself splendid: canny, cunning, idiosyncratic, revelatory; sentences that are full of ideas that no one else has ever had.''

Sender, Ramón. *A Man's Place. Translated from the Spanish by Oliver La Farge* (New York: Duell, 1940) First published, 1939. Noted for his interest in social justice and his keen sense of the symbolic, Sender merges both in a finely wrought story of a young Spaniard. The time is 1910 and Sabino suddenly disappears from a small Spanish town. Taken back and forth over a fifteen year period, the reader gradually discovers why Sabino left and the far-reaching importance of his departure. Two innocent men are tried and jailed by a system which demands an explanation for any untoward event. Several women find new loves and political parties are re-aligned. With a sardonic, vigorous twist, the author ends the novel in a manner that once again propels the town into violent turmoil. Simple prose, a powerful and logical plot, and superb character development are this author's means of exposing the nature of pre-Civil War Spain and its peoples.

George P. Elliott recommends it.

Shakespear, Olivia. *Uncle Hilary* (London: Methuen, 1910) O. S. P. writes, "Olivia Shakespear (1864-1938). Close personal friend of W. B. Yeats; related to Lionel Johnson; mother-in-law of Ezra Pound.

"*Uncle Hilary* [is] an Edwardian novel about the British in India in the nineteenth century. A novelist's tale of the personal involvements of individuals in India, the ironies and the illicit relationships emanating both in England and India from Chance. Well-constructed plot (slightly reminiscent of Trollope). Lucid almost Voltairean prose, more succinct than Henry James, and more 'Buddhist' in its perceptions. A subtle portrait of a period and set of circumstances now unknown."

Shetzline, David. *DeFord* (New York: Random House, 1968) DeFord, a carpenter, is set down suddenly in New York City, which is to him a totally grotesque world. After years of working on Western ranches, he comes East to bury his last relative. Then, suffering a heart attack and destitution, he is forced to move to the Bowery. All of this wild adventure is recounted with humor, imagination and erudition as it traces people and places and events.

Ken Kesey recommends this.

Shiel, Matthew. *Children of the Wind* (New York: Knopf, 1923) Searching for fortune and adventure, an Englishman sets off for Central Africa to find his cousin, the white queen of a native tribe. Pitting modern science against the natives, the adventurer finally overcomes all obstacles to win the queen. While the plot is clearly a yarn, the author's wild and sometimes bizarre treatment of characters and situations is remarkable.

Paul Bowles says, "I remember being fascinated by Shiel's narrative style [in *Children of the Wind*], an interest which was reinforced when I later read Shiel's *How the Old Woman Got Home*."

Shreve, Susan Richards. *A Fortunate Madness* (Boston: Houghton, 1974) Driven to the edge of insanity by guilt over her husband's death, a young widow is forced to come to terms with herself. Her disintegrating marriage which ends in tragedy could possibly prove a turning point toward a better life. The characters of both the husband and wife are vivified through telling dialogue, so true as to sometimes seem to have been tape recorded. The gradual unfolding of the young woman's consciousness is extremely moving.

Richard Bausch writes, "Shreve's novel was attacked by the feminists, for all the wrong reasons; her characters have life, not theories, and this neglected first novel is a strong evocation of a young, gifted woman in circumstances which threaten to overwhelm her. Shreve's greatest strength is her ability to render characters as palpable as one's own face in a mirror. She is one of our most important writers and *A Fortunate Madness* is one of her best books."

Sienkiewicz, Henry. *With Fire and Sword*. *Translated from the Polish by Jeremiah Curtin* (Boston: Little, 1890) First published, 1886. The opening novel in a trilogy which charts the drama of Polish history during the seventeenth century, this author uses the techniques of Scott with the vision of Tolstoy. Sienkiewicz recreates the war between the Ukrainian Cossacks and the Poles. The culmination of episodes, which are historically accurate, are made fascinating by careful attention to characterization. While the focus is on war and the striking personalities of its leaders, there is also concern for village life and peace. The other novels in this trilogy are: *The Deluge* (1888) and *Pan Michael* (1893).

William F. H. Lamont cited this is *Books Abroad*, Vol. 27:3.

Sigal, Clancy. *Going Away* (Boston: Houghton, 1962) The history of the American left from the 1930s to the 1960s is dramatized through the experience of a young man. The novel opens with the protagonist beginning a journey from Hollywood, where he has quit his job as an agent, to New York. The son of two Communist trade union organizers, he travels across the nation visiting friends and enemies out of his radical past. Upon the publication of *Going Away*, Nelson Algren called it "a first-hand novel by a first-rate writer driven by the discovery that he is a man fully equipped to live his life, but with no place to live it. . . . The recklessness of the protagonist's driving is matched by the reckless honesty of Mr. Sigal's writing."

Larry McMurtry recommends this as "an original and too-little-known novel."

Simenon, Georges. *The House by the Canal*. *Translated from the French by Geoffrey Sainsbury* (London: Routledge, 1952) First published, 1950. Typically tense in style, these are two of the French mystery writer's finest short novels. The first, which is the title of the book, concerns the emotions of a city girl doomed to spend time in almost complete isolation by a canal. It is particularly effective for its evocation of the Flemish countryside. The second, "The Ostenders," tells an amusing, yet equally gripping story about French trawlers locked by war in a Belgium port.

Shirley Ann Grau calls the lead story, "The House by the Canal," a "brooding study of evil. Not a detective story, but the best of all [Simenon's] many novels."

Simon, Claude. *The Flanders Road.* *Translated from the French by Richard Howard* (New York: Braziller, 1961) First published, 1960. Three French cavalry troopers are in retreat from Belgium after the Nazis have overrun the country in 1940. They relate the story of a Captain de Reixach, a distinguished Frenchman, who brings about his own death. The narration is worked out as the three men separate, are captured, and then meet once again in prison. The time sequences are as imaginative as they are illustrative of the mood of defeated France. The style has been compared to that of Faulkner's.

Gilbert Sorrentino says, "This is the most subtle, beautifully constructed, and masterfully composed novel of one of the masters of the *nouveau roman*, and can serve as entry to all his other novels."

Sinclair, May. *The Three Sisters* (London: Hutchinson, 1914) Like the Brontë sisters, three women are confined to a small moorland vicarage under the domination of their thrice married father. Striking out to find some kind of happiness, one of the daughters thinks she finds romance. The other two actually marry, but find little satisfaction. The great moors, the careful studies of the three sisters, and the more analytical aspects of nineteenth-century hysteria among women make this an unusual and gripping novel. The admirably presented story is matched by the writer's command of her subject matter.

Virago Press is reissuing this book.

Skvorecky, Josef. *The Cowards.* *Translated from the Czech by Jeanne Nemcova* (New York: Grove, 1970) Covering only a week in May 1945, this Czechoslovakian novel captures the sweep of the Russian invasion as the Nazis move out of the country. A jazz musician, Danny Smiricky, is caught up in the tide of the two armies sweeping through his town. While fictional, this work outlines an important time in history and delineates the impending change in Eastern Europe. Furthermore, it records what it means to be young, idealistic and innocent in a period of profound turmoil. *The Times Literary Supplement* called this "a major Czech novel."

Milos Forman recommends it.

Smith, Clark Ashton. *Lost Worlds* (Sauk City, Wisconsin: Arkham House, 1944) Dealing with the gothic, the horrible and the occult, this collection of short stories is in the tradition of H. P. Lovecraft, Henry Whitehead and, of course, Edgar Allan Poe. Dealing with primordial monsters and various other instruments of death and decay, the yarns are wildly imaginative and move briskly from one strange episode to the next. While the style may be too gothic for some readers, anyone who loves this genre will be delighted.

Harlan Ellison recommends all works by Clark Ashton Smith.

Smith, Lee. *Fancy Strut* (New York: Harper, 1973) The good citizens of Speed, Alabama, are planning a sesquicentennial celebration in the 1960s. At the same time, they are involved in, and slightly mystified by, the developments in the New South which not only call for racial equality, but for considerably more personal freedom. There are numerous characters steeped in everything from alcohol to promiscuity, who seem determined to ruin the celebration by too many injections of reality. The lively, humorous pace makes this a genuinely funny book that is satirical without being cruel. The title derives from the stride of the drum majorette that resembles the goose step, and the town is determined to have the best fancy strutter to lead their parade.

Annie Dillard calls this an "extremely funny, well-made contemporary American novel: [a] cross between Dickens and Woody Allen. Beautifully put together, very funny characters."

Smith, Mark.*The Middleman* (Boston: Little, 1967) As he moves through a private world verging on insanity, the middleman constantly puts this problem to the reader: limited by our five senses, can we really appreciate the difference between reality and illusion? Living on the shore of Lake Michigan, the narrator is a member of an old family who moved to the town during its earliest logging days. They are eccentric, infected with the notion of isolation and a sense of superiority in both intellect and imagination. When the middleman's brother dies and he becomes the guardian of his brother's children and trustee of a large insurance policy on their lives, the story takes a murderous turn. The tale is told with great skill through recollection and dream, and it builds to a tremendous climax. *The Middleman* is an extraordinary existential novel.

John Irving says that he "recommends it *highly*."

Smith, Mark. *Toyland* (Boston: Little, 1965) Caught in a hideous dilemma, two criminals must decide whether to murder two children, or in lieu of that, to have one of the would-be killers murder the other. These intelligent and pensive criminals are trapped by an agreement with an eccentric, vicious man to slay the children. No reason is given for the deed, but if they fail to carry out their mission, their credibility will be diminished and their honesty discredited. No matter what they decide, the fate of all persons involved seems absolutely inescapable.

John Irving recommends this novel "*highly*" as well.

Smith, Stevie. *Novel on Yellow Paper* (London: Cape, 1936) Due to the film *Stevie*, Stevie Smith is by now an international figure—an English poet perhaps more famous in death than during her lifetime. Here, her cultivated and thoughtful mind is turned to a novel about common, everyday events in an ordinary life. Actually, this is more a series of impressions on everything from sex and religion to bringing up children than it is a standard narrative. Her odd and very individual method may not appeal to everyone, but the satirical lightness of her touch gives the novel a charming, occasionally whimsical character rarely found in modern fiction.

Mary Gordon recommends this.

Sologub, Fyodor. *The Little Demon* *Translated from the Russian by Ronald Wicks* (London: New English Library, 1962) First published, 1907. A remarkable study on two levels, this is, first, a portrait of the progressive insanity of a stupid provincial schoolmaster played out before the indifference of his friends and co-workers, and, second, an indictment of Russian lower middle-class society in a small town. Both the teacher and his friends take perverse delight in defiling those who embody imagination and beauty. In contrast, Sologub introduces two characters who live for higher values but are misunderstood. Eventually, the teacher is possessed by "the little demon" who is a representation of evil. This is a masterly mingling of the natural and the supernatural, of horror and joy, and the ultimate confusion of life.

William F. H. Lamont cited this in *Books Abroad*, Vol. 27:3.

Sologub, Fyodor. *The Old House and Other Stories.* *Translated from the Russian by John Cournos* (New York: Knopf, 1916) The innermost feelings of a young revolutionary, hardly more than a child, are portrayed in the first story of this, by now, classic collection. Betrayed by an *agent provacateur*, the young man is doomed. The vividness and fanciful realism of the other stories make them equally absorbing. Few writers have given a more accurate picture of Russia in the ferment before the Revolution and drawn more telling sketches of petty official actions directed against the change than has Sologub.

Sanford Friedman says, "The peculiar sensibility that created the masterpiece *The Petty Demon* [also translated as *The Little Demon*] is perfectly evident in Sologub's singular stories."

Somerville, Edith and Martin Ross. *The Real Charlotte* (London: Longmans, 1900) First published, 1894. In a classic concerning manners, familial ties and dreams of rising from the lower middle class, the authors spin out an Anglo-Irish social comedy based on a harsh, fierce vision of life. The "real" lower middle-class Charlotte Mullen is contrasted with the part of herself that tries to break into higher society. As rich in character as she is in imagination, Charlotte is a strong, unique personality who is determined to outwit her landagent employer. Often compared to Balzac's *Cousin Bette*, the novel is humorous, observant and sometimes tragic. There are numerous characters besides Charlotte, including her niece Francie, a Dublin girl who is mad for men and Christopher Dysart, the gentle aristocrat who loves poetry and photography. The two female novelists (Martin Ross is Violet Martin, a cousin of Edith Somerville) are inherently snobbish but endowed with the ability to portray good people with genuine simplicity. In writing of this work, V. S. Pritchett observed that it was "the most substantial and powerful Anglo-Irish novel of the last half of the nineteenth century"

(*New Statesman*, March 9, 1973).

William Trevor recommends it.

Soto, Pedro Juan. *Spiks.* *Translated from the Spanish by Victor Ortiz* (New York: Monthly Review Press, 1973) First published, 1956. In the vanguard of Puerto Rican writers, Soto suggests the anguish, pride and political turmoil of his people in New York City. The six short stories focus particularly on Puerto Rican women and their struggle to break away from tradition and family ties. The strong characters include an unwed mother-to-be, an artist, and a misplaced vendor. Most are victims of a system which condemns them to the streets of Spanish Harlem or the empty lots of the South Bronx. The translator says in the introduction, "In all his work Pedro Juan Soto brings his readers or viewers a world sparingly drawn. He depicts scenes, characters, situations with a few quick, carefully planned strokes, devoid of unessential elaboration."

William Kennedy recommends this volume.

Spackman, W. M. *Heyday* (New York: Ballantine, 1953) Reminiscent of an F. Scott Fitzgerald character, Webb is a proper Princetonian married to a woman who is in jail. The story is of their separation. The efforts of Webb to maintain his detachment from his fate and the times are handled with considerable ability. The dialogue is not only realistic, it is shrewd and telling, and the characters in Webb's life are frequently fascinating.

Christopher Cox says, "[Spackman] is one of our great writers, but almost no one knows it yet. Spackman, like Henry Green and Lawrence Sterne, is a storyteller, a comic, an enchanter, but first and foremost a master stylist" (*Soho News*, November 5, 1980).

Speilberg, Peter. *Twiddledum Twaddledum* (New York: Fiction Collective, 1974) These are slices from contemporary life about a youth who learns the ropes in Vienna and America. The jumble of his experiences are contrasted with wit and satire against the greater American experience of disorder. The writing style is as lively as is the message.

Ronald Sukenick says that this novel is "like Kafka's *Amerika* Americanized."

Stafford, Jean. *Boston Adventure* (New York: Harcourt, 1944) *Boston Adventure* concerns the gradual climb of Sonia Marburg from the position of a chambermaid's daughter to that of an enviable figure in Boston society. The dazzling virtuosity of the author—in particular her portrait of a wealthy Bostonian, Miss Pride—offers a wonderful and memorable experience in reading. In a contemporary review, *The New Yorker* critic said, "It will probably invite plenty of comparison with Proust and should stand up under [that comparison] amazingly well."

Paula Fox recommends it.

Stapledon, William Olaf. *Last and First Men: A Story of the Near and Far Future* (London: Cape, 1931) An English philosopher traces the history of the human race from 1931 to its eventual demise some two billion years in the future. Science fiction? Perhaps, although many critics see it as an imaginative analysis of the human condition, and most particularly as a careful consideration of social, scientific, and religious problems facing the human race. Although the style of writing is sometimes awkward and cumbersome, the central ideas burn so brilliantly as to captivate the reader.

Susan Sontag calls it "an unclassifiable book of imaginary history."

Stead, Christina. *House of All Nations* (New York: Simon & Schuster, 1938) Published two years before her now famous *The Man Who Loved Children*, this, like most of her fiction, can be read on two levels. The plot concerns a Parisian banker who dominates the world of international finance in the 1920s and 1930s. Although he is the central character, the people about him, from his family to his business associates, are equally absorbing. As the tale moves from Europe to America, one senses the author's distaste for capitalism, but beyond that there is the second level of enjoyment—the technical brilliance of the author's style. She elevates what might be sociological commentary to the heights of art.

Saul Bellow recommends this work.

Stead, Christina. *The Man Who Loved Children* (New York: Simon & Schuster, 1940) The work of Christina Stead continues to gain respect and popularity, yet this, her most famous novel, is still not that well known among the general public. Ironically titled, the narrative shows the disastrous effects of a liberal minded, well-meaning scientist upon his family living near Washington, D. C. Too self-righteous and egocentric to realize what effect he is having, Sam Pollit believes he can save the world through a combination of science and humanism. And to this end, he rejects everyone, including his wife and his self-absorbed eldest child, Louisa. Sam is only happy when he is with much younger children who seem to be his emotional equals. A funny, painful and absorbing masterpiece, this novel is a profound work.

Lillian Hellman says that it is "among the best novels of our time." And Roger Straus also recommends it.

Stegner, Wallace. *The Big Rock Candy Mountain* (New York: Duell, 1943) Spanning the years 1906 to 1942, the author carries the reader through the development of the Western United States, Canada, and Alaska. The title comes from the dream of Bo Mason since he is continually on the move in search of fortune. The makeshift dwellings and places in which Bo and his family live are authentic in the smallest detail and the drama of poverty and cruelty is vividly conveyed. There is no finer novel about early twentieth-century homesteading, and the lure of the mountains and prairies.

Raymond Carver recommends this novel.

Stein, Gertrude. *Things As They Are* (Vermont: Banyan, 1950) Written in 1903, six years before her first novel was published, this is a three part work, circulated for the first time in 1950, portraying three young women who are involved in a muted lesbian love affair. Jane Mayhall writes, "*Things As They Are* exposed a fierce strength and creative focus that few novels of that period (and later) have equalled. The book is neither a study in pathology nor a sociological exploitation of abnormal types (as so many books about homosexuals and lesbians have been). The characters are openly portrayed, without resorting to literary gimmicks or caricature sensationalism. In the face of Stein's current success, too, as forerunner of avant-garde prose, it is still ironic that her actual *literary* radicalism has been so severely overlooked."

Stewart, Donald O. *Mr. and Mrs. Haddock Abroad* (New York: Doran, 1924) Sometimes compared favorably with the English classic *Three Men in a Boat* by Jerome K. Jerome, this is a truly funny satire of American manners and family life. Mr. and Mrs. Haddock and their daughter are from the midwest, and they set out to discover New York and Europe. Along the way, they meet memorable characters and the mad nature of their adventures is hilarious. Although now all but forgotten, Stewart can be ranked with Clarence Day and James Thurber as a major American humorist.

Southern Illinois University Press is reissuing this book.

Still, James. *Pattern of a Man* (Lexington: Gnomon, 1976) Here is a collection of eleven stories about isolated settlements in the Kentucky hills. Jane Mayhall writes, "James Still is a much unappreciated American writer. He has published over the past forty years some of the best American prose around. Between the mid-30s and '50s his stories and novels appeared in *The Atlantic Monthly*, *The Yale Review*, *The American Mercury*, and *The Prairie Schooner*. Although two volumes of his short stories and a novel were reissued in recent years by Kentucky publishers (James Still lives in Appalachia, in the heart of a coal mining area) there has been no national recognition of a truly subtle, brilliant and accomplished writer. His work has been unjustly relegated to that species of the merely 'regional.'

"I am particularly admiring of a book of short stories, 'Pattern of a Man'....Many of his stories are on a par with those of Frank O'Connor and Chekov. The uses of a sometimes dense 'idiom' resembles James Joyce, in Joyce's employment of Irish vernacular, with the same wit and poetic dazzle. Two of James Still's very short tales, 'Mrs. Razor' and 'The Nest' have a psychological depth (and even greatness) akin to the swift vision of Tolstoy—in concepts relating to death, and the wild play of inner imagination. Still's work is also very self-contained, and does not rely on superficial (explanatory) pointers to achieve effects."

Stowe, Harriet Beecher. *The Pearl of Orr's Island: A Story of the Coast of Maine* (New York: A. L. Burt, 1861) Set in nineteenth-century New England, this is a strongly feminist analysis of the relations between the sexes in a typical Puritan population. Commenting on her novel, Stowe said it was "as pale and colorless as real life, and sad as truth." The truth that is revealed in this story of two young children who know each other first in youth and then in adulthood is the absolute incompatibility of what is traditionally considered feminine, embodied in the character of Mara, and masculine, embodied in the character of Moses. The sad result of this observation is that Mara, in adopting the only heroic role open to a woman, must die so that Moses may be saved. In fact, she chooses death at a time she is about to enter into the soul-destroying abnegation of feminine values she encounters in the process of romantic love, courtship and marriage. This is a classic novel about a woman's place in our culture.

Judith Fetterley recommends this as well as the author's *Dred* (1856), an anti-slavery manifesto published four years after *Uncle Tom's Cabin*, and *Oldtown Folks* (1869).

Strachey, Julia. *The Man on the Pier* (London: Lehmann, 1951) In an admirable, amusing way, the author counterpoints the conventions of English intellectuals with the realities of passion and emotion. Setting her story in a country house in 1936, she portrays Ned and Aron who are staying in the house before they take over a boys' school. The two partners seem to excel one another in egotism, but Ned is brought up short when he inadvertently falls in love with Aron's wife. With wit and economy of style, matters are nicely resolved.

Eva Figes says, "A restrained, stylish writer, this novel is very moving in an unpretentious way."

Stuart, Francis. *The Pillar of Cloud* (London: Gollancz, 1949) The Second World War is just over, and the inhabitants of a partially razed town in the French zone of Germany are forced to find their way back to normality. The characters are Germans, displaced persons, officials and an odd assortment of people who make this community their home. The truly representative group of Europeans are tracked through both their thoughts and actions, and are found to have little or nothing in common with each other. They rely on themselves alone. In drawing what is alternately a dismal and a heroic way of life, the author offers a cast of marvelous personalities, true in their conversations, thoughts and lives. In addition, there is a debate in the novel on the pros and cons of Christianity, which is particularly powerful in this context.

Derek Mahon calls this "an autobiographical novel set in post-war Germany, by an Irish Dostoevsky."

Sturgis, Howard. *Belchamber* (New York: Putman, 1905) This novel, which some contemporaries compared to Thackeray's, concerns an old English family and its heir, Lord Belchamber, who wishes to abandon his position so that he can carry out meaningful work. However, the call of his family name proves too compelling, and he returns to the estate and marries. In reviewing it, Edith Wharton hailed it for its "freshness of sensation and perception." Both as a character study and a view of England this is an exceptional work.

Joseph Alsop writes, "*Belchamber* [is] of no enormous significance but deeply interesting for the insight it gives one into a most curious, now vanished, way of life."

Taylor, Elizabeth. *At Mrs. Lippincote's* (London: Davies, 1945) Over the past thirty years, Elizabeth Taylor has published numerous novels and short stories, but this, her first novel, remains one of her best and one of her most typical. It is a character study of Julia Davenport, a charming, unconventional woman who goes to live in an English seaside town where her soldier husband is stationed. While there is little plot, the unwinding of her days advances an ironic and penetrating vision of human nature. This is a charming comedy of manners which has the virtue of being considerably more, for in this distinctly English milieu the author deals with the difficult and elusive problem of loneliness.

Keith Thomas says of Taylor's novels, "They give an astringent and precise picture of English middle-class domestic life in the 1940s and 1950s." And William Trevor recommends all the novels and short stories of Elizabeth Taylor.

Taylor, Elizabeth. Hester Lilly and Twelve Short Stories (London: Davies, 1954) Her mother dead, the adolescent Hester Lilly is sent to live with her English cousin, who is a headmaster, and his hysterical wife. Blundering from one to the other, from situation to situation, Hester acts like an unwelcome catalyst to complete the decay of their marriage. Here, as in the twelve short stories in this collection, the theme is the prevalence of loneliness and misunderstanding which pervades all classes and places. More as witness than reformer, the author gently introduces her characters through telling dialogue and shrewd metaphors. The drama beneath the surface of seemingly quiet lives is wonderfully revealed in this collection.

Elizabeth Cullinan recommends it. (See next entry.)

Taylor, Elizabeth. The Soul of Kindness (London: Chatto, 1964) Rather ordinary people who partake in daily activities such as gardening and cooking populate the finely styled and intelligent novels and short stories of Elizabeth Taylor. This novel, published midway through her career,

is typical. It has the virtue of a quiet yet gripping plot, and shows how a well-meaning person can cause havoc by failing to appreciate the power of words. Here Flora, an innocent, bland and good wife, nearly destroys her family and friends by either asking too much, or, more frequently, too little of them. Within a typical English home, the author draws a telling picture of loneliness, despair and inadequacy. The juxtaposition of inner frustration and, at times, horror with outer calm is conveyed with Elizabeth Taylor's usual sensitivity and impeccable style. An enchanting balance is struck between humor and grief, subtle narration and daily, meaningless conversation.

Elizabeth Cullinan writes, "Elizabeth Taylor's books are graceful and precise renderings of vital and sometimes savage feeling. In her civilized world and her beautiful sentences, the motor accidents, faithlessness, eccentricity, and death that occur may be clean but they're no less shattering."

Elizabeth Cullinan also recommends Taylor's *In a Summer Season* (1961), *Blaming* (1976), and *Hester Lilly* (See above entry).

Thaxter, Celia L. Among the Isles of Shoals (Boston: J.R. Osgood, 1873) Drawing from her childhood experiences among the islands off the coast of New Hampshire, the author chronicles the history of what was once a thriving community. The articles, which first appeared in the *Atlantic Monthly*, are impressive for their deep appreciation of both nature and people. Whether describing an eccentric weather front or the peculiar antics of the crab, the prose pieces are some of the most beautiful and accurate ever written about American natural life. Alternating between enchantment and sorrow, Thaxter also paints the daily lives of the people.

Judith Fetterley recommends this as well as Thaxter's *An Island Garden* (1874), and Mary Cantwell writes, "Some of the pages of *Among the Isles of Shoals*, those about the islanders and their stunted lives, foreshadow Robert Flaherty and his documentary film 'Man of Aran.' Others, about the scents and sights of the isles, are close to incantatory in their passion" (*The New York Times Book Review*, August 8, 1982).

Theroux, Alexander. *Three Wogs* (London: Chatto, 1972) The first "wog" is a Chinese storekeeper who, faced with a less than appreciative English matron, finds a peculiar method of ridding himself of her prejudice. The second story shows a confrontation between an illiterate and a university educated Indian. The last in this collection of stories concerns the efforts of an English minister to maintain the services of an African singer. Thanks to a splendid ear for verbal anomalies, a sense of humor, and compassion for the embarrassed "wogs," the author accurately portrays an important aspect of contemporary life. Incidentally, "wog" is a denigating English term for a poor foreigner from the Third World.

Thomas, Dylan. *Portrait of the Artist as a Young Dog* (London: Dent, 1940) Describing incidents in his Welsh childhood and adolescence, Thomas combines fact with fiction, fancy with reality. The result is an autobiography and a group of short stories. Where one begins the other leaves off, in no way detracting from the unusual imagery and rhythmical flare. Contemporary reviewers were unanimous in noting its "unnecessary coarseness" and its use of expressions "commonly classed as impolite." But that was 1940. Today, the robust prose is singularly modern.

Keith Waterhouse says, "It may be that these early short stories, published I think originally during the war, are available in one edition or another, but I have been unable to find them in twenty years."

Thomas, John. *Dry Martini: A Gentleman Turns to Love* (New York: Doran, 1926) Paris, as seen by Americans as much in love with themselves as with their drinks, is depicted in the 1920s. Willoughby Quimby and his daughter Elizabeth are currently residing there. And the Paris of actual Parisians is present as well. All facets of the city and the times are caught in the graceful, light, amusing prose. Here is a significant contribution to humor and the social structure of a long past European-American community.

Southern Illinois University Press is reissuing this.

Thomas, Ross. *Chinaman's Chance* (New York: Simon & Schuster, 1978) Hired by a billionaire to find his sister-in-law, two soldiers of fortune are plunged into mystery and political intrigue. The missing woman is caught in the middle of a murder of a congressman and his wife, and as key witness is the target of mobs and government agents. The two unorthodox detectives manage to avoid all traps, and in a logical, suspenseful way finally discover the key to the involved, dangerous plot.

John D. MacDonald says of Thomas' novels, "These are quirky action stories by a professional who, because of his reading and his close attention to his work, manages to avoid the grotesqueries of the tin-ear writers of far greater notoriety. His stories move in unexpected patterns, and do not take themselves too seriously. He does violence well, and there is always something going on under the surface."

Thurber, James. *The White Deer* (New York: Harcourt, 1945) Take three princes, add an enchanted princess, mix them with imagery and imagination and you have this story which is reminiscent of Lewis Carroll and James Joyce. An unusual element in this fantasy is that it is set in modern times. There is a subtle mixture of prose and poetry as well as illustrations by the author and Don Freeman. As one critic put it: "If you miss this book, you deserve a good head cold."

John Unterecker says, "*The White Deer* is neglected because it doesn't fit into Thurber's pigeonhole. By any standards, this wonderful fable on the order of *Alice in Wonderland* should be reprinted perpetually. Appealing to children for its invention and to adults for its wit, it is a work that has never had the opportunity to locate its proper audience."

Thurman, Wallace. *Infants of the Spring* (New York: Macaulay, 1932) A contemporary black writer looks at Harlem during the Renaissance of the 1920s and 1930s. His concern is with the characters who make up the Bohemian circle of creative blacks. Most of the plot and the dialogue concern their affairs and the events of the period. Although a novel, it is one of the more accurate descriptions of black life. It captures the color snobbery within the community and the various methods of passing as white, as well as other manifestations of prejudice.

Southern Illinois University Press has reissued this book.

Towers, Robert. *The Monkey Watcher* (New York: Harcourt, 1964) A fifty-two-year-old conservative art historian and scholar switches his style of life, and the novel traces the result of his break from an expected pattern. (The title derives from the historian's sudden interest in watching the monkeys at Central Park Zoo.) Here one finds some unusual development of the traditional patterns along which we think: conservative versus liberal, marital faithfulness versus flexible morals, even traditional art versus modern art. As a convincing exploration into the secret, sometimes aberrant, life of a middle-aged male, this has few rivals.

William Weaver says, "The Towers novel still seems to me an exceptionally subtle work, told with sobriety and elegance, but with tension. Its neglect remains a mystery to me."

Traven, B. *March to Caobaland* (London: Hale, 1961) Published in United States as *March to the Montería*. First published, 1933. A sensitive, fast moving adventure story, this details the political and social conditions in Mexico prior to the revolution. A young Indian is the central character. In order to earn money to enable him to marry, he signs up for a two year hitch on a mahogany plantation where he becomes bound to the montería under the practice of debt slavery. Embittered, he joins the forces which will soon revolt against Diaz. A successful case study of the Mexican proletariat, this is as much a documentary as an intriguing novel.

Robert Roper recommends this as well as Traven's *The Treasure of Sierre Madre*.

Tressall, Robert. *The Ragged Trousered Philanthropists* (London: Richards, 1914) Comparable to Zola's *Germinal*, this is a closely observed picture of working-class life in early twentieth-century England. The author was a socialist laborer who wrote this one novel shortly before his death. The characters are a group of painters, plasterers, and carpenters who are not aware of their truly awful economic condition and the causes which keep them perpetually poor. Just how effective the author is in stating his case is seen in a contemporary review which said, "His unbalanced statements about landlordism and property and money is likely to do a great deal of harm if placed in the hands of uneducated or half educated people" (*Saturday Review*, April 25, 1914). However, even this reviewer had to admit that the novel is a unique and fearless record of true experiences.

Eric and Ilse Moon write, "Robert Noonan, who wrote this novel under the penname of Tressall, was a housepainter in Hastings, England. He died in 1911 and this book was first published three years after his death. It is *the* best book about working class life in England in the early part of this century, and might do much to enlighten many Americans who do not appear to understand that there is a difference between socialism and communism."

Trevor, William. *The Boarding House* (New York: Viking, 1965) Combine a run-down boarding house, a failed blackmailer, an eccentric nurse and a group of old people whom the blackmailer and nurse plan to swindle and one has the beginnings of the Irish writer's third novel. The macabre interplay between the two main characters and the aged borders in a southwest London suburb is the driving force of the novel. What makes the work so peculiar is not only the nature of this semi-respectable home, but the style of writing wherein the characters are noted by their mental or physical idiosyncrasies and a fantastic atmosphere is thus created. It is also a very deft portrait of evil.

Stanley Elkin recommended this in *Antaeus*, Autumn, 1975, along with Trevor's *The Old Boys* (1964) and *Mrs. Eckdorf in O'Neills Hotel* (1969).

Trocchi, Alexander. *Cain's Book* (New York: Grove, 1960) The journal of a New York junkie, this is an almost perfect tough and forceful autobiographical novel. The often savagely alive adventures of the writer contrast with the tenor of affluent American society. Rarely has a writer so brilliantly portrayed those on the outer fringe, from hustlers and shoplifters to drug pushers. The writing captures these characters with great success.

Edwin Morgan says, "Trocchi has not been a very productive author since the 1960s and this very remarkable book has been neglected; it is one of the most distinguished novels of the Beat period, well-written, evocative, disturbing."

Trollope, Anthony. *Castle Richmond* (London: Chapman, 1860) One of Trollope's early novels, set in Ireland during the famine, this is probably one of his lesser known works. The plot is excellent, focusing on the Fitzgeralds of Castle Richmond and, in particular, Owen Fitzgerald. The love interest is explained by the author: "The heroine has two lovers, one of whom is a scamp and the other a prig. As regards the scamp, the girl's mother is her own rival." The dialogue, descriptions of Ireland and the incidental characters are as lively and fascinating as those found in any of Trollope's later works.

Quentin Bell recommends this, saying that it has not been republished.

Uhlman, Fred. *Reunion* (London: Adam Books, 1971) A shy Jewish boy explains how, in 1932, a new student enters his gymnasium in Stuttgart. He is the son of an aristocratic German family. A strong friendship develops between the two adolescents but their companionship lasts just one year. Then, the Jewish boy is sent off to America, while the aristocrat is drawn into the Nazi circle. Some thirty years later, the novel comes to a devastating ending.

Sybille Bedford says, "A perfect novella. Immense emotional depth revealed under cool treatment. Story flawlessly told. The sense of place—a small German town (Stuttgart) in the 1930s. . . .The Nazi's; two schoolboys, one a Jew, the other an aristocrat. . . .No trace of self-pity. A small masterpiece (to me). Published with some, but not nearly enough recognition both in the United States and the United Kingdom in the 1970s."

Valera, Juan. *Pepita Jiménez*. *Translated from the Spanish by Mary Serrano* (New York: Appleton, 1891) First published, 1874. This is an unusual romance in that the heroine woos the hero who is in a seminary, and the author uses letters to reveal the passions of the two lovers. The sardonic, skeptical attitude of the author is in contrast with the romantic fiction of the time. This epistolary novel is a turning point in the development of modern Spanish fiction.

William F. H. Lamont cited this in *Books Abroad*, Vol. 27:3.

Van Greenaway, Peter. *The Judas Gospel* (London: Gollancz, 1972) Combining mystery with religion, villainy with heroism, the author takes an unlikely Dead Sea scroll as the focus of his exciting novel. The scroll shows that Peter, not Judas, betrayed Christ. While the idea is startling, the author handles it with real virtuosity. Commentary, action, revolution, spirituality and simple deduction combine to turn this story into a unique experience.

Shirley Ann Grau calls this, "An interesting blend of four novel types: detective, roman ā clef, intrigue, and serious philosophical. I don't know anything like it. Fascinating failure."

Van Vechten, Carl. *Parties.* (New York: Knopf, 1930) At a constant round of parties, in and out of Harlem, the wealthy, the bored and the hangers-on conform to a style of living associated with the 1920s. The drama derives from a limited number of people confined to even more limited spaces. Their reactions to one another are reflected in their trivial dialogue. As a sophisticated satire on New York life and a study of what seem to be completely futile existences, this is an early existential novel of considerable merit.

Truman Capote recommended it in *Antaeus*, Autumn, 1979.

Vare, Daniele. *The Maker of Heavenly Trousers* (London: Methuen, 1935) Peking is never more romantic than it is in this love story told by Vare who was the Italian minister to China. Thoroughly familiar with the China before World War I, the author gives cultural details which enhance this delightful romance. The central character is a recluse who falls in love with a young Italian girl whom he found living above the shop of a Chinese tailor, "the maker of heavenly trousers." So delicately does Vare mix facts with fiction that you become totally submerged in the absorbing tale.

Noel Perrin calls this, "Romance in high style, set in Peking around 1900. What *Harlequins* should be, and are not" (*Washington Post Book World*, January 17, 1982).

Vassilikos, Vassilis. *The Plant, the Well, the Angel: A Trilogy.* *Translated from the Greek by E. and M. Keeley* (New York: Knopf, 1964) First published, 1961. Drawing upon his facility for mythmaking, this modern Greek author develops, in these three separate yet closely related short novels, the emotional involvement of adolescents with one another, with love, and with the Greek countryside. The odd mixture of reality and fantasy is successful even in the last novel where a young man writes a letter from heaven to a former girl friend. The matter-of-fact style, the true details and the careful attention to unusual possibilities soon encourage the reader to accept even the most fantastic turns in the plot.

Edmund Keeley writes that this is "still the most interesting and substantial work of fiction produced by Greece's most prolific novelist."

Vliet, R. G. *Rockspring* (New York: Viking, 1974) Set in Texas in the 1830s, this is a lyrical short novel which describes a strange relationship. A young woman is kidnapped by three outlaws, and her life with the men is detailed in unusually fine and hard prose. The theme of evil achieving something good is brought off here with remarkable success.

Paula Deitz says this is "a wonderous novel about a Texan girl in the frontier days, who is kidnapped by Mexicans and taken across the border. She becomes part of the Spanish world and falls in love with one of her captors, who is killed when he tries to return her. Brilliant use of bilingual technique."

Voynich, Ethel. *The Gadfly* (New York: Holt, 1897) Set in Italy before the 1833-1846 revolution, this late nineteenth-century spy and conspiracy novel is concerned with multiple characters, from patriots and spies to assassins and ecclesiastics who are involved in trying to overthrow or maintain Austrian domination. At the center of the action is "the Gadfly", the son of a priest who, in the assault on authority and religion, eventually comes into conflict with his own father who has become a famous cardinal. The result is tragic, yet within the tragedy the conflicts both between and within human beings are wisely resolved. While not ideological nor politically biased, the story is anticlerical, and its central theme is the struggle against political tyranny. At the same time, the novel rings true not only because of Voynich's skills as a writer but because the hero seems based upon the author's experiences as the wife of a Polish revolutionary.

Jerzy Kosinski recommends this saying that Bertrand Russell called it "the most exciting novel I have ever read in the English language."

Vreuls, Diane. *Are We There Yet?* (New York: Simon & Schuster, 1975) Setting out with her four-year-old daughter and a cart containing all her possessions, Emma is on her way to a small farm in southern Ohio. Traveling by foot, boat and truck, the pair meet a great number of people and live through humorous, sometimes touching, episodes on their slow, pleasurable journey. Through flashbacks, the reader learns of Emma's past, her life with Arthur, and an affair with a guitar teacher. The combination of fun and

poignancy is gently achieved through a precise literary style and a fine sense of the rhythms of speech.

Anne Tyler says this is "remarkable for its freshness and a unique speed and dash in its style. With a few bold slashes, it creates a heroine I've thought back on often and fondly ever since I first read about her."

Wagoner, David. *Where is My Wandering Boy Tonight?* (New York: Farrar, Straus, 1970) It's a great life when you are young and living in a small Wyoming town in the 1890s. Just what it feels like is conveyed through the narration of a youth who tells how he loses and then finds his father, learns to ride a horse, and finally decides to become a cowboy. It is much funnier than this plot summary suggests, and the author has a peculiar ability to create memorable dialogue.

Bill Ott says, "Wagoner is known primarily as a poet, but he is also the author of numerous novels, some of which are middling at best. *Where is My Wandering Boy Tonight?*, though, is the great exception. Irreverent, comic, ironic—a delightful romp, and a much better book than the somewhat similar *True Grit*."

Walser, Robert. *Jakob von Gunten: A Novel.* *Translated from the German by Christopher Middleton* (Austin: University of Texas Press, 1969) First published, 1909. The story opens with students studying from one and only one textbook. There is only a single class and one lesson which is repeated time and again. The school is a training institute for German servants, and the narration concerns the musings and discussions of one student with his fellows. Sometimes it is difficult to separate the students, as they seem to be no more than the alter ego of the narrator. This work, in fact, is so inventive as to make modern experimental novels seem excessively structured. The narrator is both ingenuous and sophisticated, a combination that makes him extremely sympathetic. A gem of a novel, this is carefully and imaginatively translated.

Susan Sontag recommends it.

Warnke, Janice. *The Narrow Lyre* (New York: Harper, 1958) While the plot is not uncommon—a discontented, married, middle-aged man becomes involved in a love affair—the style and the perceptive treatment of the people and their emotions are outstanding. From the moment the reader is introduced to Robert Crossfield until the time he works his way out of his loveless marriage, the author's sure command of her material is apparent. There is a judicious measure of satiric irony and humor to balance the intensity of the characters emotional lives.

Sybille Bedford writes, "A very good novel indeed, of great literary merit, written in the grand style, with much depth and beauty. Utterly neglected because it came out during the great newsprint strike of 1958. When the strike was over and the *New York Times* and the *Herald Tribune* reappeared, backlogs had accumulated and the book was not reviewed (or so I understand). A great pity, because it prevented this—to me—first rate American writer from being properly recognized; I feel that with some public awareness of her potential much can yet be expected from this writer."

Wassermann, Jacob. *Doctor Kerkhoven*. *Translated from the German by Cyrus Brooks* (New York: Liveright, 1932) Doctor Kerkhoven has the psychic power of healing, a revelation which is slowly disclosed to him just before the First World War. After the war, he takes on a disciple who eventually forces him to rethink the entire direction of his life and his powers. Despite a sometimes complicated plot, the essential beauty of the prose and the profound and burning seriousness of Doctor Kerkhoven's mission offer innumerable rewards. Essentially, the author has a morbid view of life which is consistent and, finally, memorable.

Morton Sobel says, "Wassermann's work is a very romantic novel—which is probably dated by now. At the time I read it, it spoke to me in very personal terms."

Waters, Frank. *The Man Who Killed the Deer* (Denver: University of Denver Press, 1942) This is a very serious novel about the American Indian. The story concerns the conflict between the whites and the Pueblo Indians as typified by the experiences of one of the young Indians. Stimulated by a white education and the tradition of his tribe, the young man is torn between what are essentially two different approaches and philosophies of life. His efforts to resolve the conflict, and return to his tribe (both physically and emotionally) are the primary concern of the novel.

William Stafford says, "*The Man Who Killed the Deer* conducts the reader into the world of a Native American—a way of life that feels foreign to most of us, but is at hand, and is rich with attitudes that relate to our twentieth-century poverty of culture." And Ronald Sukenick says this "may be the best novel ever written about American Indians."

Weesner, Theodore. *The Car Thief* (New York: Random House, 1972) At the age of sixteen, Alex Housman is an accomplished car thief who gets his kicks from joyriding through a backwater, Michigan, factory town. He is caught, freed, and sent back to high school where he is savagely beaten for previous gymnasium thefts. He drops out of school, drifts, and eventually joins the army. While the plot is simple, the characterization of this sad delinquent is complex. Written with sensitive understatement, the novel is in the tradition of James Farrell's *Studs Lonigan,* and as good.

Roger Sale said this is "the best novel I have read since, say, *Herzog*" (*American Scholar,* Winter, 1979).

Welch, Maurice Denton. *A Voice Through a Cloud* (London: Lehmann, 1950) Denton died in 1948 at the age of thirty one, and this unfinished novel closely follows his life and the thirteen years of suffering he endured after a serious accident. While the theme is grim, the novel actually is lyrical, at least in terms of depicting a human being able to overcome even the most trying situation. More prevalent is the rebellion of the author-hero who simply refuses to submit to self-pity, although he experiences moments of great fear and despair. Along the way to death, the writer offers marvelous insights into life in hospitals, medical treatments, and the reaction of the living to the near dead.

Laurie Colwin recommends this novel.

Wells, H. G. *The Passionate Friends* (New York: Harper, 1913) The eternal triangle—here two men and a woman—is the concern of Wells who, along the way, brilliantly describes social, political, and class problems in England at the turn of the century. Stephen Stratton is in love with Lady Mary Christian, but she marries Martin Justin. Later, Stephen and Lady Mary meet, there is a passionate affair, and Martin then learns about it. While the plot is hardly new, the eloquent reflections on people and events and the absorbing conversations make this probably Wells' best work of fiction.

Vladimir Nabokov called this "my most prized example of the unjustly ignored masterpiece. . . .A touch of high art refused to Conrad or Lawrence" (*Times Literary Supplement,* January 21, 1977).

Welty, Eudora. *A Curtain of Green* (New York: Doubleday, 1941) The deceptively simple stories about ordinary people are collected in this first publication by the now famous Southern writer. As in her future stories, the focus is on regional characters and sometimes extraordinary events. The writing is particularly impressive for its economy and the force of its impact.

Nadine Gordimer recommended this in *Antaeus,* Autumn, 1979.

Werfel, Franz. *The Forty Days of Musa Dagh.* *Translated from the German by Geoffrey Dunlop* (New York: Viking, 1934) First published, 1933. It is 1915, and the Armenian community of Musa Dagh in Syria is under siege by the Turkish army. The siege will continue for forty days until it is finally lifted by the French who save the members of seven villages from extermination. Central to the plot are the astonishing details concerning the military operation and the analysis of the spirit of a people who refuse to be conquered.

D. J. Enright says, "Immeasurably superior to Franz Werfel's better-known and over-sweet *Song of Bernadette.* . . .The most powerful presentment I know of the syndrome of persecution: distrust and then hatred of the foreigner, and lust for the foreign woman, 'in whom you possess the God of your enemy'; the fear that lives in the bones, along with the stoicism; the limits to human endurance, and, as well, human unexpectedness" (*Observer Magazine,* November 25, 1979).

Wesker, Arnold. *Love Letters on Blue Paper* (New York: Harper, 1974) Here are five short stories by the English playwright, only three of which are included in an earlier English edition under this title. In almost all the pieces, family memory is a major concern, and the author, as in his plays, is vitally engaged with working-class people. His inherent respect and affection for all his characters and his wholehearted commitment to their vision make these original and satisfying stories. For a fairly current example of his plays, see "The Merchant" in the English periodical *Adam*, 1977-1978.

West, Rebecca. *The Thinking Reed* (London: Hutchinson, 1936) A comedy of manners, quite unlike most of the author's other works, this concerns a St. Louis widow who goes to France to seek a new life and a new husband. She finds both, and in the process reveals an astonishing capability for adapting to a decaying society. But what makes the novel memorable is neither plot nor characters, but the author's observations. Elizabeth Bowen wrote, *"The Thinking Reed* seems to me to be the classic novel, such as is not often written today: imagination (or vision) and sheer top-form professional ability now seldom go together; it is hard to find a mean between satire and good faith. . . . The book as a book appears to me to have almost no imperfections; it rounds itself off, it is impossible to think beyond it" (*New Statesman & Nation*, April 11, 1936).

Liz Smith recommends this saying, "No one seems ever to have noticed West's romantic novel. She became more celebrated for nonfiction."

Westcott, Glenway. *Good-Bye Wisconsin* (New York: Harper, 1928) Set in Wisconsin, the short stories in this collection depend heavily upon the landscape, and the author is as absorbed with the background as he is with his singularly well-defined characters. Particularly noteworthy are the recurrent themes of the beauty and power of the landscape and the

drive for individual expression. Along with his novel *The Pilgrim Hawk* (1940), these short stories are considered among Westcott's finest achievements.

Wallace Stegner recommends this volume.

Westheimer, David. *Lighter than a Feather* (Boston: Little, 1971) If the United States had not had the atom bomb, how would the war with Japan have ended? The imagined answer is graphically portrayed in this novel which has America invading Japan. With accurate detail, fine characterization and a talent for depicting action, the author presents a graphic, almost documentary, description of the invasion and the subsequent reaction of the Japanese.

Weston, John. *The Walled Parrot* (New York: McGraw, 1975) A psychological thriller with a dash of appreciation for the Arizona landscape, this opens when Caroline Sheridan shoots her husband. She disposes of his body, along with that of his similarly slaughtered female friend, by shipping them in a truck to Los Angeles. She is caught, and the finest part of the novel is concerned with the question of her state of mind when she killed the pair.

David Westheimer says this is "a well-written story of a woman's psychological disintegration."

White, Antonia. *Frost in May* (London: Harmsworth, 1933) Describing her first novel, the author explains that she began writing it at the age of sixteen, "but did not finish till I was over thirty. [It] deals only with the predicament of a child who did not become a Catholic till she was seven—the automatic result of her parents being converted—in the bewildering atmosphere of an ultra strict convent school of old pre-World War I type." Out of the four years in the life of a child, the author has fashioned a book of unusual charm and power.

Maureen Cleave recommended this, saying, "The passionate intensity makes one read it, as it were, all in one breath" (*Observer Magazine*, June 4, 1978).

White, T. H. *Mistress Masham's Repose* (New York: Putnam, 1946) Written both for children and adults (as are most of his works from *The Once and Future King* to *The Sword in the Stone*), this is a witty social satire about a little rich girl in a community of Lilliputians. They are secreted on the grounds of a deserted English castle, living on a miniscule island in the middle of a lake. The heroine, among other activities, witnesses a dramatic lecture on human rights and is saved by the charge of a rat cavalry. Charm, laughter and excitement are everywhere.

Patricia Abercrombie recommends this as "a fantasy, beautifully and convincingly written."

Whitechurch, Victor L. *The Canon in Residence* (London: Benn, 1904) Reminiscent of Anthony Trollope and the more modern view of the Anglican church of Barbara Pym, this is an amusing, distinctly original novel which has a very proper and scholarly canon as its central character. While traveling in Switzerland, he loses his clerical garments and is forced to put on more sporty clothing. He becomes a layman, for all intents and purposes, and thus learns how others live. Beneath the humor is a serious undercurrent of criticism of religion and the clergy, particularly the dull prejudices of country life.

Whitman, Stephen F. *Predestined: A Novel of New York Life* (New York: Scribner, 1910) Here is an accurate, realistic portrait of New York at the turn of the century. Its people are seen through the eyes of a struggling young writer who is primarily involved with the "tenderloin" and Bohemian sections of the city. The naturalistic style, particularly the authentic dialogue, was much admired by F. Scott Fitzgerald, if not by other contemporary critics.

Southern Illinois University Press is reissuing this novel.

Wiebe, Dallas. *Skyblue the Badass* (New York: Doubleday, 1969) Skyblue is the name of the hero who suffers from the "badass" complex, which means he simply cannot conform to what society expects from him. Yet, he overcomes his better judgment and earns a Ph.D. in order to become an English teacher at a midwestern college. From there on, it is pure disaster ... and wild humor with verbal pyrotechnics.

X. J. Kennedy says, "For years, whenever I have felt glum, this comic novel has been my cheer and consolation. The academic life has seldom been depicted with less charity. It is about an innocent from Kansas who goes to the big city, discovers literature, and tries to teach the stuff, only to be found out. There is an incredible chapter about an official tea party. College teachers may adore this book or detest it, but they owe it to themselves to read it. Wiebe's style can roughly be described as the way S. J. Perelman might have written had he been revved up on speed."

Wilder, Thornton. *The Cabala* (New York: Boni, 1926) At the pinnacle of Roman society, a group of people have formed a cabala with extraordinary powers to influence individuals and governments. Outwardly diverse, it is difficult to perceive what holds them together, although the common wisdom is that wealth, education and aristocratic heritage is the tie. Through a series of individual character studies, casual meetings and conversations, the reader gradually comes to appreciate the true nature of the cabala. Wilder's first major novel, this remains one of his most distinguished ones as it is marked by his uniquely beautiful style and uncanny observations.

Gore Vidal recommends this.

Wilder, Thornton. *The Ides of March* (New York: Harper, 1948) During the months preceding Caesar's assasination, there is fervent planning and plotting which is all revealed through the ingenious device of structuring the novel around imaginary documents, private letters, journal entries and reports. Due to superb writing and careful attention to actual data, the fictional account is a fascinating and original piece of creative historical rewriting. The motives and the manners of numerous characters are perfectly understood and portrayed. It is a brilliant tour de force with fine shadings of satire, humor and tragedy.

Gore Vidal recommends this as well.

Williams, Charles. *All Hallows' Eve* (London: Faber, 1945) Praising Williams' supernatural work, T. S. Eliot said, "There are no novels anywhere quite like them. They are very good thrillers. . . .They are the work of a man who had something very serious to convey." Equally at home with the supernatural and the natural world, Williams gained fame through the efforts of such supporters as Eliot and W. H. Auden. Today, his intensely fascinating prose is too often neglected. *All Hallows' Eve* opens with a confrontation between a dead wife and husband on Westminster Bridge. The evolution of their relationship in death is the central theme. There are powerful subplots and credible characters that increase the authenticity of this grand reading experience.

Noel Perrin says it is "one of the most powerful works of supernaturalism to appear in our century" (*Washington Post Book World*, January 17, 1982).

Williams, John A. *The Man Who Cried I Am* (Boston: Little, 1967) A black American writer dying of cancer would prefer to leave the hospital, and so he goes to Holland to see his Dutch wife. During his twenty-four hours in Amsterdam, the writer is finally able to say "I am" and come to terms with his past and his future. Primarily, the narrator recalls his journalistic, military and literary careers, and brings back, in vignettes, his experiences which range from civil rights struggles to forays with literary critics. The novel is called by some a roman à clef because there are recognizable portraits of prominent civil rights workers, reviewers, writers and politicians.

Eric and Ilse Moon write, "Nearly everything written by John A. Williams has been undeservedly neglected—from his marvelous first novel, *Night Song* (perhaps the best novel about New York's jazz world), to *The Man Who Cried I Am*, which is probably his best novel. It is in a sense an updating, vintage late 1960s, of Ralph Ellison's classic of the fifties, *Invisible Man*, conveying much the same theme, but with more passionate anger: the black person's tragic lack of identity and recognition. In these years, it is a terribly appropriate book for revival and recognition."

Williams, Joy. *State of Grace* (New York: Doubleday, 1973) Trapped by her father's engrossing love and all enveloping idea that a daughter is an extention of his own clerical will, Kate vainly tries to break away. She goes to college and takes up photography, but her father makes her dispose of her camera. Finally, she marries, enjoying some relief from her dominating parent, and giving birth to a child. But when her husband is fatally injured, she returns to her father, hands him the baby, and tries to obliterate herself. This bleak, marvelously written novel takes an essentially sad story and turns it into a credible myth which holds the reader's attention from the opening sentence to the last.

William Gaddis recommends this.

Williams, Thomas. *The Night of Trees* (New York: Macmillan, 1961) A successful New York businessman is in New Hampshire on a hunting trip, attempting to pull himself together after his wife has walked out on him. He is joined by his college-aged son, and the novel develops the father-son relationship in all its negative tones: they are completely at a loss to understand one another or even communicate successfully. The spirit of hunting is explored as well. Both as a splendid outdoor novel and a deft portrayal of fascinating, intense characters the story has great strength. The plot is as engaging as the evocative descriptions and the fine ending.

John Irving says that he recommends this *"highly."*

Windham, Donald. *The Warm Country* (New York: Scribner, 1960) Set in Georgia, with one or two diversions to Italy, the fourteen short stories in this early collection represent some of the author's finest observations about people. There is little plot, little action, but there is a telling appreciation of Southern approaches to living. E. M. Forster, who wrote an introduction to this volume, says of Windham's stories, "[They] are simply written . . . and . . . completely free from the slickness that comes from attending courses in Great Literature."

Truman Capote recommended this in *Antaeus*, Autumn, 1979.

Winslow, Anne Goodwin. *The Springs* (New York: Knopf, 1949) It is near the turn of the century, and a Southern girl and her family are caught up in the excitement surrounding the springs (waters suddenly discovered to have medicinal qualities) and a new summer hotel. Focusing on Alice and the effects of the commercial change on her and on the community, the story develops through several brief events that parallel the growth of the girl's consciousness. Diana Trilling has suggested that the novel is reminiscent of those by Henry James. "Its young heroine has the fragile durability of a James girl, and the construction of the hotel has the same import as the European experience in a James novel." Throughout Winslow's writings, much the same approach and style are employed: in verse, *Long Gallery* (1925), in fiction, *A Quiet Neighborhood* (1947), and in autobiography, *The Dwelling Place* (1943).

Jacques Barzun recommends these novels.

Wittlin, Josef. *Salt of the Earth.* *Translated from the Polish by Pauline DeChary* (London: Methuen, 1939) First published, 1935. In the early days of World War I, an unknown Polish soldier, an everyman of the armed forces, is called upon to go into battle. Covering only the first six weeks of the war, the novel has a deceptively simple style but a vivid effect. The Polish author concentrates on an intimate, usually ironic picture of the war. He is involved with the small events which determine the degree of success or failure of vast strategic military movements. The novel has extreme sympathy for downtrodden characters and a fine, compassionate means of expressing that emotion.

Mavis Gallant says, "I read it about ten years ago. . . .I'm apt to hang on to books I love, and I'm probably not aware of it when they fall out of print."

Wolf, Christa. *The Quest for Christa T.* *Translated from the German by Christopher Middleton* (New York: Farrar, Straus, 1971) First published, 1954. Charting the life of what appears to be an ordinary woman who grows up during World War II, goes to a university, marries and has children, the author appears to be writing a conventional novel. Not so. For after Christa T. dies at the age of thirty seven, the quest to discover her real life begins. Through letters, poems, diaries and dialogue it develops that her unassuming, unexceptional life was a mirror of the tragic times through which she lived. Her sobering glimpses of reality which contrast with the promise and fulfillment presumably offered by the future provide a necessary corrective to the optimism of the period. It is worth noting that the author is an East German, and for years the book was limited to only a small public by the government.

Virago Press is reissuing this work.

Woolf, Douglas. *Fade Out* (New York: Grove, 1959) Faced with being relegated to an old folks home, Mr. Twombly "fades out" of his middle-class life and hits the highway for an Arizona ghost town. The story concerns his cross country trip, accompanied by an ex-prize fighter. The bizarre events match the wildest surrealism found in any modern novel. An exceptionally fine balance is struck between depicting human behavior and eliciting humor, and the final victory of the old over their families and society makes this a truly inspiring novel.

Ronald Sukenick says, *"Fade Out* is a geriatric *Huckleberry Finn."*

Woolf, Leonard. *The Village in the Jungle* (London: Hogarth, 1913) Although today he is best known for his autobiography, Leonard Woolf's two novels deserve considerably more attention than they have been given. This, the first, is based upon his early experiences in Ceylon and concerns both the natives and the English civil servants. It is as sympathetic as it is intelligent, and the horror and the desolation of life in the jungle has rarely been better described.

Arthur C. Clarke writes, "Woolf wrote this novel after he had resigned from the Colonial Office and it was one of the first books he and Virginia published at the Hogarth Press. As an account of Ceylon village life at the beginning of the century it is unsurpassed (it is used as a textbook in the schools here [in Ceylon]) and many consider it superior to *A Passage to India.* (Forster encouraged Woolf in its writing.)

"It is a tragic (indeed, heartbreaking) account of the struggle of simple villagers to survive in the face of drought, disease, wild animals, and superstition—and even worse, the greed, corruption and indifference of their fellow men.

"I must declare my interest, as I took the role of Woolf in Lester James Peries' Sinhalese film of the book, *Beddegama* (the literal translation of the title.) It was shot on actual locations, including the courtroom at Hambantota on the south coast of Sri Lanka, where Woolf was Assistant Government Agent (and hence magistrate) in 1910. *Beddegama* has just been screened in London, Paris & the U.S; it will shortly be appearing on BBC TV. . . ."

Paul Theroux also recommends this book, as does Leon Edel who says, "Leonard Woolf's picture of life in rural Ceylon of his time, the marginal existence on the edge of the jungle, [is] as vivid and empathic a novel of 'survival' as any westerner has ever written about a way of life totally different from his own. It is a masterwork of its kind."

Wright, Austin Tappan. *Islandia* (New York: Farrar, Straus, 1942) There are certain underrated, neglected novels which appear time and time again on reading lists, gain a certain following, yet somehow never become well known. *Islandia* is a classic example, particularly among dedicated readers. (It is over one thousand pages long.) The name of the novel comes from the name of an imaginary continent in the South Pacific. On one side of a dividing range of mountains live the natives, on the other the white intellectuals. The divisions represent two obvious clashes of culture, and they are thoroughly explored through the eyes of John Lang, an American consul. While the novel sometimes suffers from oversimplification, the characters tend to be quite real. The work may have some faults, but it manages to rise above them.

Ursula K. LeGuin says, "*Islandia* of course is beloved by its lovers—but it ought to be taken more seriously as probably the finest American Utopian novel."

Wright, Patricia. *Journey Into Fire* (London: Collins, 1977) A former aristocrat, turned ardent communist, Konstantin helps to contain the Germans and later defeat the Whites during the Russian Revolution. He is elevated to the position of Red Army general and takes part in the collectivization of the 1920s as well as the 1930 purges. The episodic events are carefully detailed and the novel follows fact very closely. So closely that one sometimes has the sense of taking part in a living documentary. It is a stunning experience; one that is not to be missed.

Sybille Bedford writes, "An epic about the USSR from the 1917 revolution to post-World War II. Powerful, intuitive, harrowing—a truly extraordinary book going to the tragic roots of that unhappy country. It is not particularly well-written in any literary sense . . . yet it sweeps one along. I was deeply moved and shaken. Patricia Wright is an English scholar (history don) and novelist. Author of an excellent forerunner, a novel about nineteenth-century Russia seen through an English governess stranded there. . . .Both novels essential for anyone who wants to understand the horrors and tragedy of the USSR. The author even tackles Stalin head on. . . ."

Wright, Richard. *Lawd Today* (New York: Walker, 1963) Jake Jackson is a black postal clerk in Chicago. It is the time of the Depression and during the single day with which the novel is concerned, Jake tries to find a way out of his troubles. Primarily, they concern exasperating relations with his wife and his inability to cope with financial debts. The day, described in unsparing detail, focuses on the total frustration of a black man in a white society. This novel, published posthumously, was written before *Native Son* (1940).

Olivia Cole recommends this as well as Wright's other works.

Wright, Richard. *Uncle Tom's Children* (New York: Harper, 1938) Written two years before his well known *Native Son*, this is a collection of four short stories. It is Wright's first work and the conflict between whites and blacks in the South is its focus. There are accurate, sometimes painful accounts of racial hatred. The powerful prose and the vigorous attention to detail makes this a moving and historically important work.

Clancy Sigal recommends these stories.

Yates, Richard. *Eleven Kinds of Loneliness* (Boston: Little, 1962) The title describes the main theme of this collection of short stories. Almost without exception, the characters are fighting loneliness. The range of the fiction is broad and includes a wide variety of people in different social situations. In fact, each work nicely stands by itself, and while there is the theme of disappointment and need, the compassionate style makes each story a fresh discovery.

Gordon Lish recommends this volume.

Yates, Richard. *Revolutionary Road* (Boston: Little, 1961) Having lost interest in both his work and his marriage, Frank Wheeler decides to pack it all in and go to Paris. His similarly disappointed and bored wife agrees that the trip may save their marriage, and she is as anxious as Frank to find a way out of their suburban trap. The two constantly bicker and highlight the pain and emptiness of their financially secure way of life. While it is dramatic, this first novel is neither sensational nor far-fetched. In fact, the dialogue is brutally real and Yates' ear for conversation is brilliant. The excellence of the novel lies in the integrity with which the author depicts the disintegrating marriage.

William Styron says this is "a superb, moving first novel by one of our best and most-overlooked writers. It is a book which, in its way, is as well-shaped and perfect as an egg."

Yglesias, Rafael. *Hide Fox, and All After* (New York: Doubleday, 1972) In a situation faced by a number of young people, a fourteen-year-old boy strives to find himself among well-meaning teachers, parents, and friends. There are numerous memorable sections in this first novel, and it is unquestionably a landmark in the literature dealing with brighter-than-average adolescents. The author was only fifteen when he wrote this, and seventeen when it was published.

Young, Emily Hilda. *Miss Mole* (London: Cape, 1930) Miss Mole is a stereotype—the housekeeper in an English minister's home. As the story progresses and the reader learns how the efficient and kind Miss Mole keeps the family functioning, it gradually becomes obvious that she is more than typical. She is a fascinating and clear-sighted individual with a witty, happy perspective on life. Free from sentiment and with a fine appreciation for people and

their motives, the novel is as subtle in its character delineation as it is vivid in the delightful scenes of English life.

Virginia Clark writes that this is "better than Young's more acclaimed *William* (1931) or *Chatterton Square* (1947). . . . Hannah Mole is a strong and eccentric woman character of just the sort that appeals to women readers at present, but it is sad to have to recommend it solely as a 'woman's novel.' It wonderfully conjures up Bristol (called Clifton) and a whole host of characters and attitudes epitomising Britain between the wars."

Young, Marguerite. *Miss MacIntosh, My Darling* (New York: Scribner, 1965) Is Miss MacIntosh a deceptive creation of Vera Cartwheel, or is the dream of Miss MacIntosh the only reality? No matter, because the dream or the reality is a charming old woman who speaks in proverbs and axioms to her young friend. The setting is a baroque New England seaside house where Vera's mother languishes under an opium cloud. The sometimes nonlinear events and characters build toward a poetic climax. The lyrical skills of the author are strong enough to keep the whole, marvelous fabric of the story in place. In reviewing the book for *The New York Times*, William Goyen called it "one of the most arresting literary achievements in our last twenty years" and he termed it "a masterwork."

Yount, John. *The Trapper's Last Shot* (New York: Random House, 1973) A skillful interpretation of what it means to be trapped into a way of life while searching for possible means of escape, this novel is set in Georgia in the 1960s. It concerns two brothers. One wants to break away through education, while the other wishes to do it through returning to the land. Each leads the other into a firmer trap that holds them securely. Few writers have so well portrayed a modern, Southern, rural community for, paralleling the brothers' stories, we witness life in their vicinity during the civil rights movement.

George P. Elliott and Vance Bourjaily recommend this novel.

Yourcenar, Marguerite. *Memoirs of Hadrian.* *Translated from the French by George Frick* (London: Secker, 1955) The French-American author carefully documents the Roman emperor's life (76-138 A.D.). His story is told primarily in the form of a letter written by Hadrian to his grandson Marcus Aurelius. First published in France in 1951, this is one of the few historical novels often read by professional historians as well as lovers of fine literary art.

Jon Anderson recommended it in *Antaeus*, Winter, 1975.

Zhabotinsky, Vladimir. *Samson the Nazarite.* *Translated from the Russian by Cyrus Brooks* (London: Secker, 1930) First published, 1926. Samson is a man living on two planes. He is a severe Israeli judge who uses his strength to defend the weak. Yet, among the Philistines, where he spends much of his time, he is considered a *bon vivant* in a hedonistic society. The situation is resolved when the Philistines recognize Samson as a Jew and disarm him in the famous Biblical story. There are several messages running through this novel, but they in no way intrude into what is essentially a carefully developed plot.

S. J. Goldsmith said: "[Zhabotinsky] is remembered primarily as one of the finest journalists of his generation and a novelist of great stature" (*The Times*, July 12, 1980).

NONFICTION

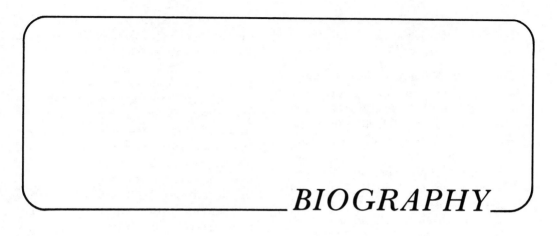

BIOGRAPHY

Aadland, Florence (with Tedd Thomey).
The Big Love (Los Angeles: Lancet, 1966)
Written by Thomey, the words are those of
Florence Aadland.

William Styron writes, "A camp masterpiece by the mother of Errol Flynn's
fourteen-year-old mistress, Beverly. Much
admired by W. H. Auden (among others), it
has been long out of print and deserves
resurrection."

Ackerley, J. R. *My Father and Myself*
(London: Bodley Head, 1968) A posthumous memoir, this concentrates on the author's libertine Edwardian father and the
contrasting style of his homosexual son.
Thanks to a remarkable means of expression, a sense of humor and a degree of self
mockery, this autobiography of the former
literary editor of the BBC's *Listener* magazine is a minor classic. Christopher Isherwood pronounced each of Ackerley's
books, including this one, to be "in a different way a masterpiece." Some notions of
the superlative flavor of the book may be
seen in the final sentences: "Of my father,

my mother, myself, I know in the end practically nothing. Nevertheless I preserve it,
if only because it offers a friendly, uncon-
ditional response to my father's plea. . .'I
hope people will generally be kind to my
memory.' "

Grove Koger recommends it.

Aiken, Conrad. *Ushant: An Essay*
(New York: Duell, 1952) The Pulitzer
Prize winner for poetry in 1929, Aiken, a
poet and a novelist, relates in this lesser
known autobiography what it means to be
a writer in America. The narrative is in the
third person and there are constant time
shifts. The prose style, which can be as inventive as it is sometimes confusing, is
concerned with what he calls "the soul's
landscape." The author retains a persistent
belief in the importance of creativity, and
has himself created what Mark Schorer
called "one of the most profoundly original documents to have come out of the
United States."

Malcolm Cowley, who recommends
this, considers it "one of the great Ameri-

can autobiographies," and Anthony Burgess terms Aiken "the most underrated American" writer.

Allingham, William. A Diary (London: Macmillan, 1907) This is an exceptionally fine book about literary life in London during the Victorian era. In diary form, the London magazine editor, who lived from 1828-1889, offers sketches and anecdotes about every well known person of the period. There is considerable talk about Lord Tennyson, a close friend, the Rossettis, and other Pre-Raphaelites. Allingham writes, too, about Carlyle, Emerson, Thackeray and Browning. There are instructive comments on general literary conditions and sketches of such nonartistic figures as the fighter Tom Sayers. The gusto, the obvious delight in gossip, and the joy of knowing just about everyone worth knowing makes this a great pleasure to read.

Roy Fuller calls this "marvellous Victorian literary chitchat."

Babb, Sanora. An Owl on Every Post (New York: McCall, 1970) The time is the eve of World War I. The place, a rugged area of Colorado. And the subject, the memory of the author's family's struggles to make a living in the Colorado wilderness. While there is a certain joy in their efforts, the notion of children learning to read from a single book and from old newspapers that cover the walls of their home gives the modern reader pause. The essence of the autobiography is an eloquent appreciation of family, the out-of-doors, and the individual.

Ann Stanford writes, *"An Owl on Every Post* is a beautifully told account of an adolescent and her family, who live in a dugout on the plains of eastern Colorado in the years just before World War I."

Baehr, Consuelo Saah. Report from the Heart (New York: Simon & Schuster, 1976) Hour by hour, what does it mean to be a suburban housewife with three chil-

dren? While the details are now familiar, the author gives her depiction a new twist. With uncanny skills of observation and a dry wit, she turns the usual domestic trivia into high, sometimes comic, drama. While the subject is deeply serious—the emotional and intellectual deprivation of a mother trapped in her home—the narrator appreciates that there is a certain amount of real joy in her routine and in her marriage. One may question the purpose, one may wallow in self-pity, while still appreciating the delight of one's vantage point. The balance between disillusionment and pleasure is as unusual as the author's clarity of vision and intelligent appreciation of paradox.

Susan Isaacs calls this "a simple, elegant report from a housewife who is neither mad nor blissful, a diary of a wife and mother. It is a special book because it is written with intelligence, passion, and considerable wit."

Bagger, Eugene. For the Heathen Are Wrong: An Impersonal Autobiography (Boston: Little, 1941) With the conscious intention of portraying both the political and the social events which led to the fall of France in World War II, Bagger perhaps unconsciously gives the reader an intimate view of the French way of life. Historian and philosopher, the author is also a brilliant stylist. The result is a book filled with challenging ideas and beautifully phrased epigrams.

R. F. Delaney recommends this.

Bagnold, Enid. Enid Bagnold's Autobiography: From 1889 (London: Heinemann, 1969) Published in America as *The Autobiography of Enid Bagnold* (Boston: Little, 1970). The English novelist and playwright surveys her life, her career, and the people she met in the course of eighty years. Replete with glamour and excitment, her experience is captured in her style, which haphazardly blends events, personalities, and startling adventures. A splendid memoir which seethes with energy, this book has a fabulous vitality.

Donald Hall recommends it, as does William Rossa Cole who says, "Bagnold was upper class: spirited, beautiful, talented; she knew all the English literary [society] in the 20s and 30s (lost her virginity to Frank Harris—and writes very amusingly about it), a wonderful, lively book."

Bannister, Roger. *The Four Minute Mile* (New York: Dodd, 1955) In 1954, the young Bannister, an English medical student, did the impossible. He ran a mile in less than four minutes. The author of this tribute to running, with spectacular effectiveness and a winning style, describes the moment of his great success and the background to its achievement.

Herbert Warren Wind writes, *"The Four Minute Mile* is an extremely good book. In this day and age, most books on sports are mediocre, but Bannister wrote his book himself, and it is one of the best descriptions of the joy, the burden, and the lure of running for those who do it seriously. Of course, the fact that Bannister was the first man ever to run the mile in under four minutes makes this book, in its field, a book of importance."

Barbellion, W. N. P. *The Journal of a Disappointed Man* (London: Chatto, 1919) Doomed to die at the age of thirty from an incurable disease, Barbellion (the pseudonym for Bruce F. Cummings) crammed fifty years of living into the last decade of his life. Living with brave intensity, the young English naturalist recorded his actions and emotions in one of the most poignant and moving personal journals ever written. In his introduction to the posthumous volume, H. G. Wells called this a work of "unpremeditated and exquisite beauty."

James Dickey recommended this as did Noel Perrin who wrote, "This journal is one of the great affirmations in our literature. If I had a friend who found life tedious, who was maybe even suicidal, and I had the power to make him read or her read one book it would be this soul stirring diary" (*The Washington Post Book World,* March 15, 1981).

Baring, Maurice. *The Puppet Show of Memory* (London: Heinemann, 1922) A truly modern man of letters, Baring (1874-1945) wrote essays, novels and poems and served as a diplomat and an editor. He came into contact with almost every major political and literary figure of his time. In this memoir, he moves effortlessly from Eton and Cambridge to Petrograd and Istanbul, and along the way portrays an extraordinary assortment of people and events. The comedy of the English diplomatic corps is contrasted with the intimate details of his home life and childhood reminiscences. As a record of a former style of living, this is fascinating.

Roy Fuller writes, "Remarkable childhood memories, not quite kept up to same standard in adulthood, by earlyish twentieth-century man of letters."

Beaglehole, J. C. *The Life of Captain Cook* (Stanford: Stanford University Press, 1974) Drawing upon the journals of Captain James Cook and Joseph Banks, the author weaves the story of one of the most exciting of all explorers. While meticulously tracing the voyages which took Cook around the world two and a half times, the narrative gives equal consideration to Cook's personal motivations, his judgment and massive talents which were disguised under a calm, almost bureaucratic, approach to the sea. A remarkable historian writing of a remarkable English gentleman, the result is a day-to-day seafaring chronicle which is an adventure of giant proportions.

Geoffrey Moorhouse recommended this in *Antaeus,* Winter, 1975.

Beauvoir, Simone de. *Force of Circumstance*. *Translated from the French by Richard Howard* (New York: Putnam, 1965) First published, 1960. In this third volume of her autobiography, the French author considers, among many subjects, her life with Jean Paul Sartre, the course of the Algerian war, and the literary personalities of the time. Her searching mind investigates both the philosophical and practical problems of an active woman's aging. Particularly impressive and informative is her detailed discussion of the methods liberals use to cope with anti-Communists, on the one hand, and Communists, on the other. Her wonderfully sensitive and rich prose gives the reader a sense of the total commitment the author has to life.

Joseph Chaikin recommends this volume.

Bolitho, William. *Twelve Against the Gods* (New York: Simon & Schuster, 1929) From Alexander the Great and Christopher Columbus to Casanova and Isadora Duncan, the thread of adventure is traced in a brilliantly woven biographical tapestry. The twelve biographies are brief, and there is not a dull one in the book. The conclusions are as credible as the documentation is accurate, and the result is a striking combination of history and dramatized portraiture.

Liz Smith recommends this.

Cardozo, Nancy. *Lucky Eyes & a High Heart: The Life of Maud Gonne* (Indianapolis: Bobbs, 1978) This sympathetic and moving biography is about the woman best known for her relationship with William Butler Yeats and her militant Irish nationalism. A heroine of some proportions, Maud Gonne's love life moved from a fixation with her father to an affair and a sordid, brief marriage. None of this was, however, as important to her as art and the Irish cause. We see in this portrait the

reason for her position as a major figure in Irish history. The author's research and enthusiastic, yet controlled, style gives the reader the best biography of Maud Gonne yet to be published.

Eugene Rachlis recommends it.

Carlyle, Thomas. *Reminiscences* (London: Longman, 1881) Actually, this is a fascinating collection of essays which adds up to a portrait of Carlyle's character. Written for himself, they contain personal reflections on the people closest to him who had recently died. The author offers vivid and acute portrayals of his father, James Carlyle, his wife, Jane Welsh Carlyle, and others. At the same time, he reveals much about himself, his deep attachment to these figures and his overwhelming sense of loss.

Roy Fuller calls this "arguably Thomas Carlyle's best book."

Cayton, Horace. *Long Old Road* (New York: Simon & Schuster, 1965) Cayton is a black sociologist and newspaperman who, over a long lifetime, knew many famous American writers. Here, he talks about them all, from Sinclair Lewis to Richard Wright. With wit and consummate style, he vividly portrays the condition of the black writer in America before the 1960s. And while this is about the quest for liberation, it is also about one man's search for intellectual independence.

David Reisman recommends this work.

Cecil, Algernon. *A House in Bryanston Square* (London: Eyre, 1944) A memoir about life and its meaning, primarily during the period before World War II, this represents a Catholic point of view. The work puts much stress on the meaning of the Catholic faith to an upper-class English person during the first part of the twentieth-century.

G. B. Harrison writes, "It is the spirited autobiography of a cultured aristocrat of ancient family and rare sensitivity, a wide reader of everything ancient and modern, but a book for an inner circle of people of like mind and temperament. Difficult to assess it in the usual critical theory or jargon; it is a communication in the depths. One can only compare it with some rare experiences or the first visit to Chartes, a red sunrise on Mount Kinchinjunga, a rare perfume, an unknown island full of scarce birds and flowers to which popular excursions should be strictly forbidden. Rereading it last night, I found it in parts deeply moving, and sadly prophetic. It should be on the same shelf as Montaigne's *Essays*, Burton's *Anatomy of Melancholy*, and *The Imitation of Christ. Not* suitable for the Reading List of English 2."

Chaplin, Ralph. *Wobbly* (Chicago: University of Chicago Press, 1948) The Industrial Workers of the World, known as the Wobblies, from 1906 to 1923 proved to be a colorful militant labor group. Their history and Chaplin's role in their movement is told by the author at the age of sixty two. While no longer a radical, Chaplin explains the attraction the Wobblies had for the idealists of their period. He describes as well the methods the group used to fight with violence equal to that of their foes, and how, eventually, they failed. The modesty and humor of the author enhances the vivid story of an important labor organization.

Ray Olson recommends this.

Chapman, Guy. *A Kind of Survivor: The Autobiography of Guy Chapman.* Edited by Storm Jameson (London: Gollancz, 1975) The title of this autobiography derives from the fact that Guy Chapman survived the First World War in which he served first as a member of the 12th Battalion of the Royal Fusilliers (from 1914 to the war's end) and after that in the Army of Occupation (until 1920). His experiences in the military are the most vivid and moving parts of this book. But he also writes effectively and nostalgically about his privileged middle-class childhood in Kensington and his careers after the war in publishing and finally in education as a historian. He was a particularly lively and stimulating personality, and these qualities come through in his writing.

Storm Jameson writes, "I gave up writing myself in 1974, when I had finished deciphering and putting into the best order I could the dishevelled mass of manuscript on which my husband, Guy Chapman, was still working until two months before he died in 1972. . . .It was not really completed, but it was published here [in England] and praised. . . ."

Chaudhuri, Nirad. *The Autobiography of an Unknown Indian* (New York: Macmillan, 1951) The author describes his growth and development in a small Bengali town, and reveals how he was influenced by his parents, their extended families and the chain of ancestral relations. While this is an autobiography, it is also a history of the nationalization of India and a startling response to it.

Paul Theroux recommends this.

Conroy, Frank. *Stop-Time* (New York: Viking, 1967) A moving excursion into the realm of childhood and youth, this is a documentary account of the author's perceptions of being young in America. Extraordinary as it is exciting, the autobiography moves from happy years spent in Florida to New York, back to Florida and finally to Europe. An achievement of both intellect and style, the remarkable volume is one of the finest evocations of growing up ever written. Stanley Kauffmann went so far as to say, "On its own level and scale, there are reminders of Wordsworth's *Prelude* in the book: discovery of the self en route to art" (*New Republic*, November 11, 1967).

Mary McCarthy recommends this.

Contreras, Alonso de. *The Life of Captain Alonso de Contreras [1582-1635]*. *Translated from the Spanish by Catherine A. Phillips,* (London: Cape, 1926) First published, 1905.

An audacious, bold and intrepid adventurer, Captain Contreras looked back on his life and wrote one of the few seventeenth-century Spanish autobiographies or memoirs. Ably translated and published in the twentieth century, it traces the man of action from his enlistment in the Spanish navy at the age of thirteen until, as a captain of a galleon, he is chasing Sir Walter Raleigh away from Puerto Rican waters. In between, he saw action in the infantry and the cavalry, killed both his wife and her lover, and for a time became a hermit. The careful and cool style of the memoirs, the almost complete lack of self-congratulation or pride in his checkered career, is as winning as the cruelty he depicts is appalling.

Geoffrey Household recommends this.

Crews, Harry. *A Childhood* (New York: Harper, 1978) What it means to grow up poor on a succession of Georgian farms in the 1930s and 1940s is the subject of this novelist in his "biography of a place." The "good old days" are not quite so good when they are viewed in terms of leaking roofs, half-empty plates, and constant backbreaking work. The loving family is contrasted with the faith healers, evangelists, and other poor dirt farmers. Told with candor and zest, the work is as much an accurate picture of a section of the American South before World War II as it is an autobiography of the immensely talented Mr. Crews.

Sam Shepard recommends this book.

Crowley, Aleister. *The Confessions of Aleister Crowley* (New York: Hill, 1970) Self-styled magician and saint of his own Gnostic Church, notorious for drug addiction and love affairs, Crowley is the hero of this fantastic life which is a peculiar mix of fact, fiction and other modes. The close to one-thousand pages leave out no detail as "The Beast," as he called himself, rambles all over the world in search of adventure. A surprising amount of space is given to his exploits as a mountain climber. Although the confessions lack any real sense of introspection or awareness of others, the book is exceptionally entertaining. It is full of surprises which hold the reader's attention even when Crowley is most undisciplined in his prose. He ended up, as Augustus John said, a nice old gentleman, and died in 1947 at the age of seventy two.

Paul Theroux recommends this.

Dahlberg, Edward. *Because I Was Flesh* (New York: New Directions, 1964) An unconventional autobiography by an American original, this work describes Dahlberg's life with his mother, a hairdresser by trade and an Eternal Woman by nature, and contrasts it with the years spent in a Jewish orphanage. He later rides the rails to California, and finally settles in New York. Much of his experience is incorporated in his novels and poems, but it is particularly vivid here. Frank MacShane described it as "an absolutely original contribution to American autobiography" (*New York Times Book Review*, May 29, 1964).

Fraser, Ronald. *In Hiding: The Life of Manuel Cortes* (New York: Pantheon, 1972) Just before the Spanish village of Malaga fell to the forces of Franco, the mayor went into hiding. That was in the 1930s. He did not emerge until 1969 when general amnesty was declared by the Spanish government. The absorbing, personal account of Cortes' activities and thoughts during those thirty years, which he spent hidden away in his own home, provide a study of courageous characters under extraordinary stress.

Philip Levine recommends this work.

Jameson, Storm. *Journey from the North* 2 volumes (London: Harvill, 1969, 1970) This autobiography begins with the writer's childhood in Whitby, Yorkshire, and covers her two marriages, the first, an anguish, and the second a success—with Guy Chapman, the distinguished historian. It also details the nature of British society during the early part of this century up to the 1960s. The characterization of the writer herself is startling and complex, and signifies a great deal about human ambition, human accomplishment, and human judgment.

Naomi Mitchison says, "Her autobiography . . . throws a lot of light on politics and social conditions in a less well known part of the United Kingdom. She is an outstanding writer and I, at least, think this is better than any of her novels. She is in her eighties but still very much alive."

Elaine Feinstein calls this "one of the finest and sharpest self-portraits ever set down, by a writer with a wide knowledge of Europe throughout the century, who is Yorkshire in her very bones."

Kauffmann, Stanley. *Albums of Early Life* (New Haven: Tickner, 1980) How does one become a world famous film critic? The *New Republic's* cinema reviewer reveals his path to success. He tried acting. Then he did some comic book editing. His early life is recounted in clear, sharp images as are his varied work experiences, which included such additional diverse jobs as hospital volunteering and play doc-

toring. The wit, humor and aesthetic perceptions complement the author's fine style.

Stanley Kauffmann recommends this.

Kilvert, Robert Francis. *Kilvert's Diary* 3 volumes (London: Cape, 1938-1940) This delightful, artistic diary was written by an English curate who was born in 1840 and became vicar of a small town on the Welsh-English border in the 1860s and 1870s. The author saw rural England with a clear eye and interpreted it with a simple yet luminous mind. The descriptions are as lucid as they are sensitive, and while Kilvert left little besides these pages, the diary is a literary experience of a pure and rare nature.

William Rossa Cole writes, "This lovely book was discovered by William Plomer, who has written an introduction. . . . Wonderful evocations of nature; touching entries about young girls he admired; humorous encounters with the parishoners. I note that a recent English guidebook has a whole section devoted to Kilvert Country."

Kingsmill, Hugh. *Frank Harris* (London: Cape, 1932) An intimate friend of Frank Harris, who was one of the world's greatest liars and literary geniuses, the author treats his subject with sly humor and satire. Harris, a British American, lived from 1856 to 1931, and gained lasting fame for his autobiography, *My Life and Loves* (1923-1927), and his uncanny ability as an editor. Later biographies have included more facts about Harris, but this early effort remains one of the most convincing, exciting and literate explanations of someone who was known as "an exasperating scoundrel." (*Note:* This was originally published under Kingsmill's pseudonym of H. K. Lunn.)

Michael Holroyd recommends this saying, "Hugh Kingsmill knew Frank Harris well, having been a youthful admirer of his first book on Shakespeare. This early admiration turned into disenchantment after working for Harris as an editor. The tone of this biography, expertly maintained throughout, is one of affectionate irony that seems to expose and to excuse his weakness—and by implication the weaknesses of us all."

Arthur Schlesinger, Jr. writes, "Hugh Kingsmill's *Frank Harris* is a model of essay-biography—efficient and exact in its delivery of information, unsentimental in its characterization, economical in its wit, and informed throughout by a delicious sense of irony. It is both very sad and very funny."

Lazarre, Jane. *On Loving Men* (New York: Dial, 1980) The novelist gives an intense account of her childhood attachment to her father, her adolescent loves, and her marriage. This relentlessly revealing autobiography traces her emotional development. Numerous political and psychological insights are incorporated into the work, along with a marvelous portrayal of her father. Her graceful style and compassionate, honest approach to her life makes this an unusual and riveting document of our times.

Jane Lazarre writes, "These autobiographical essays . . . are about sexual passion in a woman and its links to other passions—like the need for self-expression, or the need for autonomy." The author also recommends her novel, *Some Kind of Innocence* (New York: Dial, 1980).

Leiris, Michel. *Manhood*. *Translated from the French by Richard Howard* (New York: Grossman, 1963) First published, 1939. In the tradition of Rousseau, this French poet, anthropologist, and art critic traces his "journey from childhood into the fierce order of virility." As a confessional autobiography, this is a perfect

demonstration of the existential mode. The deepest feelings and experiences of the author are illuminated, and the sophisticated, often bizarre, style of living is surrealistic and compelling. As both a revelation about an artist and French society in the 1920s and 1930s, this is extraordinary.

Mark Strand recommended this in *Antaeus*, Autumn, 1977.

MacCarthy, Desmond. *Portraits* (New York: Putnam, 1931) Reflections on people he knew directly or through books, *Portraits* is one of the English literary critic's most fascinating works. Among those considered are Conrad, Disraeli, Goethe and Rossetti.

Evan S. Connell, Jr. writes, "MacCarthy did not write many books. *Memories* (1953) concerns literature: criticism, occasions, celebrities. *Humanities* (1954), except for two short stories, consists of dramatic criticism. Whatever else he wrote has been absolutely neglected. Yet he was . . . the last of a school of which Dr. Johnson was the first. . . . You must read *Portraits* with a pencil in hand because quite a few passages plead to be underlined, and there are splendid reasons for doing so. First . . . for your own enlightenment and satisfaction. But also, if you memorize enough of what you have underlined, you will very often be invited to supper" (*The Washington Post Book World*, February 21, 1982).

Mair, John. *The Fourth Forger: William Ireland and the Shakespeare Papers* (New York: Macmillan, 1938) This is an account of the man who was believed to be the fourth known forger of Shakespearean items, including such artifacts as a play and a mortgage deed. Ireland was famous when he was only nineteen years old, but completely discredited by the time he reached twenty one. He lived another forty years as a nonentity and since his death he has remained unknown. This biography effectively brings him back to life.

Mandelstam, Nadezhda. *Hope Against Hope.* *Translated from the Russian by Max Hayward* (New York: Atheneum, 1970) A two-part biography of her husband, the poet Osip Mandelstam, this is a magnificent picture of Russians over the past half century. Most of the celebrated poets and writers of the time appear in these pages, both before and after Osip Mandelstam's arrest and subsequent death in the 1937-1938 purges. Writing in *The National Review* (December 29, 1970), Guy Davenport said, "The beautifully paced plot of these memoirs in which digression and ancedote flow with rhythmic ease . . . is in itself an allusion to the brilliant school of writers in which Mandelstam was one of the most inventive."

Diana Trilling recommends this, saying, "A memoir of her life, and of her poet husband's death, under Stalin, this is one of the major books of this century, deserving of the same kind of attention that has been properly given to . . . say . . . Lincoln Steffens's *Autobiography.*"

And Joseph Alsop says, "Madame Mandelstam's book is the most beautiful and the most moving book that has appeared since the Second World War."

Martin, Frederick. *The Life of John Clare* (London: Macmillan, 1865) With the publication of *Poems Descriptive of Rural Life and Scenery* (1820), Clare became famous in England and throughout much of the world. Terming himself a "Northamptonshire peasant," the poet built an uneasy reputation. His fame dwindled by the time of his death in 1864. Martin perfectly develops the story of this remarkable English poet, and as a biography of a writer this has few rivals.

Charles H. Sisson writes, "Published in 1865, the year after Clare's death, by an author in touch with 'friends and admirers of the poet' and with access to a mass of letters and 'other original documents.' A narrative told with great personal sympathy and near enough to the time, place and people involved to make it irreplaceable. Extremely readable."

Maxwell, Gavin. *The House of Elrig*
(New York: Dutton, 1965) What it means to have too much wealth, too many benefits as a child and youth, is considered in this memorable autobiography covering the first seventeen years of a life spent first in Galloway and, later, at English boarding schools. As V. S. Pritchett wrote, "The attraction of this book is that it makes a spirited recovery of the past. He has grown out of his angers. Allowing for his being a special case, we can see that he records a lot of the common experience" (*New Statesman*, October 8, 1965).

Raymond Elgin recommends this.

Mehring, Walter. *The Lost Library: The Autobiography of a Culture.* *Translated from the German by Richard and Clara Winston* (London: Secker, 1951)

Bernard Levin writes, "The Library of the title was his father's; they lived in Vienna, and Mehring inherited it just before the Nazis marched in. He fled to the United States, and by a series of chances his library was packed up and sent to him. The book is, in effect, his thoughts as he unpacks and shelves it. The point is that his father was a man of deep liberal European culture; Heine was his great hero. And Mehring set himself to answer the question: how did the culture of Europe, which for his father enshrined all the virtues of mankind, succumb to the Nazis, who represented everything evil? His answer, conveyed in a book of fascinating literary, political and psychological analysis, is that we paid too much attention to the eighteenth century and its rationalism, too little to the nineteenth and its insights into evil. If his father had set more store by Baudelaire than Heine, things might have turned out differently. *The Lost Library* is a very serious and important contribution to an understanding of Western culture, but I have never met anybody else who has even heard of it, much less read it. The author, incidentally, died recently.''

Morley, Helena. *The Diary of Helena Morley.* *Translated from the Portuguese by Elizabeth Bishop* (New York: Farrar, Straus, 1957) First published, 1942. Barbara Howes writes, "We are indeed indebted to Elizabeth Bishop who, on going to Brazil in 1952, naturally asked people she met what books of note she should read. Many brought *Minha Vida de Menina*, (*My Life as a Young Girl*) by 'Helena Morley' to her attention, and it made such an impression she subsequently translated it into English. . . .

"The book concerns itself with Senhora Brant's (the real name of 'Helena Morley') young days growing up in Diamantina, a small provincial town in the state of Minas Gerais—as E. B. tells us, a state bigger than Texas. Helena Morley's father was English, and the two names she used are family ones. Her grandfather had come as physician to an English gold mining company and had stayed on, six of his eight children being born in Diamantina. H. M.'s father, Alexandre, however, mined diamonds by hand, or tried to, an exercise then similar to the panning of gold. If diamonds were found, the family prospered briefly, but it was in general a life of poverty and making do.

"The book, then, is made up of sketches, notes, brief compositions the child was encouraged in by her father, and also required by her school, to write, and these she came upon in later years, sorted out and had privately printed. Here are the brief obser-

vations, accounts, opinions of this young girl during her twelfth to fifteenth years, and a remarkably original and perceptive lot they are. A few examples will show their liveliness and variety. It was a fine time for a talented small being to be writing, as there she was, one might say, hovering on the borderline between child and grown-up, her child's sensibility making forays into the adult mind; by her fifteenth year, she had moved on to a somewhat darker apprehension of what life can be.

"Her mother has picked out Father Florencio to hear the children's confessions: 'He is very nice and gives very small penances, but we leave the confessional worn out with all the stories of the lives of the saints that he takes the opportunity of telling, and advises us to imitate. As if it were up to us. I decide for myself; I admire good and holy people but I can't possibly stop being the way I am. . . .' How true.

"Here is H. M. on the subject of her appearance: ' . . . I said that I knew I was homely but that it didn't bother me because Mama Tina (Negro nurse) had brought me up knowing that "The homely lives, the pretty lives, they all lives." When I said that . . . Ester exclaimed, "You homely? Just let me fix you up and you'll see." I agreed, and she got the scissors and cut my bangs and combed my hair, then she put rice-powder on my face and when I looked in the mirror I saw I wasn't homely at all. They laughed when I told them that what we do down here is to grease our hair with chicken fat to keep it plastered down. . . .'

"It is a radiant book, a dazzling pirouette on the edge of childhood, moving toward wisdom.

"Something should be said about the splendid job Elizabeth Bishop has done in her translation. This is a literary form often marred by sentimentality, linguistic ignorance, or simply by missing the right tone, but she has instead produced a wonder of bringing us the swift changes of pace and feeling, the lively intelligence so vividly apparent in H. M.'s journal."

Mozart, Wolfgang Amadeus. *The Letters of Mozart and His Family.* 3 volumes. *Translated from the German by Emily Anderson* (London: Macmillan, 1938) The abundant gaiety, humor and intelligence in these letters is rarely matched in literature, or captured in the history of music. Chronologically arranged, they provide a month-by-month account of the composer's life and that of his family from 1762 to 1800. All the extant letters of Mozart are included, as well as those of his father and mother, his sister and wife. The merit of Miss Anderson's translation and editing is that she retains the puns, the play on language, the alliteration and unusual spelling.

Emanual Ax calls this "invaluable reading for all musicians, and some of the most fun reading for everyone that I can think of. It would be wonderful to have these available again, especially at an affordable price."

Muir, Edwin. *An Autobiography* (London: Hogarth, 1954) A brilliant English poet describes the Scotland of his childhood and youth as well as his extensive travels in Germany, Italy and Austria. There are anecdotes about famous personalities, but the real strength is in the author's illuminations and moments of vision about himself and society. Muir's highly descriptive style equals that in the better known autobiographies of Yeats and Coleridge.

Donald Hall recommends this.

Mumford, Lewis. *Green Memories: The Story of Geddes Mumford* (New York: Harcourt, 1947) Elmer Newman writes, "With the literary grace and perception that is the hallmark of Lewis Mumford, we have here the story of Mumford's relationship with his son from the boy's early years until his tragic death on the Italian front in World War II. This is a neglected work of America's great man of letters."

Powys, John Cowper. *Autobiography* (London: Lane, 1934) "One of the greatest autobiographies of the English language," J. B. Priestly is reported to have said about this work. Powys, an English author and lecturer, shows his ability not only in drawing unforgettable characters, but also in relating his own character and many of his most personal thoughts and activities in this original treatment of himself as a fictional creation. This work is continually challenging and brilliant.

Denis Lane wrote that while Powys is well known in England, he is "now largely unknown in America, except among a coterie of devoted scholars. . . .For almost a quarter of a century Powys crisscrossed [America]" as a public speaker. His subject was culture. The *Autobiography* "represents a unique and impressive achievement."

Raverat, Gwen. *Period Piece: A Cambridge Childhood* (London: Faber, 1952) Recalling the delights of high Victorian life, the daughter of Charles Darwin's second son shows how charming it is to be surrounded by Cambridge faculty and other Darwins. It is an amazingly candid and accurate picture of Victorian English upper middle-class life.

Noel Perrin noted, "Besides writing the text, Mrs. Raverat drew and captioned about seventy-five illustrations, which come to have a life of their own. They exhibit the same positive delight in the absurdities of human life that the writing does, and the same child's-eye-freshness. If you were going to read only one book in your life about a group of Victorians . . . read *Period Piece*" (*The Washington Post Book World*, May 17, 1981).

Renard, Jules. *The Journal of Jules Renard.* *Translated from the French by Louise Bogan and Elizabeth Roget* (New York: Braziller, 1964) Renard was not only an early twentieth-century French writer, but a family man, a small town mayor, and a friend of the famous such as Andre Gide and Henri de Toulouse-Lautrec. In his journals, he records his gradual development from a young, unsophisticated man to a popular literary figure. While the journal is filled with epigrams, there are longer comments on people and events. Due to his sincere, honest nature and his sensitive observations, the diary is a trove of pleasures.

Louise Bogan, in the preface to this volume, observed that this journal had been almost totally neglected in England and America. Still, "critical praise of a high order has been tendered the author over the years. Albert Thibaudet in 1927 named Renard's *Journal* . . . along with Gide's *Si le grain ne meurt*, as incontestably the two autobiographical masterpieces of the twentieth century. . . .The final impression received from the *Journal* is one of delicacy backed up by power—power of character and power of intellect."

Rukeyser, Muriel. *Willard Gibbs* (New York: Doubleday, 1942) Rarely has the imaginative side of science and scientists been more appreciated than in this sensitive, skillful biography of a nineteenth-century Yale professor and genius in the field of thermodynamics. As a poet, Rukeyser offers a new dimension and interpretation to scientific accomplishment. She finds in Gibbs a perfect example of the characteristic American search for unity.

Linking the experiences of Gibbs with those of other great figures, including Herman Melville, Walt Whitman, Henry Adams and William James, the author provides a necessary bridge between the artistic and scientific cultures.

Marchette Chute calls this "a biography of a too-little-known American told with strength and poetry."

Russell, Osborne. *Journal of a Trapper: Or Nine Years in the Rocky Mountains* (Portland: Oregon Historical Society, 1955) A member of Wyeth's Columbia River Fishing and Trading Company, Russell took an active part in the discovery and exploitation of the West during the nineteenth century. He kept a meticulous journal of his activities which ranged from fur trapping to politics. A man of exceptional intelligence and imagination, he created a work which is unmatched among the scores of such journals written by early settlers.

Edward Hoagland calls this the "best mountainman's journal I know."

Sackville-West, Victoria. *St. Joan of Arc* (Garden City: Doubleday, 1936) Bringing to her biography of St. Joan the verve and imaginative understanding of a fine novelist, Sackville-West offers a model of this genre. On the one hand, the scholarship and research are impeccable; on the other, she manages to breathe life into St. Joan so that she lives as a dramatic character in a tragic, historical romance.

Raymond Elgin recommends it.

Scott, Geoffrey. *Portrait of Zélide* (New York: Scribner, 1925) Denied the career her natural wit and precocious intelligence suited her for, the eighteenth-century Zélide was forced to marry a dull and considerably less talented husband.

Before her nuptials, she was wooed by James Boswell, but apparently her forthright nature defied even his conception of the role of a wife. Later on, she inspired Benjamin Constant as well as numerous other famous people. Between the documentation, the author is able to capture the subtle temperament of Zélide. This brilliant woman's erratic life finally outpaces the most dramatic fiction.

Francis Steegmuller recommends it.

Seager, Allan. *The Glass House* (New York: McGraw, 1968) As much a discourse on the genesis of his poetry as it is on the life of the poet Theodore Roethke, this biography is a classic of its type. Seager gives a detailed account of his friend's sometimes tragic life and fills his book with unobtrusive documentation. This is a rich and superlative portrait of a great American poet.

Donald Hall recommends this.

Segal, Lore. *Other People's Houses* (New York: Harcourt, 1964) At the age of ten, Lore Segal left Vienna for England—a Jewish child in flight from the Nazis. "Other people's houses" is a reference to the numerous places she lived in England, the Dominican Republic and later in New York where she was married. The linked sketches of people, places and events results in a substantial narrative account of what it means to be a refugee, and, more particularly, an uprooted child developing through a succession of transitory experiences. The precise evocation of the child discovering other cultures, especially that of the English, is as rewarding as the author's obvious, yet unsentimental, courage.

Cynthia Ozick writes, "Lore Segal's *Other People's Houses* achieved a certain celebrity through being published, in sections, in *The New Yorker*, and it remains, I think, a basic document essential to an understanding of the history of Europe under Hitler. Beyond that, it is an absorbing and highly intelligent commentary on childhood and unexpected changes. . . ."

Simpson, Louis. *North of Jamaica* (New York: Harper, 1972) The son of a Scottish farmer and a Russian mother, the young poet describes how he is brought up in Jamaica to be the prototype of the average English boy. The parents divorce; Simpson is given a strange education, and eventually he leaves for New York at his mother's request. In the second part of the autobiography, he discusses his career, his return to Columbia University after the war, and the inevitable journey to Paris. The highlight of the book, however, is his early years, although the final part includes excellent discussions of poets and poetry. The reflections on Robert Bly and Saul Bellow are outstanding.

Donald Hall recommends this.

Steegmuller, Francis. *Cocteau* (Boston: Little, 1970) Cocteau (1889-1963) spent most of his life in the arts as, among other things, poet, filmmaker and novelist. The author takes the reader with grace and style through the life of this complex personality. While never ignoring Cocteau's limitations as a person or an artist, Steegmuller sharpens the focus on his portrait of a fascinating individualist.

Julia Child writes, "I suppose the main reason this book has been neglected in America is that Cocteau is not really known in this country. He was an extremely important figure in French literature, art, music, theatre, and also an extremely flamboyant character. Steegmuller did enormous research on this book and has written a very lively account of Cocteau and his peculiar personal life as well as his really great importance in the French scene from the very beginning—which for him was the first of the great Russian ballets in Paris, on up to his inauguration in the French Academy, and finally his death, which wasn't so many years ago."

Strong, George T. The Diary of George Templeton Strong. 4 volumes. Editors Allan Nevins and Milton Thomas (New York: Macmillan, 1952) A fascinating view of American urban life during much of the nineteenth century can be discovered in this diary. A founder of the Columbia University Law School, Strong proved to be an enthusiastic New Yorker. From the age of fifteen, in 1835, until his death in 1875, he kept a four-million-word diary which is magical in its ability to transport the reader back to the time it was written.

Noel Perrin says, "Strong loved to imagine what New York would be like a hundred or even a thousand years after his time. Once as a young man, he imagined his descendants in the far-off twentieth century thumbing through the diary. They would believe it, he decided 'a queer old journal . . . that nobody could read through, but which contains curious illustrations of old times.' Curious, wonderful, and intensely real" (*The Washington Post Book World*, September 20, 1981).

Symons, Julian. A. J. A. Symons (London: Eyre, 1950) The subject of this intimate biography is best known for his study of the eccentric author Frederick Rolfe, in *The Quest for Corvo* (1934). In private life, A. J. A. Symons was an imaginative liar, bibliographer, gastronome and dandy. No one, for example, could be quite sure of his family history. He changed its genesis from situation to situation, although his brother, the author of this book, does divulge the actual background of his subject and explains the reasons for his sibling's concealment. Despite A. J. A. Symons' love for material things, he proved an attractive romantic and the perfect biographer for Corvo. His megalomaniac self-importance brought him some misery, yet it resulted in his becoming a compelling personality.

Roy Fuller says, "Gripping delineation of a remarkable character . . . by his brother. An early work by a writer who has become a noted critic and crime-novelist."

Talbot, Toby. A Book About My Mother (New York: Farrar, Straus, 1980) Here is a portrait of an archetypal, nurturing, independent Jewish mother. The drama derives from the death of this plain and strong woman in her seventy-fourth year. Her daughter enters a period of deep mourning, and from her grief comes this compassionate, beautiful story of a mother-daughter relationship. These life-affirming portrayals avoid sentimentality and pathos. The author's preoccupation with trying to understand her mother and herself results in the depiction of almost any essential relationship. It is a celebration of love.

Susan Isaacs says, "This is a book by an ordinary woman which is extraordinary. It is a lament for the author's mother, and it evokes, brilliantly, a life that was and illuminates a life that is."

Trollope, Anthony. Autobiography (Berkeley: University of California Press, 1946) First published, 1882. Rarely has such a successful author told so much about the craft of writing as Trollope does in these candid memoirs. His sturdy business attitude in regard to the economics of writing did much to harm his reputation, although by then he was dead. (The autobiography was published a year after his death.) The outspoken character of this book is matched by Trollope's typical, brilliant writing.

Russell Baker recommends this, saying, "The *Autobiography* of Anthony Trollope . . . I believe is the finest book ever written on the mechanics of writing and has the best advice ever published on how to be a writer. This book ought to be a standard required text for every college department of writing, yet it is almost impossible to find except in antique shops.''

Walburga, Lady Paget. *In My Tower* 2 volumes (London: Hutchinson, 1924) The author, a German-born aristocrat, moves with her husband, Sir Augustus Paget, in the highest circles of English society. Insights into the lives of the wealthy in the late nineteenth century are plentiful in the diary. For Lady Paget cannot escape the social whirl even when she retreats to a tower, opulently refurbished of course, above Florence for the purpose of appreciating the simple (though very costly) pleasures of life. Purple prose coupled with social insensitivity and aesthetic arrogance makes this, in the words of Quentin Bell, "a masterpiece of unconscious humor."

Wells, H. G. *Experiment in Autobiography* 2 volumes (London: Gollancz, 1934) A frank portrayal of an extraordinary writer who drew material from, and helped to shape thinking in, both the nineteenth and twentieth centuries, this deals with Wells who lived from 1866 to 1946. This "experiment" is a major literary treatment not only of his climb to fame but also of people and events of his time. Wells knew most of the famous, and he is quick to point out their glories and their faults. The book includes his ideas on politics and society as well, and he concludes the work with his notion of the ideal world. Few autobiographies have been so interesting in so many different ways.

Alex Colville recommended this in *Saturday Night,* May, 1976.

Yeats, John Butler. *Letters to His Son W. B. Yeats and Others 1869-1922* (London: Faber, 1944) Artist, raconteur, philosopher and critic, Jack Yeats spent long hours recording his thoughts in letters to his son and to friends.

Lord Dacre of Glanton (Hugh Trevor-Roper) writes, "As is clear from the title, J. B. Yeats was the father of the poet W. B. Yeats. He was a marvellous letter writer, he wrote beautifully and his letters dealt with every conceivable question of literature, art, England, Ireland, and the whole range of human interest. I think they are wonderful letters, and of course they have a special interest since they come out of that very civilised Anglo-Irish world of the time, and are largely addressed to a famous poet."

LITERATURE

Auerbach, Erich. _Mimesis_. _Translated from the German by Willard R. Trask_ (Princeton: Princeton University Press, 1957) First published, 1953. The study of mimesis involves examining the imitation of life in art. In this case, the focus is on Western literature. The work opens with the professor and critic closely analyzing passages from Homer and the Bible. He then explicates portions from the works of such writers as St. Francis and Dante, Virginia Woolf and Proust. His remarkable knowledge of history, sociology, art and politics combines to produce a work in the finest modern European tradition of criticism. Delmore Schwartz believed "the compass and the richness of the book can hardly be exaggerated" (_New York Times_, November 29, 1953). By now, _Mimesis_ is a classic of literary analysis, yet it is not that well known among the general public.

James Michener calls this "the best book on the problems of narration."

Balakian, Nona. _Critical Encounters_ (Indianapolis: Bobbs, 1978) This is a collection of thirty-eight book reviews and es-says, by a writer for _The New York Times Book Review_, which is nicely prefaced with an overview of the world of American literature for the past twenty-five years. The argument is that book reviews can be a major literary form, a source of insight for the general reader and the scholar. While primary focus is on the American novel, attention is also given to poetry, drama and criticism. Highly articulate without being academic, the essays are written in a fine conversational style. Joyce Carol Oates said it is "one of those rare books of which it can be said: one does wish it longer" (_New Republic_, May 20, 1978).

Eugene Rachlis recommends it.

Barfield, Owen. _Poetic Diction: A Study in Meaning_ (London: Faber, 1928) Writing with the same passion and color as the poetry he explicates, the English critic explains and defends his thesis. "There are two important functions which poetry is there to perform. One of them is . . . the making of meaning, which gives life to language and makes true knowledge possible. And this it does inasmuch as it is the vehicle of imagination. The other, lying much nearer the surface of life, is to mirror, not necessarily by approving, the characteristic response of the age in which it is written." Barfield is a compelling writer who emphasizes the emotional, metaphorical content in poetic diction.

Richard Wilbur recommends this work, adding that other books by Barfield are also worthy of examination. He mentions *Saving the Appearances*, which is a finely argued theory of perception and knowledge.

Bespaloff, Rachel. On the Iliad. *Translated from the French by Mary McCarthy* (New York: Pantheon, 1948) In reviewing these essays on Homer's *Iliad*, the translator and critic Robert Fitzgerald said, "This book is about the best thing I have ever read on the art of Homer and unless you have tasted the poem in Greek, Mme. Bespaloff will serve better than the translations to convey how distant, how refined an art it was" (*New Republic*, April 26, 1948). As a brilliant and evocative analysis of a classic work of literature, this has few rivals, and the author's style approaches the majesty of her material.

Blackmur, Richard P. Language as Gesture (New York: Harcourt, 1952) A leading American literary critic addresses himself primarily to twentieth-century poetry in this collection of essays. A thoughtful, highly learned and brilliant observer, Blackmur's views are as original as his presentation is compelling.

Edmund Keeley writes, "*Language as Gesture* is perhaps the most important work of purely literary criticism produced by an American critic in this century."

Burroughs, William. The Job (New York: Grove, 1970) In a series of interviews, the author of *The Naked Lunch* explains the purpose behind his Bosch-like land-scapes. A devoted anarchist and drug enthusiast, Burroughs is the antitype of the American hero. His intellectual brilliance and biases are never more apparent than in these detailed discussions concerning his friends and his milieu.

Allen Ginsberg recommended this in *Antaeus*, Autumn, 1975.

Chute, Marchette G. Geoffrey Chaucer of England (New York: Dutton, 1946) A lucid introduction to the life and times of Chaucer, this is particularly impressive since the author ably constructs an amalgam of biography and literary analysis. Chute's deceptively simple style carries the reader into the center of English political and social history, making it read like a continuing and current series of events. And while she never loses sight of Chaucer, she is equally involved with the course of English history.

Isaac Bashevis Singer recommends this.

Connolly, Cyril. Enemies of Promise (London: Routledge, 1938) What is required to prepare oneself for the literary life? And, after all, is it really a worthwhile pursuit? About midway through his own literary life, Connolly set down his thoughts on these subjects. He begins with a discussion of contemporary writing, moves on to the pitfalls which face young writers, and concludes with his own Georgian boyhood, in a year-by-year account of his experiences at Eton. Both a warning and an encouragement, the study is as engaging as it is idiosyncratic. Above all, the author is a perfectionist who expects the same from life . . . and other writers.

James Atlas writes, "I'm not sure if this book qualifies as overlooked, since it still has quite a reputation, but I've never seen it in print. It is a vivid memoir of the author's own youth and a wry account of the perils of the literary vocation."

Elliott, George P. Conversions: Literature and the Modernist Deviation (New York: Dutton, 1971) In evaluating the essays of Elliott, Stanley Edgar Hyman noted that he pioneered a new approach to literary criticism, that of criticism by autobiography and parable. Here both approaches are illustrated. Published between 1964 and 1971, the essays cover a wide variety of subjects from pornography and the teaching of writing to modern art and Tolstoy.

Lore Segal writes, "I recommend to the reader who does not want to lose the books that matter the work of the late George P. Elliott. He was a 'man of letters,' who wrote novels, short stories, poetry, essays. His style of writing and thinking fell out of style in his lifetime but a steady readership persists in admiring the work and the man. His most famous—that is to say most anthologized—story *Among the Dangs* fascinated the sixties. In it, a black anthropologist's studies take him through a religious trance: it sends him back home. Elliott's novels are uncompromisingly thoughtful, argumentative and perhaps his least successful work, but read *In the World* about marriage, and about goodness and find what you've always suspected: the good is quite as complicated as the bad or the unhappy. His essays (like Plato's) intersperse thought with scenes from experience so that each illuminates each; here are, perhaps, George Elliott's most extraordinary and eloquent productions."

Ford, Ford Madox. The March of Literature (New York: Dial, 1938) A relaxed and entertaining yet authoritative overview of literature, this proceeds from ancient Egyptian writings to the fiction of Ernest Hemingway. With a boldness reminiscent of H. G. Wells' history of the world, Ford is as biased as he is secure in his aesthetic selections. Written for the average reader, this literary history succeeds in communicating its author's exhilarated appreciation of reading. Ford always keeps in clear view his sense of what masterly writing should be.

Gilbert Sorrentino writes, "Ford's mammoth, encyclopedic, idiosyncratic 'history' of world literature from Confucius to the classic moderns. Replete with brilliant opinions and rich with examples, it is unique in its field, a private seminar in comparative literature."

Ginestier, Paul. The Poet and the Machine. *Translated from the French by Martin Friedman* (Chapel Hill: University of North Carolina Press, 1961) First published, 1954. The influence on poetry of the material progress of society is the theme. Employing psychoanalytic techniques, the author offers an outline of a method of literary aesthetics.

X. J. Kennedy writes, "*The Poet and the Machine* . . . is one of the most intriguing critical books I've seen. A French critic of high originality, Ginestier offers a profound idea: in attempting to encompass the machine and industrialism in modern poetry, recent poets are seizing upon the same powerful, archetypical images that classical poets seized in writing of gods and colossuses."

Greene, Thomas. Rabelais: A Study in Comic Courage (Englewood Cliffs: Prentice-Hall, 1970) After a fascinating background chapter, the study turns to a discussion of the works Rabelais wrote between 1532 and 1553. The importance of those works to subsequent literature and the clues they give to the development of Western thought are brilliantly outlined. The author probes "the problem of the fertile, exasperating conjunction of 'serious' and 'comic'" modes. The elegance of Greene's style conveys some of the magnificence of Rabelais' work.

Donald Frame recommends this.

Holmes, John Clellon. *Nothing More to Declare* (New York: Dutton, 1967) In a thorough analysis of the Beat movement and its adherents, Holmes explains the literary, social and political attributes of its loosely knit members. The author's creative abilities, obvious in his short stories and novels, are used graphically to depict the Beats from their inception through to their decline.

William Harrison recommended this in *Antaeus*, Winter, 1975.

James, Henry. *The Notebooks of Henry James.* Edited by F. O. Matthiessen and Kenneth B. Murdock (New York: Oxford University Press, 1947) In his own words, James explains the purpose, scope and, once in a while, the mystery of many of his writings. These are the working notes for most of his novels and short stories, supplemented with useful and intelligent commentary by the compilers. The notebooks cover the period from November, 1878, through May, 1911. There are several additions as well, including project notes for *The Ambassadors*. Altogether, there are 418 pages of sheer joy for devotees of the Master.

François Truffaut recommended this in *Antaeus*, Autumn, 1979.

Knight, G. Wilson. *Lord Byron's Marriage: The Evidence of Asterisks* (London: Paul, 1957) The historical principle of covering up one vice with another is used by critics of Byron, claims Knight. His argument is that Georgian society preferred to believe in incest between Byron and his half sister rather than in the poet's homosexual tendencies. The incest argument is frequently based upon a series of Byron's letters. Knight's argument derives from two major sources: the asterisks in those same letters (hence, the title of the book) and, to a lesser extent, an interpretation of the poetry itself. Knight's response to former critics of Byron results in his painting a fearless, fascinating portrait of his subject.

Frederic Raphael says this is " . . . a good instance of ingenious hagiography (no prizes for identifying the hag)."

Lawrence, D. H. *Fantasia of the Unconscious* (New York: Seltzer, 1922) A fascinating effort is made by Lawrence to explain systematically the philosophy which governs his novels. At some levels, this work is generally instructive, based on Lawrence's wide readings. Much of it, however, is grounded solidly in his own imagination and recapitulates his views of men and women and his insights into philosophy and his art. The style is delightful, and the psychoanalytical material easily understood.

Robert Bly recommends this.

Leavis, Queenie. *Fiction and the Reading Public* (London: Chatto, 1932) The reading public considers "a book" a synonym for "a novel," and most people read a novel for entertainment and relief from daily activities. The result is a less-than-critical approach to fiction. Indeed, the reading public has a willingness to accept any type of trash which is easy and exciting to read. The author traces the development of popular taste and the probable size of the reading public in England in the early 1930s. Her methodology is still useful, and her conclusions comparatively sound. But the essential notion that the reading public may be neatly divided into lowbrow, middlebrow and literary types is open to question. Still, it is a pioneer work in the study of what people read.

Mowatt, Anna Cora. *Autobiography of an Actress: Or Eight Years on the Stage* (Boston: Fields, 1853) Married at the age of fifteen to a wealthy New York lawyer, the author had the good fortune to have a loving husband who helped further her education and career, which began when she was seventeen and published her first story in verse. When her husband's wealth declined, she took up writing for magazines, and reached real success with her play *Fashion* in 1845. Although no longer worth reading, it turned its author into an actress, and she was on the New York stage from 1845 to 1854. It is this career which she chronicles in one of the earliest, one of the best autobiographies of the acting profession in America.

Nowotiny, Winifred. *The Language Poets Use* (New York: Oxford University Press, 1962) In a clear, nontechnical fashion, the author shows how to analyze the content, meaning, style and other facets of a poem. The lucid approach is considered a model of literary criticism, and it increases the reader's enjoyment and respect for the complexity of poetry.

Fred Levinson recommended this in *Antaeus*, Winter, 1975.

O'Connor, Flannery. *Mystery and Manners* (New York: Farrar, Straus, 1969) One of America's most brilliant short story writers explains her themes and characters, at least in a general way. Here is her philosophy of the art of fiction writing, the central theme of which is an imprecation to readers to accept the authors and their stories for what they are. This work provides a fine insight into the mind of a creative genius, and gives some new perspectives on her art.

Aaron Asher recommends it.

Roth, Philip. *Reading Myself and Others* (New York: Farrar, Straus, 1975) The author of *Goodbye, Columbus* and *Portnoy's Complaint* turns to his first work of nonfiction, a collection of essays and interviews. The work is remarkable because the author treats himself as though he were a stranger and, interviewing himself, answers questions about his work and his character. The second half of the book consists of essays which successfully explain the position of Roth and his literature in the context of American Jewish culture and Jewish stereotypes.

Aaron Asher recommends this volume.

Routley, Erik. *The Puritan Pleasures of the Detective Story* (London: Gollancz, 1972) While describing another fan, the author could be describing himself—"a profoundly learned and experienced connoisseur of detective stories." As a record of what he reads in bed, the compilation opens with Sherlock Holmes, moves on to the classics (John Thorndyke to Father Brown), and ends with enthusiastic, though lesser tributes to "puritans and romantics" such as the writers John Dickson Carr and Georges Simenon. There is a brief section on American authors and two concluding chapters which serve as a justification of the detective genre. Edmund Wilson, who hated detective stories, might not be swayed by the arguments, but the average reader will be delighted and instructed. In his preface, Routley comments, "I simply do not see how anybody can fail to get some sort of perverse pleasure out of this book." Agreed.

Virginia Clark writes that this should "rank with Julian Symons's *Bloody Murder* (1972; title in the United States *Mortal Consequences*, 1972) or Colin Watson's *Snobbery with Violence* (1971) as one of the truly readable, thoughtful looks at its genre before the waves of 'scholarly' popular culture studies broke. Alas, Routley has never found an American publisher. In an alter ego, he is an outstanding organist and Anglican church music scholar."

Said, Edward. *Joseph Conrad and the Fiction of Autobiography* (Cambridge: Harvard University Press, 1966) This is a brilliantly written study of Conrad's philosophy of life as reflected in his letters and shorter works of fiction. The focus is on psychological criticism, and numerous insights are glimpsed beneath the surface of Conrad's glittering rhetoric.

Christo recommends this as well as Said's other works, including *Arabs and Jews* (1974), *Beginnings* (1976), *Orientalism* (1978) and *Literature and Society* (1980).

Schutze, Martin. *Academic Illusions In the Field of Letters and Arts* (Chicago: University of Chicago Press, 1933) Critical of the objective, scientific analysis of literature, a professor of German literature calls on teachers to adopt a new, humanistic approach. His comments are concerned with the theories current in the academic study of literature in the 1930s. He then moves on to explain his own carefully conceived concepts about the nature of literary art and what it really means to appreciate and understand its value.

Lionel Trilling recommends it.

Sewell, Elizabeth. *The Orphic Voice* (New Haven: Yale University Press, 1960) Linking poetry to the mind's awareness that order in the world is part of its own making, the poet and critic traces the history of imagination and myth. She considers the work of Bacon, Goethe, Rilke, Shakespeare, Erasmus, Darwin, Wordsworth, Linnaeus, Hugo and others who help her develop her theme. Orpheus comes into this because "Orpheus is poetry thinking about itself, and every significant mention of Orpheus by a poet or scientist may bring the working methods a little nearer the surface."

George Steiner wrote, "As one lays down the book, the intricate argument and the evidence offered by Miss Sewell's own poems begin resounding inside one like remembered music. It is a great work" (*Nation*, February 4, 1961).

Smith, James. *Shakespearian and Other Essays* (Cambridge: Cambridge University Press, 1974) This is one of the best and most complete studies of Shakespeare's comedies. The prose style is remarkable for its vigor and imaginative use of illustrative metaphors. The dozen essays, written in the 1930s and 1940s, display great erudition. Smith's analyses are highly individualistic, and never more so than in his primary contention that Shakespeare's tragedies and comedies are closely linked. He manages to connect disparate characters convincingly in order to prove his point, and his views are always stimulating.

Roy Fuller recommends this, saying that it is "literary criticism of the highest order."

Sperry, Willard. *Wordsworth's Anticlimax* (Cambridge: Harvard University Press, 1935) After 1808, the English poet seemed to have peaked in his creativity and started on a downhill course. It is Professor Sperry's belief that there is a clear explanation for this failure. Not only does he explain and justify his theory, but in the process elucidates other factors which might explain the poet's period of decline.

Sanford Friedman says this is "one of the very few studies I know of a great writer written by a writer equal to his subject."

Strand, Mark. *The Monument* (New York: Ecco Press, 1978) In some fifty short prose passages, the poet offers thoughts on as many subjects in the course of playing a sophisticated literary game. The subjects range from rationales for writing to the mystical and puzzling fusions of life and poetry. In section thirty, he pays a lovely tribute to Elizabeth Bishop and her poem "The Monument." All this is set within a fictitious context—a writer, in the midst of a translation of his work, is communicating with a translator from a future age. As a game with substance, this is great fun to read.

Daniel Halpern recommends it.

Williams, Charles. *The English Poetic Mind* (Oxford: Oxford University Press 1932) As the poetic mind matures, it passes through certain recognizable stages which tend to conclude in catastrophic disillusionment. Yet, the true genius survives this stage. While *The English Poetic Mind* is under two hundred pages, it contains a subtle and rewarding analysis of the creative process. The thoroughness of the study is apparent, particularly in its treatment of the minor poets and in its understanding of Shakespeare, Milton and Wordsworth.

Christopher Fry writes, "It contains insights of a kind not to be found in any other critical work that I know of. Its chapters on The Cycle of Shakespeare, Milton, and Wordsworth fascinated me when I first read the book, and, whenever I have dipped into it since, still do. It has always seemed to me a great pity that a paperback edition was not available for students."

Wolfe, Thomas. *The Story of a Novel* (New York: Scribner, 1936) Wolfe's description of how he came to write *Look Homeward, Angel* is a revealing self-analysis of the germination of his idea and the methods he employed while writing the novel. His constant fear of failure is echoed throughout the book, and he also discusses the final, drastic editorial alterations. It is an appealing profile of an author at work.

Cynthia Buchanan recommended this in *Antaeus*, Winter, 1975.

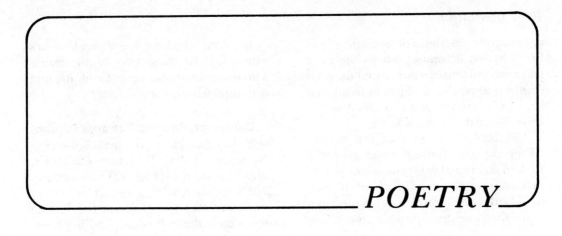

Adams, Leonie. *Poems: A Selection* (New York: Funk, 1954) "[A] poet who should be on your list [of unjustly neglected works] is certainly Leonie Adams," writes John Unterecker. "Though no collected poems was ever issued, a skimpy selected poems came out in the fifties. The list of poets who learned their trade through study of the works of Leonie Adams (or through study with her) could go on for pages. Theodore Roethke considered her one of the great poets of his time, and Louise Gluck would be a far different poet than she is had she not been taught by Adams. Difficult and a bit crabbed, the poems are charged with the same brilliance that one finds in the best of Hopkins and Dickinson. It is extraordinary to see that she is no longer anthologized. Though her total body of work (like Elizabeth Bishop's) is very small, it is uniformly thrilling. It has the power that the very greatest poetry has. Eventually, one hopes, she will be rediscovered and properly celebrated."

Ann Stanford also recommends Leonie Adams's poems.

Anderson, Jon. *In Sepia* (Pittsburgh: University of Pittsburgh Press, 1974) A third collection, and in some ways the most successful, these poems are by an extraordinary poet. The subject matter is familiar, running from death to compassion and grace. What makes the collection noteworthy is the extreme credibility of the poems and the lyrical innocence of the style.

Daniel Halpern recommends this.

Austin, Mary. *American Rhythm* (New York: Harcourt, 1923) John R. Milton writes, "The first third of Austin's book is a long essay on rhythm, or, more specifically, what she identifies as the American rhythm. The rest of the book is a collection of Amerindian songs, reexpressed from the originals. Austin has received credit, justly, for making the Indian songs available. But the essay, often ignored, is even more significant. Austin approaches rhythm through psychology, biology, landscape, and work movements, all of which can be related to 'primitive' Indian song. The American rhythm is assumed naturally from aboriginal songs, from the rhythms of land and nature, and even from a democratic way of life. Rhythm becomes perhaps the most pervasive influence in our lives; but, what Austin is also talking about in terms that need to be revived and examined is free verse. She makes sense of it.''

And Ray Olson says of the poems, "They are still concrete in imagery and stark in emotional expression: fine poems that conjure the conditions of human life—birth, toil, death, love, contemplation—with awesome spiritual power.''

Bogan, Louise. *The Blue Estuaries: Poems, 1923-1968* (New York: Farrar, Straus, 1968) Including poetry from five previous volumes as well as a selection of new poems, this collection shows the strain of Bogan's art over a period of forty-five years. The poems are lyrical and intellectual, and they represent the most dignified tradition in modern American poetry. Her language is responsive to the various subjects she treats, and it is always on key.

Daniel Halpern recommends this volume.

Brown, Sterling. *Southern Road* (New York: Harcourt, 1932) The poems of this young black poet (now a venerated man of letters) hold their fascination and power. The dialect pieces are evidence of acute observations on the part of the poet. And as portraits of Southern black people, the poems provide character studies and social protests, depictions of home life and humor.

Philip Levine recommends this.

Bullen, A. H. *Weeping-Cross and Other Rimes* (London: Sidgwick, 1921) Charles H. Sisson writes, "This posthumous book of poems by a man who performed great services as an anthologist and editor of 16th- and 17th-century poets is slight in bulk and, most would say, in content. But, the attractive personal flavour

apart, there are here a few small verses which will be recognised by any reader who understands poetry as being the rare and unpretentious article.''

Carpenter, Edward. *Towards Democracy* (London: Heywood, 1883) Following the model of Walt Whitman, Carpenter, who lived from 1844 to 1929, was an English poet who, over a period of twenty years, wrote a series of poems to celebrate democracy, the individual, and the liberated style of Whitman. Striving to reach "everyman," Carpenter chose to write about the most common experiences. His free verse is both effective and beautiful.

Allen Ginsberg recommended this in *Antaeus*, Autumn, 1975.

Clarke, Austin. *Flight to Africa and Other Poems* (New York: Oxford University Press, 1963) John Unterecker writes, "Austin Clarke is one of those almost-major figures who fascinate the reader because of excellences that should give him major status but who is blocked from popularity; in Clarke's case it is because he had the bad luck to be born at the wrong time. A little younger than Yeats, Clarke wrote almost all of his poetry in Yeat's shadow, limiting its international appeal by a narrow focus on things Irish. Very late in his career, he wrote one great poem (the title poem in *Flight to Africa*) that remains unread because the book was published in a very limited edition that had virtually no critical coverage. Brilliant and quirky, the poems in that volume reveal Clarke to be a poet of great range and intensity. Nothing else in his considerable publication history anticipates this late and extraordinary power.''

Coxe, Louis O. *The Sea Faring* (New York: Holt, 1947) In his first book of poems, the author draws from his experience on a PC boat in World War II. Much of the sea is here, trenchantly observed by a person heading toward danger. The poems are original in style and the ideas are devoid of sentimentality.

Richard Hugo calls this "a lovely and underrated book of American lyrics. Coxe captures the power and sadness of his New England heritage, the stern ways people survive harsh winds and pounding surfs."

Cuney, Waring. *Storefront Church* (London: Breman, 1973) X. J. Kennedy writes, "William Waring Cuney (born in 1906) is a poet whose reputation rests on a single poem, the perfectly realized 'No Images,' so often anthologized. Although his production has been small, he is surely one of the finest American black poets of the century; and I have never seen a poem of his that I didn't admire. Cuney never wastes words, as in this complete poem:

> Jesus' mother never had no man.
> God came to her one day and said:
> Mary, child, kiss my hand.

As far as I know, Cuney's work has appeared only twice in book collections, neither of them from an American publisher: *Storefront Church* . . . and *Puzzles* (1960), issued in a limited edition by a society of Dutch bibliophiles. This neglect appears to have been to some extent at Cuney's own choice. A reticent man unwilling to promote his poetry, he came out of his seclusion in 1973 when he supplied some poems to a little magazine I co-edited, *Counter/Measures*; but when I had a Boston publisher eager to look at a full collection, he declined to show any. Cuney's poems are not many, and not all are strong, but they are never wrong about anything. A 'poet who knew, and said it,' Don L. Lee has called him."

Davidson, Donald. *The Tall Men* (Boston: Houghton, 1927) Poems in blank verse,

these concern the tall men of Tennessee and their adventures as pioneers, hunters and soldiers on foreign battlefields. The vivid poetry of action and ruggedness has a strange unique beauty.

Russell Kirk writes, "Davidson . . . has been neglected as a poet: his volume of poems *The Tall Men*, among his several volumes of poetry, is particularly important."

Denby, Edwin. *Collected Poems* (New York: Full Court Press, 1975) Better known as a dance critic than a poet, this septuagenarian proves that Frank O'Hara, whose essay on the poet is included in this volume, was right. Denby is expert at bringing out the qualities of the places he observes, from New York to the ancient cities of the Mediterranean. As a poet of the city, he has few equals, and he uses his talent to explore a variety of moral complexities.

X. J. Kennedy calls this "very outstanding poetry."

Doughty, Charles M. *The Dawn in Britain* (London: Duckworth, 1906) Guy Davenport writes, "*The Dawn in Britain* (1906, six volumes). It is, I believe, the only English epic. I recognize the absolute grandeur of 'Paradise Lost' but as a Baroque poem closer to Michelangelo and Bach than to Homer.

"I admire Doughty for his narrative invention, his mighty line, his wholly original diction, his nobility, his grandeur of heart—the very qualities in Homer which no translator since Chapman has got anywhere near. Indeed, Doughty is 'before' Chapman. Doughty's idea was that poetry is outside time, and that in the twentieth century he could chart the birth of England in its two great heritages (the aboriginal British people, Christianity). His Christians are not doctrinal missionaries but

Graeco-Roman Stoics bringing the full measure of Mediterranean culture.

"Aside from being a poet who does not weaken anywhere, Doughty is one of the best storytellers in our literature. I think his neglect is simple fate. Look at the date of publication. His tradition is that of Hardy, Hopkins; but in a sense he made his own tradition. He hated modern English. His real love was geography and Arabic. His masterpiece has always been taken to be the magnificent *Travels in Arabia Deserta* (his Odyssey). The *Dawn* (his Iliad) must be put beside it.

"G. B. Shaw admired the *Dawn*, as did Yeats (Pound read it to him), E. M. Forster, Bridges, and of course T. E. Lawrence, who became who he was because of Doughty.

"Poetry by 1906 was becoming all entwined with philosophy, aestheticism, and everything except narrative. Doughty is simply a narrative poet whose concern is to make us see and feel a pattern in history: the convergence of the people who buried a king at Sutton Hoo, built Stonehenge, and wrote *The Beowulf* with some stray Romans and Syrians who had a drinking cup used by a rabbi who had been crucified by Roman legionaries, which rabbi they believed to be God, who as a man had brought a vision of mercy and brotherhood.

"But it is the *texture*, so good to read. The poem (two editions only, and those small) has never been available to the public. It will never be 'popular.' But is has Old Testament bigness and solemnity. It is alive. It is decidely the work of a man who has walked across Arabia with the most Fundamentalist of the Bedouin, never hiding from them that he was an infidel; and a man who thought English was ruined as a language by the Renaissance. His greatest imaginative triumph was to write as if Spenser had not yet begun *The Fairie Queene*."

Fearing, Kenneth. *New and Selected Poems* (Bloomington: Indiana University Press, 1956) M. L. Rosenthal writes, "Kenneth Fearing was probably the best poet to make his mark in this country during the 1930s, a forerunner of Allen Ginsberg but with a much finer ear and sardonically more cutting and economical [in] style. Edward Dahlberg compared his style with Corbiére's and wasn't altogether wrong; he was a Catullus of the American Depression and of New York City streets as well—rasping, angry, touching, absolutely wry and witty."

Roy Fuller also recommends this volume, saying it is "almost as good as his crime novel, *The Big Clock!*"

Feinman, Alvin. *Preambles and Other Poems* (New York: Oxford University Press, 1964) In a review of this collection, Harry Strickhausen of *Poetry* magazine wrote, "Each one of Mr. Feinman's poems seems perfectly finished and inevitable, and each has a strangely compelling authority. . . ." The poet has a technique in line with Wallace Stevens and W. H. Auden. In craftsmanship and intellect, this first book of poems is remarkable.

Harold Bloom called this volume "really astonishing . . ." (*American Scholar*, Spring, 1970).

Field, Michael. *Works and Days* (London: Murray, 1933) This is a journal kept by Michael Field from 1888 to 1914. Field, actually, was the joint pseudonym of two women poets, Katherine Bradley (1848-1914) and Edith Cooper (1862-1913) who, as aunt and niece, lived together most of their lives socializing with numerous British authors. The diary, which the women ordered to be held from publication until 1929, consists of comments, observations and correspondence about the Brownings,

Meredith, Hardy, Ruskin, George Moore and countless other writers. Their delicate style and careful attention to detail are balanced by acute, often witty insights.

Roy Fuller describes these as "vivid extracts from the journals, etc. of this 90s poet, really two maiden ladies, Katherine Bradley and Edith Cooper."

Gascoigne, George. *The Posies* (Norwood, NJ: Johnson, 1979) First published, 1575. Charles H. Sisson writes, "[Gascoigne is] still one of the most readable and most neglected of 16th-century poets, remarkable for his direct and familiar style and, as to content, in particular for fascinating insights into the life of a soldier in the Low Countries." *Note:* Gascoigne's complete works were edited by J. W. Cunliffe, 1907-1910, and they remain the authoritative compilation.

Ghiselin, Brewster. *Against the Circle* (New York: Dutton, 1946) Sensuous detail coupled with a command of prosody mark this collection of imagist poems. The deft technique and the gracefully wrought images create a type of effortless music which may be traced back to the author's other art, painting.

Richard Hugo calls this "a solid collection of imagistic and colorful poems by perhaps America's most unjustly overlooked poet. Ghiselin is truly a father of western American poetry."

Goodman, Paul. *The Lordly Hudson* (New York: Macmillan, 1962) M. L. Rosenthal writes, "Paul Goodman wasn't the equal of Fearing or Guthrie as a poet, but his work has a special spirited quality, staunchly frank and in some of the lyrical pieces remarkably and gaily alive and colloquially contemporary, or harsh and self-revealing. And Goodman took some of his

stance as a citizen of a betrayed republic, with clear, forthright political emotions, from the model of Wordsworth's political sonnets. He used his intelligence poetically far better than most."

Greenberg, Barbara. *The Spoils of August* (Middletown: Wesleyan University Press, 1974) This collection of highly personal poems presents the events of everyday life in an extraordinary way. With a mixture of wit, imagination and insight, the poet steers her way through her poems. In one, for example, she imagines herself an old woman instructing her great-granddaughters by relating her life story which they beg to hear. Not surprisingly, the world of the poems becomes a useful and unusual reference point from which to view the self and others.

Marilyn French says, "This was certainly overlooked. It is a fine volume by one of our finest poets, known, unfortunately, mainly by other poets."

Gunn, Thom. *Jack Straw's Castle* (New York: Hallman, 1975) The importance of detail is evident in the series of eleven poems which comprise the heart of *Jack Straw's Castle*. In the castle of the self, a forceful and simple syntax carries the reader through the everyday events from living with television and hi-fidelity to the haunting aspects of the daily news. The experience is intensified by the poet's mature distillation of the common issues of the day.

Aaron Asher recommends this volume.

Guthrie, Ramon. *Maximum Security Ward, 1964-1970* (New York: Farrar, Straus, 1970) M. L. Rosenthal writes, "*Maximum Security Ward* is still for the most part an unknown masterpiece, one of our best American poetic sequences, written by a poet with a lovely lyric ear, a sometimes bitter comic sense on the order of Mark Twain's, and a heartbreaking gift for projecting pain and grief. Ramon Guthrie is probably our outstanding neglected modern American poet."

And Malcolm Cowley calls this "Ramon Guthrie's testament, a summing up of his adventurous life and a tribute to the creative spirit."

Hecht, Anthony. *Millions of Strange Shadows* (New York: Atheneum, 1977) Few poets write with the precision and inventive wit of Hecht, and here he is at his best in a volume which details many facets of human experience. Whether he is writing about war, love, exile or the problems of youth, he invokes the common experience in a fresh way. These are distinctive, urbane poems distinguished by a high level of sensitivity.

Anthony Hecht writes, "And, since the opportunity offers and poets often suffer neglect, I beg leave to propose my own work as having been largely 'overlooked.' "

Howes, Barbara. *A Private Signal: Poems New & Selected* (Middletown, CT: Wesleyan University Press, 1977) The poet, whose first volume of verse was published in the late 1940s and who continues to write today, is well-anthologized and highly acclaimed by other poets. This collection was nominated for the National Book Award in poetry in 1978. Her verses are lyrical, beautiful and moving. She records experiences that are sensuous and deeply felt through her precise language and her vivid images. Not fashionable, not adhering to the latest styles, her work seems fresh and timeless in its devotion to the piercing impact that life has on the mind.

Dana Gioia wrote in *The Cumberland Poetry Review* that, "Reading *A Private Signal*, one sees Howes very clearly as a woman writing in one of the oddest but most important traditions of American po-

etry. Howes stands with Marianne Moore, Elizabeth Bishop, and ultimately Emily Dickinson in a group of women writers absolutely committed to the independence and singularity of the poetic imagination. . . .They form an eccentric but influential club. In most ways they are modest, even self-deprecating writers, but in matters they deem important they are bold and self-assured. . . .Perhaps what unifies them most obviously is the affirmative quality of their vision."

Jones, David. *The Anathemata: Fragments of an Attempted Writing* (London: Faber, 1952) A highly personalized version of English history which combines poetry and prose, this is also an intellectual's tribute to spiritual and mythic reality. Reminiscent of the author's *In Parenthesis* (1937), the fragments cohere in a long, carefully annotated poem. The fundamentally religious perspective is applied to a consideration of the salvation of man. In fantastically rich diction, with indebtedness to historical research, this work becomes commanding and inspiring.

Donald Hall recommends it.

Kees, Weldon. *The Collected Poems of Weldon Kees* (Iowa City: Stonewall Press, 1960) Robert Mazzocco writes, "The most unjustly neglected poet of his generation—that of Berryman, Lowell, Bishop—Kees, though obviously rooted in modernism (Baudelaire, Eliot, Auden) has, nevertheless, a voice of his own, distinctively American, if unusually suave. He was also, I believe, the first American to give *vers libre* an existential overtone. A few of his dramatic monologues, the woefully witty Robinson poems, in particular, and some of the extended lyrics, seem to me a permanent addition to the literature."

Kenyon, Jane. *From Room to Room* (Cambridge, MA: Alice James Books, 1978)

The primary interest and theme of these poems is the experience of being a woman. These poems explore the feminine sensibility from a position of quiet strength, with a remarkable ability to portray details of ordinary people inhabiting various places. The poet clearly demonstrates her substantial talent in these literal pieces with symbolic reverberations.

X. J. Kennedy calls this " . . . very outstanding poetry."

Kessler, Jascha. *Whatever Love Declares* (Los Angeles: Plantin, 1969) Due to a classical orientation and a deep appreciation of the aesthetic sensibility, Kessler's stunning poetry is concerned with subjects of daily concern to all. Whether he is addressing himself to ideas about family, love or landscapes, he is clear and original. His later works include *In Memory of the Future* (1976) and *Bearing Gifts* (1979).

Cynthia Ozick calls him " . . . a composer of beautifully wrought parables. . . ."

Kirstein, Lincoln. *Rhymes of a Pfc.* (New York: New Directions, 1964) Portraits of World War II figures, from General Patton to the typical Pfc., offer the true face of war. The poet is particularly effective in drawing the individual soldier who emerges as the hero of these rhymes.

W. H. Auden, writing in *The New York Review of Books*, said, "As a picture of the late war, [this] is by far the most convincing, moving and impressive book I have come across" (November 5, 1964).

Kunitz, Stanley. *Intellectual Things* (Garden City: Doubleday, 1930) A first book of poems by a distinguished American poet, these demonstrate his substantial themes, his superb craftsmanship, and his imaginative, figurative language.

John Ciardi wrote, "I know of no book of poems more unjustly neglected" (*American Scholar*, Autumn, 1956).

Mazur, Gale. *Nightfire* (Boston: D. R. Godine, 1978) Evocative poetry of a highly personal nature which deals with everyday events requires considerable skill. This poet has that ability, and her poems therefore are unusually involving. With precise attention to detail and an impressive technique, this collection is a delight.

X. J. Kennedy calls this " . . . outstanding poetry."

Morgan, Frederick. *The Tarot of Cornelius Agrippa* (Sand Lake, NY: Sagarin Press, 1978) Using beautifully engraved illustrations from a seventeenth-century Tarot deck, the poet offers a short selection facing each figure; there are twenty two in all. This is a highly unusual method for exploring human consciousness, and the poems work by altering, radically, our normal perceptions.

Paula Deitz writes, "Parables based on the Greater Trumps of the Tarot Deck, illustrated with reproductions of the Greater Trumps from the 1664 Mitelli Deck. Of this book, the poet Daniel Hoffman comments, 'These fables have the imaginative power of the great folk tales.' "

Olson, Charles. *The Maximus Poems* (Frankfort: Jargon, 1970) Olson's theory of projective or open verse pushed poetry into energetic new areas of development, and this American remains a lasting influence on the art form. There is greatness in these last poems of Olson's, the final volume of which was published in 1975.

Gilbert Sorrentino recommends the "incomprehensibly out-of-print final volume of Olson's great *Maximus Poems*. It is the summation of the life's work of arguably the most important American poet of the post-war years."

Parsons, Clere. *Poems* (London: Faber, 1932) Charles H. Sisson writes, "Clere Parsons died [in 1931] at a very early age and the book contains only a handful of poems. They are, however, if slight and evidently the work of a poet only beginning, of great clarity, not to say luminosity, and are unlike anything else. They certainly deserve reprinting.''

Pitter, Ruth. *Collected Poems* (New York: Macmillan, 1969) According to the preface, the poet is trying "to capture and express some of the secret meanings which haunt life and language; the silent music, dances in stillness, hints and echoes and messages of which everything is full.'' She succeeds.

John Unterecker writes, ''Ruth Pitter ... is a poet who through a long life produced quiet but authentic poems that consistently won her a small but devoted following of readers. Though no Emily Dickinson, she is far too fine a poet to be forgotten.''

Putnam, H. Phelps. *The Collected Poems of H. Phelps Putnam* (New York: Farrar, Straus, 1970) These poems were written between 1924 and the poet's death in 1948. The collection opens with an appreciative note by Edmund Wilson who says, "To young people of the present period [the poetry] will at once appear very old-fashioned, because it is versified in conventional meters ... but ... his genuine originality comes through.''

James and Anne Wright recommended this in *Antaeus*, Winter, 1975.

Reverdy, Pierre. *Risques et Perils.* *Translated from the French by Kenneth Rexroth* (Paris: Gallimard, 1930) Reverdy's first poems appeared in 1915, and he gained early fame as a friend and editor of Apollinaire and other cubist writers. Cubism strongly influenced his poetry. The simplicity in these poems indicates an interaction between things, ideas and acts.

There is a sense of the reorganization of scenes along cubist principles.

John Ashbery recommends this volume.

Riding, Laura. *Collected Poems* (New York: Random House, 1938) The author of this collection was a prolific writer of poems that are tough and uncompromising in their vision. The experiences that she documents tend to be ones that all readers can empathize with if they allow themselves to dwell on the essentials of existence. Her verses are not lyrical but strong, thoughtful, and perceptive. She treats her ideas and insights honestly and respectfully in a modern idiom that W. H. Auden said had a strong effect on his own poetry. The author chose some of these poems to be included in *Selected Poems: In Five Sets* (London: Faber, 1970).

Kenneth Rexroth and Carol Tinker recommended Laura Riding's poetry, prose and fiction in *Antaeus*, Autumn, 1979.

Schubert, David. *Initial A: A Book of Poems* (New York: Macmillan, 1961) Theodore Weiss writes that *"Initial A ...* not only anticipated qualities prominent in more recent poetry, the so-called New York school and others, but realized those qualities and others with a clarity and dramatic immediacy that makes Schubert's volume pioneering and original indeed. It continues to be fresher, more telling, more gripping than most of our present poetry.''

Spencer, Bernard. *Aegean Island and Other Poems* (Garden City: Doubleday, 1949) Most of the patterns of description found in these fine poems relate directly to the author's military service in Greece and Egypt between 1940 and 1942. They are particularly devoted to painting accurate landscapes, accompanied by an intellectual appreciation.

Richard Hugo calls this "a beautifully innocent and profound love affair between a poet and a new found land. For anyone who ever had an obsessive private fixation on real places in the world."

Stickney, Trumbull. *The Poems of Trumbull Stickney* (Boston: Houghton, 1905) Although now largely ignored, this is a collection of truly remarkable poetry. Stickney died at the age of thirty in 1904. He left behind what John Hollander describes as "sonnets and strophic lyrics full of a romantic Hellenism and a formal sense sometimes stronger than their rhetoric." Several critics now consider Stickney a central figure in the development of American romantic poetry.

Malcolm Cowley says, "He was the greatest poetic talent of the American 1890s."

Tessimond, A. S. J. *Voices in a Giant City* (London: Heinemann, 1947) Typified by the poem "London," this collection of poetry centers in and around the metropolitan style of living. Beyond that, the poet focuses on urban delights and dilemmas that could pertain to any part of the world, particularly the apparent helplessness of people to enhance their lives. The style is as neat as it is perceptive and sensitive, and the poet is often compared to W. H. Auden and Stephen Spender.

John Simon recommends this.

Thribb, E. J. (pseudonym for Barry Fantoni) *So, Farewell Then* (London: Elm Tree Books, 1978) These are really dreadful, awful poems, and I would not have included them at all if my co-author hadn't insisted. Actually more than poems, these are jokes. Or perhaps, I should say, less than poems. . . .At any rate, they are amusing commentaries on the passing English, and sometimes American, scene. They are most notable for egregious plays on the names of people who have died or done something else which has spirited them into the public eye. Or, should I say, the private eye, since all of them first appeared in that outrageous, funny, gossipy, social and political satiric magazine, *Private Eye.*

Valentine, Jean. *Ordinary People* (New York: Farrar, Straus, 1974) In this collection of poetry (the author's third), the marked lucidity and imagery are outstanding. Here one finds the daily experience of living given a new dimension. The translation of the Dutch poem, "Twenty Day's Journey" is the basis for the title:

I was afraid. You were just saying
ordinary things.

Rarely have ordinary things been said in such a splendid fashion.

Aaron Asher recommends this volume.

Walcott, Derek. *Another Life* (New York: Farrar, Straus, 1973) A four-part poem, this offers a realistic picture of life in the Caribbean. The autobiographical work is memorable because the poet captures the sights and sounds of the region as well as the imaginative realm of childhood.

Aaron Asher recommends this.

Walcott, Derek. *Selected Poems* (New York: Farrar, Straus, 1964) Walcott often makes reference in his poems to his original home in the Caribbean and to the pervading sense of racial tension both there and in America. This collection includes poems from 1948 to 1964, and shows Walcott's special gifts such as musical overtones, a painter's eye and a strong moral and imaginative response to injustice. In reviewing this collection, James Dickey noted, "One is left . . . with a complex, troubling sense of the Caribbean Islands, their reality and unreality, their filth and foam . . . doubly welcome in a time of timidity and correctness" (*The New York Times Book Review*, September 13, 1964).

Roger W. Straus recommends this.

Woiwode, Larry. *Even Tide* (New York: Farrar, Straus, 1977) Without the confessional tone of much personal poetry, the poet speaks to his family and friends about intimate matters. Due to the coolness in his tone and style, and his devotion to matters of emotion which are common to all, the poems offer a lyrical tribute to people and nature. His imagery is as precise as his understanding is deep.

Aaron Asher recommends this.

Wylie, Elinor. *Collected Poems* (New York: Knopf, 1932) While much appreciated during her own short life (1885-1928), Elinor Wylie is not well known to the general reading public today. The *Collected Poems* should remedy the situation. They show her gradual, breathtaking development from what one critic called "mere brilliance and erudite polish to work of unquestioned genius." Writing about the collection, Louis Untermeyer said that the more than three hundred pages range over a vast number of emotions and experiences, and he called some of her work "among the rarest offerings of our time."

Vance Bourjaily says, "I think the poetry of Elinor Wylie is overlooked . . . and well worth reviving."

Young, Marguerite. *Moderate Fable* (New York: Reynal, 1944) Between metaphysical themes of perfection, time and reality, the poet develops her quasi-surrealistic style and offers readers numerous memorable lines. Her achievements are as impressive as her technique is bold. She is a poet of remarkable subtlety and complexity and this is one of her best collections.

Ann Stanford recommends this.

Zaturenska, Marya. *Collected Poems* (New York: Viking, 1965) Winner of the 1938 Pulitzer prize for poetry, and author of a definitive biography of Christina Rossetti, Marya Zaturenska is a distinctive voice. She is primarily an expert craftswoman with a sensitive ear. Probably best known for her lyricism, this collection represents most of her published work.

Ann Stanford recommends this.

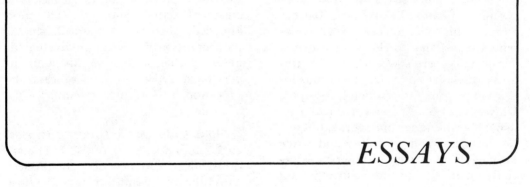

ESSAYS

Baring. Maurice. *Unreliable History* (London: Heinemann, 1934) Through the ruse of fictitious diaries, letters and dialogue, the author takes us on an unconventional tour of history and myth. We meet Hamlet, Henry the Eighth and Catherine Parr (the latter two at breakfast), among other intriguing figures. This good-natured parody of the historian's craft (or art) is as skillful as it is humorous, and while the tales are completely unfaithful to reality, they are unflinchingly personal and human.

Dwight MacDonald recommended this in *American Scholar*, Summer, 1970.

Bowen, Elizabeth. *Collected Impressions* (New York: Longman, 1950) While best known for such novels as *Death of the Heart,* this Anglo-Irish novelist (1899-1973) is an equally fine essayist as evidenced by this collection of book reviews, miscellaneous writings, articles on plays, places and pictures. The work is distinguished in both style and content.

Howard Moss wrote, "Elizabeth Bowen may be an unknown writer to the present generation . . . her books have been hard to find for years" (*The New Yorker*, February 5, 1979).

Brenan, Gerald. *Thoughts in a Dry Season: A Miscellany* (Cambridge: Cambridge University Press, 1978) In his eighties, the English writer examines his notebooks, and from them extracts short passages about his thoughts and his reading. The sometimes poetic, sometimes aphoristic pieces are arranged by broad topics. A man of moderately skeptical nature, Brenan relishes original ideas and provocative entertainments. This is illustrated in the variety of the sequence which begins with people and moves to literature, death and architecture.

George Core writes, "This collection of 'aphorisms, descriptive pieces, brief essays, memoirs, opinions and quotations' offers some of the richest and most rewarding occasional reading that I have ever encountered. I may be mistaken, but my impression is that the book was all but ignored when it was published . . . in 1978. Brenan is a brilliant stylist and a very shrewd and engaging author."

Burnet, John. *Essays and Addresses* (London: Chatto, 1929) David Daiches writes, "This collection of essays . . . represents lectures and articles written over a considerable period of time by a distinguished scholar and teacher who was for thirty-four years Professor of Greek at the University of St. Andrews. He had a remarkably wide range of learning, linguistic, historical and scientific, and wrote memorably on Greek philosophy, especially on Plato. But the most important essays in this collection, and those that had a sustained influence on my own thought about education, about the nature of university teaching and—most of all—about the relations between science and the humanities (especially science and literature), were the two entitled 'Humanism and Education' and 'Ignorance'. In the former he documented with great persuasiveness the close relation between Renaissance Humanism and Renaissance Science and went on to show how the two depended on each other and how modern science was born out of a fusion between the two. The separation of humanistic from scientific studies, which is a modern development (in Britain, a 19th-century development), was to him an evil, and in his arguments for their reassociation he tried to heal a disastrous division in the modern mind. His essay on 'Ignorance' begins by pointing out that when Professor Ferrier invented the word 'epistemology' in the mid-19th century he also invented another word, 'agnoiolgy', which has been forgotten. The former word means "theory of knowledge" and the latter means "theory of ignorance." In a world of rapidly increasing specialized knowledge it becomes less and less possible for any individual to know more than a tiny fraction of all possible knowledge. Whereas in earlier phases of Western civilization it was possible for one man to master all available knowledge, that possibility has long since disappeared. Increase of potential knowledge means increase of actual ignorance. The more knowledge there is in the world the smaller the proportion of it that any individual can master. Burnet starts from this point and goes on to reflect on its significance for education. It is all most relevant for our own time."

Child, Lydia Maria. *Letters from New York* 2 volumes (New York: C. S. Francis, 1843-1845) The founder of the first American children's monthly magazine (*Juvenile Miscellany*, 1826), the author soon turned her interests to the abolitionist movement and eventually operated a Massachusetts station in the Underground Railroad. She later became a suffragist and an early pioneer in sex education. Her background is central to an understanding of *Letters from New York*, which is comprised of articles and columns written originally for the *Boston Courier* and *The National Anti-Slavery Standard*, which she edited at the time. The letters do two things exceptionally well. First, they give an accurate, fascinating account of urban social life in the 1830s and 1840s. Second, and more importantly, they examine the pressing social questions of the day—questions often overlooked in books by men of the same period. The work was an instant success, going through at least eleven printings. As a first hand account of the excitement, the controversies and the various roles of ordinary people in American life, these articles are as vivid today as when they were written.

Judith Fetterley recommends this volume.

Curtis, Charles and Ferris Greenslet. *The Practical Cogitator or the Thinker's Anthology* (Boston: Houghton, 1945) Under approximately a dozen subject headings, from "Man in search of himself" to "They must have peace, security, and liberty" and "He seeks solace and beauty," the compilers include excerpts from the best writing of the ages. While their choice is highly personal, it is vastly urbane and of high aesthetic quality.

Henry Cabot Lodge says, "*The Practical Cogitator or the Thinker's Anthology* is indeed an anthology put together by two gifted men—Charles Curtis, a discerning Boston lawyer, and Ferris Greenslet, who was the editor of Houghton Mifflin at the time. Rare indeed is a bit of prose which will not somehow be appropriately touched by these pages."

Day, Clarence. *This Simian World* (New York: Knopf, 1920) Ours is a civilization directly descended from the monkeys, and all our actions and ideas are determined by our simian heritage. So goes the message of Day's whimsical and witty social analysis. He also considers what we might have been had our ancestors been cats or even elephants. Beneath the cumulated centuries, Day chooses those human traits which simply refuse to disappear. "Every simian [for example] will wish to know all the news of the world, but he'll forget what he's read the very next hour."

Alfred A. Knopf was quoted in *The New York Times* as saying, "It's the cat's pajamas" and "[it's] still relevant to an understanding of the human animal in New York, Washington, or anywhere else" (August 18, 1981). The *Times* was celebrating the republication of the book by Knopf.

Dodds, Eric Robertson. *The Greeks and the Irrational* (Berkeley: University of California Press, 1951) Here is a series of essays on Greek religion and culture. Kelly Cherry writes, "E. R. Dodds' *The Greeks and the Irrational* is a remarkably lucid and persuasive examination of the role in Greek culture of matriarchal, Dionysian, and other cults of the irrational. From origins that can only be deduced and speculated upon, Dodds's work traces the development of these cults as a counterpoint to

the official religions, showing how they influenced later cultures and religions and in ways persist even today. Despite the subject matter, Dodds' documentation is thorough, his reasoning sane, his tone (shall we say) Apollonian, and his prose a marvel of syntactical clarity. This is a book essential for cultural anthropologists, theologians, psychologists, and classical historians; it is also, however, a book that any writer of fiction and poetry will want to read, for the sake of its ideas, it images, and its implications."

Huneker, James G. *Ivory Apes and Peacocks* (New York: Scribner, 1915) While wielding his literary tomahawk against the foibles and reputations of some distinguished writers, artists and composers, Huneker does separate his heroes from his victims. Here, for example, among the numerous subjects one finds excellent, relevant remarks concerning Conrad and highly amusing and imaginative comments on the heroines of Ibsen, George Moore and Edith Wharton. But the magic of the book is Huneker's infectious interest in all forms of art.

Arno Karlen writes of Huneker that he is "strangely neglected now. It is a scandal of ignorance and lapsed taste that [he is] missing from anthologies of American writing. . . .The four most distinguished American critics of this century have been Huneker, Pound, Eliot and Wilson . . . [Huneker] is a delightful man who stands in the front rank of American criticism and the fine second rank of American writing" (*The Antioch Review*, Autumn, 1981).

MacCarthy, Desmond. *Humanities* (Oxford: Oxford University Press, 1954) This is a collection of book reviews, reminiscences, and short stories by the late British critic who lived from 1877 to 1952 and knew as much about human nature as he did about literature. Sometimes called the last of the Edwardian essayists, Mac-Carthy was a man of varied interests, yet he had one identifiable sensibility, one voice. Here are many facets of the critic who was a close friend of Virginia Woolf and a member of the Bloomsbery group.

Leon Edel recommended this in *Antaeus,* Autumn, 1979.

Martí, José. *The America of José Martí.* *Translated from the Spanish by Juan de Onis* (New York: Noonday, 1953) Selected writings by a Cuban author about the United States, these are considered some of the most precise and beautiful pieces ever written by a foreigner about this country. Particularly compelling are his portraits of Peter Cooper, General Ulysses S. Grant, Walt Whitman and Buffalo Bill.

German Arciniegas wrote, "One of the greatest writers of America, Martí had a clearer vision of the United States than any other Latin-American writer" (*American Scholar,* Autumn, 1956).

Michaux, Henri. *Selected Writings: The Space Within.* *Translated from the French by Richard Ellmann* (New York: New Directions, 1952) The Belgian-born poet and painter moved to Paris where he became editor of a leading French literary review and established his reputation as one of France's leading intellectuals. His writings have two major elements or themes: the pervading sense of nothingness, as captured in some of his characters' emotions; and the sense of the millenium which is part of a fantastic world he creates in other of his writings. He triumphs in making the most natural thing seem strange, the strangest most ordinary. This collection includes much of his best work, and has the added advantage of having the French text on the page opposite the excellent translation.

Richard Ellmann writes, "I consider Henri Michaux one of the most original and profound French writers of the century. He excels in imagination, in wit, and in his understanding of modern consciousness."

Mitchell, Joseph. *Bottom of the Harbor* (Boston: Little, 1960) In this volume, *The New Yorker* writer considers the kinds of people who make a living in and near the harbor of New York. Whether he is reproducing a conversation about rats or oysters, or describing a once prosperous waterfront hotel, Mitchell intimately acquaints one with personalities, activities and events. In his typical low-keyed style, he is a master of observation and muted enthusiasm.

Calvin Trillin recommends this (see below).

Mitchell, Joseph. *McSorley's Wonderful Saloon* (New York: Duell, 1943) The collection of real people who are assembled here are essentially Dickensian characters with American accents, and they are as vivid as any found in the best American or English literature. An adroit and sensitive writer, Mitchell wrote most of these sketches for *The New Yorker,* but they were revised and rewritten for this collection. Masterpieces of observed detail and evocative style, the studies are as compassionate as they are accurate, as enchanting as they are sincere. Most of the people are from New York, but others are out of the author's home town in North Carolina.

Calvin Trillin recommends this saying, "I think Mitchell has written among the best nonfiction pieces that ever appeared in *The New Yorker,* and I think a lot of writers agree with me. The above books [*McSorley's Wonderful Saloon* and *At the Bottom of the Harbor*] are collections of pieces, mostly about New York and the waterfront. Other titles are *Old Mister Flood* and *Joe Gould's Secret*."

Montesquiou, Robert de. *Les Hortensias Bleus* **(Blue Hydrangeas)** (Paris: Les Editions des Autres, 1979) A man who set about perfecting the "art of being disliked," Montesquiou, who lived from 1855 to 1921, enjoyed provoking controversy. He was, in addition, immensely talented, writing like a brilliant conversationalist. His essays reveal a man with a quick wit who has a fine appreciation for both normal and strange human situations.

Francois Bott wrote, "The selected pieces...reveal a man who was as sensitive as he could be vicious, and as enthusiastic when admiring beauty as he was mordant when denouncing mediocrity" (*The Manchester Guardian Weekly*, November 18, 1979).

Morris, William. *The Unpublished Lectures of William Morris* (Detroit: Wayne State University Press, 1969) This major nineteenth-century English poet, artisan and political liberal not only wrote, but delivered numerous popular lectures. These were collected from holograph manuscripts in the British Library. With characteristic lucidity, wit and imagination, Morris speaks of the dignity of labor, the relation of art to society, the value of medieval culture and many other topics including the pleasure and exhilaration he felt in discovering Icelandic literature. The man emerges as modest and unobtrusively intellectual.

Quentin Bell recommends this as "some of the best persuasive writing of the last century."

Namier, Lewis. *Skyscrapers and Other Essays* (New York: Macmillan, 1931) Although Namier is famous for his study of eighteenth-century England, the essays collected here deal primarily with political personalities and events in the early twentieth century. His brilliant style, flawless scholarship and imaginative conclusions are all evidenced in this sterling collection.

Joseph Kraft says it is his "feeling that [Namier] is the foremost historian of the twentieth century, unrivalled in intellectual penetration...."

Péguy, Charles. *Basic Verities.* *Translated from the French by Ann and Julian Green* (London: Kegan, 1943) The voice of a Catholic idealist, killed at the Battle of the Marne in the first World War, is heard here in a wise selection of his prose and poetry. This collection is an excellent introduction to the mind and works of Péguy, and there is a fine explanatory preface by Julian Green.

Eugene McCarthy recommended this in *Antaeus*, Autumn, 1979.

Rozanov, Vasily. *Solitaria.* *Translated from the Russian by S. S. Koteliansky* (New York: Boni, 1927) First published, 1912.

A collection of aphorisms and thoughts, these, while fragmentary in style, reveal the mind of an early twentieth-century intellectual of uncommon originality. In the opening pages, Rozanov describes his literary medium. "The wind blows at midnight and carries leaves....So also life in fleeing time tears off from our soul exclamations, sights, half thoughts, half feelings....I have always somehow liked these sudden exclamations." Written without any overall plan and on the slightest of pretexts, the various ideas and impressions move from a description of "Three men I have met" to the concluding remark, "No man is worthy of praise. Every man is only worthy of compassion." Discussing this work, Renato Poggioli notes that, "None of the Russian critics who have written on Rozanov . . . has failed to agree that *Solitaria, Fallen Leaves,* and *The Apocalypse of Our Times* are those of his literary remains that recommend him to posterity."

Vladimir Nabokov called Rozanov "an extraordinary writer combining moments of exceptional genius with manifestations of astounding naïveté" (*The New York Times Magazine,* August 23, 1981).

Sassoon, Siegfried. *The Memoirs of a Fox-Hunting Man* (London: Faber, 1928) This work begins by describing an idyllic childhood in the English countryside. Ostensibly a work of fiction, this autobiography first appeared anonymously and won several literary prizes. No matter whether it is classified as autobiography or fiction, it remains extremely charming and frequently satirical. The title derives from the second part of the book when the young boy is taught the vagaries of fox-hunting. Many consider this to be a major contribution to sporting literature. The final section records a change in mood and scene, taking the reader to the trenches during the First World War. This is a singular and strangely beautiful book.

Betty Comden recommends it.

Tagore, Rabindranath. *A Tagore Reader*. *Translated from the Bengali and edited by Amiya Chakravarty* (New York: Macmillan, 1961) Poet, artist, educator and philosopher, Tagore wrote a vast amount of material. Much of the best of it is found in this collection which includes passages from all the genres that the Indian author explored and enriched. Even travel diaries and letters are included. Each section consists of an introductory preface by Chakravarty, who was Tagore's literary secretary. One segment of the book explores the problem of translation and Tagore's personal methods for translating his Bengali poems.

The Reverend Theodore Hesburgh writes, "Tagore was one of the best Indian poets of all times. His secretary, Amiya Chakravarty, has rendered his Bengali poems in beautiful English. I highly recommend them for their beauty and understanding of the human condition."

Yeats, William Butler. *Essays and Introductions* (New York: Macmillan, 1961) Published about thirty years after his death, this collection includes early essays of the Irish poet and the unpublished, revised introduction to a collected American edition of his poems. The focus is on aesthetics, social issues and metaphysics. The gracious style and the wit sometimes cover fairly diffuse ideas. Still, a brilliant, poetic mind exploring issues of worth more than makes up for the minor flaws.

Eugene McCarthy recommended this in *Antaeus,* Winter, 1975.

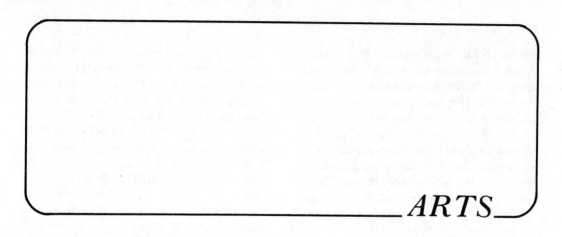

Beaumont, Cyril W. *The Complete Book of Ballets* (New York: Putnam, 1938) While some of the stories of ballets, nicely recounted here, are as ridiculous as the plots of operas, it does help to know what the dancers are portraying. More useful is the approach which makes this book so valuable. The author groups the stories by various choreographers and gives complete information on costumes, scenery, the composers of the music, the place of the first production, the initial cast, and so forth. In addition, the monumental encyclopedia includes frequent quotations from contemporary reports and criticism. The redoubtable scholarship and detail is matched by the author's lively style—the style of a balletomane. There are numerous, marvelous illustrations.

Deborah Jowitt writes, "I grew up on this book. I think it's out of print because people assume that it has been superseded by the Balanchine-Mason book [Balanchine's *New Complete Stories of the Great Ballets*. Editor Francis Mason (1968)], but this isn't true. Beaumont only goes up to the 1930s, but he gives scenarios of many 18th- and 19th-century works."

Bottomley, Gordon. *King Lear's Wife; Gruach* (London: Constable, 1920, 1922) A vigorous, imaginative poet, Bottomley wrote as much for the theatre as he did for the art of recitation. Many of his works, including the five collected under the title of *King Lear's Wife*, were offered in rooms without the benefit of stage props. He is inevitably concerned with historical circumstances, and the lead work traces the early years of Lear's wife. His deep, sympathetic understanding of women is evident in each of these plays, as is his uniquely beautiful poetic gift.

Gruach is a collection of two plays. The leading work investigates the youth of Lady Macbeth.

Naomi Mitchison says, "These are poetic plays but with a wonderful sense of history. Beautiful use of language. Perhaps out of fashion now but might come back."

Chambers, Frank. *Cycles of Taste* (Cambridge: Harvard University Press, 1928) *The History of Taste* (New York: Columbia University Press, 1932)

Joseph Needham writes, "In *Cycles of Taste* and *The History of Taste*, two books for which I have the warmest admiration, Frank Chambers took up a theme derived originally, perhaps, from Oswald Spengler. We used to characterize it jokingly as the doctrine that 'history was composed entirely of dark ages and decadent periods.' In other words what Chambers was trying to show was that there are long periods in history during which works of brilliant artistic creation are produced, but there are few literary or artistic critics. These then are followed by long periods of time when the really original artistic works are few, but there is plenty of literary and artistic criticism. I suspect that this is probably basically true, but only within the aesthetic realm. I don't think it's true of either humanistic scholarship or scientific advance—but then Frank Chambers never said it was.

"I have always greatly admired Frank Chambers' work, and I would strongly recommend it. . . . It has never had very much influence on my own work as a historian of science, technology and medicine in Chinese culture; but that is probably because scientific creation is so far apart from artistic creation, in spite of genii who bridge the two, like Leonardo da Vinci."

Delacroix, Eugene. *Selected Letters, 1813-1863.* *Translated from the French by Jean Stewart* (New York: St. Martin's Press, 1972) This illustrated and annotated volume contains selections from the correspondence of the famous French artist, chosen and translated by Jean Stewart. The letters follow Delacroix's career, relating his continual financial difficulties and his friendships with various well known and unknown personalities.

John Russell says in the introduction "Delacroix was a natural writer who at one time might have turned professional. . . .He needed to write. Orphaned by the time he was fifteen, left with the slenderest possible financial prospects and cared for—if

that is the word—by an older sister, he needed to establish relations of security with somebody, somewhere: his men friends helped towards this and he remained grateful to them for the rest of his life, but he was enough in need of female assurance to undertake the most desperate and implausible of manoeuvres. I know of few relics more moving, in their kind, than the drafts of the letters which he hacked out in English when his sister's housemaid, Elizabeth Salter, was the object of his affections. . . ."

Drinker, Sophie L. *Music and Women: The Story of Women in Relation to Music* (New York: Coward-McCann, 1948) A feminist (one reviewer called it "aggressively feminist") history of music from the caves to the mid-twentieth century, its thesis is that women lost their roles as leaders of society and, in the process, their powers to compose music and, to a lesser extent, to play it. Inhibited in social expression, they became inhibited in musical expression. When freedom from intellectual and economic bondage becomes more widespread, women will regain their early position as a dominant force in music.

Judy Chicago says of this work, "I wept when I read it, particularly the part about how when women's political and social authority ended, they stopped making music. Thus, music is an expression of power, human power, personal power and authority."

Feild, Robert. *The Art of Walt Disney* (New York: Macmillan, 1942) In 1981, the Whitney Museum in New York City devoted a floor to an exhibition of the art of Walt Disney and his studios. Long before this event, however, Feild realized the peculiar place Disney occupied in the American artistic milieu. Here, he traces the development of the Disney studio, the techniques which were employed in animation, and the Disney genius for promoting his art.

Howard Mumford Jones recommended this book, saying it was "the first close aesthetic analysis of a unique American art, that of the animated cartoon brought to a level of genuine artistic achievement" (*American Scholar*, Autumn, 1956).

Fergusson, Francis. *The Idea of a Theatre* (Princeton: Princeton University Press, 1949) While he was director of the Princeton seminars in literary criticism, the author wrote this dramatic and author- itative history of basic theatre. The author explains the art of action underlying the language in drama—how each character has a primary reason for exerting power which results in the central action of the play. Using this as a premise, the work ex- amines the great landmarks in dramatic art. It assuredly is one of the most signifi- cant books to be published on the art of the theatre in America.

Allen Tate recommended this in *An- taeus*, Autumn, 1977.

Field, Joanna. *On Not Being Able to Paint* (London: Heinemann, 1950) Robert Motherwell wrote, "The book . . . is about a psychoanalyst who had no talent for art, who wanted to be a holiday painter, and, through that rigorous psychoanalytical honesty at its best, discovered that every- thing she had been taught about how to paint was unreal. . . . I think only a person of extreme intelligence and implacable self-honesty could write a book with [this] self-directed title" (*American Scholar*, Spring, 1970).

Fry, Roger. *Reflections on English Painting* (London: Faber, 1934) With such artists as William Hogarth, William Turner and William Blake there is hardly any need for the English to apologize for their art and their artists. The author, one of the first English critics to recognize the contri-

butions of modern French painters, is in- fectiously enthusiastic about English paint- ing and writes of it as though it were a new discovery. His singularly fresh approach, his incisive critical remarks, and his thor- ough understanding of art makes this an exceptionally valuable guide. Among the other artists discussed are Peter Lely, Joshua Reynolds, Thomas Gainsborough, Thomas Lawrence and John Constable.

Quentin Bell recommends this, saying, "Like all the smaller works, too little known, due for revival."

Gottlieb, Carla. *Beyond Modern Art* (New York: Dutton, 1976) What is concep- tual art, pop art, earth art, optical art? The author gives the attributes of each of these movements as well as others which have flourished since the end of World War II. She then offers counter-arguments to de- fine and redefine her definitions. The me- thod serves to move the reader from one description of a work of art to another, and to consider carefully the statements of the artists about their work. There is a mass of information about some older European artists who are still unknown in America and a fine bibliography of quotations.

Christo recommends this book.

Green, Martin. *The Problem of Bos- ton: Some Readings in Cultural History* (New York: Norton, 1966) The cultural history of Boston, particularly from the nineteenth to the twentieth century, is real- ly the story of America's striving for artistic independence. Green charts the course of this struggle in a truly original study of America's intellectual growth and devel- opment.

Irving Kristol calls this "a thoughtful examination of the rise of Brahmin culture."

Haggin, B. H. *Thirty Five Years of Music* (New York: Horizon, 1974) Famil- iar with almost every type of classical music from opera and ballet to concerts and vocal recitals, Haggin wrote criticism unmatched for its liveliness and its effortless scholarship. Here are essays written between 1929 and 1964 in which the critic's indignant surprise about the inadequacies of other critics is reflected in his appreciation of the true points about the music under review. Sometimes his reaction to other critics is overdone, but his musical assessments and instincts seem utterly persuasive.

Tim Page wrote, "Perhaps [Haggin's] name is not as well known as it once was—his form of passionate subjective criticism has been out of fashion for a while. The fact remains . . . that Haggin is one of our great critics" (*Soho News*, November 5, 1980).

Hawes, Elizabeth. *Fashion Is Spinach* (New York: Random House, 1938) Combining liveliness with indignation, an American dress designer reveals the secrets behind fashion. No less fascinating is the story of her own rise from unpaid assistant at Bergdorf Goodman's to apprentice in New York and Paris and finally to ultimate success in her profession. Entertaining as well as informative, this work combines autobiography with the history of modern fashion. It was one of the first of its kind. Among designers it is deemed a classic even when they challenge her irreverent, unconventional approach. For all, it is an honest, witty and knowledgable exposé of fashion.

Clancy Sigal calls Hawes a "badly neglected late 1930s-40s *haute monde* fashion designer turned union organizer and radical writer. Pre-movement feminist."

Heath-Stubbs, John. *Helen In Egypt and Other Plays* (New York: Oxford University Press, 1958) Turning to drama, the English poet offers three verse plays which are rich in ideas. The dialogue is well paced, the characters lively, and the action credible.

X. J. Kennedy writes, *"Helen in Egypt and Other Plays* seems to me one of the few attempts to write actable poetry in our time that succeeds in being both actable and worth reading. The finest play in the book is 'The Talking Ass,' based on the Biblical story of Balaam; it was first performed in a London church in 1950. It manages to encompass both a beautiful angel who speaks in sweet pentameters and a braying ass who sasses falsehood and pomposity. I am somewhat prejudiced in this play's favor, having taken part in a production of it in Ann Arbor in 1961, under the direction of the author. I played the first half ass. But it is a splendidly stageable play, at moments hilarious, at moments deeply moving. 'The Harrowing of Hell,' also in this volume, is the only convincing contemporary miracle play I know."

Heilpern, John. *Conference of the Birds* (Indianapolis: Bobbs, 1978) A running account of the theatrical methods of Peter Brook, the great director, and his experimental theatre company, this charts the development of the production of *Conference of the Birds*. The time is 1972-1973, and the narrative is concerned with the group's tour of West Africa. A capable and sensitive writer with a strong instinct about people, the author captures both the spirit of the company and the reactions of its numerous audiences. Brook wished to break through language barriers with newly created sounds and movements which would have universal significance. Just how well he succeeded makes this a memorable theatre book.

Eugene Rachlis recommends it.

Herriman, George. *Krazy Kat* (New York: Holt, 1946) Krazy Kat proved to be one of the first successful, long-lived, American cartoons, which was surprising to almost everyone because of its intellectual and satirical content. Somehow Americans should not like such material. But they did. Why was the newspaper strip so popular? Walt Disney believed it was that Herriman had "the common touch" which made people think "without too much puzzlement at his parodies and ironies which carried punch without being bitter."

Clarence Brown recommended this in *Antaeus*, Autumn, 1979.

Jowitt, Deborah. *Dance Beat: Selected Views and Reviews 1967-1976* (New York: Dekker, 1977) Drawing upon her background as dancer, choreographer and critic, the author offers a compelling view of dance. She considers almost every conceivable aspect of dance from ballet and modern to post-modern and non-Western forms. She writes about that art form with exceptional clarity and the reader can easily visualize the various performances. Few books offer such an informed opinion on dance and dancers. Most of the entries are reviews for *The Village Voice*, but many have been reworked with additional comments and different points of view as her judgment seasoned.

Deborah Jowitt writes, "You'll have to forgive my putting myself forward! Marcel Dekker printed this collection of my dance reviews in 1977 and is now out of the dance book business. I get many inquiries still and would love to see the book reissued as a cheap paperback that students could afford."

Mandel, Oscar. *Collected Plays* 2 volumes (Santa Barbara: Unicorn Press, 1971-1972) This is Mandel at his best. The twelve plays are a fascinating mixture of morality and parody, allegory and humor. Constant, careful consideration is given both to fantasy and reality. The subject is people, their reactions to one another and to the society in which they happen to find themselves. Unexcelled dialogue leads the reader through a marvelous world.

Cynthia Ozick calls Mandel "a writer of great brilliance who has gone unnoticed for three decades. He is a poet and playwright of exquisite lyricism (in the poetry) and wise comedy (in the plays). . . .He is a writer of "classical" style, European in bent . . . his grain is immaculate and pure, and goes off in a direction entirely his own; and he is an exquisite humorist and ironist. . . ."

Mellers, Wilfred H. *Music in a New Found Land: Themes and Developments in the History of American Music* (New York: Knopf, 1964) A British musicologist analyzes and explains the history of popular and classical music in America. The interweaving of sociological, literary and musical history results in a splendid panorama of American life, incorporating such figures as Stephen Foster and Harry Partch. The central section is a challenging exploration of jazz, followed by an entertaining yet scholarly discussion of pop, rock and country music. Refreshingly free of jargon and preconceptions, the history is as skillfully written as it is enthusiastic.

Aaron Copland and Virgil Thomson recommended this in *Antaeus*, Autumn and Winter, 1975.

Motherwell, Robert, editor. *The Dada Painters and Poets* (New York: Wittenborn, 1951) One of America's most famous modern painters is the editor of this collection of memorabilia which furthers an understanding of Dadaism, a phase in the history of modern art which peaked in the 1920s. There is material from Jean Arp, documents relating to the Dada artists, objects of their work, excerpts from journals, reviews, manifestoes, photographs, catalogues, and even invitations to exhibits. This serious and lively book provides important documentation of a major artistic movement.

Virgil Thomson recommended this in *Antaeus*, Winter, 1975.

Neuhaus, Heinrich. *The Art of Piano-Playing.* *Translated from the Russian by K. A. Leibovitch* (New York: Praeger, 1973) A distinguished piano teacher at the Moscow Conservatory, Neuhaus offers much sensible advice for young pianists. He is concerned with every element of the art, from the spiritual content of music to the need for better music departments. Neuhaus stands apart from other writers because of his wisdom and his devoted, humanistic sensibility.

Emanuel Ax writes, "This book is the most interesting of its kind, because the author taught both Richter and Gilels, two of the greatest modern-day pianists."

Powell, Ann. *The Origins of Western Art* (New York: Harcourt, 1973) The history of art is the history of us all, and the author offers a broad survey of art and civilization from Paleolithic to Roman times. The cave paintings are discussed in view of what is known about the development of early human beings. As she moves to Mesopotamia, Egypt and Asia Minor, careful attention is given to significant events which shaped artistic expression. There are, in addition, intertwined themes of magic, myth and ritual, short biographical pieces, and perceptive aesthetic judgments. This is a tour de force, accompanied by fine illustrations throughout the text.

M. Hamel-Schwulst recommends this.

Reid, Louis Arnaud. *A Study in Aesthetics* (New York: Macmillan, 1931) In recommending this clearly written, brilliantly conceived philosophy of aesthetics, Jacques Barzun observes, "[This] should be the bedside book of every critic and every amateur of the arts; it is the only work since Santayana that expounds a philosophy of art while giving evidence that the little three letter word is to the author a living reality." Among other topics, Reid discusses beauty and ugliness, the relation of art to truth, reality and moral values, and the competition of interests in various arts.

Jacques Barzun says, "Reid is as unappreciated in the United States as is Collingwood." (Robin G. Collingwood, a British philosopher, was the author of major works on aesthetics.)

Sackheim, Eric, editor. *The Blues Line: A Collection of Blues Lyrics* (New York: Grossman, 1969) In the firm conviction that blues is a unique form of American poetry, the editor brings together more than two hundred and seventy American black songs. Among the composers one will find Leadbelly, Muddy Waters, John Lee Hooker and every important figure in the development of this art.

Allen Ginsberg recommended this in *Antaeus*, Autumn, 1975.

Smyth, Ethel. *Impressions that Remained* (New York: Knopf, 1946) There are few more radiant and moving autobiographies than this, which is about the career of an eminent British composer. Working against the odds of being a woman in a man's world, Smyth established close friendships with many male composers, from Brahms and Grieg to Tchaikovsky and Wagner. These luminaries as well as famous women, such as Clara Schumann and the Empress Eugenie, populate this work which relates Smyth's wildly varied and fascinating career.

Alfred A. Knopf writes, "My interest in Ethel Smyth goes back to the far away and long ago. She was a woman composer and respected one of my idols, Beecham. I read *Impressions that Remain* in the English edition when it was first published, and admired it greatly. So much so that later, in 1946, I went to the considerable expense of setting up the book and publishing a one-volume edition of it."

Steinberg, Leo. *Other Criteria: Confrontations with Twentieth-Century Art* (New York: Oxford, 1972) In this collection of essays, the art critic is concerned with the particular qualities of modern art and artists, and the necessity of formulating new approaches in order to appreciate them. He opposes formalistic models and encourages a more personal point of view. Few critics so forcefully deal with the errors in modern art criticism and the dogmas associated with that criticism. In addition, his excellent style beautifully expresses his meaning.

Christo recommends this.

Young, Stark. *The Theatre* (New York: Scribner, 1927) A description of events which helped to shape the American theatre, this is the work of an expert who speaks on almost every aspect of his subject, from acting and directing to costume and scenic design. Both a novelist and a prominent drama critic, Young knew his subject intimately and had an elegant prose style. Of particular interest today are the sketches of people prominent in the theatre of his time, as well as the useful comments on the plays.

Sanford Friedman writes, "Stark Young remains for me America's finest theatre critic, as well as one of our finest critics *per se.*"

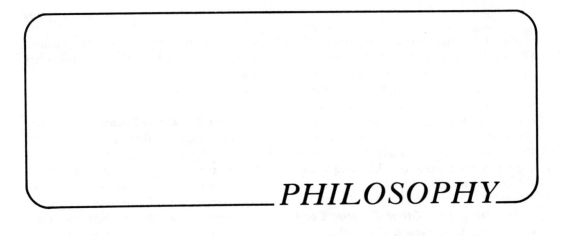

PHILOSOPHY

Adorno, Theodor. _Negative Dialectics._
Translated from the German by E. B. Ashton (New York: Seabury, 1973) Until his death in 1969, Adorno, along with Herbert Marcuse, was involved in applying themes derived from Marx and Freud to the nature and function of society. Here he demonstrates how "critical theory" shifted during the Nazi years from focusing on capitalism to analyzing western civilization as a whole. The numerous motifs which have come to dominate Western thinking over the past decades are carefully considered. Adorno points out that man's failure to recognize his role as part of nature has resulted in his creation of monumental problems.

Marvin Cohen recommended this in _Antaeus_, Winter, 1975, along with Adorno's _The Jargon of Authenticity_ (1973), two books which are often called classics of the twentieth century.

Bergson, Henri. _Creative Evolution._
Translated from the French by Arthur Mitchell (New York: Holt, 1911) Alden Nowlan writes, "I've never been able to understand the neglect—general disparagement, in fact—of Henri Bergson's _Creative Evolution._

"It may be due to snobbishness—a belief that because he was once a fad he can't possibly have been any good.

"My own discovery of Bergson came during a process of self-education very similar to that of the title character in Jack London's _Martin Eden._

"Most of the philosophers whom I had read up till then seemed to be discussing a different cosmos than the one I inhabited. Reading _Creative Evolution_ I felt that the author was saying what I had always sensed but had been too clumsy to express.

"I remember that I had to stop underlining sentences—because I was underlining them all!

"I still think that Bergson succeeded in putting into straightforward expository prose concepts that others have been able to communicate only by implication through images and metaphors.

"Many, many times since I was a very small child I've stopped for a moment and thought to myself how very strange it is to be alive. Such feelings must be common, and yet they're seldom mentioned in either philosophy or literature. All of *Creative Evolution* stems from that recurrent feeling of naked wonder."

Breasted, James. *The Dawn of Conscience* (New York: Scribner, 1933) Based on his experience as a scientist and his extensive archaeological research in Egypt, the professor concludes that conscience and morality were born in the Nile Valley. He associates the dawn of human beings with the religion of the sun god, Ra. While some of the speculation is a bit too assured, the ability of the author to support his premises with personal experience and scientific data add to its credibility. Due to his storytelling abilities, the work reads like a well-constructed novel.

Karl Helicher recommends this.

Brunner, Constantin. *Science, Spirit and Superstition: A New Enquiry into Human Thought.* *Abridged and translated from the German by Abraham Suhl* (London: Allen & Unwin, 1968) First published, 1908. Combining a decisive style of writing with an imaginative new approach to how one perceives reality, Brunner's philosophical thoughts are gathered in this selection from his writings. The primary focus is on the theory of faculties, or the three modes of conceiving of reality which he calls faculties of thought. The first is practical understanding and its content can be defined as a part of science. The second faculty is the spiritual one expressed in philosophy, art and love. And the third is analogous thought, which takes its form in religion, metaphysics and moralism.

Yehudi Menuhin writes, "Constantin Brunner formed my philosophy, to the extent that I have one. I have never come across a thinker or writer who had a better grasp of human nature and the relation of man to his aims, thoughts and ideals, nor who expressed these more succinctly."

And Colin Wilson calls *Science, Spirit and Superstition* "excellent and fascinating."

Burtt, Edwin. *Metaphysical Foundations of Modern Physical Science* (New York: Doubleday, 1954) Written in a relatively simple, direct style, this is an illuminating treatise on the relation between science, man and the universe. The author gives a clear, detailed history of metaphysics, both from the point of view of the scientist and the philosopher. He also develops his theory of the origin and development of the universe.

Henry Guerlac recommended this in *American Scholar*, saying, "I can think of no work that has had such reverberations among our little band of brethren" (Autumn, 1961).

Chazal, Malcolm de. *Plastic Sense.* *Translated from the French by Irving Weiss* (New York: Herder, 1971) First published, 1948. In a wildly imaginative collection of aphorisms, meditations and thoughts on human behavior and the physical world, the French writer and painter offers startling new ways of looking at things. He moves from topics such as body language, which he discusses in poetic rather than psychological terms, to acute perceptions of extraordinary human behavior in social situations. In the appreciative foreword by W. H. Auden, the reader is encouraged to use the book for browsing and return to it for reference.

Anthony Hecht calls this "a collection of the most extraordinary and original *pensées* of virtually any writer of modern times."

Cioran, Emile. *The Temptation to Exist.* *Translated from the French by Richard Howard* (New York: Quadrangle Books,

1968) First published, 1956. The Rumanian-born philosopher analyzes man's fate in view of a new interpretation of existence. This forceful existential treatise is one of the most passionate and subtle ones in modern times, and it is particularly rewarding for the author's thoughts on nationalism and religion. Cioran assumes the reader is well versed in modern literature and thought.

Susan Sontag recommends this book.

Cohen, Morris R. *Reason and Nature: An Essay on the Meaning of the Scientific Method* (New York: Harcourt, 1931) How may the scientific method be applied to almost all subjects in life and scholarship? Answering this question, the famous American philosopher, who lived from 1880 to 1947, shows how reason and the scientific method are suited to the study and history of all fields. His precise, clear prose makes this fairly easy to follow.

John H. Randall recommended this in *American Scholar*, saying, "[Cohen's] appraisal and clarification of the intellectual issues in both the natural and the social sciences remains unsurpassed" (Spring, 1970).

Cuddihy, John Murray. *The Ordeal of Civility* (New York: Basic Books, 1974) Subtitled "Freud, Marx, Levi-Strauss, and the Jewish struggle with modernity," this stimulating study provides a revisionist approach to some fundamental ideas of the past century. His basic theory is that the outstanding Jewish thinkers of our times refused to imitate Gentiles and shunned old-fashioned Jewry. With their subsequent isolation, they worked out profound theories for different modes of existence. It is a provocative and stimulating analysis.

Edgar Z. Friedenberg says, "It has a keenly ironical sense of moral paradox, rooted in the tragedy of culture. Also, wit."

Dixon, William Macneile. *The Human Situation* (London: Longman, 1937) This is an eloquent, lucid statement on the differences and similarities among science, philosophy and religion. Exploring modern scientific and philosophical speculations about the nature of human beings and their world, the professor's lecture shines with wit and fitting allusions. He places particular emphasis on the significance to religious thought of Darwin's efforts, and also provides a clear explanation of the theory of relativity.

Ashley Montagu calls this "an inspired work. One of the most important, beautiful, and wisest books of this or any century."

Foss, Martin. *Symbol and Metaphor in Human Experience* (Princeton: Princeton University Press, 1949) The author delves into the philosophy and the meaning of various symbols and metaphors. He is especially interested in showing how his interpretations give new meaning to the arts. While a relatively technical work, the sensitive style of writing and the highly imaginative speculations are noteworthy. They call for considered rethinking of some of our common assumptions about language.

Marianne Moore recommended this in *American Scholar*, Autumn, 1956.

Lovejoy, Arthur. *The Great Chain of Being* (Cambridge: Harvard University Press, 1936) A history of ideas from antiquity to the close of the eighteenth century, this is a study of intellectual vigor and critical precision. The professor's amazing knowledge and his concepts of governing principles are as impressive as his writing style.

Marjorie Nicolson called this "one of the great books of our generation" (*American Scholar*, Autumn, 1961). And Mike Benedict says, "Lovejoy is well known, a classic mentioned in the best bibliographies . . . but unread."

Mehta, Ved. *The Fly and the Fly-Bottle: Encounters with British Intellectuals* (Boston: Little, 1963) What do England's leading philosophers and historians think about the nature of philosophy and the purpose of historical studies? In a series of remarkable interviews, the Indian-born journalist relates their answers to his questions. The summaries of their philosophical and historical thinking are nicely spiced with a light, human touch. For example, the book concludes with a charming study of the famed historian Sir Lewis Namier and his wife. Among others with whom the blind author has conversations are Bertrand Russell, Ernest Gellner, A. J. Ayer, Iris Murdoch and A. J. P. Taylor.

Meyerson, Emile. *Identity & Reality.* *Translated from the French by Kate Lowenberg* (New York: Macmillan, 1930) First published, 1908. A consistent, sparkling argument, this develops a theory of knowledge which depends upon basic scientific ways of thinking for proof. Drawing on a deep and extensive knowledge of scientific history, Meyerson conceives of rationality as pure, undifferentiated identity. The vigorous style and historical scholarship help to make an otherwise complex argument relatively popular.

Howard Nemerov recommends this.

Onions, Richard. *The Origins of European Thought About the Body, the Mind, the Soul, the World, Time, and Fate* (Cambridge: Cambridge University Press, 1951) Early European thought on fundamental problems are considered from linguistic, literary, and archaeological evidence. Among the eternal questions addressed are those on the nature and function of human consciousness, the role of

fate, and the soul's relation to the body. While this is a work for specialists, the reader with any religious or philosophic curiosity will find it fascinating.

N. O. Brown recommended this in *American Scholar*, Spring, 1970.

Seidenberg, Roderick. *Posthistory Man: An Inquiry* (Chapel Hill: University of North Carolina Press, 1950) What is the meaning of history, particularly to the average person? A nonprofessional historian (the author was a New York architect) suggests a breathtaking and original answer. Seidenberg believes man passed from a prehistoric evolutionary period, where instinct prevailed, to a modern period of rational, intelligent evaluations, but he avers that this alteration came about at great cost. "The depersonalization of the individual will increase until a final state of automatism will be reached." Readers may take strong exception to the viewpoint, but there is no question but that the author bases his opinion on an impressive knowledge of science, psychology, sociology, anthropology, philosophy and history. He brings all this to bear on his treatise, yet he always writes in a pleasing, understandable style.

Crane Brinton wrote, "Seidenberg's suggestive inquiry into the possible future of mankind deserves, I think, something of the same kind of critical consideration Toynbee received" (*American Scholar*, Autumn, 1956).

Shah, Idries. *The Sufis* (Garden City: Doubleday, 1964) Doris Lessing writes, "*The Sufis*. Idries Shah. A Doubleday Anchor Paperback.

"This has proved itself a key book for our time, transforming East-West studies, explaining how the Sufis have influenced the West in ways previously not suspected. It is also the authoritative work on an ancient mystical tradition which is very much alive and influential in all parts of the world. Essential for scholars—and for aspiring Sufi students who need information so they may know how to choose the genuine contemporary Sufic study from ever-proliferating spurious sects. This book has been allowed to go out of print in hardback, yet it is an essential reference book."

Doris Lessing also recommends *Oriental Magic* by Idries Shah.

Shestov, Lev. *In Job's Balances.* *Translated from the Russian by Camilla Coventry* (London: Dent, 1932) First published, 1929. Considered by many to be a leading philosopher, Shestor analyzes the works of Dostoevsky and Tolstoy as well as Spinoza and Pascal. His breadth of penetrating analysis and appreciation of these writers is as impressive as it is instructive. In fact, his style is reminiscent of the eloquence of Pascal himself as he rages against scientific inquiry. The result is an astonishing clarification "on the sources of the eternal truths," which is the subtitle of this volume.

R. D. Laing recommends it.

Still, Colin. *The Timeless Theme: A Critical Theory Formulated and Applied by Colin Still* (London: Nicholson, 1936) The timeless theme is that of myth, and Still is convinced that all works of literary art achieve universal significance in the degree to which they are derived from myth. The myth is the archetype to which a work of literature seeks to conform. Many examples are given to make this point, although the second part of the book involves a lengthy study of Shakespeare's *The Tempest*. While Still's theme is debatable, the argument is so well devloped and the prose so clear that even when one takes exception to a single point, one is left with a new way of looking at literature.

Howard Nemerov recommends this.

Suttie, Ian D. *The Origins of Love and Hate* (London: Kegan, 1935) After many years of research and experience, Suttie concludes his detailed examination of the classical Freudian position with some basic questions. His findings lead him to renounce much of the Freudian theory of personality. There is a brilliant explanation of the reciprocal love between the child and the mother. The study concludes with a long chapter on religion. Suttie believes that the primary appeal of religion is its assuaging a guilt-ridden mind.

Ashley Montagu recommended this, saying it was "the first effective constructive criticism of the Freudian view of human nature I had read. It opened my eyes to the meaning of many human behavioral traits that I had previously not clearly understood. . . .The whole book glows with originality and stimulating ideas . . . " (*American Scholar*, Autumn, 1961).

Upward, Allen. *The New Word* (London: Fifield, 1908) Donald Davie writes, "*The New Word* . . . is one of several books by the maverick British intellectual Allen Upward, who died 1926, which had a deeply formative and abiding influence on Ezra Pound—something that Pound scholars have been slow to acknowledge, though Pound himself never ceased insisting on it. The argument of *The New Word* is extraordinarily original and powerful; and Upward's prose is admirably trenchant."

Woodbridge, Frederick. *Nature and Mind* (New York: Columbia University Press, 1937) Epistemology and metaphysics are the focus of thirty-seven essays by this Columbia University professor who became a legend in his own lifetime. Weaving through the essays is a philosophy of life which is as coherent and as significant today as when it was composed. The vigorous style is matched by the originality and clarity of the ideas. This is one of the few works of this genre which has as much meaning for average readers as it does for professional philosophers.

John H. Randall called this a work of "enduring significance . . . [for] all those concerned with human wisdom" (*American Scholar,* Spring, 1970).

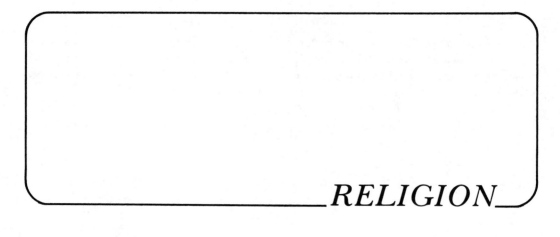

RELIGION

Baskerville, Geoffrey. *English Monks and the Suppression of the Monasteries* (London: Cape, 1937) One of the most readable and entertaining of histories, this is a carefully documented study of life within the English medieval monasteries, and the fate of the monks when Henry VIII suppressed the Church. The historian is in complete control of his data, and with a touch of malice, which the subject calls for, he humanizes the Tudor world.

A. J. P. Taylor recommends this for telling, "What really happened to the Monks."

Bolton, Herbert. *Rim of Christendom* (London: Macmillan, 1936) One of the most indefatigable Jesuit missionaries in southern California was Father Eusebio Kino, a wise pioneer who helped to settle the West. Based on his letters, diaries and unpublished works, the biography offers a fine picture of the Spanish frontiers and the area's first white settlers.

This was cited in the *Journal of American History*, September, 1952.

Coppe, Abiezer. *A Fiery Flying Roll* (Exeter: The Rota, 1973) Reprint of the 1649 edition. Christopher Hill writes, "A fiery flying roll, some sweet sips of some spirituell wine, Copps Return to the wayes of Truth. Fascinating experimental prose from the mid-seventeenth century, unjustly ignored by literary historians and critics."

Eckenstein, Lina. *Woman Under Monasticism* (Cambridge: Cambridge University Press, 1896) Judy Chicago writes, "*Woman Under Monasticism* by Lina Eckenstein—originally published in 1896 and reissued—brilliant—an analysis of the changeover from matriarchy to patriarchy through the changes in specific female roles and also an analysis of the convent and what it was (positively) for women."

Fausset, Hugh L'Anson. *The Lost Dimension* (London: Stuart & Watkins, 1966) Phyllis Theroux writes, "A small, very popular among students of spiritual thought, book, which I currently own in a reproduced (by photocopy) form, which is how this book now travels, from hand to hand, copy machine to copy machine. I consider it extremely insightful and keep it on my desk for frequent reading."

Grant, Robert M. *The Secret Sayings of Jesus* (Garden City: Doubleday, 1960) This is a study of how the Gnostic religion, an early rival of what was to become modern Catholicism, was shaped. The author gives an account of Jesus as he was known and interpreted by the Gnostics in the Gospel of Thomas, which was discovered in 1945. This is an admirable and clear commentary for the average reader.

Robert Bly recommends it.

Hamilton, Edith. *Witness to the Truth* (New York: Norton, 1948) The life of Jesus Christ has had as many interpreters as his teachings, and in a successful effort to summarize and explain the numerous approaches, the author offers a brief, intense and quietly brilliant study. It is suffused with learning, and marked by her great perceptiveness.

Brooks Atkinson wrote, "Without being in any sense a crusading or pious book, it penetrates the mystification that surrounds the name of Christ to the simplicities of His teaching. Although Miss Hamilton is a prodigious classical scholar, she writes with modesty, humility and kindliness. *Witness to the Truth* is the most illuminating book on Christ and Christianity that I have read" (*American Scholar*, Autumn, 1956).

Harrison, Jane. *Themis: A Study of the Social Origins of Greek Religion* (Cleveland: World Publishing Company, 1912) Using the Hymn of the Kourites as her basis for research, the author analyzes what it meant to be an ancient Greek. While her focus is on religion, many other themes are considered. They range from the Olympic games to initiation rites.

Sanford Friedman writes, "*Themis* is a stunning feat of the creative imagination—how many of its shrewd insights derive for instance from Harrison's painstaking and ingenious numismatics; as a writer I find the book inexhaustibly stimulating and suggestive."

Hay, Malcolm. *The Foot of Pride* (Boston: Beacon, 1950) Reissued in 1960 as *Europe and the Jews*. Taking the ideas of Christian anti-Semitism one after the other, the author refutes each charge and examines the fallacies of inhumanity and exaggeration connected with the prejudice. This close, objective study covers the past 1900 years. It is the scholarly work of a sincere Catholic layman. His technique is to produce ancient and contemporary evidence to answer each charge, and the ultimate tragedy of Hitler's Germany is traced back to its frequently overlooked roots.

Frederic Raphael calls this "a volume of merit."

La Barre, Weston. *The Ghost Dance: Origins of Religion* (Garden City: Doubleday, 1970) Ashley Montagu writes that this is "the best book ever written on the nature and evolution of religion." La Barre, basing his analysis on anthropological, historical and psychological findings about religion, believes that religions stem from troubling situations when an individual steps forward to straighten things out. The ghost dance is an example of this event. La Barre holds that now modern people can liberate themselves from the clutches of religion.

Lecomte Du Nouy, Pierre. *Human Destiny* (London: Longmans, 1947) The author, a scientist and philosopher, offers a moving argument for placing greater emphasis on spiritual values and less on material ones. He sees an inevitable disaster in store for civilization unless goals are drastically altered in favor of spirituality. While the main thesis is not especially novel, the uniqueness of the book resides in its clear and simple restatement of this perception. Its sincere vision is buttressed by scientific evidence and a thorough knowledge of history.

James Fixx writes, "An argument, surprisingly fresh although it was published in 1947, that human life has ultimate purpose."

Maritain, Jacques. The Things That are Not Caesar's. *Translated from the French by J. F. Scanlan* (New York: Scribner, 1930) First published, 1927. The French philosopher and Catholic apologist examines and documents the old problem of the separation of church and state. He reviews the events which led to the division and concludes with a prediction for the future. The discussion of the relation of spiritual and secular authority is one of the best ever written.

Peter Glenville recommended this in *Antaeus*, Autumn, 1979.

Mencken, H. L. Treatise on the Gods (New York: Knopf, 1930) James H. Gray writes, "To appreciate the importance of *Treatise on the Gods* you must realize it came upon the American scene at a time when religious orthodoxy was supreme. Huxley, Darwin and Haeckel and Bradlaw had had a profound impact on the thought of Europeans, a full generation earlier. But the great debates in England had made little impression on the United States. Books were still being banned in Boston, including Mencken's own *American Mercury* which contained the Hatrack story. The *Treatise on the Gods* said to the American people: 'Hey, look, back off and see if we can come to some rational explanation for the existence of religion.'

"It seemed to me then, as it seems to me now, that Mencken's conceptualization of the invention of the first god was one that clothed our first ancestors with dignity, courage and an indomitability of spirit. He imagined the first man, confronted with the overwhelming force of nature that was about to destroy him, fighting back, lunging desperately at the encroaching flood and beating it back.

"I retrieve this from memory because my copy of *Treatise on the Gods* was loaned out and lost many years ago and I was unable to replace it. My God, how the United States needs a Mencken today to take on the 'moral majority' and the plague of Bible-pounding television preachers!"

Murray, George Gilbert. Five Stages of Greek Religion (Oxford: Clarendon, 1925) This is a delightfully clear and intelligible explanation of the development of Greek religion by one of the world's leading scholars. The first two lectures concern Saturnia regna and the Olympian conquest. The third is called "The failure of nerve" and traces the decline of religion. The series ends with a brief history of the revival under Julian, followed by the author's translation of a little known text, a treatise by Salustius. This is basic for every student or lover of Greek culture.

Sanford Friedman writes, "Despite Eliot's debunking of Murray, the translator, Murray, the writer, endures as one of the great spirits and teachers of our time."

Sabatier, Auguste. Religions of Authority and the Religion of the Spirit. *Translated from the French by Louise S. Houghton* (New York: McLure, 1904) First published, 1901.

External authority is heinous to this nineteenth-century French writer. He believes that the individual must decide important matters of the spirit, relying on reason rooted in morality. Neither the Church nor the Bible are to be slavishly trusted. The author, employing persuasive exposition and argument, divides his work into three sections: "The Roman Catholic Dogma of Authority," "The Protestant Dogma of Authority," and "The Religion of the Spirit." In the first two sections, he quite democratically challenges both Catholics and Protestants, as he finds almost as much to fault in one as the other. In the final section, he offers what many consider to be a theologically sound argument for individual decisions about religion.

Herbert McArthur says, "Auguste I believe is the brother of the better-known Sabatier; this book is a study of Catholic and Protestant Christianity, arguing for a third version—a kind of Unitarianism. An old-fashioned book and one calculated to infuriate a lot of Christians, I suppose; but it ought not to be forgotten."

Senden, Marius Von. *Space and Sight.* *Translated from the German by Members of the Laboratory of Psychology* (Ithaca, NY: Cornell University Press, 1950) First published, 1932.

Annie Dillard writes, "Sober study, nonfiction, of nineteenth-century Europeans, blind from birth, who had congenital cataracts removed: their learning to see, their learning our concepts of space. Absolutely fascinating. I get six letters a month from people who are trying to find this book."

Suzuki, D. T. *Mysticism: Christian and Buddhist* (New York: Harper, 1957) In a relatively few pages, the world's most prominent authority on Zen Buddhism explains to the lay reader the similarities and differences between Buddhism and Christianity. In a second section, he points out that Shin Buddhism has much in common with Zen, and he makes distinctions between the various approaches to mysticism. His style is clear, his point of view objective, and the overall sense the reader gets is that the author has long ago understood the meaning of life, even if there is no particular meaning.

Nancy Wilson Ross recommended this in *American Scholar*, Autumn, 1961.

SOCIAL SCIENCES

Astell, Mary. *Some Reflections Upon Marriage* (London: J. Nutt, 1700) An early eighteenth-century English bluestocking, Astell wrote this witty and acerbic satire "about the inequality of husbands and wives in marriage, concluding that no woman ought to marry unless the man she chose could prove himself to be of sufficient moral stature to play the part of disinterested custodian to his wife's virtues." So says Ruth Perry.

Perry recommends this saying that Astell's "prose is lucid and lively; her voice is engaging: by turns it is earnest, satiric and steadfastly rational. . . .Many a scholar . . . has opened one of Astell's books in idle curiosity, [and] has been surprised by the passion and conviction issuing from its pages" (*Antioch Review*, Autumn, 1981).

Bates, Marston. *The Prevalence of People* (New York: Scribner, 1955) Ranging over a wide field, from the biology of reproduction to Malthusian theories, the author offers nonprofessionals a direct, easy to understand summary of population studies. He explains plague, disease and other factors limiting growth, and then turns to reproductive elements which encourage population expansion. The clarity of the presentation is matched by Bates's clear understanding of history and the problems inherent in studying populations.

Donald Poroda recommends this.

Berkman, Alexander. *Prison Memoirs of an Anarchist* (New York: Mother Earth Publishers, 1912) Tried and sentenced for the attempted murder of Henry Clay Frick, who employed armed men to crush strikers during the 1892 Homestead steel strike, Berkman, an avid anarchist, tells of his years in prison.

Kay Boyle writes, "*Prison Memoirs of an Anarchist* (like the same author's *The Bolshevik Myth*) creates an alien and wholly convincing world, a world as foreign to the author as to the reader, but a world which in the end becomes our own. Berkman spent sixteen years in American prisons, ten of them in solitary confinement, and emerged a patient, gentle, humorous man who never ceased seeking with determination the salvaging of his own dignity and his own identity, and the dignity and identity of other men."

Blake, James. *The Joint* (Garden City: Doubleday, 1971) In the realm of prison literature, Blake's account is outstanding. Both in jail and out, between sentences, he wrote the letters which make up most of this collection. He often is compared favorably to Genet because of the truthfulness of this account of himself and his experiences.

George Plimpton recommended this in *Antaeus*, Autumn, 1975.

Burney, Christopher. *Solitary Confinement* (New York: Coward-McCann, 1952) What does it feel like to be in solitary confinement for eighteen months? The answer is given by the author who, captured by the Germans in 1942, was put into solitary confinement. Rollo May, in reviewing this work, said, "This is a beautiful, simple and moving book. To my mind it deals with a question more important than even the war and intrigue . . . how a man may find and build his own self."

Francis Steegmuller recommends it.

Caillois, Roger. *Man, Play and Games.* *Translated from the French by Meyer Barash* (New York: Free Press of Glencoe, 1961) First published, 1958.

Applying historical and social perspectives to the topics of play and games, the author divides his fascinating study into two sections. The first deals with a definition and classification of the subject and the second with a theory and practical application of games in daily living and education, especially mathematics. In a careful analysis of just what constitutes play and its various forms, the author offers new insights into an ordinary activity. The style of writing, the author's historical knowledge and his general verve quickly involve the reader in a remarkable literary experience.

Alison Lurie recommends this.

Cornford, F. M. *Microcosmographia Academica: Being a Guide for the Young Academic Politician* (Cambridge: Bowes and Bowes, 1908) Although only fifty-three pages long, this is a definitive study of politics in the English university. The focus is on the students, and the tone is both ironical and serious. The common sense of the discourse makes it applicable to American universities as well, with ramifications for any situation where politics are a necessary ingredient. The economy of language and the deceptive simplicity of the style makes this as enjoyable today as when it was published.

Theodore H. Hesburgh recommends it.

Cox, Oliver Cromwell: *Class, Caste and Race: A Study in Social Dynamics* (Garden City: Doubleday, 1948) A Tuskegee Institute professor amasses a wealth of material to support his theory about the history of race relations and the position of the black person in the United States. Drawing upon scores of studies, and hundreds of quotations, his analysis is exceptionally thorough. Not everyone will agree with his conclusions, yet this comprehensive history is basic for arriving at a reasoned judgment about racial friction.

Kenneth B. Clark wrote, "This is one of the most profound and penetrating analyses of racial and related problems I have ever read" (*American Scholar*, Spring, 1970).

Cunard, Nancy. *Negro Anthology* (London: Wishart, 1934) One of the earliest collections of material on black life, this was published at the expense of the author to show that there was "no superior race, merely cultural differences." Almost every aspect of the black experience is covered, either by black authors or by white people sympathetic to the Negro cause. History, literature, law, education, theatre, politics, art and music are among the many topics considered. The book is not limited to America or England, but touches on black culture in other parts of the world as well.

Virgil Thomson recommended this in *Antaeus*, Winter, 1975.

Davidson, Donald. *The Attack on Leviathan* (Chapel Hill: University of North Carolina, 1938) John R. Milton writes, "During the 200-year course of American life and letters, a kind of literature called 'regional' has been both cherished and vilified. Since 1940 a prevalent pseudo-sophistication and quasi-nationalism among too many critics and professors has led to a rather general condemnation of many excellent novels, and some poems, that give importance to the geographical, environmental, or physical context (setting) of their action. Usually the term 'regional' is applied to nonmetropolitan areas, to literary works arising from somewhat rural landscapes and people.

"The real question is whether regional literature is by its nature prevented from expressing universal qualities. The obvious answer—obvious but not always recognized—is that almost all great art is simultaneously regional and universal. Davidson's book is a stimulating and important discussion of these matters, correcting a great number of misconceptions."

Russell Kirk also recommends this book.

Deming, Barbara. *Prison Notes* (New York: Grossman, 1966) The author kept notes during her stay in a Georgia prison after a 1964 march for freedom. The writing is direct and deceptively free of ran-

cour. Her work is a graphic testimony to the courage of the author and her friends. Deming's experience is one of frustration, for, as she puts it, "One thing that makes nonviolent struggle difficult is that usually one must wait so long to see the effects of one's actions. The effect of a violent act is immediately visible."

Dwight MacDonald recommended this in *American Scholar*, Summer, 1970.

Elias, Norbert. *The Civilizing Process.* *Translated from the German by Edmund Jephcott* (New York: Urizen Books, 1978) First published, 1939.

The roots of social behavior, good and bad manners, and the way these rituals have affected history are presented in an almost breathless, yet credible, fashion by a truly fascinating observer. The intellectual brilliance of this study has won Elias a place among the top historians and social commentators of Europe, but he is too little known in the United States. Moving from the medieval period to modern times, with numerous pauses and digressions, the narrative shows how everyday rituals, from table manners to blowing one's nose, developed as both a mirror of and an operative mechanism in history. The fascination lies with the sudden recognition that today's etiquette, and even routine manners, are in no way simply spontaneous.

Figes, Eva. *Patriarchal Attitudes* (New York: Stein & Day, 1970) Christianity, Freudian analysis and the rise of capitalism are among the factors which the author believes have helped to mold rigid attitudes about women in Western society. Her historical overview of the role of women is paralleled by a close examination of the patriarchal motivations which lie behind manifestations of male domination.

Alison Lurie recommends this as "one of the best feminist works."

Frank, Jerome. *Law and the Modern Mind* (New York: Bretano, 1930) Matching theories of law with social and psychological concepts, the noted jurist suggests that the law is a father substitute. As such, it "stirs up unconscious attitudes, concealed desires, illusory ideals, which get in the way of realistic observation of the . . . law." Given the belief that the law and the father are united, the predictable result is that numerous people think the law must be certain and absolute. Judges are oracles passing down the "word," and lawyers tend to be involved in the deception. The potential chicanery of those who practice law has never been better exposed.

Bruce A. Ackerman recommended this in *Daedalus*, Winter, 1974.

Harrington, Michael. *The Other America: Poverty in the United States* (New York: Macmillan, 1962) In what is now a classic study, yet not that well known to many people, the author discusses the underclass, that invisible subculture which prevails despite America's wealth. In this journey through an economic subterranean world, the author demonstrates the extent of the desperation and the needs of this group. His solutions are debatable, but his findings are horrendous.

Eugene McCarthy recommended this in *Antaeus*, Winter, 1975.

Kempton, Murray. *The Briar Patch* (New York: Dutton, 1973) The focus is on the trial of the Panthers, a black militant group. But the book is actually about black people in America, and their sometimes futile efforts to win justice. Although this won the 1973 National Book Award, it is now difficult to locate it.

Nat Hentoff said, "What lifts this book beyond a journalistic account is, of course, Kempton—his flavorful appreciation of all kinds of ambiguities and contradictions; his extraordinary sensitive ear as well as eye . . ." (*The Village Voice Literary Supplement*, October, 1981).

Keyserling, Count Hermann von. *The Book of Marriage* (New York: Harcourt, 1926) The Russo-German philosopher contributes to this work which he edited. It consists of papers from twenty-four members of a symposium on the principles and philosophy of marriage. Among the topics concerned are romantic marriage, the Indian ideal of marriage (Tagore), marriage as a psychological relationship (Jung), love as an art (Havelock Ellis) and marriage as a sacrament. There are numerous conflicting attitudes and approaches to the subject and the collection effectively presents points of view from everyone, feminists and traditionalists, psychologists and moralists. An outstanding achievement, this continues to be important today.

Gail Godwin recommended this in *Antaeus*, Autumn, 1977.

Legman, Gershon. *Love and Death: A Study in Censorship* (New York: Breaking Point, 1949) Censorship laws, at both the local and national level, are a constant threat to imaginative literature, forcing it into areas of perversity because vital subjects are denied direct expression. And while this was written many years ago, before the present easing of censorship (particularly as it relates to sex) the arguments are still valid. In fact, the case the author sets forth is almost totally applicable in fighting today's censor. As an added bonus, there is an excellent chapter on comic books.

Larry McMurtry recommends this.

Lilge, Frederic. *The Abuse of Learning: The Failure of the German University* (New York: Macmillan, 1948) Why did so many German universities and faculty members fail to oppose Hitler? After a careful study of the records, the author draws the cultural and ideological backgrounds to a truly complex situation. If there is no single answer to his question, there are several reasonable explanations. Much of what the University of California professor (and former student in Germany) reports serves as a significant reminder of the role of education in both the totalitarian and democratic states.

Herbert McArthur says, "A short book, it's a striking analysis of the German universities, their 19th-century background and what happened under the Nazis. I wish more people had read it during the 'troubles' of the 60s; but it's still very much worth reading."

Madge, Charles. *Society in the Mind* (London: Faber, 1964) What are the ruling ideas of our society and how can they be modified to assure a more pleasant life for all? This is the major question which concerns Professor Madge as he investigates our basic body of ideas about society and social institutions. He shows how the ideas developed historically, and how the pictures of society in our own time differ from those of earlier eras. Later, he discusses how appropriate values are evolved.

Donald G. MacRae writes, "Professor Madge won distinction as a poet, as a sociologist and as one of the pioneers of empirical research in industrial society employing methods derived from anthropology. *Society in the Mind* is the best statement known to me of an unfashionable but, I think, correct theoretical position which one might call something like 'Sociological Subjectivism.' He writes beautifully and with admirable brevity."

Mannheim, Karl. *Ideology and Utopia.* *Translated from the German by Louis Wirth and Edward Shils* (London: Kegan, 1936) First published, 1929. Revolutionary in its import, Mannheim's book puts forth the significant, critically central idea that people, far from indulging in "pure"

thought, are promoting their own interests through the ideology of their social groups. As a result, Mannheim justifies the need for discovering people's unconscious motivations in order to understand their perspective. The technique for this reflection is called the sociology of knowledge, and here he applies it to the complementary concepts of "ideology" and "utopia." Mannheim's method makes room for the social and personal equations, and he puts what people think into a social context.

Edward Shils recommended this in *Daedalus*, Winter, 1974.

Moberly, Walter. *The Crisis in the University* (London: S. C. M. Press, 1949) Acting as a mediator between the state and the universities in England, the author was chairman of the University Grants Committee. His background is enough to insure the quality of his knowledge about the growth and development of universities, and while not all readers will agree with his conclusions, they are built on a strong foundation. He deplores the emphasis on the sciences and social sciences at the expense of the humanities, the shift away from focusing on quality, and the failure of the university to address itself to problems facing society at large. This is a worthy addition to such deeply impressive works as Ortega y Gasset's *Mission of the Universities* (1944).

Theodore H. Hesburgh writes, "Sir Walter Moberly's book considers an aspect of university education which is largely neglected today. I highly recommend it."

Mumford, Lewis. *The Culture of Cities* (New York: Harcourt, 1938) One of the most careful analyses of urban life, this is a pioneer study which traces the history of the development of cities and declares a need for radical change. Although written over forty years ago, the primary arguments are as valid today as when they were written. While some of the conclusions are debatable, the discussions are important for the questions they raise. In addition, we have Mumford's highly personal and lively style, so the work is as much a joy for its literary merit as for its perceptive analysis of the issues.

Eugene McCarthy recommended it in *Antaeus*, Winter, 1975.

Murie, Margaret. *Island Between* (Fairbanks: University of Alaska Press, 1977) Eskimo life on St. Lawrence Island before the advent of outsiders is the focus of this extraordinary account. The author, who is familiar with the far North and the wilderness areas, shows what the ultimate effect of modern technology upon Eskimo culture amounts to. The book is illustrated by the author's naturalist husband.

Ted Ryberg recommends this.

Parker, Tony. *The Frying Pan: A Prison and Its Prisoners* (London: Hutchinson, 1970) Taped interviews with almost one hundred prisoners and half the staff of a psychiatric prison in England reveal the success and failures of a new, innovative approach to disturbed criminals. Scrupulously objective, Parker records without comment and makes no assessment about the functioning of the prison. His purpose is to expose the kinds of people involved in daily prison life, and the result is intensely engrossing.

Eve Auchincloss writes, "Several books of interviews by the English Tony Parker have been published here but little noticed. . . .They are extraordinary for their imagination and compassion. I will never feel the same again about sexual offenders, criminals, lighthouse keepers, etc. after reading his self-effacing and deeply moving examinations of lives that most people would rather not notice. He is almost entirely neglected here." (See next entry as well.)

Parker, Tony. *In No Man's Land: Some Unmarried Mothers* (London: Hutchinson, 1972) While the role of the unmarried mother is now more acceptable, it is still a difficult one. Here six mothers talk about themselves. Using a tape recorder, Parker transcribes the voices of the "new" women, most of whom are British. The honesty and sensitivity of the presentation is matched by the deep satisfaction the mothers find in their children. Due to careful editing, the book may be read as literature, not simply as social research. The book provides outstanding insights into the lives of these women.

Eve Auchincloss recommends this too, as well as Parker's *The Hidden World of Sex Offenders* (1969), (published in England as *The Twisting Lane*); and *Lighthouse* (1976).

Polak, Frederick. *The Image of the Future: Enlightening the Past, Orientating the Present, Forecasting the Future.* *Translated from the Dutch by Elise Boulding* (New York: Elsevier, 1973) First published, 1961. Written by a Dutch sociologist, this is a study of the dynamics of culture. Here one finds analyses of people's conscious efforts (their foreknowledge) and unconscious efforts (their dreams and desires) to shape their civilization in light of different clusters of expectations and ideals. The author moves from a study of ancient Greece to Israel, to medieval Christianity, and to recent images projected by psychoanalysis. It is a profound study, as impressive for its scholarship as for its literary form.

Kenneth Boulding calls this "one of the early classics of the futurology movement and indeed can almost be credited with starting the movement."

Slater, Philip. *The Glory of Hera* (Boston: Beacon, 1969) Proceeding from an objective, social-scientific point of view, the Brandeis professor offers a startling revisionist assessment of Greek's Golden Age. Actually a comparative cultural analysis based upon psychoanalytical and sociological perspectives, the study examines the realities of Greek family life from our current understanding of the emotional consequences of family dynamics. The book is as provocative as it is unique,

particularly in the close, psychoanalytical interpretations of classical Greek life and mythology. Furthermore, the author has some pertinent observations about the role of women in ancient times.

Frederic Raphael calls this "a very good instance of a dubious tradition, the psychoanalytic treatment of Greek myth."

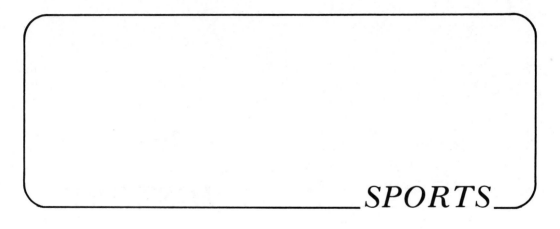

SPORTS

Asinof, Eliot. *Eight Men Out: The Black Sox and the 1919 World Series* (New York: Holt, 1963) Many claim this scandal to be the most spectacular scandal in the history of American sports. It happened during the 1919 World Series when eight members of the Chicago White Sox allegedly plotted with gamblers to let Cincinnati carry off the winner's prize. The eight were tried in 1921, and in this detailed and sympathetic reconstruction of the series and the trial, the author, who was once a ballplayer, builds a suspense story rarely found in fiction or nonfiction about the sport. In sympathy with the underpaid players, he finds their action understandable, if not justified. So what at first appears to be a clear case against the eight becomes clouded not only by the unresolved points brought out at the trial, but by the entire history of the game, a history which the author copiously draws upon. This is a superb and comprehensive account.

Vance Bourjaily calls this "well worth reviving."

Bourjaily, Vance. *The Unnatural Enemy* (New York: Dial, 1963) While best known as a novelist (*The Hound of Earth* [1955]; *The Violated* [1958]; *The Man Who Knew Kennedy* [1967], etc.), Bourjaily has written a superb book on hunting, his first work of nonfiction. He contends that the sport heightens the spiritual and aesthetic experience of being out of doors. The ethical question about killing is met with an astute analysis which is as provocative as it is honest. Beyond this, there is the heart of the book which is a sensitive, graceful argument for the moving power of the environment to intermingle with our senses. One must, he suggests, heighten one's sensitivity to the beauty of nature, whether it be an open field or a bird in flight. Also, there are some mildly bizarre and humorous episodes dealing with violence and insensitive hunters. An intelligent, questioning book, this illuminates the love of one man for the wonders of nature.

HISTORY

Adams, Henry. *The Degradation of the Democratic Dogma* (New York: Macmillan, 1919) History, its vital aspects, and its relation to modern man are the topics of these three essays collected after the death of Adams (1838-1918). While not as distinguished as his masterpiece, *The Education of Henry Adams*, it does afford a refreshing view of history and the universe by an original thinker. Interestingly, when this was first published, it received mixed reviews, with most of the professional historians taking a negative stand.

Howard Nemerov recommends this volume.

Arnstein, Walter L. *The Bradlaugh Case* (London: Oxford, 1965) Subtitled "A Study in Late Victorian Opinion and Politics," this is a historical classic. Several critics claim it to be a model of historical investigation, and the style of writing keeps one in suspense from beginning to end. The case concerns Bradlaugh who was prevented from taking his seat in Parliament in 1880 because he was a professed atheist. For six years, the English conserva-

tive religious elements denied him his position, although each time he presented himself for re-election, he was elected. The confusing nature of the law and the character of Bradlaugh, the man and his politics, are excellently explained.

A. J. P. Taylor says, "Along with Geoffrey Holmes' *The Trial of Dr. Sacheverell*, the finest legal-political *affaires* in England."

Babeuf, François Noël. *The Defense of Gracchus Babeuf before the High Court of Vendome*. *Translated from the French by John A. Scott* (Amherst: University of Massachusetts Press, 1967) First published, 1794. The defendant (1760-1797) began work as a keeper of local manorial rolls and, after the French revolution of 1789, became involved in the defense of the common Paris worker. Seen as a foe of the government, as a possible rallying figure for the dissatisfied underclasses, Babeuf was arrested and tried in 1796 for treason. Determined to deny actual conspiracy, yet anxious to justify the right of the people to revolt, he prepared his ingenious defense. As a document of human rights, it is unsurpassed, yet it failed to win him his freedom and he was executed in 1797.

Anthony Hecht writes, "*The Defence of Gracchus Babeuf* is a valiant, generous and intelligent plea, addressed against all odds, to unsympathetic ears, with the speaker's very life itself at stake, in behalf of the elementary decencies of human life, of judicial and governmental fairness, of political freedom. Its eloquence derives both from the justness of its cause and the hopelessness of its occasion. Babeuf was a genuine martyr, and, though uneducated, an extremely intelligent and thoughtful one."

Beard, Mary. *Woman as Force in History: A Study in Traditions and Realities* (New York: Macmillan, 1946) Carl Degler wrote, "...a striking thing about the book is that it is frankly antifeminist ... The book, indeed, argues openly and forcefully against feminists, both male and female. Among those singled out for extended criticism, for example, are Mary Wollstonecraft and John Stuart Mill.

"To put the matter quite bluntly, a central point of the book is that the feminist conception of women's history is wrong. As Beard reads the literature of feminism she finds that the subjection of women is taken for granted rather than proved ...

"[Her] larger purpose ... is to examine critically the tradition that 'women were members of a subject sex throughout history.' Her method is to bring together a great number of examples of women's past activities that historians and others have either overlooked or subordinated in writing about the activities of human beings. ... Beard's rejection of the thesis of subjection may place her outside the grand feminist tradition, but her emphasis upon the constant and active role of women in the past

puts her squarely in the midst of those who are fundamentally feminist in outlook ... " (*Daedalus*, Winter, 1974).

Bell, Daniel, editor. *The Radical Right* (New York: Doubleday, 1963) What is the radical right? What does it want? Here a number of prominent historians and social scientists (Daniel Bell, Nathan Glazer, Richard Hofstadter, Herbert Hyman, Seymour Lipset, Talcott Parsons, David Riesman, Peter Viereck and Alan Westin) explore these questions. The final section provides a summary of three of the most radical rightist movements: McCarthyism, Coughlinism, and Birchism. The clear explanation of the difference between conservatism and radicalism makes the book as useful today as when it was written.

Frances Fitzgerald writes that this is "a collection of essays by some of this country's best sociologists and intellectual historians including Hofstadter, Glazer and Riesman. It is once again timely—and should not be out of print."

Bevan, Aneurin. *In Place of Fear* (New York: Monthly Review Press, 1964) First published, 1952. In the 1945 elections in England, the Labour Party won a landslide victory and Ernest Bevin became Foreign Secretary while Aneurin Bevan became Minister of Health. A few years before his death, Aneurin Bevan summarized his political, economic and social beliefs. A fine stylist with a clear understanding of his role in history, he wrote what a critic for the *Times Literary Supplement* called "a significant and important book ... It will be examined by historians either as a summary of fulfilled hopes, or as an epitaph on their destruction."

Desmond Morton wrote, "Today the book is obviously dated ... The humanism remains ... I have always envied his clarity and force, and because of the impact of his writing, I have never begrudged the time I have myself given to that most transient of forms, political writing" (*Saturday Night*, May 1976).

Bradford, William. *Of Plymouth Plantation, 1620-1647* (New York: Knopf, 1952) First published in 1856. Sometimes titled *History of Plymouth Plantation 1620-1647.*

Written between 1630 and 1650, this history is the work of a Mayflower Pilgrim who became the first governor of Plymouth in 1621 and was re-elected to that post every year until 1656. The manuscript, prepared for his descendants and not for publication, was stolen by English soldiers during the Revolution and taken to England, where it was identified only in 1855. With the 1952 edition, painstakingly edited by Samuel Eliot Morison, the work was finally presented in an exact and authoritative manner. While the history is, by common consent of historians, among America's first important classics, it is not that well-known. It is a pleasure to read. What saves the sometimes mundane passages is the author's obvious love of the good life and his exceedingly intelligent style. America as it really was, not distorted through a romantic lens, comes through on almost every page.

This will be included in the Soviet Union's "Library of the Literature of the United States," comprised of the works of sixty prose writers and eighty poets.

Briffault, Robert. *The Decline and Fall of the British Empire* (New York: Simon & Schuster, 1938) Drawing upon his knowledge of anthropology and history and his considerable skill as a novelist, Briffault sounds the warning note which, in fact, was to prove all too true. His contention is that the British Empire (in 1938) is on the verge of collapse. While his basic assumption is now beyond debate, the true delight

for the modern reader lies in examining the evidence. Briffault develops a stirring narrative about the hidden worm in such things as public schools, cricket matches, and ruling class procedures. The attack is a masterpiece of vituperative writing.

Morton Sobell writes that this book "clearly delineates the West's role in the rise of Hitler, and projects a scenario—which was quite accurate—of the development of World War II, *viz.* Germany attacking Great Britain, instead of the Soviet Union, which was not the way Great Britain wanted it."

Burckhardt, Jakob. *Force and Freedom: Reflections on History. Translated from the German by M.D. Hottinger* (New York: Pantheon, 1943) First published, 1905. A famous historian interprets, explains and comments on the flow of cultural history. He examines religion, culture and the state, and has a penetrating chapter on "The Great Men of History." Along with his perceptive insights, this Swiss historian had some peculiar notions by today's standards. For example, he believed that war was a necessary factor in the higher development of civilizations. While the translation does not always faithfully render Burckhardt's dynamic style, it does capture his admirable scholarship and breadth of learning.

Dennis Barnes writes, "This is not so much a history as lectures and notes for lectures about various events including those leading up to the French Revolution. It is a detached, mid-nineteenth century, skeptical and learned view, with some striking ideas and phrases."

Burke, Kenneth. *Attitudes Toward History* 2 volumes (New York: New Republic, 1937) In two slender volumes, the philosopher and literary critic explores the meaning of history for the modern age.

The reflections are often from a Marxist perspective, although there is more emphasis here on cultural anthropology than on political stances. The highly personal digressions and sometimes detailed footnotes give the work a particular flavor which neatly emphasizes the problems of applying and understanding history. Burke's lucid prose and marvelous imagery carry the reader to new interpretations and a closer appreciation of the value of history.

Stanley Edgar Hyman called this "the outstanding book of the last thirty years [in literary criticism] . . . With its concepts of symbolic action, it profoundly revolutionized the study and teaching of literature."

Carr, Edward. *Romantic Exiles: A Nineteenth Century Portrait Gallery* (London: Gollancz, 1933) Alexander Herzen, the Gogol of Russian political writers, is the central character in this study of nineteenth-century Russian and German exiles who settled in other parts of Europe, primarily in London. Carr not only examines the political and economic struggles of the period, but he is equally concerned with the lives of people surrounding Herzen. V. S. Pritchett said, "Carr's book combines the virtues of introducing us to the pre-Marxian political and social panorama and of placing the involved domestic histories of his Romantics against it. The material . . . is so fantastic that it might well be the basis of biography dressed up as fiction" (*Christian Science Monitor*, May 6, 1933).

Francis Steegmuller recommends this book.

Cochrane, Charles N. *Christianity and Classical Culture: A Study of Thought and Action from Augustus to Augustine* (New York: Oxford, 1941) A scholarly contrast is drawn here between the Christian and Graeco-Roman view of life. Ethics, political action and social thought are considered. The author begins with Augustus, the Roman dictator, and concludes with the fourth-century attempt of St. Augustine to sever connections with the earlier traditions.

Whitney J. Oates wrote that this is "a landmark in the history of classical scholarship . . . [It] studies and interprets the first centuries of our era when Graeco-Roman civilization amalgamated with Christianity . . ." (*American Scholar*, Autumn, 1961).

Collier, Richard. *The Sound of Fury: An Account of the Indian Mutiny* (London: Collins, 1963) Drawing upon almost every printed source (approximately six hundred are listed), the author gives the best, most accurate, and most thrilling account of the Indian Mutiny of 1857. An impartial and well-rounded picture presents the Mutiny from the side of the Indians as well as that of the British. Today's readers feel as though they are sharing in the actual experiences surrounding the revolt of the Bengal Army and the subsequent explosion in northern and central India. This book explores the nature of Victorian virtues and flaws as well as the Mutiny itself, and this makes for extremely compelling reading.

Marie Seton recommends this book.

Commission of Inquiry Into the Charges Made Against Leon Trotsky in the Moscow Trials. *Not Guilty* (New York: Harper, 1938) Chaired by John Dewey, the American Commission found Trotsky "not guilty" of the crimes charged by the Soviet Union. (Two years later, in 1940, Stalin reversed the decision by hiring an assassin to kill Trotsky.) The Commission's report is based on evidence from the Moscow trials of the early 1930s, and an evaluation of the testimony by scores of expert witnesses.

Sidney Hook writes, "*Not Guilty* is the only volume in any language which contains an exhaustive analysis of the evidence presented by the Soviet prosecutor and of other relevant documents and testimony bearing on the first two frame up Moscow Trials. There are some who on the strength of Khruschev's speech before the XX Congress of the C. P. S. U. in 1956 assume that he reveals the truth about these trials and have modified their judgment of these trials retrospectively. However this is an error. Khruschev does not discuss the Moscow Trials. It is only this volume issued by the John Dewey Commission of Inquiry (together with the earlier one that presented Leon Trotsky's defense *The Case for Leon Trotsky*, consisting of the text of the hearings at Coyacon, Mexico), which contains this invaluable material."

Dobie, James Frank. *Coronado's Children: Tales of Lost Mines and Buried Treasure in the Southwest* (Texas: Southwest Press, 1930) Following Coronado and his expedition to find the seven lost cities of Cibola, Dobie also devotes himself to other treasure tales of the Southwest. The yarns of buried treasure, some true, some speculative, are well documented. There is a splendid map and numerous charts to help the reader follow along.

Bob Carmack recommends this.

Dubois, William E. B. *Souls of Black Folk* (Chicago: McClung, 1903) Dubois (1868-1963) carefully documents and explains the history of black people, particularly those in the Southern states. This is a seminal work in the field of American history.

Eugene Genovese considers Dubois "probably the greatest American of our century. [He] requires international attention. His *Souls of Black Folk* alone could educate world opinion on the depth and meaning of the Afro-American contribu-

tion to modern civilization" (*Times Literary Supplement*, January 21, 1977).

Fair, Charles. *The Dying Self* (Middletown: Wesleyan University Press, 1962) An analysis of the human mind, this concludes that man is regressing into barbarism and Western civilization probably is doomed. The thesis is based as much upon political and historical evidence as it is on neuroanatomy and neurophysiology. While the groundwork is technical, the style is clear and this is an eminently readable book.

Robert Bly recommends it.

Fuller, Thomas. *Worthies of England* (London: Printed by J. G. W. L., 1662) An abridged edition, edited by John Freeman, was published by George Allen & Unwin, London, 1952.

Fuller (1608-1661) was one of England's best known writers at the time of his death, and while he has had occasional revivals, he has been neglected in the past century. A master of the miniature life, he discusses county by county, shire by shire, the "worthies" of each section. In addition, he considers such things as natural commodities, manufacturers, buildings, wonders and even proverbs. He cannot resist a story "purposely interlaced, not as meat, but as condiment," and the characters emerge as living people. There is always immense gusto, and, as Leslie Stephens said, "no trace of dullness, and he enjoys immediate and intimate contact with the reader."

Christopher Fry recommends this.

Fülöp-Miller, Réne. *The Mind and Face of Bolshevism* (New York: Knopf, 1927) When first published, *The Times Literary Supplement* reported that this was "certainly one of the most remarkable books that have appeared on the new Russia." Today, it is valued for the historical background it supplies on the cultural development of Russia. Written when all art was dedicated to enhancing the state, the study shows the benefits and the costs of such a policy.

Peter Glenville recommended this in *Antaeus*, Autumn, 1979.

Grunfeld, Fred. *Prophets Without Honor* (London: Hutchinson, 1979) The prophets are sixteen Jewish intellectuals, including the obvious ones, such as Freud, Kafka and Einstein, and the less well-known, such as Toller, Kolmar and Broch. The time and place is the Weimar Republic, and the purpose is to illustrate the creative tensions arising from the precarious position of the intellectuals in an anti-Semetic setting. Following the form of collective, contrasting biographies, the author discusses several prominent figures in each chapter. He describes the background of each person, discussing the parallels and contrasts with the others, and when possible, quotes extensively from their writings. The discursive sketches are as fascinating as they are compassionate.

Edgar Z. Friedenberg says, "It has a keenly ironical sense of moral paradox, rooted in the tragedy of culture. Also, wit."

Hazard, Paul. *European Thought in the Eighteenth Century*. *Translated from the French by J. Lewis May* (New Haven: Yale University Press, 1954) First published, 1946. In an intellectual history of Europe from Montesquieu to Lessing, the author concentrates on the collapse of traditional values and the succession of the Man of Reason. Although there is some reference to English writers, Hazard devotes himself primarily to French thinkers and their cultural characteristics which lead them from religion to reason and then to romanticism. As learned and witty as he is scholarly, the author conveys an unusual feeling for the age and the people who helped to mold it.

Carlos Fuentes recommended this in *Antaeus*, Autumn, 1977.

Holmes, Geoffrey. *The Trial of Dr. Sacheverell* (London: Methuen, 1973) A superb and exciting story is spun from improbable material. Charging that the church was endangered by the Whigs' fondness for religious dissenters, Dr. Sacheverell preached a sermon in St. Paul's Cathedral in 1709. The Whigs were outraged, and by 1710 the Doctor was on trial before the Lords in Westminster Hall. He almost had to be found guilty, but, after being given a derisory sentence, he emerged a triumphant hero, at least to the Tories. Not only does Holmes' style and historical research revivify the age of Queen Anne, but he writes in such a way as to bring enormous suspense to the trial. This is political history as dramatic action.

A. J. P. Taylor says, "Along with Walter L. Arnstein's *The Bradlaugh Case*, the finest legal-political *affaires* in England."

Kent, Frank. *The Great Game of Politics* (New York: Doubleday, 1923) This is a manual for the politician. Thanks to the author's experience and intellectual appreciation of history and the political process, the work is also considerably more than that. It provides a vivid account of the way the human factor influences government and the governed. Most of the philosophy, if not the detail, is as applicable today as when it was written.

Henry Cabot Lodge writes, "He concentrates on politics, on how to get into it, how you get ahead in it and how you get out of it. It is all told in Frank Kent's lucid, limpid style and with an occasional tongue-lashing (as only Frank can do it)."

King, Jr., Martin Luther. *Stride Toward Freedom* (New York: Harper, 1958) Telling the story of the successful boycott of Montgomery, Alabama's "Jim Crow" bus system, King also documents the emergence of black Americans as politically powerful and important in Southern life. Furthermore, he continually demonstrates the inspiring leadership qualities which thrust him to the forefront of the struggle for justice in the United States.

Nikki Giovanni says, "i meet people who . . . want to ignore or deny the awful eloquence of martin luther king, jr. . . . *Stride Toward Freedom* deserves a reading because [it] has something both sweet and crucial to share about the human condition and [it] shares it beautifully. with words well chosen. emotions properly harnessed. thoughts well formed."

Kogon, Eugen. *The Theory and Practice of Hell.* *Translated from the Russian by Heinz Norden* (New York: Farrar, Straus, 1950) The erudite and brave author survived the Buchenwald concentration camp, and here, as a trained sociologist, he objectively surveys the social phenomenon of an S. S. dominated, miniature state. The S. S. acted as lawmakers and judges, yet the actual administration of the camp was left to the prisoners. Hitler's dream of a whole world as a concentration camp is seen here on a small scale, and aside from the intrinsic value of the book as sociology, it is a lasting monument to the necessity for sanity in an occasionally deranged world.

Roger W. Straus recommends this.

Lukacs, John. *Historical Consciousness: Or the Remembered Past* (New York: Harper, 1968) The evolution of historical consciousness is traced through national characteristics, religious history, memory and time. The author's brilliant style and his perception of historical problems which remain significant to the modern age makes this as fascinating as it is informative.

Jacques Barzun writes, "I think [this] is a remarkable work."

McManners, John. *French Ecclesiastical Society Under the Ancien Regime: A Study of Angers in the Eighteenth Century* (Manchester: Manchester University Press, 1960) A detached, sometimes ironic, yet warm portrait of Angers, an eighteenth-century town, this work portrays a community built around the church. The author has brought reality to history by showing the change in the community as it moved closer to the French Revolution. The drama of the revolution is confined to the last hundred pages. Yet, the recreation in living terms of the complex religious life of the French town is accomplished in a polished narrative style.

Peter Gay wrote, "I can think of few books that I would rather give to the student of history—even of other periods—than this one" *(American Scholar,* Spring, 1970).

McNeill, William. *The Rise of the West* (Chicago: University of Chicago Press, 1963) In approximately eight hundred pages, the historian sets out to explain the history of mankind. H. R. Trevor-Roper called it "not only the most learned and the most intelligent, it is also the most stimulating and fascinating book" of its type. The scholar considers the interdependence of economics, sociology, technology, art and other human endeavors in the progress of man from the distant past to the present time.

Harrison E. Salisbury says, "*The Rise of the West* gives us extraordinary insights of another kind; the leading role played by climatology; epidemiology; shifts of wind and weather which produced such extraordinary human movements as the Mongol invasions of Russia, Europe, China and India in the twelfth and thirteenth centuries; the role of the rats and the plague in shifting balance of power. His work shows how extra-human causes result in major historical movements."

Mahdi, Muhsin. *Ibn Khaldûn's Philosophy of History* (London: Allen & Unwin, 1957) The great Arabian historian is best known for *The Muquaddimah*, a comprehensive study of the philosophy of history written near the end of the fourteenth century. Here, the author gives a systematic account of Ibn Khaldûn's work. He tells the story of the historian's active life as well.

Melville Herskovits wrote that this was "an extremely significant contribution to history and social sciences because of the light it throws on the broader relationships of the whole of Western European culture" (*American Scholar*, Autumn, 1961).

Milton, George. *Eve of Conflict: Stephen A. Douglas and the Needless War* (Boston: Houghton, 1934) A front rank American historian introduces the idea that the Civil War was much more than a struggle to free the slaves. Neither was it entirely an economic struggle. It was more complex, and as much a mistake as it was, to some critics, a necessity. The clear style and the careful research, drawn primarily from the letters and writings of Douglas, add to the reading experience.

This was cited in the *Journal of American History's* list of books chosen by historians (September, 1952).

Muller, Herbert. *The Loom of History* (New York: Harper, 1958) This is a vivid history of the various civilizations which have succeeded one another down the ages in Asia Minor. The author moves from the ancient society of Phrygia to the modern times of Ataturk, usually with a sense of recurrent pessimism as to what has been accomplished. The scholarship, eloquent literary style and humanistic concepts make this a solid addition to the author's better known work *The Uses of the Past* (1952).

Peter Glenville recommended this in *Antaeus*, Autumn, 1979.

Namier, Lewis. *1848: The Revolution of the Intellectuals* (London: Oxford, 1946) A brilliant historian and an equally brilliant writer, Namier is a historian's historian. In this discussion of the crisis of 1848, he depicts the movement of middle-class intellectuals who set out to improve European society. The 1848 revolt proved to be a turning point in the lives of millions of people. Namier's interpretations and explanations, which include a detailed examination of early German nationalism, will interest anyone concerned with trying to understand the background of the contemporary world.

Joseph Kraft recommends this work (see below).

Namier, Lewis. *The Structure of Politics and the Accession of George III* 2 volumes (London: Macmillan, 1929) One of Namier's first published studies, this established him as an authority on eighteenth-century English politics. His initial research focused on the American struggle for independence, but as the historian became involved with the topic, he broadened his subject to go beyond the American Revolution to consider the war as it was seen in the British House of Commons.

Joseph Kraft recommends this work as well, saying, "My feeling [is] that [Namier] is the foremost historian of the twentieth century—unrivalled in command of detail (as witness *The Structure of Politics*)."

Nomad, Max. *Apostles of Revolution* (Boston: Little, 1939) The apostles of revolution are seven exceptional characters whom the historian believes represent distinct schools of thought in the development of radical ideology and action. Among those considered are Michael Bakunin, Joseph Stalin, Karl Marx and Sergey Nachayev. More iconoclastic than idealistic, more mistrustful of authority than worshipful, the author is primarily concerned with the reasons that revolutions succeed or fail. He believes most fall far short of achieving their original aims. Although disillusioned, he is not totally convinced that revolution is doomed to failure. Clear and readable, this book is particularly fine.

Clancy Sigal recommends it, calling the contents "radical political essays."

Ogle, Arthur. *The Tragedy of the Lollards' Tower* (Oxford: Pen-in-Hand, 1949) History, in the guise of both a mystery story and a compelling puzzle, is exemplified in this superbly written work. An English merchant tailor was found hanging in the London Lollards' Tower on December 4, 1514. Since he was probably murdered on the orders of the Bishop of London, the incident proved to be a turning point in the jurisdiction of the Church. In fact, it set the ground work for the ultimate destruction and downfall of the Church in 1529-1533. The author diligently and splendidly recounts and interprets history from the time of this famous death to the birth of Elizabeth.

Christopher Hill writes that this is "a neglected masterpiece in early Tudor history."

Ortega y Gasset, Jose. *Man and Crisis.* *Translated from the Spanish by Mildred Adams* (New York: Norton, 1959) First published, 1933. Marked by brilliance and imagination, this is one of the gifted Spanish philosopher's last works. In it, the author presents a systematic review of his concept of the science of history, and he makes a passionate, humane plea for the benefits of studying the past. Written in a clear and lively style, this is a worthy companion for his better known work, *The Revolt of the Masses* (1932).

Robert Bly recommends this book.

Parsons, Geoffrey. *The Stream of History* (New York: Scribner, 1928) The stream of history begins with the evolution of the earth, the introduction of man, and the scientific theories about that evolution. It ends shortly before 1928. The story unfolds in a dramatic fashion, making it comprehensible and interesting to the general reader.

Alexander Heard wrote that this was "a book that cemented an understanding of two simple concepts: that the lives of men are circumstantial segments in the seamless flow of the Life of Man, and that this enigmatic, conscious Life of Man is only a tiny second at our end of the long story of the world" (*American Scholar*, Autumn, 1961).

Reade, Winwood. *The Martyrdom of Man* (New York: Dutton, 1920) First published, 1872. Beginning with an analysis of Africa, the author proposes a philosophy of history. He takes the view, according to his own words, that "in each generation the human race has been tortured so their children might profit by their woes." War, religion, liberty and the intellect are examined as the progressive stages in man's painful upward struggle. Reade believed the last stage necessary to overcome was religion, hence the book was dismissed by most of his contemporaries. With an undeniable talent for simple, clear explanation and a direct, forceful style, the author brings to life the past. This is a history which demands to be read.

Marie Seton recommends it.

Rostovtzeff, Michael. *The Social and Economic History of the Roman Empire* (Oxford: Oxford University Press, 1926) As the title suggests, the historian treats the whole Roman Empire from an intellectual and spiritual viewpoint, on one hand, and from an economic, political and social perspective, on the other. Due to a fine prose style and an unquestionably vivid imagination, the author is able to contend with the massive amount of material in a deceptively relaxed fashion. At the same time, the detailed research and careful conclusions leave nothing at loose ends.

G. W. Bowersock writes that this is "one of the most provocative and influential studies of classical civilization to appear in the present century. . . .[H]istorians and classical scholars at the time were well aware of its monumental importance." Of its author, "a massively erudite Russian exile," he terms him "an intellectual titan," and says that "for all its errors *The Social and Economic History of the Roman Empire* was a masterpiece. . . .Today there is probably not one reputable historian who would accept the basic thesis of Rostovtzeff's book. Few, however, would question the greatness of the work" (*Daedalus*, Winter, 1974).

Rozanov, Ivan. *The Apocalypse of Our Time, and Other Writings.* *Translated from the Russian by Robert Payne and Nikita Romanoff* (New York: Praeger, 1977) First published, 1917-1918. Originally published as a series of ten pamphlets, and distributed and sold by the author, who lived from 1856 to 1919, the *Apocalypse* is a summary of the state of Russia during the Revolution. Composed of a series of aphorisms, reports, notes and comments, the work manages to reveal the tenor of the times, and, in the words of one of the translators, "the very disjointedness of Rozanov's thoughts has the effect of giving him a reality . . . By revealing himself, he reveals his age."

Edouard Roditi recommends this work.

St. Clair, William. *That Greece Might Still Be Free* (Oxford: Oxford University Press, 1972) Wishing to expose the sentimental admiration for all things Greek by the West, the author concentrates on the Greek War of Independence and the role some one thousand foreigners, including the poet Lord Byron, played in it. The strong contrast between the dreams of the Philhellenists and the Greek reality is developed through brilliant sketches of the Europeans who were determined to fight for Greece. The writing is as clear as it is intelligent, and the research is impeccable.

Frederic Raphael says this "certainly deserves reprinting; it is a story of English (largely) Philhellenists, including Byron of course."

Thompson, Flora. *Lark Rise to Candleford: A Trilogy* (Oxford: Oxford University Press, 1945) First published as *Lark Rise* (1939); *Over to Candleford* (1941); and *Candleford Green* (1943).

The life of an English country hamlet and of nearby market towns in the late nineteenth century is sketched by the author who grew up in just that environment. Both as a social history and as a work of literature, this is a real evocation of people and places. Crammed with observations and insights, the skillfully told and arranged trilogy is a delight from beginning to end.

William Rossa Cole says that this depicts "rural life in England in the 1870s and 1880s, when forelocks were pulled to the gentry, and a ten mile trip was a major undertaking. A dear, sweet girl growing up. A treasure of a book."

Thompson, William *At the Edge of History* (New York: Harper, 1971) On the edge of history, the author looks over and sees the end of Western civilization. He also sees a new culture coming out of the collapse. While this is a highly fanciful vision, it is supported by statistical data and historical research which makes it convincing reading, even for the more skeptical.

Harrison E. Salisbury writes, "*At the Edge of History* should be read not only by those interested in history, but anyone interested in human events; [Thompson] explores the remarkable fact that poets and artists tend to pre-vision history; he uses Yeats as an example, noting how closely Yeat's poems prefigured the events which were to come in Ireland, the Easter Rising and all. His theories can be demonstrated in other remarkable ways; for example in the extraordinary outburst of revolutionary creativity which preceded the Russian Revolutions of 1905 and 1917; including works which almost precisely outlined events which would follow, such as Andrei Bely's *The Silver Dove.*"

Voegelin, Eric. *Order and History* 4 volumes (New Orleans: Louisiana State University Press, 1956-1975) Professor Voegelin defines history as "the revelation of the way of God with man," and sets out boldly to recreate the historical Israel. He does this, in fact, in the first volume, aptly subtitled "Israel and Revelation", of this four volume series. Using biblical historiography the author details a theory of history which is at odds with that of many historians. No easy work to read, the study is among the most provocative ones to be published in the past fifty years.

Eugene Genovese said this "presents a learned, if irritating reading of our past" (*The Times Literary Supplement*, January 21, 1977).

West, Rebecca. *Black Lamb and Grey Falcon: The Record of a Journey Through Yugoslavia in 1937* 2 volumes (London: Macmillan, 1942) In this description of a 1937 journey through both urban and remote sections of Yugoslavia, the reader discovers one of the most vital, perceptive and fascinating combinations of history and travel literature ever published. The book came out just before World War II, and served as a kind of curtain falling on one of the great periods of Western European culture.

Edgar Z. Friedenberg writes, "I first read the book when it was published, over forty years ago. It is still probably the most influential book I have ever read—this despite the fact that Dame Rebecca's social philosophy, as reflected in her subsequent works, is quite repugnant to me. But I have never read any book that reflects a keener sense of culture and its historical roots, and the moral implications and consequences of living in a particular place at a particular time. All this enlivened by a literary style of great wit, precision, and pathos; and the keenest possible sense of personal responsibility, evinced repeatedly in scenes of breathtaking concreteness. There are whole paragraphs, pages, even, that I quote all the time to myself when not to others."

Wilson, Edmund. *The American Jitters* (New York: Scribner, 1932) Looking at an early year of the Depression, 1931, one of America's finest literary critics describes the beginning of what may have been the worst economic period in American history. As concerned with the changes the Depression brought about as he is with the people who entered this crisis, Wilson draws some marvelous portraits of individuals. The stubborn integrity of intellectuals is examined, and not always found wanting. This book includes some of the best reporting on the Depression to be found anywhere.

Leon Edel calls this "Edmund Wilson's remarkable reportage of the 1930s Depression in the United States—no one has told the story of that period better."

Young, Marguerite. *Angel in the Forest: A Fairy Tale of Two Utopias* (New York: Reynal, 1945) Employing poetic prose and brilliant insights, the author relates the history of two early eighteenth-century experiments in socialistic or communal living. She is concerned with New Harmony, Indiana, and the subsequent English movement of Robert Owen. At the time of its publication, *The New Yorker* critic observed that "it was one of the most interesting books of nonfiction . . . in some time . . . and there is not a page of her volume that doesn't show signs of being . . . very good indeed" (April 7, 1945). The vivid portrayals of scenes and the abundance of witty commentary make this as original as it is compelling.

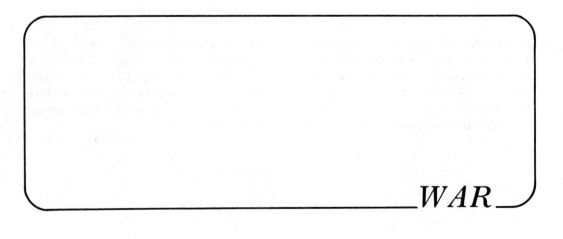

WAR

Douglas, Keith. *Alamein to Zem Zem* (London: Edition Poetry London, 1946) An English poet, Keith Douglas keeps a close account of the battle for North Africa as witnessed from his vantage point as a tank leader. His vibrant personal record of desert warfare provides a good balance to the official histories. His evocative descriptions capture almost every nuance of battle from tedium to full armored warfare. Douglas was killed in the Normandy landings at the age of twenty four.

Paul Fussell recommended this in *Antaeus*, Autumn, 1977.

Farwell, Byron. *Queen Victoria's Little Wars* (London: Allen, 1973) Many of the wars fought during Queen Victoria's reign proved less than important in historical terms, yet they were crucial to the individuals concerned. Farwell succeeds in weaving the highlights of battle into this review of campaigns. Highly readable and well researched, this goes a long way to explain the prevalence of war memorials in England.

James Rettig writes, "Farwell's popular history will disabuse anyone of the notion that Victoria's long reign was mostly peaceful. The Crimean and Boer wars were but the most prominent fought between 1832 and 1901. During every year of her reign, Britain fought at least one 'little war' somewhere in its empire. Her subjects' dedication to queen and empire are best exemplified by Garnet Wolseley, a man who appears in campaign after campaign in Farwell's book and who was rewarded with the title of Viscount and the rank of Field-Marshal for his service in wars on four continents."

Glasser, Ronald. *365 Days* (New York: Braziller, 1971) From his station in Japan, an American doctor writes about American soldiers wounded in Vietnam. Some readers believe this to be one of the best books to come out of the Vietnam war.

Robert Mazzocco writes, "Not 'fiction' at all, but rather a devastating account of a doctor's experiences in Vietnam. Glasser is no 'writer,' as such, but has a very serviceable prose, and his book seems to me the most potent, accurate, and dismaying to have come out of that war. More unnerving, certainly, than similar episodes in the novels of Robert Stone or Tim O'Brien. And you've only to compare it with *Burma Surgeon*, a famous best-seller of the Second World War, to realize not only the differences in generations, but also how the American spirit and the whole American *raison d'etre*, including American imperialism, have radically altered in a few short decades."

Graves, Robert. *Goodbye to All That* (London: Cape, 1929) While this is hardly neglected by those familiar with World War I memoirs, it remains one of the English poet's less well-known works. Yet it is surely one of his finest. The candor of his description of life in the trenches is considered by many to be the most interesting war writing of any period. Graves was only nineteen years old when he entered the conflict, high in hopes for a glorious adventure. The gradual transformation of his attitudes and his character is traced as he becomes more deeply aware of the horror of warfare. Still, he maintains a certain detachment and cooly, realistically appraises "things which are not talked about" normally in warfare. Admirably recounted, this true story unfolds like a splendid novel.

M. L. Rosenthal writes, "*Goodbye to All That* isn't really 'neglected' . . . But it's known too little: one of the important relatively early books showing the real meaning of World War I and its psychological effects (not its total subject, however), this astringent and candid autobiographical account is easily Graves' best prose and probably more enduring than his poetry."

Gray, J. Glenn. *The Warriors: Reflections on Men in Battle* (New York: Har-

court, 1959) Drawing upon journals of his experience in World War II, the author paints a fine, honest picture of the combat soldier. As beautifully written as it is true, the account is an effort to comprehend the nature of modern war. The ecstasy and the horror of warfare and their effects on the personalities of the warriors are evident on every page.

Evan S. Connell, Jr. writes, "Gray was an agent of the Counter Intelligence Corps in Europe during World War II, later a professor of philosophy at Colorado College. He kept a journal during the war and this book is a mediation or reflection upon men at war, himself included. It is a book one doesn't forget, and certainly it is relevant to the bizarre militarism of our time."

Hay, Ian. *The First Hundred Thousand* (Edinburgh: Blackwood, 1915) Written by a front line captain during the middle of the First World War, this is a little known classic. The title refers to a battalion of Argyll and Sutherland Highlanders, formed from a segment of the first one hundred thousand men who responded to Kitchener's call for enlistment. Most were lost during the war, but Captain Hay shows how they were trained and tells how they fought. Both officers and men come in for gentle sarcasm in the training stage, which occupies much of the book; the sketches of life in the trenches are filled with vivid experiences, related with strains of pathos and humor, and sometimes ferocious simplicity.

G. B. Harrison recommends this work.

Jünger, Ernst. *Storm of Steel*. *Translated from the German by Basil Creighton* (New York: Doubleday, 1929) First published, 1920.

Subtitled "From the Diary of a German Storm Troop Officer on the Western Front," this is by now a classic of World

War I. From early youth, the author believed in the romance and the glory of war. He even ran away from home to join the French Foreign Legion. With the outbreak of World War I, Jünger volunteered and joined the infantry on the Western Front. He was almost killed, being wounded fourteen times, and was finally promoted to head a shock troop unit. His descriptions of artillery barrages, bravery and cowardice, and daily life on the Front have rarely been matched by other writers. Some readers see this work as ambivalent since Jünger repudiates the slaughter of modern war yet glorifies the military tradition. In fact, contemporary reviewers strongly suggested it was a perfect portrait of the military mind refusing to face the reality of horror. Over the years, that attitude has changed, and many now believe the book to be a denunciation of war.

Lussu, Emilio. *Sardinian Brigade.*
Translated from the Italian by Marion Rawson (New York: Knopf, 1939) A personal narrative of the Italian Alpine campaign of 1916-1917, and one of the best war autobiographies published, this is particularly notable for its avoidance of self-pity and the usual tone of disillusionment. Lussu, who loathes and deplores war, depicts heroism through the use of irony and horror through wit. It is a persuasive, fast moving and exciting narrative which conveys, in a uniquely dignified style, the tragedy of warfare.

Saul Bellow recommends it.

Moss, W. Stanley. *Ill Met by Moonlight*
(New York: Macmillan, 1950) In April, 1944, the commander of the German forces on Crete was daringly kidnapped by resistance fighters led by two young English officers. One of those officers is the author of this dramatic retelling of the event. In an exuberant style, Moss fashions a masterpiece of action and narrative. Anyone who

enjoys a first rate adventure story will read this from cover to cover without pause.

Paul Fussell recommended this in *Antaeus*, Autumn, 1977.

O'Malley, Ernie. *Army Without Banners* (Boston: Houghton, 1937) As a young medical student in the Dublin of 1916-1921, O'Malley became a member of the Republican Army. Looking back to those days, he describes the struggle in an unsentimental, poetic, brutal, loving way. The autobiography affords one of the best personal views now available of civil warfare. His story is far more intelligent and graphic than most accounts of such strife, in Ireland or elsewhere.

Malcolm Cowley calls this "a marvelously fresh evocation of the author's life in the Irish Republican Army when it had a cause that every true Irishman could support."

Sajer, Guy. *The Forgotten Soldier.*
Translated from the French by Lily Emmet (New York: Harper, 1971) When writing about life on the Front in World War I, Ernst Jünger repudiated the romance of war in his classic work, *Storm of Steel*. In a sense, this is an update of the horror story, told with equal skill and verisimilitude by another German soldier, this time one who served on the Eastern Front of World War II. His reactions during the fighting through Poland and Russia are captured graphically in this combination of history and autobiography. The reader is seized with horror by the sheer suicidal onslaught of battle. Few authors have written so vividly about the sensations of fighting in a modern army.

Paul Fussell recommended this in *Antaeus*, Autumn, 1977.

Teissier Du Cros, Janet. *Divided Loyalties* (London: Hamish, 1962) Life in a small French village during the German

Occupation of World War II is depicted in a deceptively flat, matter-of-fact fashion by the author who is English but married to a French scientist. The effect of calling up past memories is almost Proustian, and the lucidity and directness of her style effectively recreates events and personalities. Furthermore, the candid descriptions of the author's fears makes this an exceptionally personal narrative and a distinguished, faithful record of an important aspect of war.

Robert Motherwell wrote, "Nothing spectacular or even especially dramatic happens; but the completeness of detail really does approach the complicated texture of everyday life" (*American Scholar*, Summer, 1970).

Unruh, Fritz. *The Way of Sacrifice.*

Translated from the German by C. A Macartney (New York: Knopf, 1928) Destined for the army because of his Prussian heritage, Unruh temporarily gave up writing, in 1914, to become a captain. Here is his war diary which is particularly noteworthy for its daily record of events as seen by Germans at the Battle of Verdun. The graphic quality of the daily fighting it records is matched by its poetic style. It is a damning piece of literature, clear in its opposition to war, although the author lets the readers draw their own conclusions. Unruh, incidentally, went on to become a playwright, a poet, and a novelist; his book *The End Is Not Yet* (1947) is a seminal study of the Nazis.

Wade, Aubrey. *The War of the Guns*

(London: Batsford, 1936) During the last two years of World War I, the author was attached to an English artillery battery. In simple, straightforward prose, he explains what it was like to live within the shadow of cannons day in and day out. Few works better demonstrate the reality of war. In fact, the story has an added impact because the author, aside from some understandable bitterness, tends to let the story tell itself. The very lack of introspection or self-pity makes this an especially effective and accurate picture of the Great War. This English edition includes more than a hundred photographs, many of them truly horrific.

David Jones was said to have admired this book and thought it neglected. "He had often wondered what the more mobile artillery man's war was like and this told him" (*The Long Conversation: A Memoir of David Jones* by William Blissett [New York: Oxford University Press, 1981]).

Zahn, Gordon. *In Solitary Witness: The Life and Death of Franz Jägerstätter*

(New York: Holt, 1965) An Austrian peasant, the subject of this remarkable biography, refused to serve in Hitler's armies. He was a devout Catholic who not only denounced Nazism as hostile to his religion, but was well aware of the result of his taking a public position on the issue. He was tried, and finally beheaded in 1943.

Pyke Johnson writes, "It is a book which affirms the importance of the individual, and which demonstrates how one person who insists on standing by what he believes can have an effect far beyond his own sphere of action. It draws added strength from the fact that it is not about an intellectual, but about a simple man who refused to be turned from his convictions by his family, his church, or the state."

Theodore Roszak, who also recommends this book, says, "I don't recall *In Solitary Witness* all that clearly after all these years. I continue to remember it as an inspiring study of moral courage—which never got the recognition it deserved. . . .It is hardly dated, any more so than the life of any saint."

ECONOMICS

Brady, Robert. *Business as a System of Power* (New York: Columbia University Press, 1943) In a hard-hitting, factual explanation of business as a major power in politics and governmental policy, the economics professor cuts through to the realities of business as a force. With painstaking thoroughness, he describes the business associations in Germany, Italy, Japan, France, Britain and the United States. The primary question is whether the people of the world are to be dominated by business or have a chance to work for and enjoy their own freedom. The author is less than optimistic.

Noam Chomsky writes, "Published in 1943, and out of print (I believe) for many years. Brady gives a penetrating account of developments in the industrial societies leading towards what some now call 'friendly (or not so friendly) fascism.' It is not only unusually perceptive, but also very timely, in my view."

Jouvenel, Bertrand de. *The Ethics of Redistribution* (Cambridge: Cambridge University Press, 1951) Let us say that to-morrow the world's income will be divided equally among all people. What would then happen? In this series of Cambridge University lectures, the author considers answers to this question in the context of Western economic systems, the socialist idea of income redistribution, and the effects of such major changes on social values. The curse is too much government, and de Jouvenel promotes this argument gracefully.

Nathan Glazer says, "*The Ethics of Redistribution* was one of the very few books I knew of some years ago which had anything good to say about inequality. Since I wrote my favorable comments on it some years ago, there has been a revival of defenses of economic inequality (*e.g.*, George Gilder . . . and the whole supply-side argument) and the book is less original or unique than it was. . . ."

Kalecki, Michal. *Essays in the Theory of Economic Fluctuations* (New York: Farrar, 1939) Essays by this professional economist explain three important currents in economic thought: the doctrine of competition, the Keynesian theory, and the ideas of the Swedish school. He also covers the business cycle theory.

Thomas Balogh has called Kalecki "the economist who initiated New Economics before Keynes and is now only recognized by a few."

Lloyd, Henry Demarest. *Wealth Against Commonwealth* (New York: Harper, 1894) Union organizer and journalist, Demarest proved to be one of America's earliest and most effective muckrakers. Today, his writing is an accurate, yet slightly biased, account of the development of American industrial reform. A fully documented and well written discussion of monopolies, this remains one of his best books, and continues to make for fascinating reading.

Marguerite Young recommends this.

Polanyi, Karl. *The Great Transformation* (New York: Farrar, 1944) Charles P. Kindleberger wrote, "The theme of *The Great Transformation* has been continuously on my mind. I referred to it first in a paper in 1951, most recently in 1970, and at least five times in between. My reference is usually a half-sentence summary: 'Polanyi believed it outrageous that economic overwhelmed social considerations in the industrial revolution,' plus, frequently, a half-sentence rebuttal: 'but to prevent adaptation to market conditions may simply store up and aggravate the difficulties, as illustrated by the refusal of France to permit the modernization of agriculture from 1890 to 1950, leaving its peasants sodden, brutalized, inefficient, demoralized.' I see the question as to whether economic and social forces converge or conflict as unresolved and well worth discussing" (*Daedalus*, Winter, 1974).

Ashley Montagu also recommends *The Great Transformation*. He terms it "a revelation, stimulating and deep-probing," and says "it represents the most illuminat-

ing account of the economic process in modern civilization I have read. As my friend Robert MacIver, the distinguished Columbia sociologist wrote of it in his foreword, 'It is a book for every intelligent man who cares to know the society in which he lives, the crises it passed through, the crises that are now upon us.'"

Rocker, Rudolf. *Anarcho-syndicalism* (London: Secker, 1938) One of the most succinct and brilliant statements of liberal doctrine, this is a logical explanation of why people should be free from state coercion. The author would replace formal government with a federation of communities, and would place economic power in the hands of the worker. While this echoes some of the work of Godwin, Proudhon and Bakunin, it is quite original in its concepts and its closely argued theses. It, equally, gives a solid history of England under industrialism, and is a protest against the political socialism of the Russians.

Noam Chomsky writes, "Long out of print, and barely known when it was in print, this is in my view one of the real classics of the libertarian left, indeed, one of the classics of social and political analysis."

Schumpeter, Joseph Alois. *Capitalism, Socialism and Democracy* (New York: Harper, 1942) Capitalism, socialism and democracy, the three governing forces in Western society, are mercilessly scrutinized and found generally wanting. Schumpeter's Germanic scholarship is as thorough as it is biting. Of primary value today is his historical survey of the beginnings of these politico-economic concepts, their triumphs and their failures. The study is as charmingly written as the conclusions are startling and thoughtful.

Leo Rosten recommended this in *American Scholar*, Spring, 1970.

Wheeler, Mortimer. *Rome Beyond the Imperial Frontiers* (London: G. Bell, 1954) Using extant literary evidence, archaeological discoveries and his own excavations, the author fills in a comprehensive picture of Rome's foreign trading practices. The book takes the reader from Europe to Africa and Asia, and the story is clear, learned and always informative. A rare combination of formal elegance and historical content, this is sometimes compared to the work of Robert Graves.

Emma Swan recommended this in *Antaeus*, Summer, 1975.

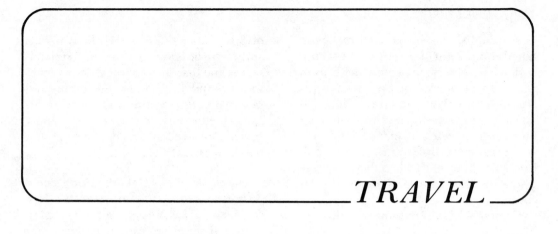

TRAVEL

Ackerley, J. R. *Hindoo Holiday: An Indian Journal* (London: Chatto, 1932) As secretary to the ruler of a small native Indian state, the young English author soon discovers his employer is more interested in conversation and companionship than work. Given this free time and talk with the Maharaja, Ackerley is able to present a delightful and essentially accurate picture of pre-World War II India. As V. S. Pritchett wrote, "Mr. Ackerley is candid and dispassionate . . . There is a delightful tenderness in [his] writing and here and there when the Maharaja ventures some wistful question concerning human existence, some quaint problem of political delicacy, Mr. Ackerley reveals himself as a man whose instinct of understanding is gentle, ready and deep. His humor is the humor of pity and love . . . "(*Christian Science Monitor,* June 11, 1932).

Patricia Abercrombie calls this "a very perceptive and extremely amusing travel book about India."

Austin, Mary. *The Flock* (Boston: Houghton, 1906) Sheep and their herders are on center stage in what is primarily a history of sheep ranching in California at the beginning of the twentieth century. The study opens with background material on the trade, and the author moves the reader, along with the sheep, to the West from New England.

Donald Davie writes, "Mary Austin, author of the acknowledged minor classic, *The Land of Little Rain*, and of other books about the Southwest, in *The Flock* recreates the already vanished or vanishing California of the migrant sheep-herders, as often French or Basque as American. She proceeds obliquely, and her style is elaborate; to be savoured, her book requires recapturing the spaciousness and the leisure of the pastoral world she lovingly evokes."

Bagnold, Ralph. *Libyan Sands* (London: Hodder, 1935) A few years after the First World War, the author found himself in the English army quartered in Egypt. Bored and in need of adventure, he set out with fellow officers to explore the Libyan wastes. In a Ford touring car, they covered almost twenty thousand miles. The separate journeys, some long, some short, took them over a widely disparate landscape where they met people from numerous cultures. The book ends when they converge upon Italians embarked on a similar course.

Carolyn Michaels recommends this.

Bowen, Eleanor Smith. *Return to Laughter* (New York: Harper, 1954) Untouched by civilization, a tribe in British West Africa is visited by the author, an American anthropologist writing under a pseudonym. Combining both fact and fictional elements (primarily to protect the tribe and related individuals), the author writes of her marginal acceptance as a member of the group. Intended for both lay readers and anthropologists, this book is highly recommended as accurate, sympathetic documentation of an almost lost African way of life. It is particularly noteworthy for the good humor, details about the environment, and descriptions of women's life and polygamy.

Donald Finkel recommended this in *Antaeus*, Autumn, 1979).

Brenan, Gerald. *South from Granada* (London: Hamilton, 1957) Traveling south from Granada, the British journalist and historian vividly describes the people and their villages in southern Spain. His attention to styles of living, politics, relations between the sexes, treatment of animals, and kinds of food, as well as quantities of general information, make this very different from the typical bull fighting travel book.

Leon Edel writes, "*South From Granada*—the story of Gerald Brenan's discovery of Spain after the First World War—his ability to be alone in unfamiliar landscapes and his remarkable capacity for absorbing and feeling the life of the old Moorish part of Spain: it is a 'Lesson for Loners,' the way in which the solitary Brenan absorbed and made the country a part of himself."

Butor, Michel. *Mobile: Study for a Representation of the United States* (New York: Simon & Schuster, 1963) Since this is a surrealistic report of modern travel in the United States, it is sometimes difficult to separate fact from fiction. But that is of little matter. The joy resides in the insights and imaginative style of one of France's leading novelists. It is a fine, stimulating book.

Joseph McElroy recommended it in *Antaeus*, Winter, 1975.

Byron, Robert. *The Road to Oxiana* (London: Macmillan, 1937) On the road to Iran and Afghanistan, Byron draws upon his lyrical powers of description and his solid knowledge of the area. He tends to measure civilizations by contrasting the ancient buildings with the modern populace, and showing both as a continuing story. The concentration on Iran and Afghanistan makes the book particularly pertinent for today's readers.

Bruce Chatwin wrote in a new introduction to this book, "[Those] who read around the books of the thirties in the end conclude that Byron's *The Road to Oxiana* is a masterpiece [of travel literature]" (*The Guardian*, August 1, 1981).

Cummings, E. E. *Eimi* (New York: Covici, 1933) One of the twentieth century's most remarkable travel diaries, this traces the sometimes comic, always perceptive, experiences of the American poet on a thiry-six day trip through Russia.

While not unsympathetic to the Russian Revolution, Cummings saw early on the danger of state control of artists, and in his descriptions indicates clearly how this censorship affects creativity. The people and places he depicts, however, are subordinated to the style, for here the technique in which the travelogue is written (imaginative combinations of prose, poetry and typography which are made to function dynamically by implying in visual terms ideas, objects, and sensations) is of ultimate interest.

Dwight MacDonald recommended this in *Antaeus*, Winter, 1975.

Douglas, Norman. *Siren Land* (London: Dent, 1911) Supported by the enthusiastic recommendation of Joseph Conrad, this finally was issued after repeated rejections by English publishers. It is the author's first major work of literature, and comes a decade before his *South Wind* (1917). The "siren land" is Capri and the surrounding area including Sorrento which Douglas uses as a backdrop for his reflections. The charming and unusual blend of history, travel, philosophy and personal impression is supported by the author's terse, vigorous and intelligent style. It is a book of generous spirit and distinctive wisdom.

The Arts Council of Great Britain recommended this as an "overlooked twentieth-century classic" in 1982. It has been republished in England by Secker & Warburg.

Ford, Ford Madox. *Provence: From Minstrels to the Machine* (Philadelphia: Lippincott, 1935) The superb writer of *The Good Soldier* and countless other novels here turns his hand to travel. As the title indicates, this is a tour, using literature as a map, through France. The guide, additionally, includes flashback scenes of an earlier London, as well as fine drawings by Biala. Historical and literary achievements of Provence are treated with great zest and delight.

Daniel Halpern recommends this work.

Ford, Richard. *A Handbook for Travellers in Spain* 2 volumes (London: Murray, 1845) *Note:* An abridged version, *Gatherings from Spain* (1846), is made up of matter deleted from later editions of the *Handbook*.

In 1824, Ford married a daughter of the earl of Essex, and spent the next four years with his wife in Spain. He became almost a native, showed a particular appreciation for Spanish art, and was the first to make the work of Velazquez known to the English. His one book is practically an encyclopedia of Spain, yet it is as readable as it is brilliant. Ford's enthusiasm for everything Spanish shows on each page. V. S. Pritchett says this is "probably the best guide book ever written" (*New Statesman*, September 2, 1966). Until the Spanish Civil War the book was much used, but the war made such a change in Spain that the handbook became somewhat outdated. Still, it holds its fascination.

Keith Thomas calls this "perhaps the best study of Spanish society by an outsider ever written. It combines Dickensian humour and Gibbonian irony with acute social observation."

Forster, E. M. *Alexandria: A History and a Guide* (Alexandria: Morris, 1922) During the First World War, Forster was in Egypt, working as a Red Cross volunteer, when he wrote most of this guide. Published two years before *A Passage to India*, the work is divided into two parts. The first consists of the history of the city, including considerable background material on its culture. The second section is a methodical guide to the city and the outlying regions.

An appendix is devoted to the various religious organizations of Alexandria. This remains one of the best guides ever published, and can be read as much for its deft style and timely background information as for practical tips on getting around Alexandria. While dated, it is still extremely useful for both real and armchair travelers.

Leon Edel says, *"Alexandria*—Forster's 'touring in time' of the ancient city; an intimate work of history and personal observation and study."

Gheerbrant, Alain. *The Impossible Adventure.* *Translated from the French by Edward Fitzgerald* (London: Gollancz, 1953) Published in America as *Journey to the Far Amazon* (1954).

Starting out from Bogata in early 1949, four young men are determined to cover over two thousand miles of jungle in the Orinoco-Amazon region. As they travel down rivers which lead to the Orinoco, the four have many adventures. Finally, they arrive at the "impenetrable green hell"— the Sierra Parima, until then almost totally unexplored, lying between the jungles of the Orinoco and the Rio Negro. After tremendous difficulties, they meet the primitive Guaharibos, a hunting tribe which enjoys the music of Mozart. In the tradition of great tales of exploration and adventure, this is an inspired work.

Frank MacShane recommended this in *Antaeus*, Winter, 1975.

Gide, Andre. *Travels in the Congo.* *Translated from the French by Dorothy Bussy* (New York: Knopf, 1929) First published, 1927. A little known travel notebook by Gide, this is a lucidly and beautifully written account of the Congo in Belgian and French equatorial Africa. There are numerous, pertinent references to Conrad, and these two separate viewpoints (Conrad's and Gide's) often parallel one another. Today, it is of particular interest for the cosmopolitan, contemporary response to what was then an almost completely foreign culture.

Daniel Halpern recommends this.

Gould, Laurence. *Cold: The Record of an Antarctic Sledge Journey* (New York: Brewer, 1931) As second in command of the Byrd expedition to the Antarctic in 1929, the author lived through the adventure related in this reserved, yet exciting story. The sledge journey to the pole from Queen Maud Mountains is accompanied by photographs taken by Gould. As a sensitive report on an explorative and scientific endeavor, this has few equals.

Paul B. Sears writes, "*Cold* by Laurence M. Gould, distinguished geologist and past president of Carleton College, is an absorbing log of a scientific journey by dogsled in the rigorous conditions of the Antarctic, probably among the last examples of the use of this means of transportation. It is a vivid picture of the hardships of an area which has become one of the few examples of genuine collaboration among scientists of nations whose relationships in other fields are being dangerously neglected."

Graves, John. *Goodbye to a River* (New York: Knopf, 1960) Weaving Indian myths and pioneer lore into his story, Graves takes the reader on a lone, two hundred mile canoe journey down the Texas Brazos. The observations of the ever changing landscape and human beings along the way enliven the already exciting adventure. A considerable amount of Comanche Indian and pioneer lore is also included in the work.

Nell Surface recommends this.

Hudson, W. H. *Idle Days in Patagonia* (London: Chapman, 1893) Published eleven years before *Green Mansions* (1904), this is a factual account of the author's study of life in Patagonia. After an accident, he was compelled to limit his studies to birds, people, and places in the immediate vicinity. His reflections on the lives of men and birds, his visualization of much that he sees, and his elegant style add up to a beautiful, scientific, prose poem.

Paul Theroux recommends this work.

Kennan, George. *Tent Life in Siberia* (New York: Putnam, 1910) First published, 1870. With a clear appreciation for the rugged natural beauty of Siberia and the manners and customs of its people, the author sets out near the turn of the century to live and travel among the tribes of Kamchatka and northern Asia. Welcoming danger and hardships, well aware of the need for reliable observation divorced from romanticism, the uncle of our Ambassador to Russia spins a fascinating adventure story. Although first published many years ago, the epic quality of the book is such that it holds the attention of the most skeptical reader. Also, the author has a fine sense of humor about himself and his companions, and is particularly amusing when he describes such bothers as mosquitoes in Siberia and the difficulties of using a peasant's Russian vocabulary at a formal dance.

Larry McMurtry calls this "one of the funnier books of the century."

Kinglake, Alexander. *Eothen* (London: Ollivier, 1844) A major, yet neglected, classic in the field of travel narration, *Eothen* conveys the witty observations of an English historian, politician and barrister. He records his travels through Turkey, the Levant and Egypt in 1835-1836. More involved with noting his impressions of the people and the landscape than in compiling anthropological material, the record is as accurate as it is humane. This sensitive memoir is as splendid today as when it was published.

Jan Morris calls this, "One of the best travel books ever written—I myself would say *the* best."

Landor, Arnold H. *Tibet and Nepal* (London: Black, 1905) Early in the twentieth century, equipped with little more than spirit and physical strength, Landor explored the primitive areas of Asia. Adventure followed his every step, and he recalls truly strange and fascinating events. At the same time, his sensitivity to other people's ways and religions is evident in the balanced picture he paints of life in Tibet and Nepal.

Frank MacShane recommended this in *Antaeus*, Winter, 1975.

Lansing, Alfred. *Endurance: Shackleton's Incredible Voyage* (New York: McGraw, 1959) Attempting to navigate Antarctic's Weddell Sea in 1915, Shackleton's ship was crushed. He and his twenty-seven men, cast away on ice, managed to survive without a single loss of life. The prolonged nightmare came to an end only after several months of near starvation, exposure, and heroic achievement by men who considered themselves little more than ordinary people. The author's account of one of the great adventure stories of our time is as accurate as it is exciting.

Annie Dillard terms this the "best nonfiction adventure I've ever read. I buy every copy I see; so do all my friends. It is *inexplicable* that this is out of print...." David Peele also recommends this work.

Lee, Laurie. *As I Walked Out One Mid-summer Morning* (London: Deutsch, 1969) Having been a wandering fiddler in Spain in the 1930s, the English poet is able to offer a lighthearted, yet arresting look at this world before World War Two. His impressions are as fresh now as when he, with many others, lived in the naive hope for a liberal victory in the Civil War. His characterizations are extraordinary, and the book has the force of a ballad.

William Rossa Cole recommends this.

Michaux, Henri. *A Barbarian in Asia.* *Translated from the French by Sylvia Beach* (New York: New Directions, 1949) First published, 1933. A famous Franco-Belgian poet takes the reader on an unconventional trip through India, Burma, Malaya, China and Japan in the late 1920s. The emphasis is on the natural fantasy of Asia as seen through the eyes of a cultivated, sympathetic traveler. Much of the prose is as reflective as it is descriptive. And this is one of the few Western travel books to penetrate the almost impenetrable Asian cultures; it is both stimulating and entertaining.

Mark Strand recommended this in *Antaeus*, Autumn, 1977.

Newby, Eric. *Slowly Down the Ganges: A Short Walk in the Hindu Kush* (New York: Scribner, 1967) During the winter of 1963-1964, the author and his wife set out on a twelve-hundred mile trip through northeast India, and the record of that adventure is related here in intensely enjoyable prose. One seems to be traveling with the two adventurers as they make their way by rail, boat, bus and bullock cart down the course of the Ganges River. The simple descriptions of the river, its people, and some villages and cities along the way are carried on without forays into politics or economics. The descriptions are delicate and true, the account thoroughly credible, and the story recounted with humor and enthusiasm from beginning to end.

Larry McMurtry calls Newby "a wonderfully amusing English writer."

O'Brien, Edna. *Mother Ireland* (London: Weidenfeld, 1976) This is both a personal narrative and a history of Ireland. Here one finds delightful vignettes from the author's own life combined with mythology, comments on books and plays, and sketches of the people who are often part of her better known novels. The book is short, yet it succeeds in capturing the true spirit of Ireland and the Irish. There are wonderful photographs by Fergus Bourke.

Edna O'Brien recommends her work.

Taylor, Edmond. *Richer by Asia* (Boston: Houghton, 1947) This is another one of the few studies by a Westerner to capture successfully the Asiatic spirit and philosophy. As an American official in southwest Asia, Taylor took the opportunity to study the Indians, Chinese, Siamese and Japanese. S. I. Hayakawa commented that, "Nowhere from the beginning to the end . . . is there a stale idea or trite emotion. . . . The style is clear and lucid." Through conversations and interviews, supplemented by considerable reading, the author documents the experiences which helped in his efforts to understand better the human condition.

Margaret Mead said, "This book more than any I know captured the ambiguities of our developing understanding of Asia."

Thesiger, Wilfred. *Arabian Sands* (New York: Dutton, 1959) Working for a Middle East locust control agency, the writer went to southern Arabia in 1945 and became one of the first Europeans to penetrate the vast "Empty Quarter" of the country. He spent five years with nomadic Arabs, and the book gives details of his life with them, including several extraordinary journeys by camel to the forbidden interior of Oman. As absorbing as it is substantial, this work offers readers a true, believable, and inside view of the Arab. The combination of semi-anthropological data, adventure, and travel writing makes this difficult to put down, especially since the author has a fine literary style.

Larry McMurtry thinks this is "the greatest twentieth-century travel book."

Yglesias, Jose. *The Goodby Land* (New York: Pantheon, 1967) A moving and graceful account, this is the record of the author's 1964 pilgrimage to his deceased father's village in Spain. While piecing together the life and death of his father, Yglesias introduces the reader to a collection of characters. The picture he offers of the primitive peasant mind rarely has been rivaled. Reviewing it at the time, Gerald Brenan said, "Mr. Yglesias is a writer of considerable subtlety and perceptiveness with a strong sense of narrative form, and I do not think that anyone can fail to enjoy or learn from his little masterpiece" (*New York Review of Books*, September 28, 1967).

PSYCHOLOGY

Bettelheim, Bruno. *The Empty Fortress: Infantile Autism and the Birth of the Self* (New York: Free Press, 1967) A leading expert on child psychology considers the phenomenon of the "wolf children" and offers a lucid account of autistic children. Beyond relating particular case histories, Bettelheim is interested in conveying the general, normal, yet mysterious, process by which all personalities are shaped.

François Truffaut recommended this in *Antaeus*, Autumn, 1979.

Boas, Franz. *The Mind of Primitive Man*, revised edition. (New York: Macmillan, 1938) First published, 1911. A landmark in humanistic studies, this book was almost completely revised in 1938. Boas, who lived from 1858 to 1942, took into account, when he updated this work, the new research on the influence of the environment upon growth and behavior, as well as new studies on the mental attitudes of primitive people. He believed that cultural differences are vital and necessary for the well being and happiness of civilization. Here he indicates the fundamental problems of development on primitive cultures. For all but the scholar, the revised edition is preferred, since it is a basic work by one of the world's greatest anthropologists.

Ashley Montagu terms this, "the classic (which means seldom read or out-of-print or both) book on the variability of humankind and its meaning."

Cobb, Edith. *The Ecology of Imagination in Childhood* (New York: Columbia University Press, 1977) In the imaginative experiences of childhood there can be found the essence of the most mature forms of human thought. This is a successful effort to explore and expand that theory. The author believes that the spontaneous and innately creative imagination of childhood is essential to human evolution and is a major factor in mental health. She illustrates her points with scientific findings and imaginative works, particularly poetry. The scope of her argument is matched by the careful development of her position and fine writing.

Ashley Montagu writes that this is "in my opinion the most valuable, beautiful, and soundest book on the nature of the child written in this century, or any other for the matter of that."

Custance, John. *Wisdom, Madness and Folly: The Philosophy of a Lunatic* (London: Gollancz, 1951) A former mental patient traces the development of his insanity and relates his eventual cure. During his manic period, for example, he discovers several major factors about himself and his world. Both as a factual report of his perilous trip in and out of manic-depression and as a study of the medical practices of the time, this is a revealing document. There is a preface by C. G. Jung.

Joseph McElroy recommended this in *Antaeus*, Winter, 1975.

Harrington, Alan. *Psychopaths . . .* (New York: Simon & Schuster, 1972) Who is a psychopath? The author provides surprising answers to this question. Using case histories, he shows that individuals may be suffering from an illness, or they may simply be adapting to a way of life which they feel is in keeping with the times. Examples range from a high powered business executive to an eighteen-year-old male prostitute. They support the wonderfully suggestive argument in this book.

Herbert Gold writes that this is "a brilliant dissection of the psychopathic personality of our time, with implications for the success-hungry, the urban-dwelling, everybody."

Lévy-Bruhl, Lucien. *How Natives Think*. *Translated from the French by* *Lilian Clare* (London: Allen & Unwin, 1926) Rodney Needham writes, "This is a pioneering and fundamental inquiry, based on a scrupulous study of ethnographical evidences, into the possibility that the ideas of people in certain less advanced societies differ profoundly from our own; that such ideas are not interconnected as in ours; and that the connections among them may not be of a logical nature. Lévy-Bruhl infers that they are governed by a 'law of participation' according to which things could be both themselves and something other than themselves: 'in other words, . . . the opposition between the one and the many, same and other, etc., does not impose the necessity to affirm one of the terms if the other is denied, and vice versa.' Primitive mentality is thus not merely mystical but 'pre-logical,' by which term is meant that primitive thought is not constrained, as is our own, to refrain from contradiction. These contentions refer only to collective modes of thought as traditionally prescribed; they do not necessarily apply to the mental associations made by individuals.

"The work is scholarly, clear, and (since it is written by a professional philosopher) rigorous. It led to a great deal of controversy and further inquiry, establishing a major concern within the field of anthropology which has culminated in *The Foundations of Primitive Thought* by C. R. Hallpike (Oxford: Clarendon Press, 1979)."

Lynd, Helen. *On Shame and the Search for Identity* (New York: Harcourt, 1958) The co-author of the classic *Middletown* analyzes guilt and shame as significant experiences in the formation of character. She concludes that shame is a reaction to failure while guilt is a reaction to wrongdoing of a destructive nature. Theodor Reik called this study "a pioneer attempt at solution of a complex sociological and psychological problem" (*Saturday Review*, May 3, 1958).

Cynthia Buchanan recommended this in *Antaeus*, Winter, 1975.

Mackay, Charles. *Extraordinary Popular Delusions and the Madness of Crowds* (New York: Crown, 1981) First published as *Memoirs of Extraordinary Popular Delusions* (London: R. Bentley, 1841).

Now considered a classic, although not that frequently consulted, this is an engaging study of what makes people act in one way as individuals and in quite another way when they are in crowds. The theme is supported by absolutely fascinating data which, while not always completely trustworthy, is stimulating and provocative. Among the topics considered are hair and beards, great thieves, slow poisoners, the tulipomania, the Mississippi scheme, the South Sea bubble, the witch mania and many others. Although he is seriously engaged with his subject, Mackay indulges in some wry humor.

Carl Sagan recommends this book.

Radin, Paul. *Primitive Man as a Philosopher* (New York: Appleton, 1927) Primitive people's thought processes by which they explain the internal and external worlds are examined in a clear, literate style. Much of the material is based on the author's careful, firsthand study of life among the Winnebago Indians. Often the Indians speak for themselves, and the more charming and revealing sections are those in which their voices are heard explaining such things as the theory of the soul and the place of the individual in society. Primitive people, it is obvious, are not that primitive; their thinking seems to be especially congruent with the nature of life.

Ashley Montagu calls this "a lovely corrective to the conventional dogma concerning the mental capacities of 'savages.'"

Scheler, Max. *The Nature of Sympathy.* *Translated from the German by Peter Heath* (London, New Haven: Yale University Press, 1954) First published, 1923. A principal follower of Husserl and the phenomenological school, Scheler has the advantage of being able to express himself with clarity. His unstudied, direct, almost journalistic prose makes the philosophical position much easier to comprehend, especially for the average reader. Involved with essence rather than existence, the author explores the principles involved in our daily emotional life. The skillful, subtle, descriptive exploration of the variety of life experiences is a revelation.

Robert Coles called this "a lovely work by a wonderfully tormented German theologian-philosopher of the human predicament" (*American Scholar*, Spring, 1970).

Shah, Idries. *Oriental Magic* (New York: Philosophers Library, 1957) An expert on magic and the occult, the author concentrates on the historical aspects of both in this delightful mixture of scholarship, enthusiasm and anthropological insight. The focus is on magic as it exists among the Arabs, Chinese, Indians and other Eastern peoples. Much of the material is based upon research but some comes from the author's own travels. All of this is carefully explained, and results in a fine introduction to the subject.

Doris Lessing writes: "This is an original contribution to anthropology. The author's unique position gives him access to magical and shamanistic traditions in several continents which he explains in relation to a continuing human development." She notes that this is available in a Dutton paperback.

Stendhal. *On Love.* *Translated from the French by Gilbert and Suzanne Sale* (New York: Farrar, Straus, 1957) First published, 1822. This is a tidy classification of the various manifestations of love from self-generation to passion and impotence.

Noel Perrin described this as "a book length meditation written long before *The Charterhouse of Parma* (1839) or *The Red and the Black* (1830). It has plenty to say about traps, shyness, old friends in new amorous moods, how to know when you're in love . . . If I were a foolish romantic teenager and reasonably literate, or just a person of any age interested in subtle reflections on love, I would [read this]" (*Washington Post Book World*, October 18, 1981).

Walter, Norman. *The Sexual Cycle of Human Warfare* (London: Mitre Press, 1950) Here, in the words of Anthony Burgess, the thesis is that "war is a psychobiological phenomenon, not a political one, and that it can best be studied in terms of such genetic phenomena as hybridizations, exogamy and the like. Norman explodes the human group with the aim of genetic recombination . . . War, like sex, is ineradicable from human society because war is very close to sex."

Anthony Burgess also remarks that "this book is shamefully neglected . . . [a]nd yet its thesis is original and highly suggestive" (*American Scholar*, Spring, 1970).

Zimmer, Heinrich. *The King and the Corpse* (New York: Pantheon, 1948) In a series of brilliant essays, the author attempts to validate Jung's theory that spiritual experiences of prehistoric people remain embedded in "the deeper unconscious layers of our soul." Moving from Oriental mythology and folklore to the West and the Middle Ages, Zimmer traces the common patterns in folk stories and myths. The book is arranged in such a way that the narratives form a kind of psychological epic. The fascination lies not only with the stories, but with the method of telling them which Zimmer accomplishes with considerable verve.

Richard Wilbur recommends this.

FOOD AND COOKING

Clark, Eleanor. *The Oysters of Locmariaquer* (London: Secker, 1964) The little French town of Locmariaquer is located on the northwest coast of France, and the special concern of the villagers is to cultivate oysters. With a fine literary style, the author carefully details how oysters are cultivated and brought to market, the type of people involved with the labor, and the particular sensibility of the French community. There is a splendid historical balance to this work in that there are frequent references to the relation of the oyster to past events, to epic heroes, literary texts, and a variety of other topics. It is unique.

Roald Dahl calls this "a marvellously evocative and fascinating book."

David, Elizabeth. *French Provincial Cooking* (London: M. Joseph, 1960) Julia Child writes, "Mrs. David is one of the most distinguished writers on gastronomy in the English language. She is deeply knowledgeable and her works are always fully researched; she is a wonderful stylist, and this happens to be one of the very best books on French provincial cooking. I think one reason it hasn't been widely used in this country is that for one thing, the book was not translated from British English into American English, which often puts people off, and two, that neither Mrs. David's publisher nor Mrs. David herself have made any effort to be known in this country. It is a very fine book and one that should be in the library of anyone who is serious about cooking and especially French cooking."

Field, Michael. *All Manner of Food* (New York: Knopf, 1970) Originally, these were articles which appeared in American national magazines. They are now collected into this volume of intriguing and reliable recipes. There is a great sense of selectivity in what the author chooses to include, and so the reader is exposed to his personal, somewhat scholarly, version of good taste. Each chapter focuses on one ingredient, such as garlic or potatoes, and describes its behavior under different culinary conditions.

Daniel Halpern recommends this.

Fisher, M. F. K. *An Alphabet for Gourmets* (New York: Viking, 1949) Employing the familiar children's book format for alphabets (B is for *bachelors*, K is for *Kosher*, T is for *Turbot*, and so forth) the author takes us on an informal and informative trip through the country of gourmet cooking. Even those who do not cook will enjoy her verve and fine literary style. It is clear why W. H. Auden referred to M. F. K. Fisher as the best current writer in the English language.

Grigson, Jane. *The Art of Making Sausages, Pâtés and Other Charcuterie*

(New York: Knopf, 1976) First published as *The Art of Charcuterie* (1968). With a flair for the practical, both in her approach to cooking and in her witty, down-to-earth style, the author explains the thousand and one variations on making the most out of that unprepossessing animal, the pig. While the focus is on French techniques, the author is aware of the peculiar needs of American and English cooks, and she manages to explain French terms, equipment and methods in such a way that the instructions can easily be followed. There are topical chapters, each with background details, on everything from pâtés and galantines to the use of the extremities and the fat.

Julia Child recommended this in *Antaeus*, Autumn, 1977.

SCIENCE

Ayres, Clarence E. *Science, the False Messiah* (Indianapolis: Bobbs, 1927) Attempting to strike a balance between science and other disciplines, the author points out the fallacies in scientific theory and machine technology, and, by the way, gives the reader a brief history of science. Decades later, Ayres' work remains impressive. Time has not withered the sarcastic quotations which destroy the holy notion toward things scientific. While a bit petulant, it is a most liberating view of a sacred cow.

Howard Nemerov recommends it.

Baker, Ernest. *Caving: Episodes of Underground Exploration* (London: Chapman, 1932) The autobiographical account of a life of potholing, or underground exploration, is written by a true English eccentric who is better known as a bibliographer and librarian. Here he confines himself to descriptions of his numerous adventures on excursions through caves and other apparently inaccessible areas. His enthusiasm is matched by his singularly personal style. Furthermore, he includes an interesting picture of English life before the Second World War.

W. A. Munford recommended this in *New Library World*, August, 1978.

Baker, J. A. *The Peregrine* (New York: Harper, 1967) Few books are so honestly and wisely devoted to animals as this treatise on the natural history and life pattern of the peregrine. The impressionistic, highly metaphorical, description opens with a section on Baker's decision to write the book. It then moves on to a definition of the peregrine's position in the animal kingdom, and concludes with a long account of the author's experiences with peregrines during nearly a year of close, passionate study.

Howard Moss recommended this in *Antaeus*, Autumn, 1975.

Bates, Henry W. *The Naturalist on the Amazons* (London: Routledge, 1905) Lacking financial and moral support from learned societies, Bates spent eleven years on the Amazon studying its course along with its flora and fauna. V. S. Pritchett described him as "one of the very few great travelers who is untainted by boasting, by dishonesty or by quarreling." Naturalists still approve of Bates' research, which he relates in loving detail, as he does his feelings about the landscape.

George Woodcock writes, "I think I have two main reasons for admiring *The Naturalist on the Amazons*, which has been one of my favorite books since childhood. First it is an example of that marvellously lucid prose which the best of the Victorian traveler-naturalists developed, highly utilitarian yet often lyrically descriptive at the same time. Secondly, it is an inimitable picture of a semi-primitive society still in its pristine state, just on the eve of disaster, for, as we know, Bates was followed by the robber barons who began the frightful exploitation of Amazonia. The subsidiary reason for remembering *The Naturalist . . .* is of course the position Bates held in the evolutionary debates, as a friend of both Darwin and Wallace, as the source of much of the information Darwin used in *The Descent of Man*, as Wallace's companion on his first journey, and as the originator of a quite important line of study of his own on mimicry in insects. However, for me it is the literary virtues of *The Naturalist . . .* that are most appealing and that made the book one of my models when I myself took to travel writing."

Beckmann, Peter. *A History of Pi* (Boulder, Golem Press, 1970) While tracing the history of the mathematical concept of "pi," the author also presents an overview of scientific progress from early Babylon to the present. So, not only does Beckmann trace the development of mathematics, but he matches it with a study of

human advancement in general. Written in a comparatively simple manner, this explanation is fascinating and stimulating.

Mike Benedict recommends it.

Bodsworth, Fred. *The Last of the Curlews* (New York: Dodd, 1954) This is a detailed account of the long flight from the Arctic to the Antarctic and back again by the Eskimo curlew. Its migratory flight is recounted with a minimum of jargon. The tragic side of this story is that after centuries of migration, the Eskimo curlew was slaughtered by man. The clear prose is nicely complemented by numerous, excellent illustrations by T. M. Shortt.

Donald Finkel recommended this in *Antaeus*, Autumn, 1979.

Brewster, William. *Concord River* (Cambridge: Harvard University Press, 1937) From 1879 to 1918, the author kept a diary of his experiences with, and reactions to, the lovely country around Concord, Massachusetts. Alone, or with friends, he studied the wild life, particularly the birds in the area. His careful observations of birds are found here, as well as his notes about excursions on the river, through the woods and in the swamps of Concord. A master of simple, natural prose, Brewster's record is as accurate as it is delightful.

Lewis Gannet recommended this as, "[A book] by a man who knew Concord's woods, fields and birds better than Thoreau and shared an inner ecstasy with John Muir. Brewster did not write for publication . . . [His] journals saw publication only after his death" (*American Scholar*, Autumn, 1956).

Céline, Louis-Ferdinand. *The Life and Work of Semmelweis.* *Translated from the French by Robert A. Parker* (London:

Allen & Unwin, 1937) First published, 1924. A Hungarian physician, Semmelweis (1818-1865) discovered that sterilization would kill germs and prevent infection some fifty years before Louis Pasteur. Completely devoted to science and the reduction of human suffering and death, Semmelweis was persecuted by fellow scientists, and driven to madness and poverty. According to Céline, his decline is worthy of a novel: mad, he broke into a dissection theatre, infected himself, and died in agony. All of the obsessions in Céline's writings are found in this early medical study, written with great passion and understanding.

Annie Gottlieb recommended this in *Antaeus*, Autumn, 1977.

Cloos, Hans. *Conversation with the Earth.* *Translated from the German by E. B. Garside* Edited by Ernst Cloos and Curt Dietz. (New York: Knopf, 1953) First published, 1947.

Geology as an extraordinary adventure—that is the promise of this combination of autobiography and geological travelogue. The German geologist takes the reader on his voyages through Europe, Asia, Africa and North America. Seeking to find basic truths about our earth, Cloos offers an abundance of facts and observations as well as enthusiastic discoveries. This is one of the few books which captures a great scientific spirit and mind.

Sherman A. Wengerd says, "Cloos was far ahead of his contemporaries in visualizing the earth as a great pulsating engine . . . Cloos makes the subject come alive—a witty vivacious tale—not overbearing as so many autobiographies tend to be. Eminently readable by almost anyone. I found it fascinating."

Collis, John S. *The Vision of Glory* (London: Braziller, 1973) This is scientific writing which is highly understandable and most entertaining. Here, the author considers three aspects of nature: the construction of atoms, with a digression concerning sun and light; the phenomenon of water; and the tree, along with ecology's effect on society. Basic subjects, these are central to an educated person's knowledge of the world.

Bernard Levin wrote, "When we read [Collis'] books we understand these natural phenomena better. . . .[H]is achievement [is] to measure man against his environment, and to see him as neither too small or too large" (*The Times*, June 27, 1978).

Collis, John S. *While Following the Plough* (London: Cape, 1946) Too old to serve in the Second World War, Collis decided to help his country by taking up farming. The book concerns his thoughts and reflections while working as a farm laborer. Not only does it offer brilliant insights into farming as an occupation and a way of life, but there are marvelous passages which convey the interlocking processes of nature, technology and agriculture. The lively, poetic prose is a perfect complement to this imaginative approach to work.

Bernard Levin wrote of Collis that he was "one of those rare beings who makes a truly original contribution to human understanding" (*The Times*, June 27, 1978).

Darling, Frank Fraser. *Pelican in the Wilderness: A Naturalist's Odyssey in North America* (New York: Random House, 1956) Darling, a Scottish ecologist, details his views of the United States, particularly Alaska. He discusses and comments on conservation methods, people, and wildlife. The sketches provoke thoughts about the nature and significance of conservation and the state of ecology in this hemisphere. They are also wonderfully entertaining.

Paul B. Sears writes, "The late Sir Frank Fraser Darling's *Pelican in the Wilderness* is the work of a master naturalist and superb writer whose talents have been generously given to American colleagues in the exploration of environmental problems in Alaska and other parts of the United States."

Dennis, Geoffrey. *End of the World* (London: Eyre, 1930) A sinister God hovers above the author's sometimes lyrical, always haunting speculation on the impending finale of the world. Not only is religion a major factor in the prognostication, but Dennis draws upon an impressive background of astronomy and scientific knowledge to make his major points. The pleasure in the book resides mainly in the author's style which is rhythmical and accurate and eloquent.

Morris Bishop wrote, "It treats of the greatest of subjects: How? When? Which first? What after? It does so by means of a glorious space time imagination, prickling humor and strange learning" (*American Scholar*, Autumn, 1956).

Eckstein, Gustav. *Lives* (New York: Harper, 1932) The "lives" in question are primarily those of animals that come under the scrutiny of the scientist who wrote this book. He examines a family of white rats, seven cats, two parrots, a macaw, a pigeon, three turtles, nine canaries and a million cockroaches. He concludes with a remarkable analysis of the human being. The lives are written with simplicity and sensitivity. The literary style and the factual details save the book from any danger of brooding sentimentality.

Tom Zimoski recommends this.

Feynman, Richard. *The Feynman Lectures on Physics* (Reading: Addison-Wesley, 1963) While Feynman's lectures are ostensibly concerned solely with providing an overview of physics for college students, the California Institute of Technology professor actually casts a wider net. The reader is struck by the extraordinary scope of the material, which often goes far afield of conventional topics in an introductory course. The scope of the book is matched by the felicity of expression and clarity of explanation.

Carl Sagan recommends this.

Hay, John. *Nature's Year* (New York: Doubleday, 1961) Starting in July, the gifted amateur naturalist follows the cycle of changing seasons in Cape Cod and, in so doing, he offers the reader lovely moments of peace in the generally hectic pace of life. Between careful descriptions of a wide range of birds, beasts, insects and natural flora and fauna, the author offers poetic-philosophic passages concerning the essence of nature. His acute observations and keen discernment reflect man's close relationship to the earth. There are also effective woodcuts by David Grose.

Annie Dillard calls this the "best nature writing since Thoreau."

Irvine, William. *Apes, Angels, and Victorians: The Story of Darwin, Huxley, and Evolution* (New York: McGraw, 1955) In the era which gave birth to the theory of evolution, the Victorians had to choose between apes and angels. The choices were influenced by Darwin, Huxley, Gladstone, Carlyle, Spenser and numerous other famous personalities. All are portrayed here with scrupulous skill, but the primary focus is on Darwin and Huxley. In a surprisingly fresh manner, the author makes their familiar stories seem astonishingly new. As carefully documented as it is thoughtful, the study captures the nature of the argument during the Victorian period.

Alan Lelchuk writes that this is "a beautifully written, witty, and elegant dual biography of Darwin and Huxley by a humanistic English professor."

Leopold, Aldo. *Sand County Almanac and Sketches Here and There* (Oxford: Oxford University Press, 1949) These essays are arranged by months so as to demonstrate the changes in nature during the year when the noted naturalist observed them on his Wisconsin farm. Other sections are devoted to forty years of the author's experiences. Each essay subtly urges people to adopt an ecological conscience.

Paul B. Sears writes, "The stature of this book as an American classic has been so clearly recognized that any further comment seems gratuitous. However, its central message under the title of 'conservation ethic' is so fundamental that it cannot be too strongly emphasized. It makes clear that behind all technical and legislative action must be the intangible but real sanctions of society."

Marais, Eugene. *The Soul of the White Ant.* *Translated from the Afrikaans by Winifred deKok* (London: Methuen, 1937) With singular charm, Marais explains his theory of the South African ant or termite. He believes that a nest is quite similar to an animal organism, with one group of termites acting as a digestive system, another as reproductive organs, and so on. Whether he is discoursing upon language in the insect world or on the structure of nests, his writing is always fascinating.

Joseph McElroy recommended this in *Antaeus*, Winter, 1975.

Mead, Kate Campbell. *A History of Women in Medicine* (Middletown: Haddam, 1938) A detailed historical analysis of the role of women in medicine, this book begins by examining records dating back to 3500 BC and concludes with the beginning of the nineteenth century. This was to be the first of two volumes, but the second was never completed. Mary Beard called it "a vivid history, charmingly told, . . . scholarly and well documented; besides,

Dr. Mead approaches her subject with imagination and feeling, and so makes the reader feel the periods described" (*Survey Guide*, May, 1938).

Judy Chicago recommends this saying that it, along with the Drinker and Eckenstein books, "shaped my theory of history and deepened my understanding of women's historic struggle. They are primers, in my opinion."

Oppenheimer, J. Robert. *The Open Mind* (New York: Simon & Schuster, 1955) In what now seems a timeless plea for sanity, the reknowned atomic scientist explains the dangers of nuclear warfare and explores related issues. Delivered as eight lectures, this collection is actually divided into two parts. The first pertains to war, the second to the relationship between science, as an intellectual activity, and the rest of a culture. The whole work provides penetrating insights into some of today's major challenges for survival. The prose is direct, easy to understand, and moving.

Kelly Cherry recommends it.

Pickles, William Norman. *Epidemiology in Country Practice* (Bristol: J. Wright, 1939) For twenty-five years, the author carried on a successful medical practice in northern England, and here he reports on his understanding of, and experience with, infectious diseases. The notes and observations are remarkably clear, literate and fascinating.

Berton Roueché writes, "Dr. William Norman Pickles of Aysgarth, Yorkshire, is to English medicine what Gilbert White (1720-1793) of Selborne, Hampshire, was to the flora and fauna of his part of England, and Dr. Pickles' memoir of his years as a health officer, *Epidemiology in Country Practice* ranks with White's classic *The Natural History of Shelborne*. They share the strengths of a lively intelligence, a gift for unbiased observation, and an ability to communicate enthusiasm. Dr. Pickles' book was first published in 1939, and was reissued in 1949, but has long since, and most undeservedly, been out of print."

Ricketts, Edward F., and Jack Calvin. *Between Pacific Tides* (Stanford: Stanford University Press, 1939) The subtitle of this book is "An account of the habits and habitats of some five hundred of the common, conspicuous seashore invertebrates of the Pacific Coast between Sitka, Alaska, and northern Mexico." This is aimed at the common reader and is copiously illustrated with lovely photographs which show the animals in their natural surroundings. It is a fine introduction to marine fauna.

Ken Kesey writes, "This is the book 'Doc' (Ed Ricketts) was working on through *Cannery Row* and *Sweet Thursday*."

Russell, Henry N. *The Solar System and Its Origin* (New York: Macmillan, 1935) The origins of the solar system and the complexity and isolation of our earth are the topics of an engaging, early attempt to make astronomy and science comprehensible to the layperson. The author, a former professor of astronomy at Princeton, has a striking ability to make even the most complex matters understandable. This, along with an excellent style, leads the reader to the concluding chapter, which today is considered brilliant though controversial. Here, Russell discusses specific theories about the origin of the solar system.

Harlow Shapley said, "These Virginia lectures have inspired both textbook writers and delvers into local cosmology. Although much recent research has been done in this fundamental astronomical field, Russell's clearly written and deeply thought out pioneering should not be overlooked" (*American Scholar*, Autumn, 1961).

Sauer, Carl. *Agricultural Origins and Dispersals* (New York: The American Geographical Society, 1952) The domestication of animals and plants is due to a combination of special human inclinations and leisure which historically caused certain people to progress in this direction while others, lacking time and interest, followed different paths. The picture of historical development which usually is advanced is that people progressed in stages from hunting to pastoral nomadism and finally to agriculture. Sauer takes exception to this belief, and in his various lectures, writings and original research thoroughly develops his theory. Aside from the primary theme, the book also offers fascinating details about plants and animals.

Henry Allen Moe called this his "candidate for the dolorous crown of the most neglected excellent book known to me, published during the past thirty years. It is a study of what man has done with the plants and animals at his disposal" (*American Scholar*, Autumn, 1961).

Seton, Ernest Thompson. *Wild Animals I Have Known* (New York: Scribner, 1898) Although this is now almost a hundred years old, it remains one of the most winning and authentic of animal books. It was written by a man who had lifelong connections to children: he helped found the Boy Scouts of America and became a father at the age of seventy eight. (He lived to help his daughter celebrate her eighth birthday.) This work contains the stories of eight different animals. They were fine enough for Kipling to attribute to Seton the germ of the idea for *The Jungle Book*.

Noel Perrin writes that while some of the stories are too good to be true, "the wonderful thing about Seton is that he offers a middle road between the frank sentimentalism of *Bambi* . . . and the impersonal biostatistics of most natural history" (*Washington Post Book World*, December 10, 1981).

Smith, Olga. *Gold on the Desert* (Albuquerque: University of New Mexico Press, 1956) Somewhat less than enthusiastically, the author sets out with her prospector husband to spend a year on the Arizona desert. In the beginning, she dislikes the life but gradually she is given the opportunity to witness some extraordinary activities of nature. Over a period of time, she comes to accept the strange land. She moves from periods of resentment to adjustment, then on to acceptance and affection. The life of the desert has rarely been so accurately described.

Maye Keith recommends it.

Thompson, D'Arcy Wentworth. *On Growth and Form* (New York: Cambridge University Press, 1917) John Hollander writes, "*On Growth and Form,* originally published in 1917, has existed in a remarkably well-edited and brilliantly annotated abridged edition, prepared by John Tyler Bonner, since 1961. It is a noble piece of literature and science, an account of how and why living things assume the shapes and forms that become characteristic of them, and what asking some of those questions about how and why may mean. A great piece of writing, it has been as beloved by poets as by scientists, and poses no conceptual problems for the general reader, so profoundly is it thought through and expounded."

Alastair Reid also recommends this.

Watts, May. *Reading the Landscape: An Adventure in Ecology* (New York: Macmillan, 1957) Here, an experienced botanist leads the reader through a portion of the environment and points out sights worthy of notice. Her informal, yet informed, tour of plant life traces its development against the background of an evolving America. This is a wonderful guide, written in a delightful manner.

Virginia L. Wilson recommends it.

Waugh, Albert E. *Sundials: Their Theory and Construction* (New York: Dover, 1973) The author lovingly takes the reader into the realm of early time measurement by describing sundials which may be constructed today. For those who have sundials, he gives explicit instructions, with numerous tables and graphs, for computing the proper time. His concern and enthusiasm are contagious, and the book is as much fun to read as it is helpful for those ambitious folk who may wish to build their own sundials.

Richard Wilbur recommends this.

Whitehead, Alfred North. *Science and the Modern World* (New York: Macmillan, 1925) The broad role of science in shaping and reflecting our culture is brilliantly explained by this English philosopher. The material remains fresh. In Whitehead's own words it "is a study of some aspects of Western culture during the past three centuries, in so far as they have been influenced by the development of science." John Dewey, in a contemporary review, called it "the most significant restatement for the general reader of the present relations of science, philosophy and the issues of life which has yet appeared." It is still good reading.

Robert D. Seeley, recommended this in *Antaeus*, Autumn, 1979.

INDEX OF RECOMMENDERS

INDEX OF AUTHORS AND TITLES